International Conference on Computer Graphics, Visualization, Computer Vision and Image Processing (CGVCVIP2022); Connected Smart Cities (CSC2022); Big Data Analytics, Data Mining and Computational Intelligence (BIGDACI2021); Theory and Practice in Modern Computing (TPMC 2022)

Held at the 16th Multi-Conference on Computer Science and Information Systems (MCCSIS 2022)

Lisbon, Portugal
19-22 July 2022

Editors:

Yingcai Xiao
Ajith Abraham
Guo Chao Peng
Jörg Roth
Piet Kommers
Pedro Isaías
Luís Rodrigues

ISBN: 978-1-7138-6091-4

Printed from e-media with permission by:

Curran Associates, Inc.
57 Morehouse Lane
Red Hook, NY 12571

CURRAN ASSOCIATES INC.
proceedings
.com

Some format issues inherent in the e-media version may also appear in this print version.

International Association for Development of the Information Society (IADIS)
Rua Sao Sebastiao Da Pedreira
No. 100, 30, 1050-209
Lisbon, Portugal

Phone: 351 21 3151373
Fax: 351 21 3151244

secretariat@iadis.org

Additional copies of this publication are available from:

Curran Associates, Inc.
57 Morehouse Lane
Red Hook, NY 12571 USA
Phone: 845-758-0400
Fax: 845-758-2633
Email: curran@proceedings.com
Web: www.proceedings.com

INTERNATIONAL CONFERENCES ON

COMPUTER GRAPHICS, VISUALIZATION, COMPUTER VISION AND IMAGE PROCESSING 2022

CONNECTED SMART CITIES 2022

BIG DATA ANALYTICS, DATA MINING AND COMPUTATIONAL INTELLIGENCE 2022

THEORY AND PRACTICE IN MODERN COMPUTING 2022

part of the

MULTI CONFERENCE ON COMPUTER SCIENCE

AND INFORMATION SYSTEMS 2022

PROCEEDINGS
OF THE
INTERNATIONAL CONFERENCES
ON

COMPUTER GRAPHICS, VISUALIZATION, COMPUTER VISION AND IMAGE PROCESSING 2022

CONNECTED SMART CITIES 2022

BIG DATA ANALYTICS, DATA MINING AND COMPUTATIONAL INTELLIGENCE 2022

and

THEORY AND PRACTICE IN MODERN COMPUTING 2022

JULY 19 - 22, 2022

Organised by

iadis

international association for development of the information society

As a member of Crossref (a non-profit membership organization for scholarly publishing working with the purpose to make content easy to find, link, cite and assess) each published paper in this book of proceedings will be allocated a DOI (Digital Object Identifier) number for its fast and easy citation and indexation.

Volume Editors:
Yingcai Xiao, Ajith Abraham, Guo Chao Peng and Jörg Roth

Computer Science and Information Systems Series Editors:
Piet Kommers and Pedro Isaías

Associate Editor: Luís Rodrigues

TABLE OF CONTENTS

CONNECTED SMART CITIES

BIG DATA ANALYTICS, DATA MINING AND COMPUTATIONAL INTELLIGENCE

THEORY AND PRACTICE IN MODERN COMPUTING

SHORT PAPERS

CONNECTED SMART CITIES

BIG DATA ANALYTICS, DATA MINING AND COMPUTATIONAL INTELLIGENCE

POSTER

COMPUTER GRAPHICS, VISUALIZATION, COMPUTER VISION AND IMAGE PROCESSING

FOREWORD

These proceedings contain the papers of the following conferences: 16th International Conference on Computer Graphics, Visualization, Computer Vision and Image Processing (CGVCVIP 2022), the 8th International Conference on Connected Smart Cities (CSC 2022), 7th International Conference on Big Data Analytics, Data Mining and Computational Intelligence (BigDaCI'22) and 11th International Conference on Theory and Practice in Modern Computing (TPMC 2022), which were organised by the International Association for Development of the Information Society. These conferences are part of the Multi Conference on Computer Science and Information Systems 2022, 19-22 July, which had a total of 608 submissions.

The Computer Graphics, Visualization, Computer Vision and Image Processing Conference intends to address the research issues in the closely related areas of Computer Graphics, Visualization, Computer Vision and Image Processing. The conference encourages the interdisciplinary research and applications of these areas. Submissions were accepted under the following 5 main topics:
- Computer Graphics
- Visualization
- Computer Vision
- Image Processing
- Other Related Topics

The Connected Smart Cities (CSC 2022) conference aims to provide a premier and exciting forum for the exchange of scientific ideas, research findings, and industrial practices among academics and practitioners, who are from different disciplines (e.g. information systems, computer science, telecommunication engineering, urban studies, and business and economics) but have common interests in smart cities. It welcomes all forms of relevant research, including conceptual, theoretical, quantitative, qualitative, and mixed-method studies. Papers with an interdisciplinary nature are particularly encouraging. In order to offer wide-ranging discussion opportunities, the conference seeks the most recent and relevant research on the following main topics:
- Wireless Connectivity in Smart Cities;
- New Business Concerns in Smart Cities;
- Data and Software Applications in Smart Cities;
- User-Centric Smart Cities;
- Security, Privacy and Identity Issues in Smart Cities;
- Greenness and Sustainability of Smart Cities;
- Smart City as an Integrated Ecosystem.

The aim of the Big Data Analytics, Data Mining and Computational Intelligence Conference is to serve as a forum to present current and future work as well as to exchange research ideas in this field. BigDaCI'22 invites authors to submit their original and unpublished work that demonstrate current research using big data analytics, computational intelligence and other intelligent computing techniques and their applications in science, technology, business and commerce. Submissions were accepted under the following areas and topics:

- Big Data Algorithms and Architectures
- Computational Intelligent Frameworks for Big Data Processing
- Data Mining Topics and Applications
- Big Data Applications
- Multi-Agent Systems: Models, Architectures and Applications

The International Conference on "Theory and Practice in Modern Computing" provides a forum for research and developments in the field of computing foundations and technology. Modern computing comes not only with efficient concepts and their application, but also it often addresses networking and mobility topics. Hence, the view in TPMC ranges from fundamentals like new or improved algorithms to very recent and modern applications like ubiquitous scenarios or even everyday computing. Complementary to these technically-oriented contents, TPMC also shall serve as discussion platform about ethics and social impact of those technologies. Submissions were accepted under the following key topics:
- Design Foundations
- Mobility Communication and Services
- Realization Aspects
- Networking and Grid Approaches

These events received 161 submissions from more than 23 countries. Each submission has been anonymously reviewed by an average of five independent reviewers, to ensure that accepted submissions were of a high standard. Consequently, only 24 full papers were published. The overall acceptance rate corresponds to about 15%. A few more papers were accepted as short papers, reflection papers and posters. An extended version of the best papers will be published in the IADIS International Journal on Computer Science and Information Systems (ISSN: 1646-3692) and also in other selected journals.

Besides the papers and posters presentations, the conferences also include one keynote presentation from internationally distinguished researcher. We would therefore like to express our gratitude to Professor Xiaoru Yuan, School of AI, Peking University, China, for accepting our invitation to be our keynote speaker.

This volume has taken shape as a result of the contributions from a number of individuals. We are grateful to all authors who have submitted their papers to enrich these conferences proceedings. We wish to thank all members of the organizing committee, delegates, invitees and guests whose contribution and involvement are crucial for the success of the conference.

Last but not least, we hope that everybody enjoyed the presentations, and we invite all participants for next year's edition of these conferences.

Yingcai Xiao, The University of Akron, USA
Computer Graphics, Visualization, Computer Vision and Image Processing 2022
Program Chair

Ajith Abraham, Machine Intelligence Research Labs (MIR Labs), USA
Big Data Analytics, Data Mining and Computational Intelligence 2022
Program Chair

Guo Chao (Alex) Peng, School of Information Management, Sun Yat-sen University, Guangzhou, China
Connected Smart Cities 2022
Program Chair

Jörg Roth, University of Applied Sciences Nuremberg, Germany
Theory and Practice in Modern Computing 2022
Program Chair

Piet Kommers, University of Twente, The Netherlands
Pedro Isaias, The University of New South Wales (UNSW – Sydney), Australia
MCCSIS 2022 General Conference Co-Chairs

July 2022

PROGRAM COMMITTEE

COMPUTER GRAPHICS, VISUALIZATION, COMPUTER VISION AND IMAGE PROCESSING 2022

PROGRAM CHAIR

Yingcai Xiao, The University of Akron, USA

CONNECTED SMART CITIES 2022

PROGRAM CHAIR

Guo Chao (Alex) Peng, School of Information Management, Sun Yat-sen University, Guangzhou, China

BIG DATA ANALYTICS, DATA MINING AND COMPUTATIONAL INTELLIGENCE 2022

PROGRAM CHAIR

Ajith Abraham, Machine Intelligence Research Labs (MIR Labs), USA

THEORY AND PRACTICE IN MODERN COMPUTING 2022

PROGRAM CHAIR

Jörg Roth, University of Applied Sciences Nuremberg, Germany

MCCSIS 2022 GENERAL CONFERENCE CO-CHAIRS

Piet Kommers, University of Twente, The Netherlands
Pedro Isaias, The University of New South Wales (UNSW – Sydney), Australia

COMPUTER GRAPHICS, VISUALIZATION, COMPUTER VISION AND IMAGE PROCESSING 2022

COMMITTEE MEMBERS

Aiert Amundarain, Ceit, Spain
Alessandro Rizzi, Università degli Studi di Milano, Italy
Angelica De Antonio, Universidad Politecnica de Madrid, Spain
Bin Chen, Max Planck Institute for Informatics, Germany
Brian dAuriol, Gwangju Institute of Science and Technology, Republic of Korea
Bruce Campbell, Rhode Island School of Design, USA
C Rama Mohan, Research Scholar, Visvesvaraya Technological University, India
Carlo Nati, Working Group for the Development of Technoscientific Knowledge, Italy
Celmar Guimarães da Silva, University of Campinas, Brazil
Cesar Alberto Collazos, Universidad Del Cauca, Colombia
Chih-Cheng Hung, Southern Polytechnic State University, USA
Chong Zhang, TigerGraph, USA

CONNECTED SMART CITIES 2022

COMMITTEE MEMBERS

Raquel Martínez España, Universidad de Murcia, Spain
Riccardo Bettati, Texas A&M University, USA
Rosaldo Rossetti, University of Porto, Portugal
Sandro Leuchter, Mannheim University of Applied Sciences, Germany
Silvano Vergura, Politecnico di Bari, Italy
Zena Wood, University of Greenwich, United Kingdom
Zhu Ye, Cleveland State University, USA

BIG DATA ANALYTICS, DATA MINING AND COMPUTATIONAL INTELLIGENCE 2022

COMMITTEE MEMBERS

Adina Florea, University Politehnica of Bucharest, Romania
Alessandro Giuliani, University of Cagliari, Italy
Anirban Kundu, West Bengal University of Technology, India
Archil Maysuradze, Lomonosov Moscow State University, Russia
Carson K. Leung, University of Manitoba, Canada
Christos Kalloniatis, University of The Aegean, Greece
Dariusz Krol, Wrocław University of Science and Technology, Poland
Filippo Sciarrone, Universitas Mercatorum, Italy
George Tambouratzis, Institute for Language and Speech Processing, Greece
Gerard Murray, Franchise Cloud Solutions, Australia
I-Hsien Ting, Kaohsiung University, Taiwan
Irina Mocanu, University Politehnica of Bucharest, Romania
Ivan Izonin, Lviv Polytechnic National University, Ukraine
Jan Platos, Vsb - Technical University of Ostrava, Czech Republic
Jose Molina Lopez, Universidad Carlos III De Madrid, Spain
Kauser Ahmed, VIT University, India
Ki Chan, Hong Kong University of Science and Technology, Hong Kong
Marco Villani, University of Modena and Reggio Emilia, Italy
María de los Angeles Constantino-González, Tecnologico de Monterrey, Mexico
Maricela Quintana, Centro Universitario UAEM Valle de México, Mexico
Matteo Casadei, Alma Mater Studiorum - Università di Bologna, Italy
Patrizia Ribino, Consiglio Nazionale delle Ricerche - Istituto di Calcolo e Reti ad Alte Prestazioni, Italy
Riccardo Ortale, ICAR-CNR, Italy
Silvia Parusheva, University of Economics - Varna, Bulgaria
Sung-Bae Cho, Yonsei University, South Korea
Sviatoslav Braynov, University of Illinois, USA
Tjeerd Olde Scheper, Oxford Brookes University, United Kingdom
Tomonobu Ozaki, Nihon University, Japan
Vincent Hilaire, Université De Technologie de Belfort-Montbeliard, France
Wiem Chebil, Monastir University, Tunisia

THEORY AND PRACTICE IN MODERN COMPUTING 2022

COMMITTEE MEMBERS

Angel Moreno, Universidad de Alcala, Spain
Antonio Munoz, University of Malaga, Spain
Apostolos Gkamas, University Ecclesiastical Academy of Vella of Ioan, Greece
Basilis Mamalis, Technological Educational Institute of Athens, Greece
Cheng-Yuan Chang, National United University, Taiwan
Felix J. Garcia Clemente, University of Murcia, Spain

KEYNOTE LECTURE

VISUALIZING THE COVID-19 PANDEMIC

Professor Xiaoru Yuan, School of AI, Peking University, China

ABSTRACT

During the still ongoing COVID-19 pandemic, visualization has demonstrated its unique power in communication of the information era. In this talk, I will first present a series of visualizations done by my team and collaborators in the beginning of 2020 on the theme of COVID-19. Among them, some visualizations have been broadcasted by the media with a large audience. Then a visual analytical platform for collaboratively collecting, annotating, and analyzing a global collection of visualizations related to the COVID-19 pandemic will be introduced. The visualization samples we have collected through this platform could inspire further research in the direction of understanding how visualizations interact with the society. Key findings from this systematic approach will be discussed.

FULL PAPERS

PROFESSIONAL COURSE OFFERED WITHIN A TECHNICAL ACADEMY CONCERNING THE INNOVATIVE BIM TECHNOLOGY

Alcínia Zita Sampaio and Augusto Gomes
University of Lisbon, Higher Technical Institute, Dep. Civil Engineering
Av. Rovisco Pais, Lisbon, Portugal

ABSTRACT

The implementation of Building Information modelling (BIM) methodology in the construction industry has been covering a wide applicability with recognized benefits in designing, constructing and operating buildings. A recent short course organized in the University of Lisbon, actualized with the most relevant achievement based in master researches, was offered to professionals of the industry, namely, architects and civil engineers coming from diverse engineering areas, environment, construction, maintenance, consult and patrimonial enterprises and also from public organizations like city councils. The proposed action covers the areas of construction (conflict analysis, planning and materials take-off), structures (interoperability, analyses and transfer of information between software) and the most recent Heritage Building Information Modelling (HBIM) perspective. The course aims to contribute to the dissemination of the potential of BIM in the areas of designing, construction and refurbishing of historical buildings. The participants followed the course with great interest and satisfaction, formulating several questions directed to the particular activity of each of the attendees.

KEYWORDS

BIM, Training Course, Up-To-Date Information, Improve Professional Skills

1. INTRODUCTION

The Building Information Modelling (BIM) methodology is currently the main digital platform applied in the construction activity. A BIM project is developed over a technological platform, in which all experts create, manipulate and add the information that is required and generated in the context of the work of each professional involved (Sacks *et al.*, 2018). In this process, the methodology supports the development of different components of the project, allows adequate interoperability between specific systems related to various types of analysis or simulation, facilitates the tasks of budgeting, construction, maintenance and management, and also controls the procedure for a possible demolition (Volk *et al.*, 2014).

The BIM concept began to be implemented in the construction industry at the beginning of this century as an immersive innovation in the sector. Its benefits were quickly recognised, reflected in the quality of the projects developed, based on effective process integration and clear collaboration between partners related to the different specialties intrinsic to construction (Lu *et al.*, 2014). BIM computational tools are a strong support for the development of the different disciplines of the project, enabling their parametric modelling and easy access to all the information concentrated in the BIM model created in the progress of the project.

In all areas of construction, the construction owner, designers, builders and managers, has verified the benefits of adopting BIM methodology. This fact has led to its growing acceptance, at a global level and in an exponential way, leading government entities to establish rules of action and mandatory implementation dates in public construction (Sampaio, 2021). In addition, the school has the mission, essential in society, to train future engineers with the fundamental teachings related to different themes in the field of construction, and should also be attentive to the technological innovations applicable to the sector. Naturally, construction-related companies follow this perspective, encouraging professionals to seek training actions that can add to professionals the knowledge, in the BIM context, required in a globalized industrial world, increasingly competitive.

A short course, presented in March of 2022, included the methodological concepts and a wide range of the applicability sectors inherent to the development of projects in BIM. This text reflects the contents of the course and the main objectives. The organizational structure of the course introduces the underlying fundaments of the methodology, such as parametric modelling and interoperability, and presents the scope of the applicability of BIM.

2. BIM EDUCATION

The attention of Civil Engineering education is oriented to BIM, and it is up to the school, as the main trainer of the future engineer, to introduce this theme, as a concept that should be transmitted, contributing to support all new subjects, included in the curriculum, on a BIM-based digital support. The requirement of BIM skills in the sector, has imposed an educational maturity of alert in relation to the need in society, which has led to a progressive adaptation of the curricula taught (Sampaio, 2021a).

The school have been contributing positively to the updating of knowledge of professionals in the sector, through the organization of BIM training courses, in accordance with the interest and expectation expressed by the offices and public entities. Industry and the school are partners in finding the best strategy for establishing effective ways of teaching useful to the community. In Europe, BIM training has been essentially introduced into postgraduate studies as curricular modules, disciplines or specialization courses. In reference universities, in Spain, Switzerland, Portugal and Italy, the curricular research points to a relatively rapid assimilation in engineering training.

- The *Escuela Técnica Superior de Ingenieros de Caminos, Canales y Puertos* of the Polytechnic University of Madrid offers two curricular actions (Lozano-Díez *et al.*, 2018): a discipline of specialization, within the framework of the Master's degree in construction and management of facilities, with the aim of training professionals in the application of the BIM methodology, covering the entire life cycle of a building (project, execution and operation of the building), and the use of software required in modelling and information management; an advanced discipline of BIM methodology, in the master course of project management, with a more specific and detailed programmatic content (concept and applicability, BIM model management, collision detection, collaborative workflow, conservation and exploitation of infrastructures);
- At the *École Polytechnique Fédérale de Lausanne*, the study plan identifies the introduction of BIM at master's level through a discipline of introduction and application of BIM, covering the teaching of concepts (interoperability, IFC standard and LOD levels), the generation of parametric models and conflict detection, the transfer of information between systems, the estimation of costs (5D) and, construction monitoring (4D);
- At the *Instituto Superior Técnico* of the University of Lisbon, at the level of the 1st cycle of teaching, the curriculum of the discipline of Technical Design includes an introduction to BIM, where the procedure on parametric modelling is transmitted, using BIM-based tools;
- The curriculum, of the *Collegio di Ingegneria Civile*, at Polytechnic University of Turin, offers in the 2nd cycle of education, a master's course in BIM applied to infrastructure, which includes aspects related to modelling and computer content, interoperability and formats, collision detection, structural dimensioning and real case analysis (bridges, tunnels, stations, schools and hospitals).

In addition, the construction industry has demanded from schools an offer aimed at the specificity of the profession, focusing on different perspectives. Engineers and architects recognize that in a globalized world, in the pursuit of their activity, the use of BIM platforms, leads to the achievement of better products and the establishment of more competitive projects. The constant demonstration of the benefit inherent to the use of the BIM methodology, which has been registered in the various sectors, motivates designers and managers to acquire knowledge related to the concept and scope of its applicability. Professionals from all sectors are interested in knowing the BIM concept and the scope of its applicability and technical schools organise BIM training activities to help to add knowledge and competitiveness to industry professionals.

3. PROFESSIONAL COURSE

The professional course, *BIM methodology: construction, structures and HBIM*, included within the activities of the Department of the Civil Engineering, of the University of Lisbon, was the most recent event offered to professionals of the construction industry. The range of professional englobes architects and civil engineers coming from consult enterprises and public organizations. The objective in attending the course was to improve their skills in order to increase competences in each particular domain of activity in construction. The program in presented in Table 1.

Table 1. Professional course BIM methodology: construction, structures and HBIM

Building Information Modelling (**BIM**) • Concept, applicability and implementation; • Parametric modelling, interoperability, and centralization; • BIM tool practice in generating model structures.
BIM in the **construction** • Conflict analysis; • Adding parameters to objects; • Construction planning; • Quantification of materials.
BIM in **structural** design • Interoperability; • Transfer and consistency check; • Graphic documentation and information centralization.
Heritage Building Information Modelling (**HBIM**) • Interoperability; • Concept and collection of information; • Digital capture of images (photogrammetry, scanner and drones); • Generation of specific families of parametric objects; • Documentation file (as-built); • Practical case: reconversion of a heritage building.

3.1 Introduction to BIM

The introduction of the main fundaments of BIM started with the principal concept, the range of applicability and the state-of-the-art of its implementation. The central BIM notion is the generation of a centralized digital model of all construction-related information. BIM is frequently defined as a digital representation of the building or infrastructure, strongly supported by parametric modelling and standard formats of data. Collaborative projects are developed over the model, requiring the use of advanced technologies and a high level of interoperability.

A practical lesson concerning the use of BIM-based tool, introduces the concept of parametric modelling, essential, to the understanding of the development of multitasking. In the modelling process, the first step is to define the base settings (work units, elevation levels, and alignments), followed by the selection and adaptation of parametric objects, associated to physical properties (Araújo, 2016). As an example of how to handling with a BIM-based tools, a structural BIM model was created (Figure 1). After, there were obtained several tables of take-off of materials and elements from the generated BIM model (Sampaio and Antunes, 2020) (Figure 2).

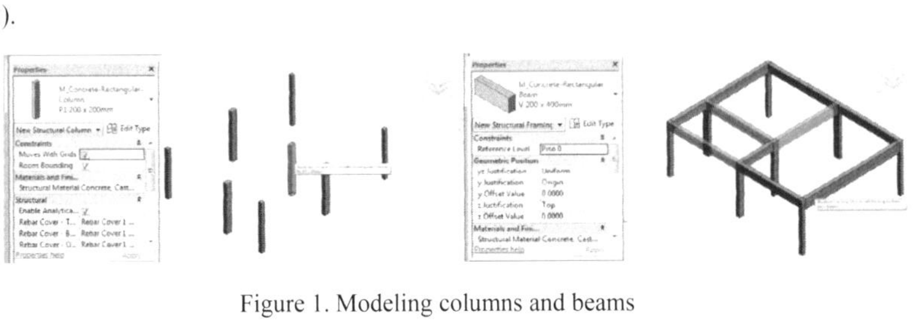

Figure 1. Modeling columns and beams

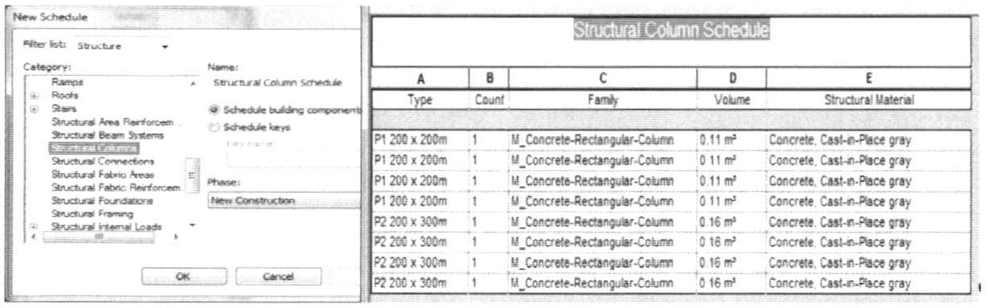

Structural Column Schedule

A	B	C	D	E
Type	Count	Family	Volume	Structural Material
P1 200 x 200m	1	M_Concrete-Rectangular-Column	0.11 m³	Concrete, Cast-in-Place gray
P1 200 x 200m	1	M_Concrete-Rectangular-Column	0 11 m³	Concrete, Cast-in-Place gray
P1 200 x 200m	1	M_Concrete-Rectangular-Column	0.11 m³	Concrete, Cast-in-Place gray
P1 200 x 200m	1	M_Concrete-Rectangular-Column	0 11 m³	Concrete, Cast-in-Place gray
P2 200 x 300m	1	M_Concrete-Rectangular-Column	0.16 m³	Concrete, Cast-in-Place gray
P2 200 x 300m	1	M_Concrete-Rectangular-Column	0 16 m³	Concrete, Cast-in-Place gray
P2 200 x 300m	1	M_Concrete-Rectangular-Column	0.16 m³	Concrete, Cast-in-Place gray
P2 200 x 300m	1	M_Concrete-Rectangular-Column	0 16 m³	Concrete, Cast-in-Place gray

Figure 2. Table of columns extracted from the model.

3.2 BIM in Construction

An analyses of the detection of conflicts between projects was also exposed to the audience. The BIM modelling tools allow the overlap of the three disciplines (architecture, structures and mechanic) and support the definition of each component by direct analysis of conflicts, identified by the system with the issuance of inconsistency messages. There are several software with conflict analysis-oriented capabilities, namely, Tekla BIMsight, Navisworks, and Solibri Model Checker tools. After running any of these systems, the modeler adjusts each conflict situation over the BIM model. In the study case show in the course, the models of MEP and structures were overlaid and an analysis of inconsistency was applied. Using Navisworks and Tekla BIMsight a set of conflicts were listed and visualized. The conflicts detected were after adjusted accordingly in order to obtain correct situations (Figure 3).

Figure 3. Changes were performed in a BIM modeler software

The course illustrates how to generate a 4D BIM model, relating to the construction process of a buildings (Mota and Sampaio, 2016). First, the complete 3D BIM model of the structural project must be defined and after the constructive sequence planning (phases and periods of implementation or placement) and allocated human resources must be established in the form of a Gant map (Figure 4).

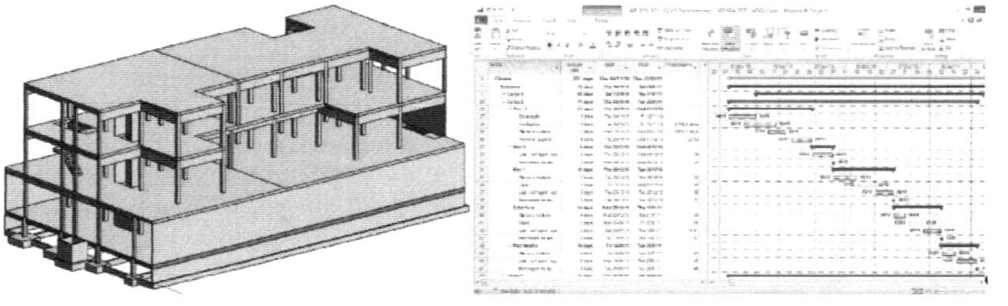

Figure 4. 3D BIM model of a structural project and the respective Gant map

The 4D model is then created in the Navisworks software. The BIM model representing the structural project is exported from the modeling system to a BIM viewer, performed in the native format. Also, the construction planning (Gantt map) file is transferred from the Ms Project system to the Navisworks. Next, it is necessary to associate the elements of the imported model, forming groups (sets), according to the activities of the schedule (Figure 5). The 4D model allows to visually simulate the planned construction.

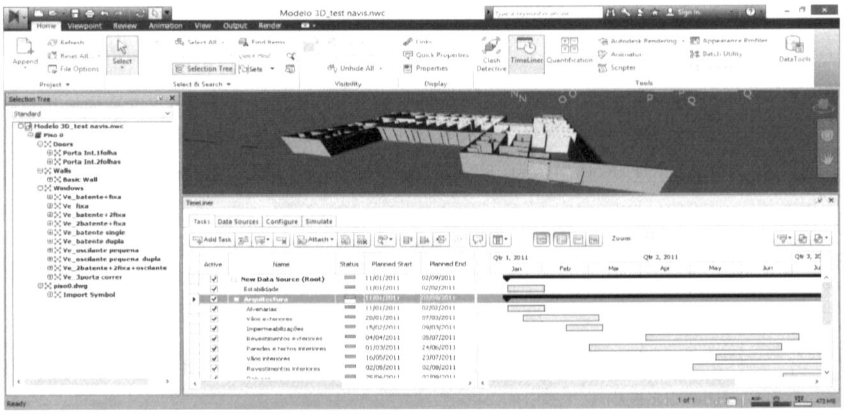

Figure 5. BIM 4D model generation

3.3 BIM in Structural Design

Throughout the development of a project and later construction and use, several processes transferring data between software, are normally performed, and for that, a high level of interoperability is required. In a structural design, the transposition of models between BIM modelling and structural analysis tools is essential. Concerning the structural design, the interoperability capacity, the transfer and verification of consistencies and the centralization of information and graphic documentation were performed (Oliveira and Sampaio, 2019).

In the course, the process of transposition of structural models between modeling and calculation systems (two-way flow) was analyzed in several situations involving ArchiCAD, Revit and AECOsim modeling tools and SAP, Robot and ETABS structural dimensioning tools (Sampaio *et al.*, 2021). The transposition of models between systems is supported: in the native format, when the software belong to the same manufacturer; by recourse to the universal data transfer standard, the Industry Foundation Classes (IFC) format. The interoperability capability analysis, verified in each model transposition process, is evaluated over several case studies of distinct volume and use (Figure 6).

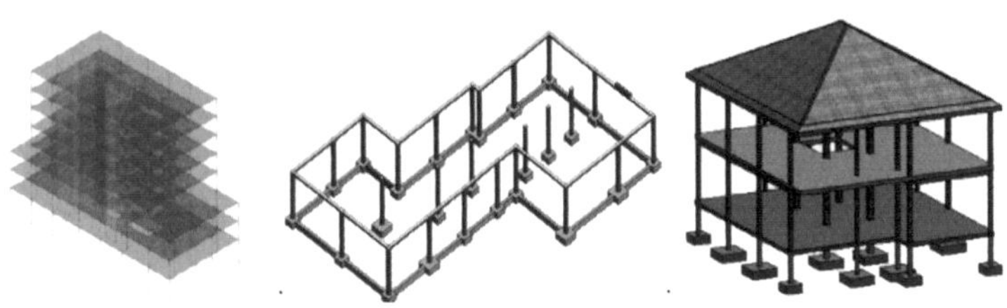

Figure 6. Structural BIM models of distinct buildings

First, the BIM models were transferred from the modeler system to the analyses software and the geometric consistency was evaluated. Several inconsistencies were observed: stair elements were not recognized (remodeled as sloped slabs in the analyses system); the foundations were not transposed (considered as supports). However, the structural elements (columns, beams and slabs), grids and material, concrete C30/37 and A500 NR SD steel were correctly transposed, but the analytical axis of some linear finite elements and rigid connections were redefined (Figure 7).

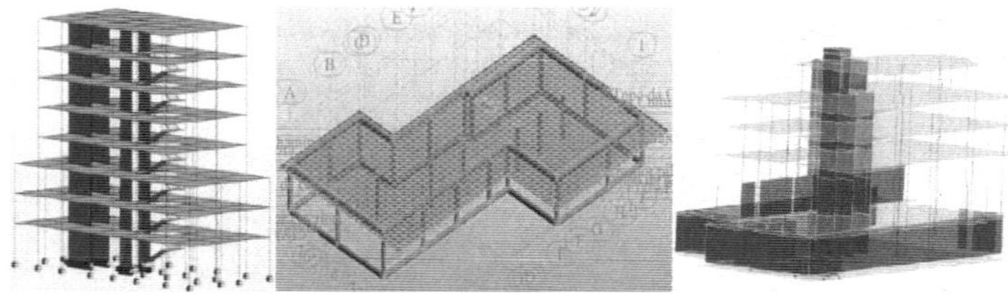

Figure 7. Structural BIM models transferred to analyses software

The level of interoperability between BIM-based modeling and calculation systems was assessed and it was found that:

- There are advantages of using Revit/Robot integrated platforms;
- The data flow modeling/calculation can be done with confidence, while the reverse flow is inefficient;
- The advantages are essentially related to the easy initial modeling, with some ability to transfer information post-calculation;
- It is appropriate to perform the detailing of reinforcements in the calculation system, as it allows a high capacity for the production of 3D designs and, subsequently, the inaccuracies are easily adjusted.

3.4 HBIM Concept and Practice

A recent implementation perspective the Historic or Heritage Building Information Modelling (HBIM) is directed towards properties of historical value or heritage relevance. Recent research related to HBIM addresses (Sampaio *et al.*, 2021a):

- The standardization of architectural configurations and creation parametric objects representative of applicable and reusable forms in the old construction;
- The analysis of constructive techniques used in order to identify the materials used and the solutions applied;
- The archive of registration documents, studies carried out or previous interventions, and their availability for consultation by experts involved in the project.

It is required to understand geometric rules, in parametric terms, from the books of architectural patterns to the HBIM modeling process. Sets of specific parametric object must be generated to allow the generation of old buildings with accuracy (Figure 8).

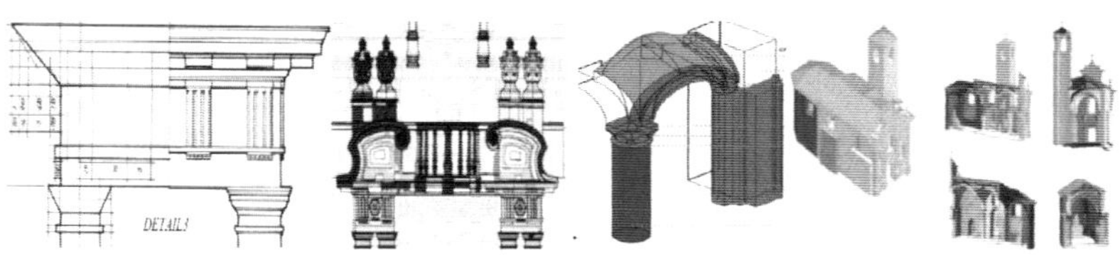

Figure 8. Architectural configurations, creation parametric objects and stratigraphic representation

The registered documentary information provides data concerning the characterization of the construction (historical epoch and traditional construction systems), the registration of refurbishing interventions and local inspection reports. In addition, the documentary collection, along with municipal archives, composed of drawings of plants, elevations and cut, referring to different dates and with yellows and reds, bring a complete description of the old building. The stratigraphic analysis covers the study of the constructive steps, which are represented through different colors, leading to a clear visual perception (Figure 10). In an HBIM process, it is also frequently necessary to establish a station of laser devices, properly positioned, so that, later, the points obtained can be unified, in a single cloud of space points.

A practical case of reconversion of a building of heritage value was presented (Sampaio *et al.*, 2021b). A proposal for the adaptation of an old building, located in Lisbon, requiring the reorganization of internal compartmentalization, but preserving their architectural characteristics, illustrated an application of HBIM (Figure 9).

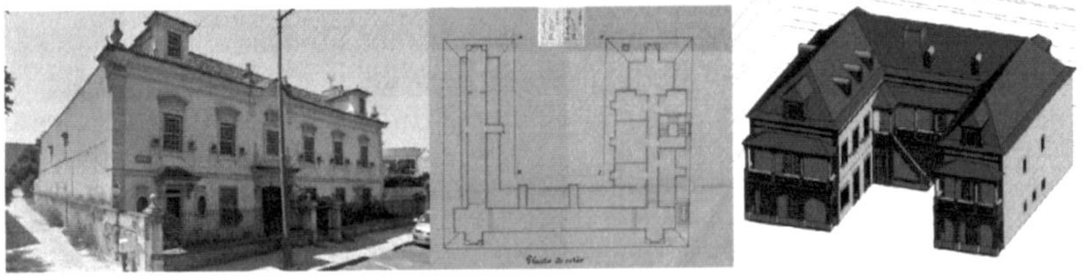

Figure 9. Building of heritage value, old drawing and BIM model of the proposal

Within HBIM, the creation of families of specific parametric objects was required for the rigorous representation of a building of patrimonial value. As a basis for modeling, it was requested to collect the existing documentation in the Municipal Archive of Lisbon, to obtain photographs from outside and inside of the building and the registration of detailed sketches. In addition, to allow a correct geometry represented in the form of parametric objects, it was necessary to add the material type and adjust the physical and mechanical properties, in order to respect the ancestral techniques of construction. The work contributes to empowering the HBIM library of parametric objects of building components.

4. CONCLUSIONS

A one-day course, *BIM methodology: construction, structures and HBIM*, was offered, at the University of Lisbon, to professionals of the construction industry. The contents of the training action was organized in order to cover a wide range of the applicability of BIM in the sector, and with the most recent achievements. The participants demonstrated a global interest in all topics presented, formulating questions oriented to their particular expertize. The global satisfaction of the attendance was good.

The main purpose of the course was to transmit the main concepts, the strategies of working in each type of BIM application and the reference to the main benefits and limitations. All parts of the course, including practice, construction, structures and HBIM, were essentially illustrated with study cases selected in accordance with the audience. Industry professionals feel the need to update themselves in the BIM context and the course contributes in a positive way to this learning. An in it the school and the industry collaborated in order to establish an interesting and useful program.

REFERENCES

Araújo, L. (2016) Development of a wall library in BIM methodology, Master's thesis in construction, University of Lisbon, Lisbon, Portugal.

Lozano-Díez, R.V., López-Zaldívar, O., Herrero del Cura, S. & Mayor, P.L. (2018) First experiences in the rule of the BIM environment: The case of the degree in Building of the Polytechnic University of Madrid, Advances in Building Education: Educative Innovation in buildings, 2 (1), 109-121, http://polired.upm.es/index.php/abe/article/view /4233

Lu, W., Fung, A., Peng, Y., Liang, C. & Rowlinson, S. (2014), Cost-benefit analysis of Building Information Modeling implementation in building projects through demystification of time-effort distribution curves, Building and Environment, Vol. 82, pgs. 317-327, ISSN 0360-1323, https://doi.org/10.1016/j.buildenv.2014.08.030, https://www.sciencedirect.com/science/article/pii/S0360132314002893)

Mota, C. & Sampaio, A.Z. (2016) BIM model of structures used in construction planning, National Meeting of Structural Concrete, Coimbra, Portugal, 10 pgs,. http://be2016.dec.uc.pt/

Oliveira, J.D. & Sampaio, A.Z. (2019) BIM in structures: analysis of interoperability, ICSAAM2019 - International Conference on Structural Analysis of Advanced Materials, Ischia, Italy. https://aip.scitation.org/toc/apc/2196/1

Sacks, R., Eastman, C., Lee, G. & Teicholz, P. (2018) BIM Handbook: A Guide to Building Information Modeling for Owners, Designers, Engineers, Contractors, and Facility Managers, Third Edition, Print ISBN:9781119287537, |Online ISBN:9781119287568 |DOI:10.1002/9781119287568, © 2018 John Wiley & Sons, Inc.

Sampaio A.Z. & Antunes, B. G. (2020) Quantity Take-Off Process Supported by Building Information Modeling (BIM) Methodology, book: Sustainability and Automation in Smart Constructions, Ch. 4, pp 21-28, Advances in Science, Technology & Innovation, Springer, Cham, https://doi.org/10.1007/978-3-030-35533-3_4

Sampaio, A. Z., Gomes, A.M. Lite, A.S., Zulueta, P. & González-Gaya, C. (2021a) Analysis of BIM methodology applied to practical cases in the preservation of heritage Buildings, MDPI - Journal Sustainability, ISSN 2071-1050, Sustainability 2021, vol. 13(6), https://doi.org/10.3390/su13063129

Sampaio, A. Z., Pinto, A.M., Gomes, A.M. & Lite, A. S. (2021b) Generation of a HBIM library regarding a palace of the 19th Century in Lisbon, MDPI - Applied Sciences, special session: Novel Approaches and Technologies for Conservation of Heritage Buildings, ISSN 2076-3417, Appl. Sci. 2021, 11, 7020. https://doi.org/10.3390/app11157020

Sampaio, A.Z. (2021) Maturity of BIM Implementation in the Construction Industry: Governmental Policies, IJETT- International Journal of Engineering Trends and Technology, ISSN: 2231-5381, Vol. 69 (7), pgs. 92-100, doi:10.14445/22315381/IJETT-V69I7P214 ©2021 Seventh Sense Research Group®, http://www.ijettjournal.org/archive/ijett-v69i7p214

Sampaio, A.Z. (2021a) BIM education required in construction, book: Sustainability and Automation in Smart Constructions, Ch. 1, pp. 3-9, Advances in Science, Technology & Innovation, Springer, Cham, https://doi.org/10.1007/978-3-030-35533-3_1

Sampaio, A.Z., Gomes, Augusto M. & Farinha, T. (2021) BIM methodology applied in structural design: Analysis of interoperability in ArchiCAD/ETABS process, JSEA - Journal of Software Engineering and Applications. ISSN Print: 1945-3116, ISSN Online: 1945-3124, DOI: 10.4236/jsea.2021.146012, IF 2.23.

Volk, R., Stengel, J. & Schultmann, F. (2014) Building Information Modeling (BIM) for existing buildings - Literature review and future needs, Automation in Construction, vol. 38, pp. 109 – 127, ISBN 0926-5805, https://doi.org/10.1016/j.autcon.2013.10.023, https://www.sciencedirect.com/science/article/pii/S092658051300191X

HEATMAP MATRIX: USING REORDERING, DISCRETIZATION AND FILTERING RESOURCES TO ASSIST MULTIDIMENSIONAL DATA ANALYSIS

Miguel Mechi Naves Rocha and Celmar Guimarães da Silva
School of Technology, University of Campinas
Limeira, São Paulo, Brazil

ABSTRACT

Visualization can help users to analyze multidimensional datasets and make better decisions related to them. The current literature presents a set of multidimensional data visualization techniques that deal with discrete variables, continuous ones, or both. Recently, the heatmap matrix was proposed as an alternative for visualizing multidimensional datasets with discrete variables. It comprises a matrix of heatmaps, in which each heatmap shows the frequency of the values of two variables in the records of a dataset. Despite its proposed utility, it only presents a static representation of the dataset, which may limit users understanding about the dataset under analysis. Therefore, we propose to add interactive resources to this visualization, aiming to provide distinct views of a dataset. To guide the choice of new features, we compared the resources of a set of multidimensional visualizations and selected the characteristics that are suitable to enhance the heatmap matrix. We added to it resources for: (a) reordering values (rows and columns) of variables in its heatmaps; (b) filtering variables and values based on correlations of variables and on association rules; (c) discretizing continuous variables to be represented in the visual structure; among others. We present two case studies in which we show the potential of the heatmap matrix, enhanced by the resources proposed in this work, to assist the analysis of multidimensional data.

KEYWORDS

Multidimensional Data Visualization, Matrix Visualization, Reorderable Matrix, Data Mining, Association Rules, Discretization

1. INTRODUCTION

The current visualization literature provides many techniques to support user analysis of multidimensional datasets. A classical example of these techniques is the *scatterplot matrix* (a.k.a. SPLOM) (Carr et al., 1987). It is predominantly applicable to datasets with continuous variables, given that scatterplots are not particularly suitable to depict discrete data, as superposition of graphical marks are likely to occur. A more recent example for scenarios with discrete data is the *heatmap matrix* (Rocha and Silva, 2018). It is similar to a SPLOM, but it is based on reorderable heatmaps instead of scatterplots. In other words, given a dataset D, with n discrete variables, a heatmap matrix is a matrix of $n \times n$ heatmaps, where a heatmap $H_{i,j}$ maps discrete variables V_i and V_j into its axes X and Y. The value of a cell $h_{p,q}^{i,j}$ from $H_{i,j}$ indicates the number of records in which $V_i = p$ and $V_j = q$ in D. Therefore, a heatmap matrix can be considered as a matrix with bidimensional histograms of all combinations of pairs of variables in a dataset. Figure 1 is an example of a heatmap matrix visualizing a dataset with six variables in a 6×6 matrix of heatmaps (details about this dataset will be discussed at Section 4).

A restriction that may hamper the exploratory data analysis in the heatmap matrix is the absence of interactive resources that could help users to tailor the visualization to their ongoing analysis. Therefore, in this work, we aimed to select interactive features that could surpass this limitation and enhance this visualization technique. We surveyed a set of features from related visualization techniques (e.g. GPLOM, generalized pairs plot, and mosaic plot) and compared them with the heatmap matrix. Based on this comparison, we proposed to add to the heatmap matrix a set of interactive resources related to matrix reordering, as well as a support to continuous data through discretization procedures. We also included filtering capabilities based on association rules and variable correlation. The results obtained in two case studies provided positive feedback regarding its potential to aid the analysis of multidimensional datasets.

The remainder of this paper is organized as follows. In Section 2, we compare a set of multidimensional visualizations (including the heatmap matrix), and list features that are absent in the heatmap matrix. Section 3 presents the features we selected to insert into the technique and how we proposed this insertion. We present two case studies in Section 4, in which we discuss the potential of the enhanced heatmap matrix as a tool for multidimensional dataset analysis. Section 5 concludes our paper and points out future work.

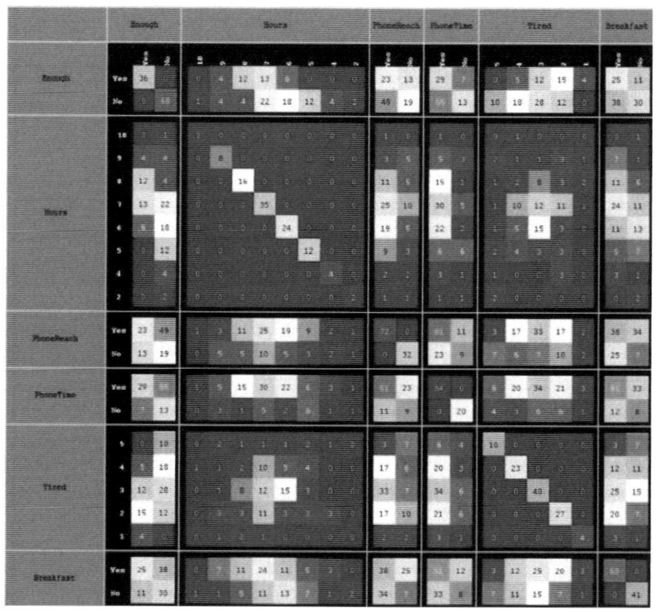

Figure 1. Heatmap matrix for the "Sleep study" dataset. This and other visualizations in this paper uses the red-white-blue diverging color scale, where red, white, and blue stand for minimal, intermediate, and maximal values, respectively

2. RELATED WORK

In our literature review, we selected a set of multidimensional visualizations that support discrete variables. Our aim was to better understand the similarities among them and the heatmap matrix, and to list possible features of these visualizations that could be inserted into the heatmap matrix to improve it.

Aiming to represent a given dataset D with n variables $(V_1, \dots, V_n)$, the *mosaic plot* (Hartigan and Kleiner, 1981) subdivides a rectangular space for each discrete value v_i^j, $j \in [1, \dots, numvalues_i]$ of a variable V_i, $i \in [1, \dots, n]$; $numvalues_i$ is the number of distinct values of V_i. The proportions of the areas $a_i^1, a_i^2, \dots, a_i^{numvalues_i}$ follow the respective proportions of the frequency of the values $v_i^1, v_i^2, \dots, v_i^{numvalues_i}$ in D. This subdivision starts with V_1 and is done recursively for all other variables $V_2, \dots, V_n$. The *mosaic matrix* (Friendly, 1999) is a matrix of mosaic plots of each possible pair of variables (V_i, V_j), $i \neq j$, from D; other properties from D may be represented by rectangle colors and dashed or solid rectangle outlines.

The *generalized pairs plot* (Emerson et al., 2012) is an extension of a SPLOM for dealing with quantitative and categorical variables. As its ancestor, it defines a $n \times n$ matrix of visualizations. A set of visualizations is available according to the classes of the two variables of each cell. For example, a cell related to two quantitative variables (QQ) may have a scatterplot matrix; when the cell is related to two categorical variables (CC), a mosaic plot can represent them; and box plots can be used to visualize data from a quantitative variable and a categorical one (QC). The *generalized plot matrix* (Im et al., 2013) can be considered as a variation of a generalized pairs plot. It uses scatterplots, heatmaps and bar charts to the QQ, CC and QC situations, respectively.

The *table lens* (Rao and Card, 1994) uses a matrix-like display, with n columns. Each record is represented by a matrix row. Each column has a starfield display (if the variable it represents is ordinal or categorical) or a bar chart (if the column represents a quantitative variable). Sorting variables in ascending or descending order is an interactive resource to reorder rows and to reveal possible correlations among variables.

The *dimensional stacking* (Grinstein and Trutschl, 2001; Ward et al., 2015) recursively subdivides the display in matrices. The X and Y axes of each matrix represent a pair of variables of D. In a recursive subdivision of the space, each cell of this matrix has another matrix with another pair of variables of D. In the last level, the matrices are heatmaps that reveal frequencies of tuples of D or the value of one specific variable.

The *parallel sets* technique (Kosara et al., 2006) does not have a tabular display. It is similar to parallel coordinates plots, but has a focus on discrete variables. Each categorical variable V_i is represented as an axis. Each value v_i^j of V_i is represented as a rectangle, whose size is proportional to the frequency of the value v_i^j in D. "Ribbons" are used to connect parallel axes instead of lines, aiming to represent the frequency of pairs of values. Users can reorder the axes as well as the values of each axis.

Pixel-oriented techniques (Keim, 1996) dedicate one part (window) of the display for each variable. In a window i, given the vector of values from V_i in D, these techniques represent each value of this vector as a colored pixel in this window. The layout of the pixels may follow space-filling curves. When the dataset is sorted according to a given variable, correlations among the variables may be revealed through the similarity among some windows of the visualization.

The heatmap at Table 1 summarizes the features we observed on these techniques. Features #1 to #4 deal with the exhibition of relationships and associations among two or more variables. Features #5 and #6 indicate the visualizations that show values of the dataset, frequencies of values, or both. Features #7 and #8 consider interaction aspects such as filtering, brushing and reordering. Features #9 to #12 point out visual mapping aspects related to which graphical property is used to show values and frequencies. Lastly, feature #13 is related to the supported types of variables (categorical, ordinal or quantitative).

Table 1. A comparison heatmap of multidimensional visualization techniques according to a set of features. A blue cell (x,y) indicates that the feature y is present in the technique x; otherwise, the cell is red

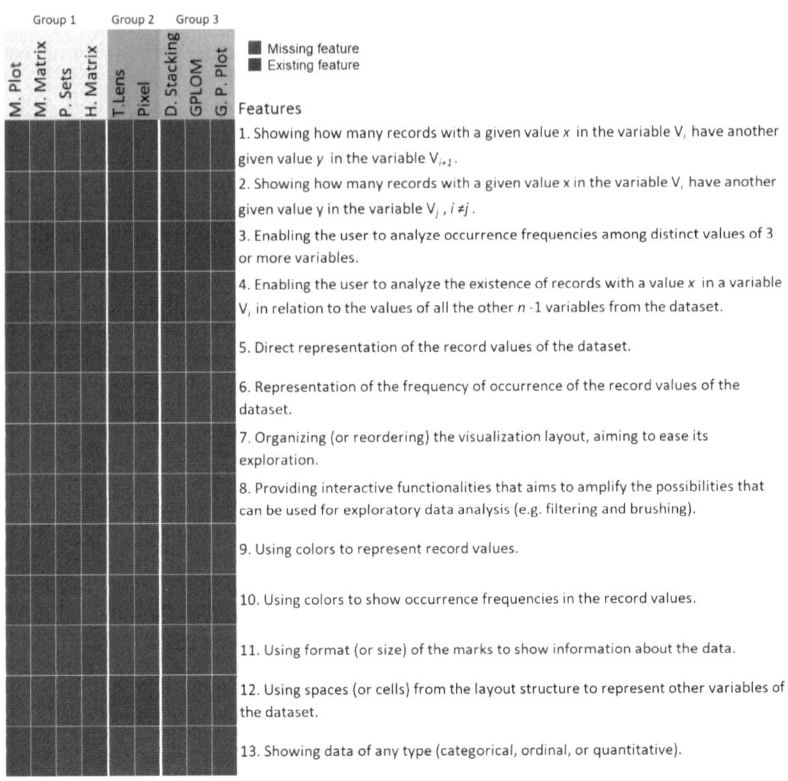

This heatmap also compares the analyzed techniques and the features they have. Three groups of techniques can be observed in this figure. Group 1 comprises mosaic plot ("M.Plot"), mosaic matrix ("M.Matrix"), parallel sets ("P. Sets"), and heatmap matrix ("H.Matrix"). These techniques cannot represent directly the values of the records (feature #5). However, they show frequencies related to values of two variables (features #2 and #6). The techniques from Group 2 – table lens ("T.Lens") and pixel-oriented techniques ("Pixel") – provide support to show discrete or continuous record values (features #5 and #13), and use color or size to represent them (features #9 and #11). However, they do not support the presentation of frequencies (feature #6). Group 3 has three techniques: GPLOM, generalized pairs plot ("G.P.Plot"), and dimensional stacking ("D.Stacking"). They enable the users to see the record values, and also the frequencies of values (features #5 and #6). Besides GPLOM and generalized pairs plot have almost all the features we analyzed.

It is worth noting that most of the analyzed techniques enable filtering, brushing or reordering (features #7 and #8). Besides, the heatmap matrix is the only technique among the analyzed ones that uses color to map frequency of values (feature #10), while the techniques that represent frequencies use sizes of rectangles (bars and boxes) (feature #11).

3. FEATURE SELECTION

After analyzing the visualizations presented at Section 2, we observed that the heatmap matrix does not have seven of the features listed at Table 1 (#3, #5, #7, #8, #9, #11, and #13). From these ones, we identified that features #7 (reordering), #8 (interactivity/filtering), and #13 (support to categorical, ordinal, or quantitative variables) could be added to the visualization, as we will present in this section. Features #5 and #9 are out of the scope of this technique, which is focused on showing frequency values instead of record values. We did not consider to add feature #11 (mapping format or size of the mark to some variable) because all variables are used in the columns and rows of the heatmap matrix. We also chose not to add feature #3 to avoid potential cognitive overload of the user. Therefore, we propose to add to the heatmap matrix the following resources:

a) Heatmap reordering. Matrix reordering algorithms search for row and column permutations of a matrix to easy the understanding of its data (Behrisch et al., 2016; Silva, 2021). We added to the heatmap matrix a resource for reordering the rows and columns of its heatmaps, in order to reveal patterns in the dataset. We proposed four ways to reorder these heatmaps – we called these ways "reordering focuses". The proposed focuses are:

1. "*Sort all heatmaps*": Individual reordering of each heatmap of the visual structure, aiming to reveal patterns regarding each pair of variables.
2. "*Sort heatmap and spread*": Reordering a given heatmap $V_i \times V_j$. The new order of the values of V_i (or V_j) is also applied to each heatmap that has V_i (or V_j) in one of its axes. Users must select which variables will be considered as V_i and V_j. The aim is to reveal patterns regarding a single pair of variables.
3. "*Sort selected variables*": Reordering each variable V_i selected by the user. To define the new order of the values of V_i, the reordering algorithm should consider a matrix composed by the concatenation of all heatmaps that have V_i in the horizontal axis (except $V_i \times V_i$), as the example of Figure 2. The goal is to reveal patterns regarding the relationship of each selected variable and all other variables.

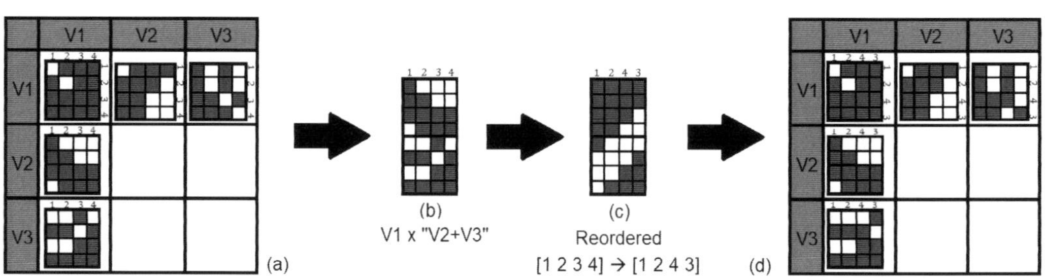

Figure 2. Reordering with "Sort selected variables" focus applied to variable V1. (a) Heatmap matrix with variables V1, V2 and V3. (b) Matrix that concatenates V1×V2 and V1×V3. (c) Reordered version of the matrix (b); (d) Heatmap matrix reordered according to the new order of V1. Cells that were not drawn in (a) and (d) are not affected by this reordering

4. "*Sort all variables*": Similar to the previous item, but it considers all variables of the heatmap instead of a subset of them.

Before reordering the heatmap matrix, it is necessary to choose one of these focuses, a set of variables related to the selected focus (when applicable), and a matrix reordering method. It is also worth to consider if the variables to be reordered are nominal, so that they really can be reordered without semantic problems.

b) Filtering by correlation and by association rules. Aiming to focus the users on possibly relevant relationships between quantitative variables, we provided a filtering capability based on correlation between pairs of variables. To use this feature, the user must provide a filtering value $\rho_{threshold}$ between 0 and 1. For each pair of quantitative variables V_i and V_j from a dataset, consider $\rho_{i,j}$ as the Spearman correlation coefficient between V_i and V_j. If $|\rho_{i,j}| > \rho_{threshold}$, the heatmap remains visible; otherwise, it is replaced with a label with the value of $\rho_{i,j}$.

Two other filtering resources are based on the analysis of which variables and variable values should be hidden, according to association rules provided by an algorithm. Given a set of association rules, the "Filter Variables" feature keeps in the heatmap matrix only the variables that are mentioned by these rules. The "Filter Labels" feature only shows the values (labels) that are cited by these rules, and their respective variables. Given that we opted by using the Apriori association rule mining algorithm (Agrawal and Srikant, 1994) in this proposal, users that want to use these filters must inform the minimal support (*minsup*) and the minimal confidence (*minconf*) values for it.

When one of these filters is applied, the visualization highlights the cells whose values are related to some rule. In our current implementation, we use a version of the Apriori algorithm that creates rules with only 1 consequent. Considering this, cells related to rules with the same consequent are colored with the same color.

c) Discretization. If a user wants to use a heatmap matrix to analyze a dataset that has quantitative variables, first they must be discretized. Among a large set of discretization methods (see Garcia et al. (2013) for a survey), we chose two unsupervised ones to add to the technique: equal width and equal frequency (Dougherty et al., 1995). *Equal width* splits the domain of a variable in a set of k intervals with the same size. On the other hand, *equal frequency* splits the domain of a variable in a set of k intervals with approximately the same number of elements. Therefore, the user must inform the desired number k of intervals (bins) and the discretization method to each variable to be discretized. These methods were selected due to their simplicity, as an initial approach to emphasize our point of view about the relevance of discretization for the heatmap matrix.

d) Global or local color mapping. Users can switch between global or local color mapping. When using *local color mapping*, the color scale is applied independently to each heatmap, considering its minimal and maximal values. On the other hand, the *global color mapping* defines that the color scale must consider the minimal and maximal values of the entire set of heatmaps of the visual structure. Therefore, the global color mapping can better reveal outliers in the entire heatmap matrix, while the local color mapping can help to reveal relationships between pairs of variables of a heatmap.

It is also worth to report that we reduced the unused space of the original version of the heatmap matrix technique by representing $V_i \times V_j$ for every pair (V_i, V_j) of dataset variables. The version of Rocha and Silva (2018) depicted only $V_i \times V_j, i > j$. As in the SPLOM, we noted that having a complete row (or column) with all the dataset variables compared to a single variable V_i is relevant when the user is focused on that specific variable. Therefore, placing V_i in the same axis in many heatmaps is useful for this kind of comparison.

4. RESULTS AND LIMITATIONS

We present two case studies in which we used a heatmap matrix to assist the interpretation of datasets. Both studies were supported by a Java-based tool that implements all the features presented in the previous section. We also present a brief discussion about limitations of this technique.

The first study comprises a dataset named "Sleep Study"[1], related to a pilot study about sleeping habits of 104 individuals within USA. This dataset has the following six variables (and respective questions and values):

- *Enough*: Do you think that you get enough sleep? (Yes/No);
- *Hours*: On average, how many hours of sleep do you get on a weeknight? (Integer);
- *PhoneReach*: Do you sleep with your phone within arms' reach? (Yes/No);

[1] "Sleep Study" dataset available at https://www.kaggle.com/mlomuscio/sleepstudypilot (February 9th, 2022).

- *PhoneTime*: Do you use your phone within 30 minutes of falling asleep? (Yes/No);
- *Tired*: On a scale from 1 to 5, how tired are you throughout the day? ([1,...,5]; 1: not tired; 5: tired);
- *Breakfast*: Do you typically eat breakfast? (Yes/No).

Figure 1, at the start of the paper, presents a heatmap matrix about this dataset. It uses the global color mapping, with no heatmap reordering and no filtering. All the dataset variables have discrete data; therefore, no discretization was needed. When exploring heatmaps individually in this figure, it is possible to perceive some interesting data. For example, suppose that we want to understand what is the behavior trend of people that do not sleep enough. In the heatmap matrix presented in Figure 1, we may start the analysis with the heatmap *Enough* × *Enough*. It shows that 68 people (65%) said that they do not sleep enough. Among them, the most common behavior we observed was: sleeping 6 to 7 hours on average per night (*Enough* × *Hours*); sleeping with cell phone within arms' reach (49 people, or 72%) (*Enough* × *PhoneReach*); using the phone for 30 minutes before sleeping (55 people, or 80%) (*Enough* × *PhoneTime*); having the tiredness level probably between 3 and 4 (46 people, or 67%) (*Enough* × *Tired*); and having breakfast (38 people, or 55%) (*Enough* × *Breakfast*).

We also can filter the visualization by association rules. In this dataset, if we configure the Apriori algorithm to run with 90% of confidence and 10% of support, this algorithm returns the following rules:

- Rule 1: {6 (*Hours*) } {Yes (*PhoneTime*) } (support: 21.15% ; confidence: 91.66%);
- Rule 2: {5 (*Hours*) } {No (*Enough*) } (support: 11.53% ; confidence: 100.0%); and
- Rule 3: {8 (*Hours*) } {Yes (*PhoneTime*) } (support: 14.42% ; confidence: 93.74%).

Based on these rules, we may apply the "Filter Variables" and the "Filter Labels" resources. In the resulting visualizations (Figure 3), note that the filter hid three variables that are not related to the association rules. These rules reinforce the idea that almost all people that sleep 6 or 8 hours per night use cell phone before sleep, and that all people that sleep only 5 hours believe that they did not sleep enough.

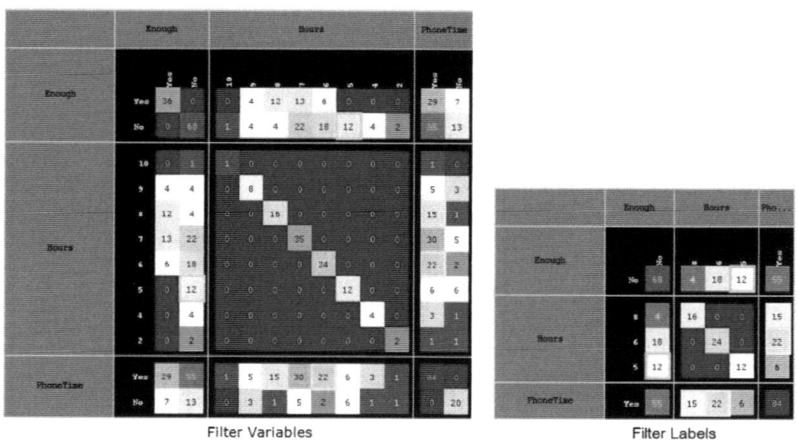

Figure 3. Filtering by association rules. Left: "Filter Variables" was applied; Right: "Filter Labels" was applied. Cells outlined in green are related to the Rule 2. Cells outlined in yellow are related to the Rules 1 and 3

In a second study case, we analyzed a dataset[2] with fictitious data about the performance of one thousand students regarding three subjects. This dataset has the following variables: Gender, Race/Ethnicity, Parental Level of Education ("parental educ. lvl."), Lunch, Test Preparation Course ("test prep"), Math Score, Reading Score, and Writing Score. Given the quantitative nature of the three scores, we need to discretize them.

For our analysis of this dataset, we used a heatmap matrix with global color mapping, equal width discretization, and no filtering (Figure 4). The visualization was reordered by the FVS algorithm (Silva et al., 2017) with the "Sort and Spread" reordering focus, based on the heatmap "*Test Preparation* × *Parental Level of Education*". In practice, it sorted the dataset according to the number of students related to each parental educational level. In this visualization, we observed a better performance of men in math scores, and of women in reading and writing scores (see the heatmaps "*Gender* × *Math Score*", "*Gender* × *Reading Score*", and "*Gender* × *Writing Score*"). We also noted that the students' scores are, in average, close to the interval [60,70],

[2]"Students Performance in Exam" available at https://www.kaggle.com/spscientist/students-performance-in-exams (February 9th, 2022).

independently of the parental level of education (see the heatmaps "*Parental Level of Education × Math Score*", "*Parental Level of Education × Reading Score*", and "*Parental Level of Education × Writing Score*"). Besides, the heatmaps that compare the Lunch variable and the variables related to scores reveal that having a standard lunch (instead of a reduced one, or no lunch) potentially helped the students in the three subjects. Also, the preparatory test seemed to be worthwhile due to the trend of higher scores for the group of students who took it (see the heatmaps related to the "*Test Preparation*" variable).

Regarding the limitations of this technique, it is worth considering that the use of colors to convey information about frequency of records provides a limited level of precision in the interpretation of the visualization. We tried to minimize this problem using cell labels that may be turned on or off according to users' needs, and zooming resources. Scalability issues may arise as the number of discrete values per variable or the number of variables increase. We provided filtering capabilities to minimize these potential problems.

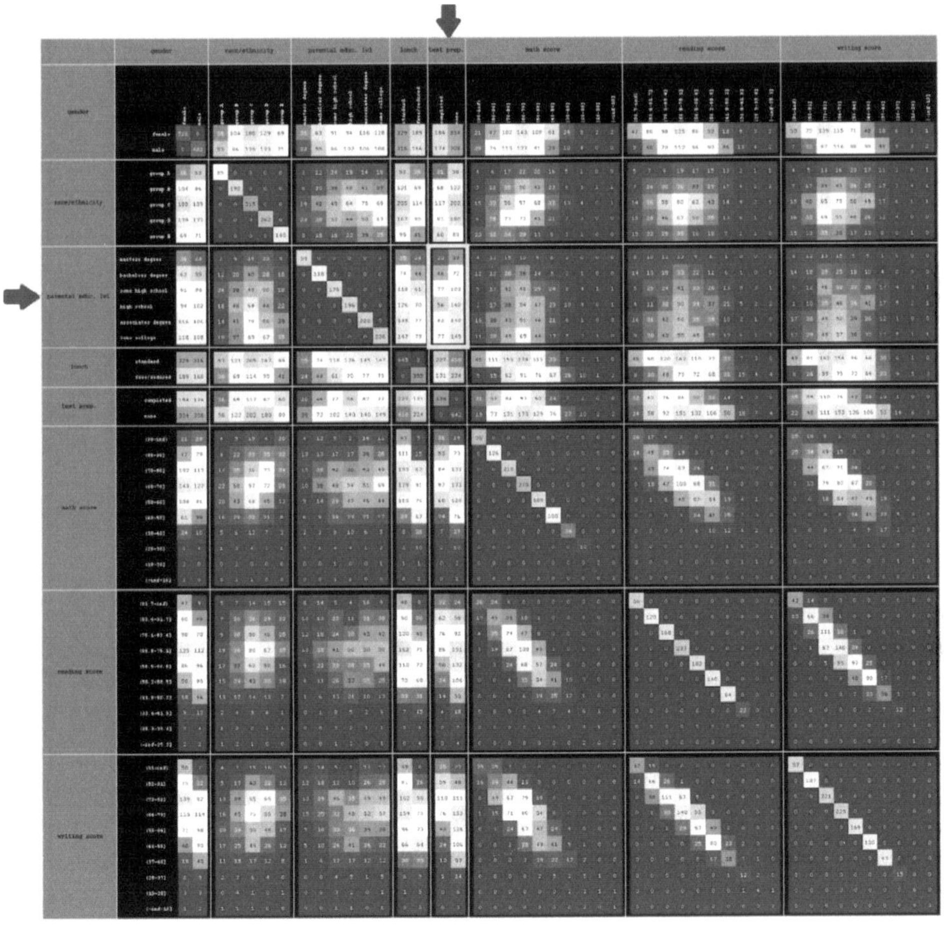

Figure 4. Heatmap matrix for the "Students Performance in Exam" dataset. Global color mapping, equal width discretization, no filtering. Matrix reordered with the "Sort and Spread" focus applied to the highlighted heatmap

5. CONCLUSION

Having a variety of interactive multidimensional data visualization techniques is essential to help users to interpret datasets. In this paper, we added to the heatmap matrix technique a set of interactive features to aid the analysis of multidimensional datasets. The users may use this visualization to analyze datasets with discrete or continuous variables, with the support of discretization methods. Filters based on correlation of quantitative variables or on the elements of association rules can be used to hide unnecessary data and to focus users on relevant values and patterns. The users may select global color mapping to make a better comparison between heatmaps, or local color mapping to focus on differences inside each heatmap. Matrix reordering capabilities complement this set of features, assisting users to perceive patterns and trends.

Future works related to this technique include: enabling the users to inform the domain and type of each variable of the input dataset; enabling manual and automatic reordering of the variables presented in the visual structure (instead of only providing reordering of values within each variable); and testing the implementation of this technique with users to evaluate how we can better enhance this technique.

ACKNOWLEDGEMENT

This study was financed in part by the Coordenação de Aperfeiçoamento de Pessoal de Nível Superior – Brasil (CAPES) – Finance Code 001. We also thank the grant #2126/22 from FAEPEX/PRP/Unicamp.

REFERENCES

Agrawal, R. and Srikant, R. (1994). Fast algorithms for mining association rules in large databases. In *Proc. 20th International Conference on Very Large Data Bases*, VLDB '94, pp. 487–499, San Francisco, USA.

Behrisch, M. et al. (2016). Matrix reordering methods for table and network visualization. *Computer Graphics Forum*, 35(3):693–716.

Carr, D. B. et al. (1987). Scatterplot matrix techniques for large n. *Journal of the American Statistical Association*, 82(398):424–436.

Dougherty, J. et al. (1995). Supervised and unsupervised discretization of continuous features. In Prieditis, A. and Russell, S., editors, *Machine Learning Proceedings 1995*, pp. 194–202. Morgan Kaufmann, San Francisco (CA).

Emerson, J. et al. (2012). The generalized pairs plot. *Journal of Computational and Graphical Statistics*, pp. 79–91.

Friendly, M. (1999). Extending mosaic displays: Marginal, conditional, and partial views of categorical data. *Journal of Computational and Graphical Statistics*, 8(3):373–395.

Garcia, S. et al. (2013). A survey of discretization techniques: Taxonomy and empirical analysis in supervised learning. *IEEE Transactions on Knowledge and Data Engineering, 25*(4), pp. 734–750.

Grinstein, G. et al. (2001). High-dimensional visualizations. *In: 7th Data Mining Conference-KDD 2001*. San Francisco, California.

Hartigan, J. A. and Kleiner, B. (1981). Mosaics for contingency tables. In Eddy, W. F., editor, *Computer Science and Statistics: Proceedings of the 13th Symposium on the Interface*, pp. 268–273, New York, NY. Springer US.

Im, J.-F. et al. (2013). GPLOM: The generalized plot matrix for visualizing multidimensional multivariate data. *IEEE Transactions on Visualization and Computer Graphics*, 19(12):2606– 2614.

Keim, D. A. (1996). Pixel-oriented database visualizations. *SIGMOD Record*, 25(4):35–39.

Kosara, R. et al. (2006). Parallel sets: interactive exploration and visual analysis of categorical data. *IEEE Transactions on Visualization and Computer Graphics*, 12(4):558–568.

Rao, R. and Card, S. K. (1994). The Table Lens: Merging graphical and symbolic representations in an interactive focus + context visualization for tabular information. In *Proceedings of the SIGCHI Conference on Human Factors in Computing Systems*, CHI '94, pp. 318–322, New York, NY, USA. Association for Computing Machinery.

Rocha, M. M. N. and Silva, C. G. (2018). Heatmap matrix: a multidimensional data visualization technique. In *Proc. Conference on Graphics, Patterns and Images*, vol. 31, Foz do Iguaçu, PR, Brazil. http://urlib.net/ibi/8JMKD3MGPAW/3S3FLDS.

Silva, C. G. (2021). Revealing band and circumplex patterns in reorderable matrices using Polar Sort and fast multidimensional projections. *IADIS Int. Journal on Computer Science and Information Systems*, 16(2):1–14.

Silva, C. G. et al. (2017). A fast feature vector approach for revealing simplex and equi-correlation data patterns in reorderable matrices. *Information Visualization*, 16(4):261–274.

Ward, M. et al. (2015). Interactive Data Visualization: Foundations, Techniques, and Applications. 2nd edition. CRC Press.

BIM TEACHING AND PROGRAMING IN DYNAMO APPLIED IN THE MAINTENANCE OF BUILDINGS

Alcínia Zita Sampaio, Inês Domingos and Augusto Gomes
University of Lisbon, Higher Technical Institute, Dep. Civil Engineering
Av. Rovisco Pais, Lisbon, Portugal

ABSTRACT

The Building Information Modelling (BIM) methodology has been applied in multi-tasks throughout a building life cycle. Its basic concept concerns the generation of a virtual model that allows centralizing and recording all the information produced in projecting, constructing and maintaining a building. The establishment of maintenance strategies requires a sustained knowledge regarding the durability of the materials and the costs involved. The research, elaborated in an academic context, is focused on the prediction of useful life, applied to materials most used as finishing of wall facades and roof terraces. A building case was analyzed considering the generation of the respective BIM model and the application of Dynamo scripts. Two scripts were created to support the estimation of the useful life of the materials, allowing professionals to obtain the lifetime of the components and to predict their state of degradation for a given year. The developed approach, allows engineers, in an early design stage, to prepare adequate maintenance plans, based on the knowledge of durability, useful lifetime and the degradation perdition of the materials. The work contributes positively to the implementation of BIM in the maintenance activity, with relevance to the high potential of the Dynamo tool when information management within BIM models is required. The proposed framework presents a novelty in the use of Revit+Dynamo in the support, in a visual perception, on the maintenance of a building.

KEYWORDS

BIM, Maintenance, Lifetime Prediction, Dynamo

1. INTRODUCTION

The Construction industry have been progressively incorporating the implementation of the Building Information Modelling (BIM) methodology, supported in the permanent and recent dissemination of its benefits in reports and in the advances of the required technology (Barlish & Sullivan, 2012). This methodology reveals a new and different way of working in the construction sector, when compared to traditional methods based in two-dimensional (2D) technical documents. The BIM work transmits more transparency, better communication and a greater level of collaboration between all partners involved in the development of building projects (Sampaio & Gomes, 2021). When developing a project, using BIM platforms, a BIM model representing a digital three-dimensional (3D) representation of the physical and functional characteristics of a building is created. The model brings together the information produced in the various phases of the life cycle forming a complete database supporting decision makers (Azhar *et al.*, 2008).

The Facility Management (FM) activity, in a building, covers several disciplines in ensuring the functionality of the built environment integrating people, places, processes and technologies. In this practice, BIM integration is still unusual (Sampaio *et al.*, 2016). However, it is recognized by several authors, who emphasize the ability to gather continuously during the various phases of design and construction, all the information necessary for FM, which allows improving the efficiency and productivity for the application of management processes (Pishdad-Bozorgi *et al.*, 2018). The ability to store a large amount of information and keep it accessible and updated with the facility of connecting with several FM systems, make BIM solutions very attractive. However, retrieving data from the model requires experience and relevant waste of time. The present study intends to contribute to use the database of the model and its application on the maintenance activity (Domingos, 2020). The text introduces the current practices in BIM-FM and the main advantages and limitations in using BIM platforms. The study describes the development of two Dynamo scripts created to improve the integration of BIM models to FM functionalities. The proposed framework presents a novelty in the use of Revit together with Dynamo programming, allowing to enhance a better perform of Revit, in a FM context.

2. BIM FOR FM: AN OVERVIEW

Although available for a few decades, it was only in recent years that BIM and its concepts began to spark more interest in the construction industry, extending their application to the entire life cycle of buildings. The types of building information that might be required in a model to manage the design, construction and operation of built assets can be described as dimensions (Sampaio, 2021): 3D model data (3D); time data (4D); costs (5D); sustainability (6D); facility management (7D); safety and accident prevention (8D). So, the 7th dimension comprises the application of BIM methodology in the Facility Management activity. It intends to gather all the information that has been developed and updated throughout the project, representing the as-built model of the building (Jamil *et al.*, 2019).

As the generation of a BIM model is based on the use of parametric objects, each component of construction includes data such as the type of materials applied in the building and its proprieties. And, the information required in the maintenance activity can ranges from manufacturer data, technical information on the products, warranties, user manuals and expectable service life among others necessary to support these activities (Sacks *et al.*, 2018). The main challenge is to integrate the accumulated information with the data acquired during the design and construction phases and provide the building management systems with relevant information at the time of operation (Araszkiewicz, 2017). In it, the degree of interoperability performed between different software is the main limitation in applying BIM in the operational phase of the building. However, using the native data format of the modeler system, the process of information transfer from BIM model to FM systems can be effectuated without loss of too much information. Additionally, the model can be permanently updated, allowing the facility manager to update the building's operation services (Gao, 2019).

The growing number of researches that address the BIM-FM topic is an indication of the industry's interest in its application. However there are some barriers for its adoption (Gouda *et al.*, 2020): a lack of guidance, protocols and standards for BIM FM; technical expertise needed for the maintenance and updating of the BIM; limited software interoperability; unclear BIM FM requirements at early project stages which reflects the fragmented nature of the construction industry. Therefore, it is possible to contribute to the reduction of investment costs and better facilities management services in a building (Sampaio *et al.*, 2021).

3. SERVICE LIFE PREDICTION

Over time, buildings and their components tend to deteriorate, naturally, and lose some of their original properties. The useful life or period of service of a building corresponds to the period of time during which its properties respond to or exceed the minimum acceptable levels for its operation of intrinsic order to the element, normative or subjective, in a situation of current maintenance (ISO 15686-1., 2000). The degradation of a component is a consequence of the natural aging process, associated with exposure to adverse environmental conditions. The evaluation of the degradation level is based on mathematical models, which consider several types of variables, and when properly adjusted, allow estimating the remaining lifetime of the element under analysis.

The awareness of the relevance of buildings' durability for a more sustainable construction led to the establishment of several methodologies for the prediction of a building's service life. According to Moser and Hovde (2004) the following prediction methods can be considered deterministic, probabilistic (or stochastic) and engineering methods.

The factor method fits into the deterministic methods as a simplified approach to support the prediction of the service life of construction components. This method consists in the prediction of a value for the estimated service life (ESL) of a given construction element, obtain by the product of the reference service life (RSL) value, under standard conditions, by several deterministic factors (Table 1).

Table 1. Formula to calculate the value for the estimated service life (ESL)

ESL = RSL x factor A x factor B x factor C x factor D x factor E x factor F x factor G		
factor A – quality of components	factor B – design level	factor B – design level
factor C – work execution level	factor D – indoor environment	factor E – outdoor environment
factor F – in-use conditions	factor G – maintenance level	

The different factors include the information listed:

- **Factor A**: represents the quality of the material or component of the construction under the conditions in which it is presented on site, being subject to the way it was manufactured, its characteristics and its conformity in relation to the technical standards that refer to the functional and environmental needs of the building;
- **Factor B**: represents the level of quality of the project according to its implementation in the building, and should reflect how the project provides each component with additional protection against degradation agents;
- **Factor C**: represents the level of quality of execution and is related to the process of execution of the work on site, with regard to compliance with the idealized constructive conditions, as well as the degree of supervision existing in the work;
- **Factor D**: represents the characteristics of the interior environment, in particular exposure to degradation agents and their severity, the type of use of the building and the location of the element in relation to relevant locations such as proximity to damp places (bathroom and kitchen);
- **Factor E**: represents the characteristics of the outdoor environment encompassing factors related to sun exposure, wind, humidity, among other degradation agents where its combination can have a critical effect;
- **Factor F**: represents the characteristics of the use and reflects the effect of using the building, namely the type of use of the space where the component is located;
- **Factor G**: represents the level of maintenance and, even if this forecast is made on the basis of the established maintenance planning, it is necessary to verify its suitability for the building under analysis, in particular the accessibility of the element or the need for special equipment. The experience of the specialist technician in relation to the maintenance activity should also be considered.

The factorial method provides only an empirical estimate based on the available information, but constitutes an expedient way of gathering the influence of each of the variables that can affect the life of the element. However, the method can be applied to carry out a systematic evaluation, even when the reference conditions do not correspond to all the intended conditions of use and also allows the incorporation, at any stage of the process, of additional information to complement the forecast of useful life:

- The RSL value is influenced by data provided by the manufacturer, homologated documentation or thematic bibliography, and by the collection of information verified in similar cases under identical conditions of use;
- The factors should have values between 0.8 and 1.2 where: the unit value is assigned when the factor has no weight for the element under study; a higher value corresponds to an increase of the ESL; a lower value is reflected in a decrease of the estimated service life.

In the present study, the bibliographical references of Raposo (2009) (Table 2), Lopes (2009) and Matos (2007) were consulted, where three cases of application of the factor method according to the guidelines of the ISO 15686-1 standard were considered. In each case a durability matrix is presented, developed by each author listed in tables, containing the factors applicable to a set of construction components:

- Cladding applied on flat roofs;
- Adherent ceramic tiling on façades; ventilated façade tiling.

The values of these tables are used in the developed Dynamo script.

Table 2. Factor A of the durability matrix of cladding applied on flat roofs (Raposo, 2009)

Factor		Description	Indice
Factor A	A1	**Declaration of Conformity and Quality Certificate**	
		With EC Declaration of Conformity and Quality Certificate	1.2
		With EC declaration of conformity or Quality Certificate	1,0
	A2	**Characteristics of thermal insulation of the cover**	1.2
		With ISOLE rating higher than recommended for coverage type	1.0
		With the recommended ISOLE rating for the coverage type	0.8
	A3	**Type of bituminous membrane armor**	
		Polyester felt of 250 g/m2 or armed with polyester and fiberglass felts	
		With polyester felt of at least 150 g/m2	
		With polyester felt less than 150 g/m2 or with fiberglass felt	

4. VISUAL PROGRAMMING IN DYNAMO

An adequate performance of buildings is becoming an important aspect to be studied by professionals involved in the construction process, concerned both in the short and long term, in terms of costs and durability, with the implicit need for the maintenance process to be discussed at an early stage of the construction process. In this context, the present study proposes to include the factor method for estimating the service life of elements in construction. The study involves the development of two scripts, defined using the visual programming tool Dynamo (Dynamo, 2020): the "Estimate Service Life" script and the "ESL Analysis". The scripts were applied over a case study allowing verifying its efficiency.

4.1 Dynamo Script "Estimate Service Life"

As a data base to be used on development of the script "Estimate Service Life" are the durability matrices of the tables of the referred authors. These were integrated in the script so that the options of each factor can be selected according to the element and material used in order to estimate the respective service life value. The script can run over projects modelled in Revit and applied over the considered constructive elements: roof waterproofing membranes; adherent ceramic tiling on facades; ventilated facade claddings. To script "Estimate Service Life" was created using Dynamo visual programming which main structure is represented in Figure 1.

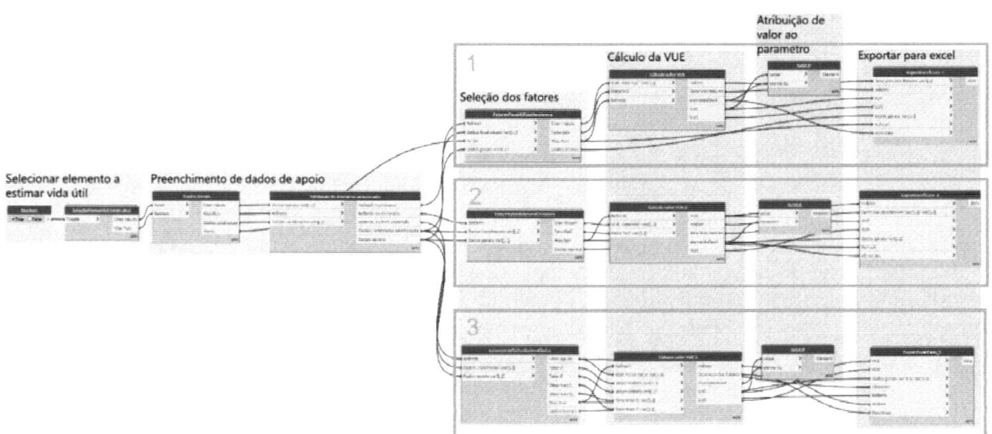

Figure 1. Dynamo script "Estimate Service Life"

In order to assist the filling of the factors (in green), a database was created using the DataBase Browser software and the nodes present in the Slingshot package were used to link the database to Dynamo. Depending of the parameters, such as the location of the project, the connection to the database provides data relating to the characteristics of the outdoor environment (summer and winter climate zone, rainfall zone, average annual number of days with frost and solar radiation index) essential to characterize the factor E.

The groups of nodes (blue) have been programmed to calculate the service life according to the factor method (depending on the indexes selected in each interface); assign the calculated value to the project parameter in Revit; and export information to the selected Excel file.

4.2 Dynamo Script "ESL Analysis"

The "ESL Analysis" script was created as a complement to the previous script, and its use requires that the first script have already been executed. Thus, for the elements of the model to which the ESL is assigned it is possible to make a prognosis of their degradation state for a given year. For this, a linear degradation of the elements was assumed, where a set of colours was assigned according to the range in which the *% of lifespan* is obtained (Figure 2).

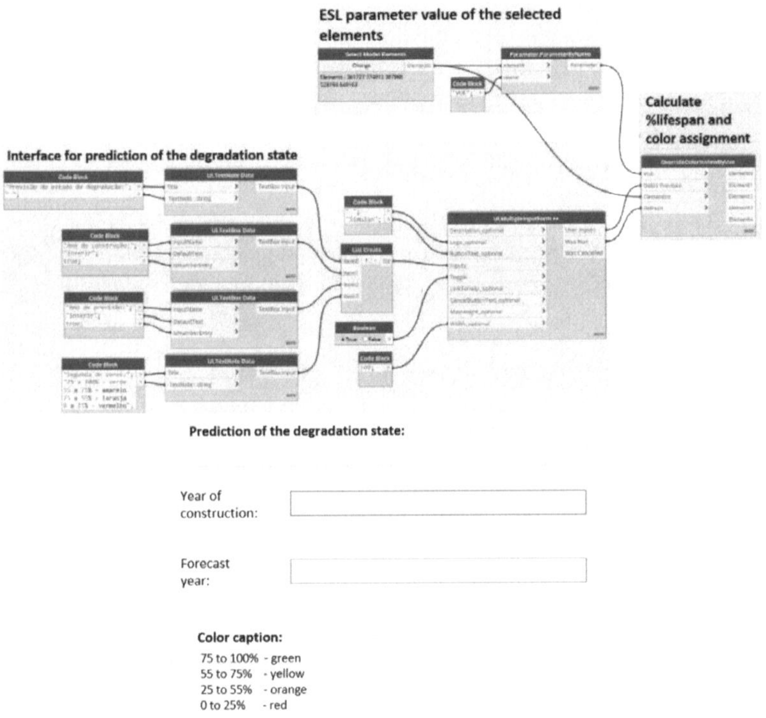

Figure 2. Dynamo script "ESL analyses" and the assignment of colors

Depending on the interval in which the calculated percentage is inserted, the element displays the color assigned to the interval. The green color corresponds to an initial degradation state, while the red color is assigned to an advanced degradation state.

5. CASE STUDY

The selected case study corresponds to a building integrated in a private complex, located in the Lisbon area, with 5 elevated floors, 3 floors in semi-basement and roof terrace. It presents two blind warps oriented to West and Northeast. The BIM architectural model was created using the Revit software (Figure 4):

- The main façade, facing north, consists of a double wall in **brick masonry**, and is covered with adherent tiles in porcelain stoneware;
- The Southeast oriented façade, a solution in **ventilated façade** clad with fiber cement plates;

- On the roof terrace was applied, as a finishing material, the **waterproofing membrane** in APP polymer bitumen self-protected with mineral granulate.

a *b* *c*

Figure 3. Main façade with tiles (a), rear façade with fiber cement (b) and flat roof (c)

The parametric objects used in the modelling process of the building were incremented with the necessary parameters related to the ESL of the components under analysis. New parameters were created, associated to the materials, in order to be able to admit, in a dynamic way, the values to be calculated through the two Dynamo scripts presented:

- **ESL**, receives the service life value estimated by the "Estimate Service Life" script;
- **Maintenance Excel**, registers the directory of the Excel file that when selected opens the file;
- **% lifespan**, variable calculated based on the ESL parameter and the forecast year, controlled in the script "ESL Analysis".

5.1 Application of "Estimate Service Life" Script

The execution of the script is running through Dynamo Player option included in the upper menu of Revit. The script was successfully executed to estimate the service life of each of the materials identified and the result is visualized in Figure 4. A table with the numerical results can be accessed and the aspect of the deterioration is illustrated by the color assumed by each element. A period of ten years, from year 2020 and 2030, were filled as an example to simulate the year of construction and the year for life forecast respectively.

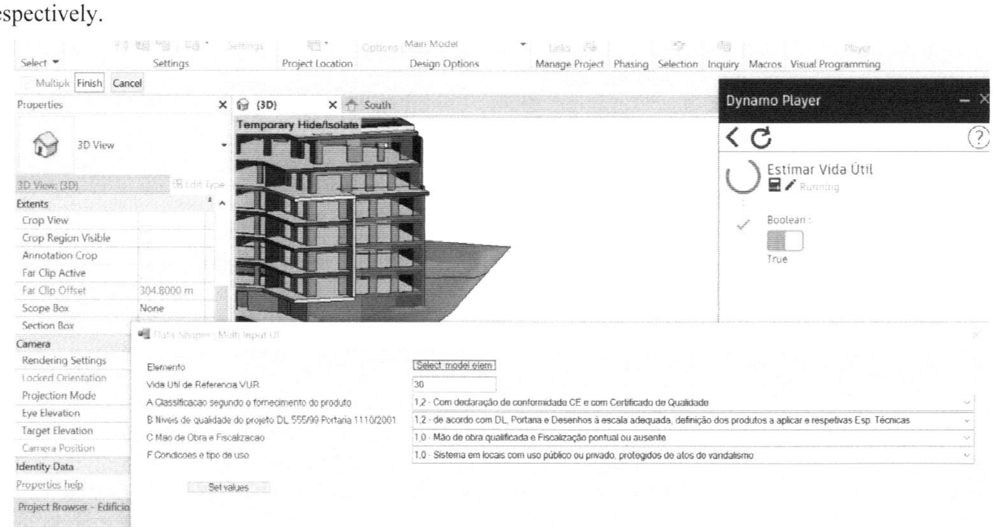

(a)

Technician's name:	Inês Domingos
Date:	2020
Element category:	Wall
Element type:	Ventilated wall
Fixing system:	At sight
Maintenance target element:	Fiber cement plates 180x100cm
Year of construction:	2020
Reference service life (RSL):	30
Estimate service life (ESL):	34,6
Total facade area [m²]:	219
Replacement cost [€/m²]:	96
Clean cost [€/m²]:	19,49
Inspection cost [€]:	70

(b)

Figure 4 (a and b). Visualization of the degree of deterioration and respective values

5.2 Application of "ESL Analysis" Script

To simplify the use of this script, the 3D view of the model was duplicated with an associated filter so that only the objects that contain the ESL parameter are visible. The new view was called "Life Analysis", and in this way the assignment of colors to the objects of the model do not overlap with the colors of the original model. This view is selected to run the script in order to see the life effects in a certain period. When the script is executed, all the elements present in the mentioned view are selected, which include the two facades and the roof under analysis. When the script is completed it is possible to observe the elements with a distinct coloring, represented in the view created. The result of the inserted values is the parameter % lifespan (automatically field) calculated for each element in Figure 4. It can be observed that the wall in porcelain stoneware (colored in green) presents a greater durability for the year 2030 than the other wall (colored in yellow) and the waterproofing membrane (colored in orange) which will be near the replacement year in 2030 if they do not receive maintenance actions.

After, an Excel table is obtained and exported supporting professionals to define or verify maintenance actions or plans. With the Excel data it is possible to explore scenarios of maintenance actions, combined with the element's costs, areas of refurbishing and periodicity of actions to be performed. The planning of the activities can be readjusted to what is necessary according to the state of degradation of the elements during the period in service.

6. CONCLUSION

The use of Dynamo allowed to show the tool's potential in the way it can explore, manipulate and export the data of the BIM model. The developed scripts allowed an analysis of the durability of the elements in the design phase where the change of solutions have less impact on overall costs. However, the BIM objects did not have the necessary parameters for the application of the factor method, highlighting the need to include in the digital catalog of each object the RSL to be able to evaluate the durability of the constructive elements in the project to which they are applied, taking into account all the factors to be fulfilled by the technician.

The execution of each of the scripts occurred without problems and no errors were reported by Dynamo. However, to apply these scripts to a BIM model it is necessary to create the project parameters: ESL, Maintenance Excel, % lifespan and all the cost's parameters, as they were named when in Dynamo. To get through this point it was necessary to include in the script the creation of each parameter. The perspective of the study was directed towards the occupation phase of the building, which since it is the phase of longer duration and where the maintenance activity increases costs that sometimes exceed the initial investment, the use of BIM has the potential to gather all the information to support this phase and reduce the associated costs. Its implementation is not yet recurrent at a business level, particularly in the national context, although as demonstrated in this study, the tools exist to allow it. The proposed framework presents a novelty in the use of Revit + Dynamo, as an important support on the visual perception of the maintenance state of a building.

REFERENCES

Araszkiewicz, K. (2017). Digital Technologies in Facility Management – The state of Practice and Research Challenges. *Procedia Engineering*, 196, pp. 1034–1042. https://doi.org/10.1016/j.proeng.2017.08.059

Azhar, S., Hein, M. & Sketo B. (2008) Building information modelling (BIM): Benefits, risks and challenges, *44th ASC Proceeding of National Conference*, USA, 2008. https://www.academia.edu/1216737/Building_information_modeling_BIM_Benefits_risks_and_challenges

Barlish, K. & Sullivan, K. (2012) How to measure the benefits of BIM: A case study approach, *Automation in Construction*, Ed. Elsevier Science, 24 (2012), pp. 129–159, doi:10.1016/j.autcon.2012.02.008.

Domingos, I. (2020). The 7D/BIM model used in the maintenance of buildings. Master Thesis in Civil Engineering, University of Lisbon. Higher Technical Scholl, Lisbon, Portugal. https://fenix.tecnico.ulisboa.pt/departamentos/decivil/dissertacao/1128253548922467

Dynamo (2020) *The Dynamo Primer*. https://primer.dynamobim.org

Gao, X., & Pishdad-Bozorgi, P. (2019). BIM-enabled facilities operation and maintenance: A review. *Advanced Engineering Informatics*, 39, pp. 227-247. Available in: https://doi.org/10.1016/j.aei.2019.01.005.

Gouda, A., Mohamed, M., Abdallah, R. & Marzoukc, M. (2020). BIM and semantic web-based maintenance information for existing buildings. *Automation in Construction*, 116, 103209. Available in: https://doi.org/10.1016/j.autcon.2020.103209.

Hovde, P. J., & Moser, K. (2004). Performance based methods for service life prediction. *In State of the art reports, CIB Report: Publication* (Vol. 294).

ISO 15686-1. (2000). Buildings and constructed assets - Service life planning - Part 1: General Principles. *ISO - International Organization for Standardization*, Geneva. https://www.iso.org/obp/ui/#iso:std:iso:15686:-5:ed-2:v1:en

Jamil, G.L., Ribeiro, F., Silva, A.M. & Lopes, S.M. (2019). *Handbook of research on emerging technologies for effective project management*. IGI Global, 2019 Edition. United States of America. ISBN 1522599940. https://books.google.pt/books?id=Z1SzDwAAQBAJ

Lopes, C. (2009). Durability in Construction. Estimated life of façade ceramic coatings. *Master thesis in Civil Engineering*. University of Porto, Faculty of Engineering, Porto, Portugal.

Matos, M. (2007). Durability as a design criterion. The factorial method in the Portuguese context. *Master thesis in Civil Engineering*. University of Porto, Faculty of Engineering, Porto, Portugal.

Pishdad-Bozorgi, P., Xinghua Gao, X., Eastman, C. & Patrick, A.S. (2018). Planning and developing facility management enabled Building Information Model (FM enabled BIM). *Automation in Construction*, 87, pp. 22-38. https://doi.org/10.1016/j.autcon.2017.12.004.

Raposo, T. (2009). Durability of the building. Estimated life of flat cover coatings. *Master thesis in Civil Enginnering*, University of Porto, Faculty of Engineering, Porto, Portugal.

Sacks, R., Eastman, C., Lee, G. & Teicholz, P. (2018) *BIM Handbook: A Guide to Building Information Modeling for Owners, Managers, Architects, Engineers and Contractors*, Third Edition Copyright © 2018 by John Wiley & Sons, Inc. New Jersey, USA. ISBN: 9781119287537, DOI: 10.1002/9781119287568

Sampaio, A.Z. & Gomes, A.M. (2021) BIM interoperability in structural design, MDPI – Civil Engineering, Special issue: *Advances in Civil Engineering*. ISSN: 2673-4109. CivilEng 2021, 2(1), 174-192, https://doi.org/10.3390/civileng2010010

Sampaio, A.Z. (2021) Maturity of BIM implementation in the construction industry: governmental policies, *IJETT- International Journal of Engineering Trends and Technology*, Volume 69 Issue 7, 92-100, July, 2021 ISSN: 2231 – 5381 /doi:10.14445/22315381/IJETT-V69I7P214 ©2021 Seventh Sense Research Group®, http://www.ijettjournal.org/archive/ijett-v69i7p214

Sampaio, A.Z., Gomes, A.M., Lite, A.S., Zulueta, P. & González-Gaya, C. (2021) Analysis of BIM Methodology Applied to Practical Cases in the Preservation of Heritage Buildings, *MDPI - Sustainability, Special issue: Strategies for the Conservation of Industrial Heritage Aligned with the Sustainable Development Goals*, ISSN 2071-1050, 2021, 13, 3129. https://doi.org/10.3390/su13063129

Sampaio, A.Z., Simões, D.G. & Berdeja, E.P. (2016), BIM tools used in maintenance of buildings and on conflict detection, Book: *Sustainable Construction: Building Performance Simulation and Asset and Maintenance Management* (Vol. 8), March 2016, ch.8, pp. 163-183, http://www.springer.com/gp/book/9789811006500, http://www.springer.com/series/10019

3D POSE ESTIMATION BY GROUPED FEATURE FUSION AND MOTION AMPLITUDE ENCODING

Jihua Peng[1,2], Yanghong Zhou[1,2] and P.Y. Mok[1,2]
[1]*Institute of Textiles and Clothing, The Hong Kong Polytechnic University, Hunghom, Hong Kong*
[2]*Laboratory for Artificial Intelligence in Design, Hong Kong Special Administrative Region, Hong Kong*

ABSTRACT

3D human pose estimation is challenging and converting it to a local pose estimation problem by dividing human body into different groups based on anatomical relationships can improve the accuracy of the resulting 3D pose estimation. Joint features of different groups are fused to predict complete pose information of entire body, in which a joint feature fusion scheme must be used for this purpose. However, the joint feature fusion adopted in existing methods has to learn a large number of parameters and is computational expensive. In this paper, we propose an optimized feature fusion (OFF) module, which requires fewer parameters and less calculations while ensures prediction accuracy. Moreover, we also propose a motion amplitude encoding (MAE) method to improve the prediction accuracy for small ranged movements. Experiments have shown that our method outperforms previous state-of-the-art results on Human3.6M dataset.

KEYWORDS

Human Pose Estimation, Feature Fusion, Motion Amplitude.

1. INTRODUCTION

3D human pose estimation is a traditional task in computer vision as it can be applied in many fields, such as cloth parsing (Dong et al., 2014), hospital surveillance (Liu et al., 2018), augmented reality (Lin & Chen, 2010), action prediction (Luvizon et al., 2018). It aims to predict the 3D space coordinates of each human body joint from an input image or video. The current 3D human pose estimation methods based on convolutional neural networks mainly adopt two approaches: 1) directly regressing the 3D locations of each joint from 2D images; 2) first predicting the 2D joint coordinates from the image and then lifting these 2D key points into a 3D space. The second approach significantly outperforms the first one, since these methods benefit from the high performance of intermediate 2D pose detectors (Chen et al., 2018; Sun et al., 2019). Some researchers proposed to group human joints into parts, such as arms, legs and torso, based on kinematics and human anatomy to improve prediction accuracy (Cai et al., 2019; Lee et al., 2018; Wandt & Rosenhahn, 2019). They first encode each part to get the corresponding features, and then fuse these features together to get a complete human pose. Although the features of each part are independently predicted, different parts affect each other and their features are also related mutually. For example, there is interaction between the arm and the head for poses in "Eating", while the hand and the foot are closely related when performing poses "Running". In these methods, a feature fusion module is used to fuse the features of different parts together; while many existing feature fusion methods just use fully connected layers, resulting in large number of parameters and high computation costs. In this paper, we propose an optimized feature fusion module for 3D pose estimation, which requires fewer parameters and has lower computational complexity, but improves the accuracy of prediction.

In order to obtain the features of each body part, we use the temporal convolutional network (TCN) (Pavllo et al., 2019) as a basic encoding structure. This network structure uses dilated temporal convolutions that process multiple 2d poses in parallel and output a 3D pose from an input 2d pose sequence. The error of one pose will not interfere with the prediction of other poses. Some follow-up works (Chen et al., 2021; Liu et al., 2020; Xu et al., 2020; Zeng et al., 2020) are proposed based on temporal convolutional network structure (Pavllo et al., 2019), but none of them solve the problem of the shallow layer of the temporal convolutional network. The shallow temporal convolutional network aggregates only a small part of the 2d pose information of the receptive field. It ignores the position and angle changes of the joints of these poses relative to the target pose joints. If the motion amplitude of some actions is very small, it is difficult for the network to learn enough information from them. Based on the above problems, we propose a method to encode the motion amplitude of human joints. This method can amplify the difference between other poses and the target pose, allowing the network to learn the angle change.

2. RELATED WORK

3D human pose estimation has been studied since a very early time. Early traditional methods utilized pictorial structures to predict 3D coordinates of human joints. These methods usually require tedious manual operations and a large amount of calculation and get bad results when encountering some complex poses. Thanks to the development of convolutional neural networks, methods based on deep learning have achieved good results. These methods can be divided into two categories. Some early works (Li & Chen, 2014; Pavlakos et al., 2017; Tekin et al., 2016) directly predict the 3D human joints from the input image or video through neural networks, which is called one-step regression method. Recently, benefit from recent advancement in 2D pose detectors, many methods first detect the coordinates of the 2D pose joints, and then use these 2D coordinates to regress the human pose joint in the 3D space.

Pose estimation based on temporal information. Estimating 3D human pose from single-view images is very challenging because of shortage of information. Therefore, researchers attempted to learn temporal information from videos to achieve more stable and jitter-free prediction results. The LSTM model is the first sequence-to-sequence model that extract 3D human pose information from videos. It mainly encodes the coordinates of 2d human joint, and then decodes them into coordinates in 3d space (Hossain & Little, 2018). Lee et al. (2018) design a propagating LSTM structure based on joint interdependency to learn the spatial position relationship of each joint of the human body. Katircioglu et al. (2018) introduce a new deep neural network based on LSTM to learn human pose features in latent space. However, LSTM cannot process multiple frames in parallel, but store them sequentially in memory resulting in many parameters. To address this problem, temporal convolutional network (TCN) is proposed for 3D human pose estimation (Pavllo et al. 2019). It performs 1D convolutions over 2d input pose sequences with fewer parameters. Liu et al. (2020) apply attention mechanism to TCN, which determine key frames and output tensor in every layer. Zeng et al. (2020) separate human joints into different groups and perform temporal convolution in each group. Finally, joints of different groups are merged into a complete human pose. Similarly, Shan et al. (2021) categorize joints into five groups and design a feature fusion module to fuse five different features after performing temporal convolution for each group. Chen et al. (2021) transform TCN to predict both direction and length of the bones.

Pose estimation based on grouping strategy. Many current methods (Park & Kwak, 2018; Shan et al., 2021; Wang et al., 2019; Zeng et al., 2020; Zheng et al., 2020) group body parts to predict 3d human pose according to the anatomical relationship of human joints. Park and Kwak (2018) propose to divide human joints into 5 non-overlapping groups (torso, left arms, right arms, left legs, right legs). Then the features learned by these 5 groups are averaged to produce the feature of the whole pose. Wang et al. (2019) define the degrees of freedom (DOF) and model limbs with higher DOFs and torso with lower DOFs. In this way, various body parts with different DOFs can supervise each other, leading to more reasonable prediction results. Zheng et al. (2020) treat each joint as a group and design a dual attention module to learn the feature relationship between each group. Zeng et al. (2020) divide the human body into local groups of joints and develop a network to learn internal dependencies within each group and weak dependencies among groups. Shan et al. (2021) split the human body into five groups (torso, left/right arms, left/right legs), encode the features of each group separately, and design a feature fusion module to fuse the 5 groups of features to obtain a complete human body.

3. METHOD

Our network framework is shown in Figure 1, which the network structure of Shan et al. (2021) is the baseline. The input of the network is the coordinate of the 2D pose that have been predicted from the images. We propose an encoding method for motion amplitude information to solve the problem of small movement range. It first processes the input 2d pose joints of target pose and other poses to obtain the angle change information, and then divides the information together with positional and temporal information into five groups (torso, left arm, right arm, left leg, right leg). Then, we input all the information into the TCN network for encoding. Next, we propose a new optimized feature fusion module to fuse the five groups of features. After feature fusion, we decode the 5 groups of features to get the coordinates of the joint points of the 5 body parts, and finally concatenate them together to get the complete human pose.

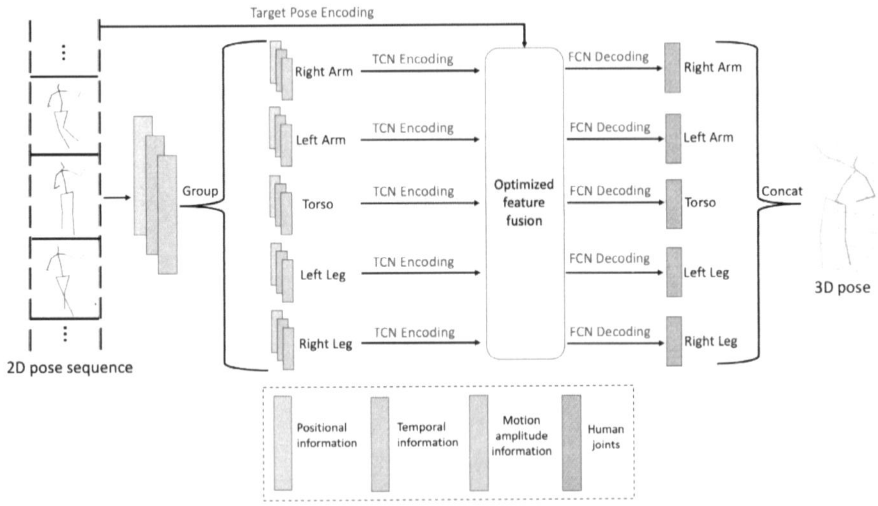

Figure 1. The proposed network framework. The input is a 2D pose sequence. In addition to calculating positional and temporal information proposed by (Shan et al., 2021), we also process the initial input into motion amplitude information. Then the three information plus the original input are divided into five groups and input into TCN for feature encoding. The encoded information and the target pose information are input to the optimized feature fusion module for feature fusion. Finally, all features are sent to FCN for decoding to produce 3d pose

3.1 Motion Amplitude Encoding

We define the input 2d pose as P, $P = \{J_1, J_2, ..., J_K\}$, J_i represents the joint of the human body, $J_i \in R^2$, $I = 1, 2, ..., K$, $P \in R^{K \times 2}$. As shown in Figure 2, we align all poses to the root joint to get the relative coordinates of each pose $P' = \{J'_1, J'_2, ..., J'_K\}$. The target pose with relative coordinates is expressed as $P'_t = \{J'_{t1}, J'_{t2}, ..., J'_{tK}\}$. The orange dots and the black solid line indicate the target pose, while yellow dots and dotted lines indicate hand joints in other poses. The orange palm point and the root joint form a green dashed vector, which is also the coordinate of the orange palm point relative to the root joint. Similarly, the yellow palm point and the root joint form a blue dashed vector, which is also the relative coordinate of the yellow palm point. The angle θ formed by the green dashed vector and the blue dashed vector represents the motion amplitude of the joint of other poses relative to the target pose. We define the encoding method of human joint motion amplitude as

$$\varphi(J_i', J_{ti}') = \exp[\theta - \pi] \quad (1)$$

where the angle θ is calculated as

$$\theta = \cos^{-1}\frac{(J_i' \cdot J_{ti}')}{\|J_i'\|\|J_{ti}'\|} \quad (2)$$

An exponential function with a base of e as an encoding method can ensure the normalization of angle information and allow learning the information of angle change accurately. Therefore, the equation of change range for all corresponding joints between the target pose and other poses is calculated as

$$I = \varphi(P', P_t') \quad (3)$$

We obtain the change range of all input poses relative to the target pose by (3), and then input it into the TCN network for encoding together with positional and temporal information proposed by (Shan et al., 2021).

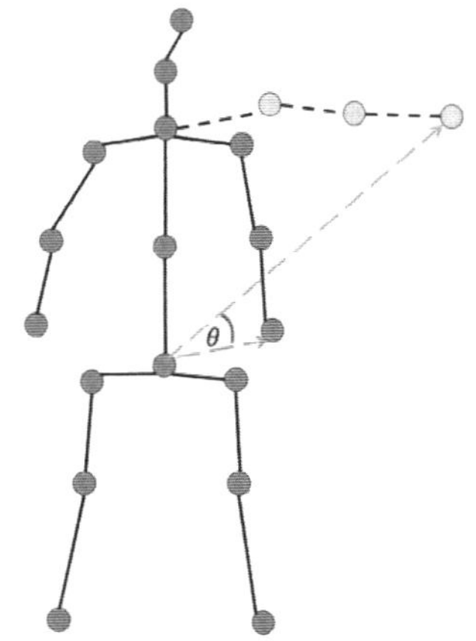

Figure 2. Human joint motion range between target pose and another pose. The orange dot and solid line represent the target poses, and the yellow dot and dotted line represent the hand joints in other poses. All joint coordinates minus the root joint coordinates to get the relative coordinates of the joint. In this way, the relative coordinates of each joint is also the vector formed by it and the root joint, such as blue dotted line and green dotted line. The angle θ between the two dashed lines is the motion amplitude f the target pose and other poses

3.2 Optimized Feature Fusion

We divide the human body into five groups (torso, left/right arm, left/right leg), and each group performs feature encoding. Feature fusion is required before the final complete human pose is obtained. Motivated by (Gao et al., 2019), we propose an optimized feature fusion (OFF) module based on 1D convolution.

Our and feature fusion modules proposed by (Shan et al., 2021) are shown in Figure 3. Both of our inputs are five local features of five body parts, four of which are concatenated together. Shan et al. (2021) use three modules composed of fully connected layer, 1D batch normalization (Ioffe & Szegedy, 2015), rectified linear units (Nair & Hinton, 2010) and dropout (Srivastava et al., 2014) to raise the feature dimension to obtain the fused features. These modules are proposed by (Martinezet al., 2017). Shan et al. (2021) also use residual connections to solve the problem of gradient explosion and disappearance when the number of network layers is deep. However, Cheng et al. (2015) illustrate that fully connected layers generally involve over 90% of the network parameters and generate redundancy of parameters in deep neural networks. Similarly, the method of (Shan et al., 2021) also generate some redundant information, since the features of each group are connected to each other when using fully connected layers to fuse the features of the four body parts. But in fact some body parts are not strongly related in some actions. For example, there is no strong correlation between head and hands in the action "Walking". Compared with the method of (Shan et al., 2021), we only use four different 1D convolutions followed by 1D batch normalization (Ioffe & Szegedy, 2015) and rectified linear units (Nair & Hinton, 2010), which can reduce the amount of parameters greatly and ensure that each part learns enough information.

Specifically, we denote each group of local features as F_i, $F_i \in R^{B\times C}$, where B and C are the batch size and the number of channels. We concatenate the four groups of local features among them together according to the channel dimension as $[F_1, ..., F_4]$. Then we aim to use the discriminative dimensionality reduction method to make the features separate and obtain a new discriminative feature F'_i for group i by aggregating features from four groups. Therefore, we need to learn the transformation W for concatenated four groups of features $[F_1, ..., F_4]$. Similar to (Li et al., 2020), we denote W as $[\mu_1^i I, ..., \mu_4^i I]^T \in R^{4C\times C}$ that is a 1D convolution with 1 stride and 1 kernel size. The input and output channels of this 1D convolution are 4C and C respectively. $I \in R^{C\times C}$ is an identity matrix. μ_i^i is the assigned learning weight. We assign more weight to the same group of features, $\mu_i^i = 0.9$, then assign the remaining $\mu_{i\neq j}^j = (1 - \mu_i^i)/(4 - 1)$, letting $\sum_{i=1}^4 \mu_i^i = 1$. Finally, the discriminative feature F_i' is obtained as follows

$$\begin{aligned} F_i' &= BatchNorm1D\left([F_1, ..., F_4] \bullet \left[\mu_1^i I, ..., \mu_4^i I\right]^T\right) \\ &= BatchNorm1D\left(Conv1D([F_1, ..., F_4])\right) \end{aligned} \tag{4}$$

After performing four different groups of 1D convolution, batch normalization (Ioffe & Szegedy, 2015) and rectified linear units (Nair & Hinton, 2010), we get four new groups of features F'_1, F'_2, F'_3, F'_4. These new features are concatenated to form the fused features $[F'_1, F'_2, F'_3, F'_4]$. Subsequently, the remaining local body features F_5 and global features (target pose) are concatenated with the fused feature and all the features are sent to the decoding layer to predict the coordinates of the 3D human pose.

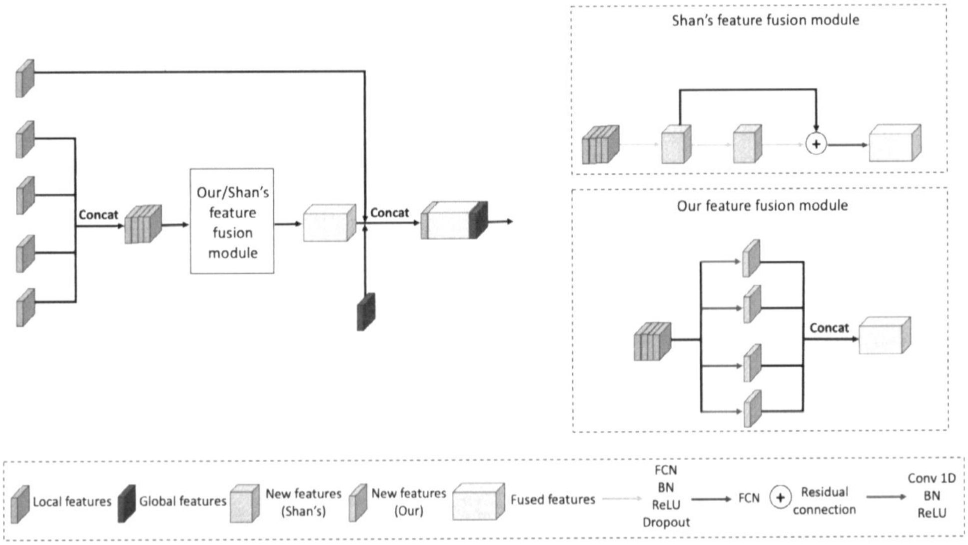

Figure 3. Our and Shan's (Shan et al., 2021) feature fusion modules. There are five groups of local features. We both concatenates the four groups of local features together. Then Shan (Shan et al., 2021) uses three modules based on FCN to raise the feature dimension and outputs fused features through a FCN, while we use four modules based on 1D convolution to obtain four new features respectively. We concatenate them together to get the fused features. Finally, the remaining local features, fused features, and global features are concatenated together to become a new feature of the body part. After performing such feature fusion five times, five new features of five body parts are obtained. (FCN) - Fully Connected Layer. (BN) - 1D Batch h Normalization. (Conv 1D) - 1D convolution

4. EXPERIMENTS

4.1 Datasets and Evaluation

We evaluate our model on the public dataset Human3.6M (Ionescu et al., 2013). Human3.6M is an indoor scenes dataset collected by motion capture system with 3.6 million video frames. It has 11 professional actors wearing clothes with markers which record the coordinates of each human body joint. These actors perform 15 actions in daily life under 4 synchronized camera views, such as walking dogs, photoing, sitting, greeting, eating and so on. Following previous methods (Liu et al., 2020; Martinez et al., 2017; Pavlakos et al., 2017; Pavllo et al., 2019; Shan et al., 2021), we adopt five subjects (S1, S5, S6, S7, S8) for training and two subjects (S9 and S11) for testing.

We use the commonly used protocols to evaluate our experimental results. Protocol 1 is denoted as Mean Per Joint Position Error (MPJPE) that is the average Euclidean distance between estimated human joint coordinates and ground-truth human joint coordinates.

4.2 Comparison with State-of-the-Art Methods

We compare our results with state-of-the-art works in recent years on the public dataset Human3.6M. Table 1 shows the comparison results between our method and recent methods on Human3.6M under Protocol#1. We use ground-truth 2D poses as input and train under the receptive field of 243 frames. Our method reaches

29.9mm in MPJPE, which is 0.2mm better than the best result. Besides, our model achieves the state-of-the-art in terms of multiple actions and also reaches the second best result in some complex actions, such as "Photo", "Sitting", "Sitting Down", "Smoking". The reason why we do not achieve the best results in these complex actions may be that these actions have severe deep ambiguity and occlusion, which requires other groups of joints to provide more information to the occluded or deeply ambiguous joints during feature fusion. Our method reduces nearly half of the parameters in the feature fusion stage, so it may lose some information for the learning of these complex actions.

Table 2 illustrates the computational complexity of different models. We compare our method with (Pavllo et al., 2019) and (Shan et al., 2021) in terms of the number of model parameters and an estimate of the floating-point operations (FLOPs) because we all use the TCN network as the baseline. Both parameters and FLOPs of us and (Shan et al., 2021) are calculated at stage 2 or 3. Although our model has more parameters than that of [30], our MPJPE result is 7.9mm lower. In addition, the number of our model parameters is much less than that of (Shan et al., 2021) and our reconstruction error (MPJPE) is also lower. As for FLOPs, our model only has 18.98 which is the least among all models, almost half of the model proposed by (Shan et al., 2021).

Table 1. Reconstruction error on Human3.6M under Protocol#1 with MPJPE (mm). The input 2d pose is ground truth. The lowest reconstruction error is bold, and the second lowest is underlined. (GT) - ground-truth

Method	Dir.	Disc.	Eat	Greet	Phone	Photo	Pose	Pur.	Sit	SitD.	Smoke	Wait	WalkD.	Walk	WalkT.	Avg
Martinez et al. (2017	37.7	44.4	40.3	42.1	48.2	54.9	44.4	42.1	54.6	58.0	45.1	46.4	47.6	36.4	40.4	45.5
Hossain et al. (2018	35.2	40.8	37.2	37.4	43.2	44.0	38.9	35.6	42.3	44.6	39.7	39.7	40.2	32.8	35.5	39.2
Lee et al. (2018)	32.1	36.6	34.4	37.8	44.5	49.9	40.9	36.2	44.1	45.6	35.3	35.9	37.6	30.3	35.5	38.4
Pavllo et al. (2019)	35.2	40.2	32.7	35.7	38.2	45.5	40.6	36.1	48.8	47.3	37.8	39.7	38.7	27.8	29.5	37.8
Liu et al. (2020)	34.5	37.1	33.6	34.2	32.9	37.1	39.6	35.8	40.7	41.4	33.0	33.8	33.0	26.6	26.9	34.7
Zeng et al. (2020)	34.8	32.1	**28.5**	30.7	31.4	36.9	35.6	30.5	38.9	40.5	32.5	31.0	29.9	**22.5**	24.5	32.0
Shan et al. (2021)	29.5	30.8	28.8	29.1	30.7	**35.2**	31.7	27.8	**34.5**	**36.0**	**30.3**	29.4	28.9	24.1	24.7	30.1
Ours (T=243 GT)	**29.0**	**29.0**	29.3	**28.4**	**30.5**	36.1	**31.4**	**27.0**	35.8	37.6	30.8	**29.2**	**28.0**	22.9	**23.7**	**29.9**

Table 2. Comparison with the computational complexity of different models. All models are trained on ground-truth 2D poses under Protocol#1 with MPJPE (mm). The input of all models is a 2D pose sequence of 243 frames. Both parameters and FLOPs of us and (Shan et al., 2021) are calculated at stage 2 or 3

Method	Parameters	FLOPS	MPJPE
Pavllo et al., (2019)	16.95M	33.87M	37.8
Shan et al., (2021)	41.78M	36.03M	30.1
Ours	24.97M	18.98M	29.9

4.3 Ablation Studies

In order to verify the validity of each part in our model, we perform ablation experiments on Human3.6M under Protocol#1 with MPJPE (mm). Our network takes the ground truth of 2D poses as input. Table 3 shows ablation experiments of different methods used in our network at stage 3. We add motion amplitude encoding on the basis of positional and temporal information encoding in (Shan et al., 2021). MAE and OFF refer to motion amplitude encoding and optimized feature fusion respectively. After adding MAE, the MPJPE result of our method is 0.1mm lower than that of (Shan et al., 2021) and the parameter of our method only increase by 0.01M. After adding two modules MAE and OFF at the same time, our model decreases the reconstruction error (MPJPE) by 0.2mm. It is worth noting that our parameter amount is almost half reduced than that of (Shan et al., 2021) because feature fusion module in (Shan et al., 2021) uses a fully connected layer, while we replace it with an optimized feature fusion module composed of 1D convolution, batch normalization (Ioffe & Szegedy, 2015) and rectified linear units (Nair & Hinton, 2010). This module can learn more useful features from grouped human poses with fewer parameters.

Table 3. Ablation study: MAE and OFF refer to motion amplitude encoding and optimized feature fusion respectively. The MPJPE results takes ground-truth 2D poses as input and is trained on Human3.6M under Protocol#1

Method	MPJPE(mm)	Variation	Parameters
Baseline	30.1	-	41.78M
+MAE	30.0	0.1	41.79M
+MAE+OFF	29.9	0.2	24.97M

5. CONCLUSION

We have proposed a motion amplitude encoding method and an optimized feature fusion module for grouped human pose in this paper. The motion amplitude encoding method can improve the 3D pose estimation for small ranged movements. Compared with other feature fusion methods, our optimized feature fusion module can use fewer parameters to fuse different groups of human pose features and it can also reduce reconstruction errors. Experimental results have proved that our method advances state-of-the-art performance on Human3.6M dataset. However, there are still limitations in our current method: we still require three stages of training and the improvement in prediction accuracy is observed but not in a significant percentage. In the future, we will research on one-stage training of the entire network and ways to further improve prediction accuracy, in both large and small ranged movement.

ACKNOWLEDGEMENT

This research is funded by the Laboratory for Artificial Intelligence in Design (Project Code: RP1-1) under the InnoHK Research Clusters, Hong Kong Special Administrative Region Government.

REFERENCES

Ailing Zeng, Xiao Sun, Fuyang Huang, Minhao Liu, Qiang Xu, and Stephen Lin, 2020. Srnet: Improving generalization in 3d human pose estimation with a split-and-recombine approach. In European Conference on Computer Vision, pages 507–523.

Bastian Wandt and Bodo Rosenhahn, 2019. Repnet: Weakly supervised training of an adversarial reprojection network for 3d human pose estimation. In Proceedings of the IEEE/CVF Conference on Computer Vision and Pattern Recognition, pages 7782–7791.

Bugra Tekin, Artem Rozantsev, Vincent Lepetit, and Pascal Fua, 2016. Direct prediction of 3d body poses from motion compensated sequences. In Proceedings of the IEEE Conference on Computer Vision and Pattern Recognition, pages 991–1000.

Catalin Ionescu, Dragos Papava, Vlad Olaru, and Cristian Sminchisescu, 2013. Human3.6m: Large scale datasets and predictive methods for 3d human sensing in natural environments. IEEE transactions on pattern analysis and machine intelligence, 36(7):1325–1339.

Ching-Hang Chen and Deva Ramanan, 2017. 3d human pose estimation= 2d pose estimation+ matching. In Proceedings of the IEEE Conference on Computer Vision and Pattern Recognition, pages 7035–7043.

Dario Pavllo, Christoph Feichtenhofer, David Grangier, and Michael Auli, 2019. 3d human pose estimation in video with temporal convolutions and semi-supervised training. In Proceedings of the IEEE/CVF Conference on Computer Vision and Pattern Recognition, pages 7753–7762.

Diogo C Luvizon, David Picard, and Hedi Tabia, 2018. 2d/3d pose estimation and action recognition using multitask deep learning. In Proceedings of the IEEE Conference on Computer Vision and Pattern Recognition, pages 5137–5146.

Georgios Pavlakos, Xiaowei Zhou, Konstantinos G Derpanis, and Kostas Daniilidis, 2017. Coarse-to-fine volumetric prediction for single-image 3d human pose. In Proceedings of the IEEE conference on computer vision and pattern recognition, pages 7025–7034.

Huei-Yung Lin and Ting-Wen Chen, 2010. Augmented reality with human body interaction based on monocular 3d pose estimation. In International Conference on Advanced Concepts for Intelligent Vision Systems, pages 321–331.

Isinsu Katircioglu, Bugra Tekin, Mathieu Salzmann, Vincent Lepetit, and Pascal Fua, 2018. Learning latent representations of 3d human pose with deep neural networks. International Journal of Computer Vision, 126(12):1326–1341.

Jian Dong, Qiang Chen, Xiaohui Shen, Jianchao Yang, and Shuicheng Yan, 2014. Towards unified human parsing and pose estimation. In Proceedings of the IEEE Conference on Computer Vision and Pattern Recognition, pages 843–850.

Jingwei Xu, Zhenbo Yu, Bingbing Ni, Jiancheng Yang, Xiaokang Yang, and Wenjun Zhang, 2020. Deep kinematics analysis for monocular 3d human pose estimation. In Proceedings of the IEEE/CVF Conference on Computer Vision and Pattern Recognition, pages 899–908.

Jinxian Liu, Bingbing Ni, Yichao Yan, Peng Zhou, Shuo Cheng, and Jianguo Hu, 2018. Pose transferrable person re-identification. In Proceedings of the IEEE Conference on Computer Vision and Pattern Recognition, pages 4099–4108.

Jue Wang, Shaoli Huang, Xinchao Wang, and Dacheng Tao, 2019. Not all parts are created equal: 3d pose estimation by modeling bi-directional dependencies of body parts. In Proceedings of the IEEE/CVF International Conference on Computer Vision, pages 7771–7780.

Julieta Martinez, Rayat Hossain, Javier Romero, and James J Little, 2017. A simple yet effective baseline for 3d human pose estimation. In Proceedings of the IEEE International Conference on Computer Vision, pages 2640–2649.

Ke Sun, Bin Xiao, Dong Liu, and Jingdong Wang, 2019. Deep high-resolution representation learning for human pose estimation. In Proceedings of the IEEE/CVF Conference on Computer Vision and Pattern Recognition, pages 5693–5703.

Kyoungoh Lee, Inwoong Lee, and Sanghoon Lee, 2018. Propagating lstm: 3d pose estimation based on joint interdependency. In Proceedings of the European Conference on Computer Vision (ECCV).

Li, Moran, Yuan Gao, and Nong Sang, 2020. Exploiting learnable joint groups for hand pose estimation. arXiv preprint arXiv:2012.09496.

Mir Rayat Imtiaz Hossain and James J Little, 2018. Exploiting temporal information for 3d human pose estimation. In Proceedings of the European Conference on Computer Vision (ECCV), pages 68–84.

Nitish Srivastava, Geoffrey Hinton, Alex Krizhevsky, Ilya Sutskever, and Ruslan Salakhutdinov, 2014. Dropout: a simple way to prevent neural networks from overfitting. The journal of machine learning research, 15(1):1929–1958.

Ruixu Liu, Ju Shen, He Wang, Chen Chen, Sen-ching Cheung, and Vijayan Asari, 2020. Attention mechanism exploits temporal contexts: Real-time 3d human pose reconstruction. In Proceedings of the IEEE/CVF Conference on Computer Vision and Pattern Recognition, pages 5064–5073.

Sergey Ioffe and Christian Szegedy, 2015. Batch normalization: Accelerating deep network training by reducing internal covariate shift. In International conference on machine learning, pages 448–456.

Sijin Li and Antoni B Chan, 2014. 3d human pose estimation from monocular images with deep convolutional neural network. In Asian Conference on Computer Vision, pages 332–347.

Sungheon Park and Nojun Kwak, 2018. 3d human pose estimation with relational networks. arXiv preprint arXiv:1805.08961.

Tianlang Chen, Chen Fang, Xiaohui Shen, Yiheng Zhu, Zhili Chen, and Jiebo Luo, 2021. Anatomy-aware 3d human pose estimation with bone-based pose decomposition. IEEE Transactions on Circuits and Systems for Video Technology.

Umar Iqbal, Pavlo Molchanov, and Jan Kautz, 2020. Weakly-supervised 3d human pose learning via multi-view images in the wild. In Proceedings of the IEEE/CVF Conference on Computer Vision and Pattern Recognition, pages 5243–5252.

Vinod Nair and Geoffrey E Hinton, 2010. Rectified linear units improve restricted boltzmann machines. In Proceedings of the International Conference on Machine Learning.

Wenkang Shan, Haopeng Lu, Shanshe Wang, Xinfeng Zhang, and Wen Gao, 2021. Improving robustness and accuracy via relative information encoding in 3d human pose estimation. In Proceedings of the 29th ACM International Conference on Multimedia, pages 3446–3454.

Xiangtao Zheng, Xiumei Chen, and Xiaoqiang Lu, 2020. A joint relationship aware neural network for single-image 3d human pose estimation. IEEE Transactions on Image Processing, 29:4747–4758.

Yilun Chen, Zhicheng Wang, Yuxiang Peng, Zhiqiang Zhang, Gang Yu, and Jian Sun, 2018. Cascaded pyramid network for multi-person pose estimation. In Proceedings of the IEEE conference on computer vision and pattern recognition, pages 7103–7112.

Yu Cheng, Felix X Yu, Rogerio S Feris, Sanjiv Kumar, Alok Choudhary, and Shi-Fu Chang, 2015. An exploration of parameter redundancy in deep networks with circulant projections. In Proceedings of the IEEE international conference on computer vision, pages 2857–2865.

Yuan Gao, Jiayi Ma, Mingbo Zhao, Wei Liu, and Alan L Yuille, 2019. Nddr-cnn: Layerwise feature fusing in multi-task cnns by neural discriminative dimensionality reduction. In Proceedings of the IEEE/CVF Conference on Computer Vision and Pattern Recognition, pages 3205–3214.

Yujun Cai, Liuhao Ge, Jun Liu, Jianfei Cai, Tat-Jen Cham, Junsong Yuan, and Nadia Magnenat Thalmann, 2019. Exploiting spatial-temporal relationships for 3d pose estimation via graph convolutional networks. In Proceedings of the IEEE/CVF International Conference on Computer Vision, pages 2272–2281.

IDENTIFYING WEAR PARTICLES WITH THEIR SHAPE ATTRIBUTE

Mohammad S. Laghari, Abdulla M. S. Alneyadi, Ahmed Y. Alawlaqi and Amr Maraqa
Department of Electrical and Communication Engineering
United Arab Emirates University, P. O. Box: 15551, Al Ain, U.A.E.

ABSTRACT

Wear particles are produced in all oil-lubricated machines when mechanical parts come in contact. These particles are generated in differing sizes, altering quantities, with specific composition, and morphology. The particles when examined by experts provide vital information concerning machine health to operate and maintain safety, efficiency, and economy. As condition monitoring becomes increasingly important and needs to be carried out regularly, a custom-designed software system is developed to investigate the wear particles by using computer vision and image processing techniques. Identifying abnormal wear at an earlier stage avoids wearing failure modes of components that may lead to the breakdown of the machinery. Conventional methods are used to diagnose wear conditions, however; the use of six morphological attributes of particle size, shape, edge details, color, surface texture, and thickness ratio is the basis of constructing an image analysis system to strengthen wear judgments. The particle shape is one of the most important attributes, which is investigated in this paper. Various parameters are used to extract shape features to identify six wear particle types including severe sliding wear, cutting edge, non-metallic, fatigue, water, and fiber particles. Particle identification is based on eight geometric features which are extracted by the image analysis system and MATLAB code. Tests are conducted to achieve 90% accuracy.

KEYWORDS

Computer Vision, Image Processing, Wear Debris, Particle Shape Classification.

1. INTRODUCTION

Mechanical machines are widely spread and commonly used in everyday life, whether it is commercial use or industrial use, there is not a field of work that does not contain some form of mechanical machines. These machines come in different types for various purposes, from vehicles to stationary motors, and generators. Regardless of the use or nature of a mechanical machine, these are always coupled with continuous maintenance, since they contain moving parts within that suffer from friction and other mechanical issues that with time wear the machine down.

Certain solutions have been implemented with time to solve some issues a mechanical machine faces during its operation time. Such a solution for example is the use of oil, specifically in the engines, to reduce the friction, thus increasing the machines' operation life. Whenever the time for maintenance is due, the first thing to get checked often is the oil of the machine, whether it requires change or not. The most basic indicator for engine oil that needs a change is its color. If it is a dark color, this indicates that the time for change is due. The dark color indicates the mixture of metallic and non-metallic wear particles with the oil separated from various machine parts.

The study and analysis of wear particles can provide valuable information about the current state of the machine and can specify if there are certain issues with the specific machine. It can also indicate specific locations from where the particles are generated and can also potentially predict an issue before it happens.

The wear particles are continuously monitored by experts to find any inconsistencies and abnormalities. For example, aberration such as abrupt changes in the particle size and quantity and/or intensity of critical wear particles. It has also been noted that experts in the field may typically have different opinions on wear judgments therefore, the conclusion of defects by such experts is conditional on their judgments and may not be consistent. An automated identification and classification system of wear particles is necessary for this respect. (Jost, 1990; Laghari, 2003).

The analysis of wear particles is commonly used for machine condition monitoring. This analysis is typically used to monitor the expensive type of machinery, such as helicopter engines, gearboxes, aircraft engines, and other large industrial production machinery. Detection of abnormal wear particles at an early stage can avoid expensive failures or even a complete breakdown of machinery (Roylance & Hunt, 1999; Seifert & Westcott, 1972; Hunter, 1975).

Image processing and computer vision techniques are extensively used in scientific and industrial inspection systems that involve detection, recognition, and classification techniques that include edge detection, segmentation, feature extraction, feature matching, etc. Edge detection is one of the primary steps of many image processing and computer vision techniques and it refers to the identification of the points in a digital image where brightness varies sharply. Segmentation is related to separating regions of interest or foreground regions from the background information in an image. It is an important step before the feature extraction process. Feature extraction refers to the estimation of the most important characteristics of an object that can be used to identify it. Feature matching can be described as the technique to find how similar are two objects based on their computed characteristic attributes.

This paper investigates the identification of wear particles by using their shape attribute. The shape attribute holds valuable information about specific machines' wear and identifies the precise location of the machines from where they generate. Eight geometric features of the area, orientation, projections, perimeter, aspect ratio, thinness ratio, Euler number, and centroid calculation are considered to detect six different wear types; where aspect ratio, thinness ratio, Euler number, and area, are of prime importance and considered. Leica Zoom 300 imaging system is used to extract these features and MATLAB code is generated for particle identification. Thirty tests are conducted with 90% accurate results as three tests resulted wrongly. However, four tests are presented here to show 100% accuracy.

2. WEAR PARTICLES

The term *wear debris* or *wear particles* is associated with the field of Tribology which is the study of friction, lubrication, and wear. The British Department of Education and Science was the first organization that used this concept in the year 1966 (Peng, 2002).

Particles mixed in the lubricating oil can be separated for examination and analysis by using many methods. Different sizes of filters are used in the machines to separate particles from the lubricant. Ferrography is one of the techniques in which wear particles are separated from the lubricant and arranged according to size on a transparent substrate for analysis, thereby allowing further observation of the particles. The particle size range is typically between 1 to 100 μm. Swansea Tribology Center's RPD (Rotary Particle Depositor) is one of the Ferrography instruments commonly used these days.

A magnetic chip detector (MCD) is another method for extracting particles. Magnetic plugs are small removable units fitted with a powerful permanent magnet and situated in convenient positions in the machine. Due to magnetism, particles stick to the plug, and later the plug is wiped on a slide. The particle size is typically greater than 100 μm.

The examination of wear particles is carried out in two ways, morphological and quantitative analysis. Morphological analysis is carried out through an optical microscope; hence, it is an offline analysis method. This process requires a detailed investigation, and it takes a considerable amount of time to collect the necessary information about the source and state of the wear. The six morphological attributes are color, shape, size, edge details, texture, and thickness ratio. These attributes help in identifying abnormal wear and possible damage in a specific part of the machinery.

Quantitative analysis is another method used for monitoring machine wear as it provides fast and empirical measurements about the quantity and size of the particles. However, relying on this method alone is not recommended, as it cannot provide information about the origin or source of the wear.

The particles generated during the wear mechanism possess certain distinguishable characteristics and are related to a specific wear process. Based on these properties and the conditions under which particles are produced, they can be classified into several types. Each type of particle can provide different signs about the performance and condition of the operating machine.

Besides morphology and quantitative analysis, particles can also be categorized in terms of their compositional properties. Comparable to morphological properties, compositional attributes can help in identifying the origin and cause of the produced particles hence predicting the machine failures. The compositional attributes can also give information on whether the particle is metallic or non-metallic, ferrous, or non-ferrous, amorphous, crystalline, etc.

3. WEAR PARTICLE TYPES

Particles generated by different wear mechanisms have characteristics that can be identified with the specific wear mechanism. There are approximately 29 different types of wear particles. The following are a few examples of wear particles. (Anderson, 2012).

3.1 Rubbing and Break-in Wear

Rubbing wear or normal wear particles are generated as the result of normal sliding wear in a machine. The wear producing this particle is benign and has a characteristic of normal rubbing wear. These are found in the lubricant of most machines in the form of platelets, typically ranging in size from 0.5 to 15 μm. Rubbing wear particles usually have a smooth surface texture.

3.2 Cutting Edge Wear

Cutting wear or abrasive wear particles are generated because of one surface penetrating another. It takes the form of spirals, loops, and long bent wires like the lathe-machining swath. The typical sizes of a cutting wear particle range from 2-5 μm wide to 25-100 μm long. Concentrations in such particles indicate severe wear mode and imminent machine failure. These particles do not have a particular surface texture, except that the spirals are very smooth and glossy.

3.3 Rolling Fatigue Wear

Rolling Fatigue particles are generated because of rolling bearing fatigue. There are three types of rolling fatigue particles. The first is Fatigue Spall particles which constitute the actual material removed as a spall opens. The second is the spherical particles that are generated in the bearing fatigue cracks. The third type is the Laminar particles.

3.4 Combined Rolling and Sliding Wear

These particle types are associated with gear systems. The particles generated are pitch line fatigue and scuffing or scoring.

3.5 Severe Sliding Wear

Severe sliding wear particles are generated when the wear surface stresses become excessive due to poor lubrication, load, and/or speed. These wear particles range in size from 15 μm up. Particles generated from severe sliding have very distinct surface features of striation marks. Again, the concentration of such particles, and with more prominent striation marks, indicate severe wear mode.

3.6 Laminar Wear

Laminar particles are associated with rolling bearing fatigue. These are very thin free metal particles between 20 and 50 μm and are generated by the passage of wear particles through a rolling contact, possibly after adhering to a rolling element. Its surface features are recognized by the repeated occurrence of holes in the particle.

3.7 Other Types

Other particle types include non-metallic, water, fiber, nonferrous metals, ferrous oxides, contaminant particles, and more.

4. RELATED WORK

Beneficial research work has been performed on the classification and identification of wear particles by using their characteristics, morphology, surface texture, and color.

Stachowiak et al. (2008) used the shape and surface texture attributes to perform automated wear particles classification using the linear support vector machine.

Peng et al. (2005) classified six wear particle types by using used a three-level search tree model approach. The authors of this reference classified black oxide, red oxide, and a few other types by using the Multi-class Support Vector Data Description "SVDD". From the other types, cutting edge particles, and spherical particles were separated by using the k-means clustering. Moreover, to distinguish between fatigue wear and sliding wear, a Secure Virtual Machine classifier was used.

Laghari, et al. (2011) used Fourier descriptors to recognize the wear particle shapes.

The authors of this reference paper collect wear particles from the cylinder-on-disk wear test. The idea is to apply a particle isolation procedure and use SEM/EDS analysis to authenticate the procedure (Akchurin et al. 2016).

Li et al. (2017) classified wear particles by using Extreme Learning Machine-based techniques. The investigators of this reference paper used wear particle surface texture, morphology, and color attributes to train a single-hidden-layer feed-forward neural network using an Extreme Learning Machine technique.

Yuan et al. (2016) have analyzed wear particle features with the use of a particle boundary signal. A Radical Concave Deviation method is used in concurrence with this analysis.

Peng et al. (2017) tried to find some correlation between wear debris and vibration analysis for machine fault diagnosis.

Laghari et al. (2021) have described two methods to deal with the edge details analysis of wear particles. Defining edges also classify shapes. One of the methods calculates the change in angle between three equidistant points on the perimeter of the particle image. The other is finding the distance between the centroid and perimeter.

Laghari et al. (2021) have classified different shape features that include the Histogram of Oriented Gradients, Rotation Scale Translation invariant features, rectangularity, solidity, and thinness ratio. The extracted features are used to train several classification models including Support Vector Machine, k-Nearest Neighbors, and discriminant analysis classifier.

Laghari et al. (2020) have classified four particle shapes by using the Histogram of Oriented Gradients, and other shape attributes including extent, eccentricity, major and minor axis length, centroid distance, and equiv diameter.

Laghari et al. (2010) have derived, processed, and stored quantitative data of wear particle shape and edge details analysis by implementing an interactive image analysis system. The stored information is analyzed to process a systematic morphological analysis of wear debris.

More & Jaybhaye, (2019) used Ferrography analysis to separate particles from oil to calculate its effective area. The ImageJ software is used to calculate the area. The experiment results predict particle concentration.

5. METHODOLOGY

Wear particles are identified by dealing with only the shape attribute. A particle dataset is established by collecting 24 images defining six different types as shown in Figure 1. Eight geometric features of the area of the particle, aspect ratio, projections, thinness ratio, Euler number, orientation, centroid calculation, and perimeter. Area and the perimeter are associated with the size of the particle which is also one of the six attributes. The above set of images is the object of study for this investigation. The aim is to extract and analyze their features so that a conclusion can be formulated as to what is common between all the particles within a certain group.

5.1 Preliminary Feature Extraction

The first step of the process is to invert the image by doing a logical NOT operation. Next, the image is converted to binary form with the help of thresholding. A universal threshold value of 128 is used to convert the image into two levels. Figure 2 shows the invert and binary conversion process.

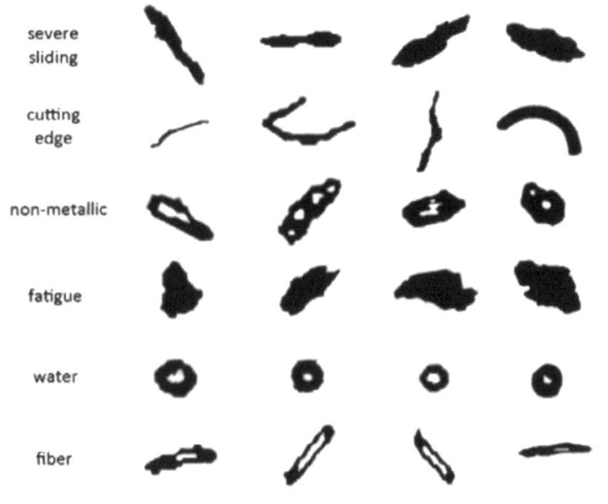

Figure 1. Wear particles dataset

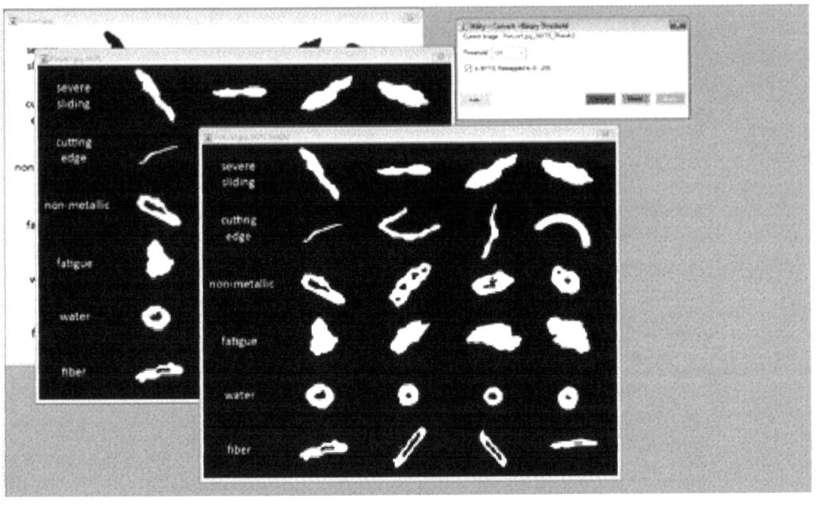

Figure 2. Wear particles invert and binary conversion

Preliminary feature extraction is performed to collect data from a few of the important features. The purpose of the preliminary feature extraction is to observe which of the eight features are beneficial to make an educated conclusion on particle identification.

It has been investigated that area, Euler number, thinness ratio, and aspect ratio are the four out of eight features used to make a fair judgment, whereas the orientation feature will be used for further image adjustment so that the particle is horizontally aligned along x-axis. The remaining three features are for particle location and position in the wear particle slide. Table 1 shows the preliminary investigation feature extraction results; the particles are scanned and selected one by one in order from the left to the right row-wise.

Based on the obtained results, it is evident that the acquired values for the aspect ratio are not accurate due to the orientation of the particle images. It is illogical to derive a conclusion when each particle is being examined based on a different orientation. Therefore, the orientation of all 24 particle images is unified before they are examined for feature extraction.

For example, the aspect ratio value of the 7th particle as highlighted in Table 1 is 0.326531, whereas a visual examination indicates that a much higher value should have been calculated. Similarly, particle number 17 from the image with a value of 1.177778 (also highlighted in the Table) is much more realistic as compared to particle # 7 which should have a value much higher than particle number 17.

Table 1. Feature extraction preliminary results

S.No	Name	Row	Column	Area	Orientation	Euler Number	Aspect Ratio
1	Picture1.jpg_NOT0	48	215	1795	37	1	0.791667
2	Picture1.jpg_NOT0	48	396	1337	-88	1	5.368421
3	Picture1.jpg_NOT0	62	544	2381	-59	1	1.53125
4	Picture1.jpg_NOT0	68	701	2553	71	1	2.085106
5	Picture1.jpg_NOT0	164	210	312	-65	1	2.181818
6	Picture1.jpg_NOT0	173	390	1597	80	1	1.983051
7	Picture1.jpg_NOT0	166	551	851	-12	1	0.326531
8	Picture1.jpg_NOT0	172	719	2001	71	1	1.721311
9	Picture1.jpg_NOT0	275	247	1792	58	0	1.45614
10	Picture1.jpg_NOT0	274	379	2419	-44	-3	0.987654
11	Picture1.jpg_NOT0	256	562	2019	-76	-1	1.777778
12	Picture1.jpg_NOT0	265	693	1892	55	-1	1.037736
13	Picture1.jpg_NOT0	354	222	2258	10	1	0.768116
14	Picture1.jpg_NOT0	345	387	2275	-52	1	1.245902
15	Picture1.jpg_NOT0	342	551	3271	81	1	2.039216
16	Picture1.jpg_NOT0	341	694	3480	59	1	1.223881
17	Picture1.jpg_NOT0	474	216	1541	77	0	1.177778
18	Picture1.jpg_NOT0	469	383	1209	-42	0	1
19	Picture1.jpg_NOT0	457	556	753	-86	0	1.058824
20	Picture1.jpg_NOT0	480	686	1176	-21	0	0.926829
21	Picture1.jpg_NOT0	563	200	1433	-78	0	2.459459
22	Picture1.jpg_NOT0	576	363	1091	-40	0	0.864865
23	Picture1.jpg_NOT0	581	563	854	39	0	0.746269
24	Picture1.jpg_NOT0	553	674	900	-85	0	5

The cause of this discrepancy is in extracting features where the 2-D images of the particles have different orientations. The orientation value of the former exampled particle # 17 is -12 compared to the latter one which is 77. The diversity of these two values is the reason why the aspect ratio values are incorrect.

Therefore, more adjustments are needed to the particle images before the final features are extracted. This adjustment is in the form of unifying the orientation of all particle images so that it serves as a common basis on which the particles are compared. The orientation of all the particles is adjusted to be 90 or -90 degrees, with an error margin of +/- 5 degrees. The reason for choosing 90 degrees, is because it maximizes the aspect ratio of all particles. Figure 3 shows a sample of this adjustment by rotating each particle image concerning the horizontal axis. The sample includes one particle from each of the six types.

5.2 Final Feature Extraction

Table 2 shows the extracted feature results after the orientation adjustment. The aspect ratio of each particle is maximized. Information from this Table is saved as a CSV file.

Notice how the orientation value has approached near-constant throughout, and the aspect ratio is reasonably accurate. The aspect ratio feature is now used effectively with this small modification.

Image horizontal and vertical projections are used to reconstruct the particle images. Typical projections are taken at an interval of 10 by 10 however, this generates a large amount of data. Therefore, an appropriate value of 40 by 40 projection is used for each particle. A higher value than this requires an unnecessary high storage area. Here, the projection values are not treated individually but as the sum of all projections as indicated in Table 2.

The thinness feature is also extracted once the aspect ratio was resolved. This feature determines how thin a particle is, which is useful when making wear judgments between cutting edge and water particles. Other useful features shown in Table 2 are the area, perimeter, and the Euler number.

The aspect ratio values of the discussed particle examples after the orientation fixations are 4.636364 (7th particle image) and 1.2 (17th) which verifies with visual inspections.

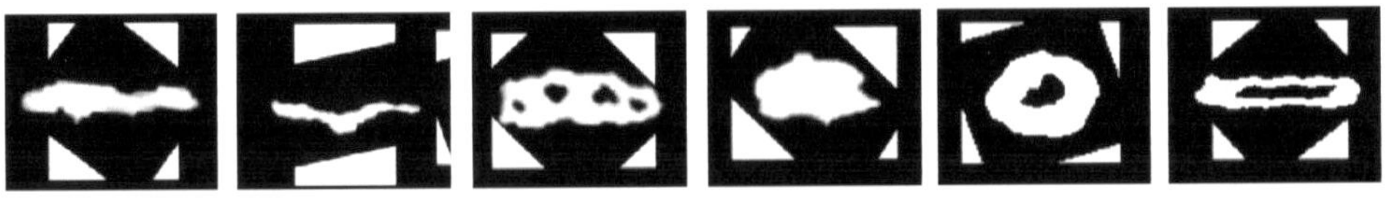

Figure 3. Samples of orientation adjustment

Table 2. Feature extraction results

S.No	Name	Row	Column	Area	Centroid_Row	Centroid_Col	Orientation	Perimeter	Euler Number	Thinness	Aspect Ratio	Proj. Sum.
1	sliding1.jpg_Thresh0	50	52	1802	56	66	89	244	1	0.380351	4.37037	410
2	sliding2.jpg_Thresh1	41	100	1338	46	81	-88	213	1	0.370601	5.368421	408
3	sliding3.jpg_Thresh2	60	84	2370	56	78	89	234	1	0.543909	3.645161	598
4	sliding4.jpg_Thresh4	54	69	2533	51	69	-89	219	1	0.663677	2.942857	778
5	Picture1.jpg_NOT2.jp	156	213	307	161	221	89	159	1	0.1526	6.583333	160
6	Picture1.jpg_NOT2.jp	167	349	1631	156	380	-89	334	1	0.183726	2.017241	376
7	Picture1.jpg_NOT2.jp	177	536	857	168	534	-89	212	1	0.239618	4.636364	270
8	Picture1.jpg_NOT2.jp	154	641	2000	149	683	89	249	1	0.40536	2.413043	524
9	nm1.jpg_Thresh18	56	78	1803	54	56	-87	201	0	0.560807	2.555556	688
10	nm2.jpg_Thresh19	60	64	2418	56	62	89	225	-3	0.600207	2.675676	792
11	nm3.jpg_Thresh20	46	76	2010	41	61	89	177	-1	0.806231	2.135135	1012
12	nm4.jpg_Thresh21	56	57	1920	43	60	89	156	-1	0.99143	1.4	1552
13	ftg1.jpg_Thresh7	53	72	2295	52	67	-89	175	1	0.941708	1.232143	1550
14	ftg2.jpg_Thresh10	46	68	2298	45	72	88	199	1	0.729212	2.15	1010
15	ftg3.jpg_Thresh11	47	74	3299	53	80	-89	242	1	0.707883	2.06	1006
16	ftg4.jpg_Thresh12	41	72	3481	52	68	-89	229	1	0.834148	1.627119	1202
17	Water 1	460	238	1573	458	220	-84	137	0	1.053168	1.2	1724
18	Water 2	454	397	1231	457	383	83	115	0	1.169694	1.04878	2162
19	Water 3	457	556	729	460	545	-87	92	0	1.082335	1.125	1816
20	Water 4	459	700	1180	463	687	-89	111	0	1.203499	1.051282	2348
21	Fiber 1	559	256	1429	558	224	89	197	0	0.462711	3.5	548
22	Fiber 2	550	421	1099	552	384	89	194	0	0.366948	4.55	430
23	Fiber 3	557	578	862	556	546	89	165	0	0.397877	4.052632	450
24	Fiber 4	548	731	929	548	696	89	182	0	0.352438	6.066667	366

5.3 Classification Criteria

Table 3 shows a matrix of the buildup criteria on which the particle types can be classified based on the geometric features. All these values are measured in microns.

Table 3. Matrix of classification criteria

Particle type	Aspect ratio	Thinness ratio	Euler number	Area
Severe sliding	> 2.9	0.3~0.7	1	large
Cutting edge	> 1.5	0.25 <	1	small/medium
Non-metallic	1~3	0.5~1	0 or 0 <	large
Fatigue	1~2.3	0.7~1	1	very large
Water	0.9~1.3	0.9~1.3	0	medium/large
Fiber	> 3.5	0.2~0.47	0	small/medium

5.4 Construction and Classification Flowcharts

The following is the flow chart in Figure 4 to show how the algorithm is constructed and the development of the software package.

The flowchart describes the main functionality of the software, where the input is the CSV file generated by the imaging system. This file of feature values is inputted into a devised MATLAB program to classify the six investigated particle types.

Figure 5 shows the classification algorithm flowchart that displays how the particles are classified. These classifications are derived from the criteria mentioned earlier. In the MATLAB code, the features will be cycled through the shown loop, and whichever block meets the appropriate criteria will be designated to a certain type.

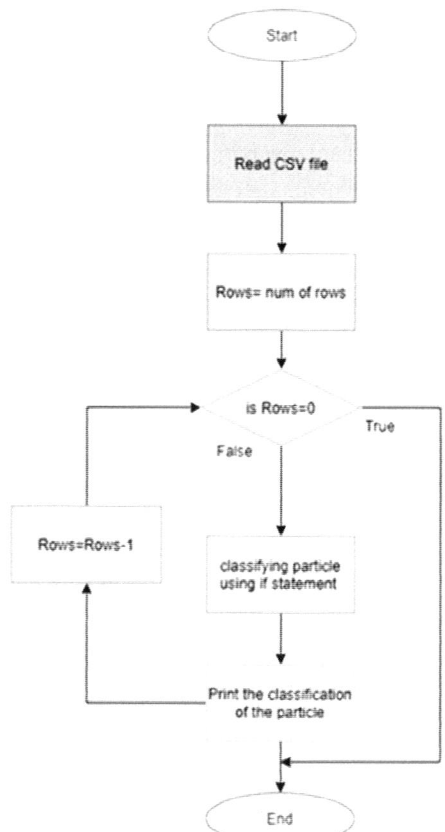

Figure 4. Algorithm construction and development software package flowchart

5.5 Testing

After the program is developed and implemented, several tests on unknown and unclassified data are performed. The following Figure 6 shows unknown test particle images to validate the devised algorithm.

Notice that none of these particles are from the original sample. Also, these particle orientations have been adjusted as described previously. After these adjustments, geometric features are extracted.

The results of the feature extraction are shown in the following Table 4, which are then read by MATLAB and the classification algorithm is applied. The output of the algorithm as shown in Figure 7 determines that particle_1 is a cutting-edge particle, particle 2 is fiber, particle 3 is fatigue and particle 4 is non-metallic.

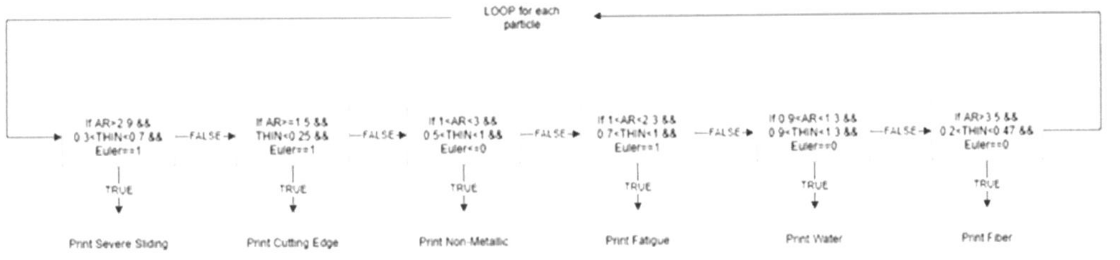

Figure 5. Algorithm classification flowchart

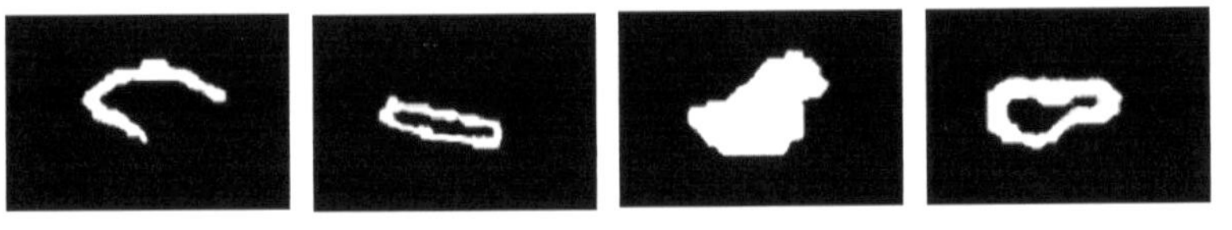

Figure 6. Wear particle test images

Table 4. Feature extraction test results

S.No	Name	Row	Column	Area	Centroid_Row	Centroid_Col	Orientation	Perimeter	Euler Number	Thinness	Aspect Ratio
1	1 jpg	71	69	2102	68	107	-89	335	1	0 235371	1 5
2	2 jpg	79	117	1534	72	122	-88	245	0	0 321146	4 111111
3	3 jpg	86	194	6974	82	141	88	343	1	0 74491	1 782051
4	4 jpg	69	109	2034	63	74	88	199	0	0 645438	1 75

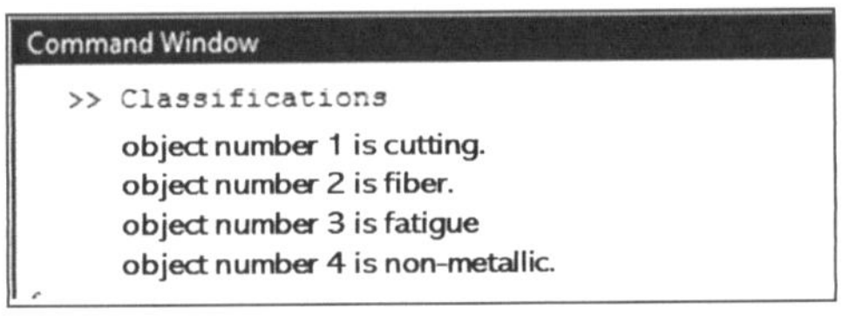

Figure 7. Classification results from MATLAB

6. CONCLUSION

In this paper, the wear particles shape attribute is investigated. The shape attribute holds valuable information about the machine's wear and identifies the specific location of the machines from where they generate. Eight features of six different wear types were extracted whereas four features of aspect ratio, thinness ratio, Euler number, and area, were of prime importance and the remaining four were used as logistics. Leica Zoom 300 imaging system was used to extract these features and MATLAB code was used for particle classification. Although, 30 tests were conducted with 90% accurate results, however, four tests are presented here showing 100% accuracy. More than six particle types need to be investigated for future work.

ACKNOWLEDGEMENT

The authors would like to express their appreciation to the UAEU SURE+ 2019 Program and the Faculty of Engineering at UAEU for their financial support.

REFERENCES

Anderson, D. P. (2012). *Wear Particle Atlas.* Noria Corporation, Oklahoma, USA.

Akchurin, A., Bosman, R., Luqt, P. M., & Mark-van-Drogen. (2016). Analysis of wear particles formed in boundary-lubricated sliding contacts. *Tribol Lett,* 63(16).

Hunter, R. C. (1975). Engine failure prediction techniques. *Aircraft Engineering*, 45.

Jost, H. P. (1990). Tribology - Origin and future. *Wear*, 139(1), 1–17.

Laghari, M. S. (2003). Shape and edge detail analysis for wear debris identification. *Computers and their Applications,* 10(4), 271–279.

Laghari, M. S., Ahmed, F., & Aziz, J. (2010). Wear particle shape & edge detail analysis. *2nd IEEE International Conference on Computer and Automation Engineering.* Singapore, pp. 122-125.

Laghari, M. S., Hassan, A., & Noman, M. (2021). Edge detail analysis of wear particles. *16th International Conference on Software Technologies.* Lisbon, Portugal.

Laghari, M. S., Hassan, A., & Noman, M. (2020). Wear debris shape classification, *LNEE*, 659, 209-217.

Laghari, M. S., Hassan, A., & Noman, M. (2021). Wear particle classification using shape features. *Advances in Intelligent Systems and Computing*, 1275, 377-385.

Laghari, M. S., Soomro, T. R., & Khuwaja, G. A. (2011). The use of Fourier descriptors to recognize particle profile. *4th IEEE International Conference on Modeling, Simulation, and Applied Optimization on Proceedings*. Kuala Lumpur, Malaysia, pp. 1-6.

Li, Q., Zhao, T., Zhang, L., Sun, W., & Zhao, X. (2017). Ferrography wear particles image recognition based on extreme learning machine. *Journal of Electrical and Computer Engineering*, 2017(2), 1-6.

More, P. P., & Jaybhaye, M. D. (2019). Evaluation of effective area of wear particles using image. *International Journal of Engineering and Advanced Technology,* 8(5), 1646-1650.

Peng, Z. (2002). An integrated intelligence system for wear debris analysis. *Wear,* 252(9-10), 730–743.

Peng, Z., Kessissoglou, N. J., & Cox, M. (2005). A study of the effect of contaminant particles in lubricants using wear debris and vibration condition monitoring techniques, *Wear*, 258(11-12), 1651-1662.

Peng, Y., Wu, T., Cao, G., Huang, S., Wu, H., Kwok, N., & Peng, H. (2017). A hybrid search-tree discriminant technique for multivariate wear debris classification. *Wear,* 393-393, 152-158.

Roylance, B. J., & Hunt, T. M. (1999). *Wear Debris Analysis*. Coxmoor Publishing, Oxford, United Kingdom.

Seifert, W. W, & Westcott, V. C. (1972). A method for the study of wear particles in lubricated oil. *Wear,* 21(1), 27–42.

Stachowiak, G. P., Stachowiak, G. W., & Podsiadlo, P. (2008). Automated classification of wear particles based on their surface texture and shape features. *Tribology International,* 41(1), 34–43.

Yuan, W., Chin, K. S., Hua, M., Dong, G., & Wang, C. (2016). Shape classification of wear particles by image boundary analysis using machine learning algorithms. *Mechanical Systems and Signal Processing*, 72-73, 346-358.

VISUAL ANALYSIS OF ENVIRONMENTAL NOISE DATA

Juan José Franco Moreno[1], Rosa Maria Alsina-Pages[2] and Pere Pau Vázquez Alcocer[1]
[1]*Universitat Politècnica de Catalunya, Spain*
[2]*Universitat Ramon Llull, Spain*

ABSTRACT

Smart cities generate a large amount of information that, if used properly, can help improve people's quality of life, while providing environmental support. Decreasing pollution generated by noise, is a prevailing concern, in today's society. A group of experts has collected data in different areas of l'Escaldes-Engordany, in Andorra. These areas have been separated according to traffic policies, i.e., the fully pedestrian ones, the fully vehicular ones, and the combined ones. Analyzing the resulting data may be a complex task, where optimal tools are not available; hence, we have developed a visualization application that allows comparisons and analysis. The main purpose is to improve the conditions in decision making, by having accurate information so that policymakers may have a better understanding of how different transit levels configure the noise landscape, and how contrasting sounds are distributed throughout time. To achieve this, we have developed a visualization application that allows overviewing, detailed individual analysis, and comparative views to parameterize the results of the policies adopted and be in a better position to improve them.

KEYWORDS

Visual Analytics, Information Visualization, Space-Filling Curves, Comparative Visualization.

1. INTRODUCTION

Urban noise, that is to say, the different sounds caused by traffic, industry, construction, and all kinds of public congregations, are environmental pollutants, that damage human, and animal health. Many studies have concluded how stress, heart disease, hypertension, loss of hearing, and sleep disorders, just to name a few, harm people, in such a way, that (Organization, 2011), one million years of healthy life are lost annually in Western Europe only, which translates into high health expenditures and a substantial loss in productivity. Currently, there is a growing concern, about the impact that environmental noise produces on health. People who live in large cities, suffer frequently from cardiovascular diseases, headaches, and decreasing eyesight, hearing, and even olfactory capacity, just to mention a few, compared to individuals living in the countryside. Thus, noise pollution is currently a threat to public health. (Alsina-Pagès et al., 2019) refer to the importance arising from the effects that noise pollution produces on public health, considering it a critical factor, especially when highlighting the relationship between road traffic noise (RTN) and various diseases in the areas affected by it. At l'Escaldes-Engordany, in Andorra, the government is taking steps toward reducing overall noise, especially traffic noise. Therefore, vehicles have been restricted on a set of main streets. Having limited traffic, the next stage was analyzing the impact that such restrictive policies, had had. Accordingly, sound recordings were taken at three different points of the town: 1) an area surrounded with lanes, where traffic is allowed; 2) an area, where vehicles are only allowed on one lane; and 3) an area, at a pedestrian zone, where vehicles are currently restricted. Up to now, information has been added-up on the size of sound intensity (that have been manually labeled). However, a deeper understanding, (on the moments of higher, and lower noise, as well as the distribution of the sound events throughout the day) is definitely necessary. Such knowledge is essential to evaluate the results. (Of the policy changes, as well as conveying the outcome to the government and citizens.) In solving these problems, we created a visualization application to help the domain experts, and policymakers to get insights on the distribution of urban noise along the day at three different locations. One of the main reasons for developing and implementing this type of visual representation is the need to make visual comparisons of overviews of total data sequences in different locations. Among our contributions, it is important to highlight: 1) the design and development of an application for a specific use that provides specific technical solutions matched with domain experts' needs which provides several comparative visual representations with interactive tools to gain insight of the behaviour of pollutant noises in three different places along the day and, 2) insight documentation about the conducted experiments, which in order to be achieved we performed: a) an informal User's Study with domain experts, that reveals it was not very clear how to follow the sound sequence or making comparisons in the visual representations, so efforts were concentrated in these areas and improvements were implemented to trace, follow-up, and compare the sound sequence, b) a guided tutorial that turned out to be very useful to generate familiarity and bring users closer to the new method of analysis, and finally, c) a formal User's Study that would be detailed in the evaluation section.

2. PREVIOUS WORK

Environmental urban noise visualizations have proved to be of great help in research related to noise mitigation and urban noise environmental analysis, although much research related has been undertaken, most approaches have been focused on specific proposals, leaving little to make comparisons; meaning either, general overviews, or specific details due to a large amount of data. Nevertheless, vital information is lost, creating loopholes that could lead to misperceptions. (A.L.Brown & K.C.Lam, 1987). A large amount of data requires visualizations of long sequences, that are usually developed for dimensional data, the visualization of large-scale data-oriented in time has been a difficult problem to solve even with the technological advances achieved, due to the limited size of screens and the limited visual perception inherent in humans. (Aigner et al., 2011) describe numerous series of visual representations to display time variating data, however, to the best of our knowledge and after extensive research, there is no evidence of any approach using segmented coloured space-filling curves (SFCs) to represent a whole dataset in a single view. The problem is increased if we consider the multiple variables in the structure of the data concerning the data creation and its goal for analysis. Among the attempts to reach solutions according to specific needs, (Bach et al., 2016) propose the use of Time Curves, a technique that folds the lines and brings similar points closer together, unfortunately, this type of representation generates overlapping of the curves and makes individual interaction, segmentation and, individual analysis arduous tasks. To use this type of representation a similar metric between points is required which is not the case with the environmental noise collected data. A preliminary proposal (Rind et al.,2010) suggests the use of horizontal representations to analyse and compare medical parameters, however, the amount of data in a single data set is limited by the horizontal screen and the number of datasets by the vertical size. Nonetheless, we consider this type of visualization to further inspect our data, but we use it as a detail on-demand interaction, not as a primary view. To improve visual representation, we developed a data aggregation algorithm to depict a whole dataset in a single horizontal view. Other approaches suggest the use of abstraction methods (Berry & Munzner, 2005) which leads to the possible loss of substantial data that in the general analysis could lead to misperceptions.

(Kaliski et al., 2007) described a project with a sound propagation model, by creating a traffic map over a certain area of the state of Vermont; however, no distinction was made about the type of noise, rendering comparisons of acoustic intensity between one street or building, to others, as a difficult task for the untrained eye.

Recent literature, acknowledges several different types of anomalous noise events (ANE) taking place every day at cities: Conversation among people, music played out loud, peddlers hawking goods, etc. Such sounds are usually mixed with roars from vehicle engines, and their combination shapes the locations' soundscapes (Socoró et al., 2017). As concerns our study, we have decided not to mix them, but instead, to consider them separately, as individual events, sizing them up in their environmental significance.

(Gleicher et al., 2011) provide a survey for visual comparisons, emphasizing that all visual designs use the taxonomy (juxtaposition, superposition, and explicit representation) either separately or in hybrid models. There is no single correct answer on how to do it, but they suggest separating comparative views to their most basic elements and introducing human interaction efficiently will result in more useful visualization to compare time series data. After reviewing the existing bibliographical notes, whose topics are related to visualizing sound, we decided to highlight some proposals, such as SONYC (Sounds of New York City), which focused on noise mitigation, through a platform of intelligent sensors, monitoring specific sounds, to understand patterns, developing interactive 3D visualizations, whereby a huge cyber-infrastructure was used. It is important to underline, due to this project's magnitude, that much research has derived from it, for example, a sound labelling system through a citizen science platform, or the use of spectrograms to visualize sound clips.

Furthermore wonder why two contrasting parts of the city feel similar or different, comparing social urban data sets, that is, noise complaints, taxi data, crimes, etc. As a result, we get colour-coded geographic views, overlain by line charts, that represent the intensity of the corresponding values according to each location.Tmote-invent is a prototype that collects data using wireless sensors, analyzing it through tinyLAB, a context tool developed for this research, however, it was not designed to display the gathered info. (Santini et al., 2008). Therefore, we believe that a visualizing tool could provide RawData insights into subtle reality.

IDEA (Intelligent Distributed Environmental Assessment), is a noise monitoring network that uses consumer hardware to collect data, while a map is trained to determine dominant sounds by category (Botteldooren et al., 2011), supplying a noise means analyzer, through quantified heat maps, which highlight different sound levels for a period of time. IDEA was developed by taking MESSAGE (Mobile Environmental Sensing System Across Grid Environments) as a reference, which monitored, noise, pollution, and air quality, using distributed sensors in two cities, to make comparisons and explore frameworks of daily correlation between humans and traffic-related noise. (Bell & Galatioto, 2013). Following the same order of ideas, the Fi-Sonic project consisted of a system built to analyze the city soundscape continuously, measuring noise and identifying, triangulating, and detecting, isolated events. (Preto Paulo et al., 2016). They did create charts to visual compare sound levels, but depict only sporadic data segments.

(Bocher et al., 2019) proposed a system to estimate the impact of noise, aiming at the production of physical indicators on urban environments, which includes maps of buildings, distances and lines to show the propagation of sound, as well as thermal maps to indicate the impact on the population. (Zhou et al., 2021), developed a multivariate and comparative visualizing tool, using data-driven curves for 2D and 3D visualization and the Hamiltonian Path. This research stated that space-filling curve (SFC) better-preserved features in space, compared to other existing methods whether there be a route in a directed graph from a beginning node, to an ending node. In this case, our data differs from their study; therefore, we used a 2D Hilbert curve which is better for mapping continuous data. (Cao et al., 2020), carrying out previous research had analyzed the problem of large-scale data visualization, generating context maps with routes and heat maps, for urban planning, using big data and Geographic Information System (GIS). (Martinelli, 2016), provided a heat map of the whole world, making several assumptions: for example, when showing the map and seeing that there is a road or a rail, it is assumed that they are generally noisy. There are visual limitations, however, that do not allow to identify specific noises or make comparisons throughout a time period.

3. DESIGN REQUIREMENTS

The current data obtained through analogue sound recordings (WAV files) which by their nature contain characteristics that make them very attractive for visualization purposes, pose a considerable challenge. Considering the extreme length of the sequences, the great variation in types of sounds or frequencies along with the intensities in decibels, the fact of identifying and categorizing, already implies an arduous task. Our objective is to visualize environmental noise behaviour over defined periods and make comparisons, nowadays the majority of research attempts address this through animated or interactive sectional views, that do not present an overview or do not allow panoramic comparisons, leaving the analysis process reduced to individual segments. The experiment we focused on for our research, consisted of a two-day, 10-hour recording campaign, at three different city locations. One was surrounded by lanes where vehicles were allowed; the other, only had a traffic lane; and the last one was surrounded by some streets, its use, however, was restricted solely to pedestrians (Alsina-Pagès et al., 2019). Sixty audio recordings, at 48KHz, were obtained, with a length of around 10 minutes each. The data was then cleaned and manually labelled with 47 different labels. Labels were classified under 4 categories: *Vehicles*, *Works*, *City Life*, and, *People*. Unidentifiable portions (where no label stands out) were classified as *Complex*. An initial analysis was carried out by domain experts, however, the software they commonly use does not allow the users to extract a general perspective on the evolution of the noise landscape throughout the day, nor does it efficiently compare the different types of noise between locations.

Our ultimate goal was to analyze the obtained data, with the main purposes of: a) helping those in charge of taking political decisions, b) helping the experts understand the data. To achieve this, a multiview visualization tool was designed that could provide a means to analyze data recordings of sound. The tool should be capable of displaying extremely long sequences, classified under labels and categories. This way users should be able to get an idea of which sounds are more frequent at certain areas, and their distribution over time. The visualization should provide a general outlook of all recorded events, and help users solve problems such as:

- **R1**: Understanding the succession of events along a day in a certain location
- **R2**: Comparing the sound levels of different locations and/or different times of the day
- **R3**: Getting insights on the types of sounds that happen along the day
- **R4**: Checking the effect vehicles' presence in the different locations influences the soundscape
- **R5**: Analyzing the differences in noise between weekdays and weekends.

Besides that, we also set up as requirement that the application should work on basic machines, and the loading time should not exceed a few seconds.

The visualization web application is designed to meet two types of fundamental needs or roles, namely: the planner, mostly interested in being able to analyze the families of noises, for which space-filling curves will be essential; the other role scientist, mostly interested in knowing specific moments of the day, requiring finer granularity and the details of the subcategories or labels. This way, the user may be able to understand what happens during the periods recorded at certain locations, instead of whether values were analyzed individually. Between the possibilities to display data sequences in comparative timelines, there is the possibility of using segmented lines from left to right and from top to bottom but SFCs are a better technique with nicer clustering properties as well as a better arrangement in recursive patterns due to a property that keeps items together either in the one-dimensional distribution or in a two-dimensional representation. (Keim, 1996) This property can help discover patterns, that in other representations would go unnoticed.

4. DATA PROCESSING

The data obtained by the experts consisted of 60 files, each one containing 24,000 records, which represent the recording time on each location and at a certain time; each record has a date; a starting hour, and an ending hour; the corresponding decibels; and an assigned label-abbreviation (Alsina-Pagès et al., 2019). To visualize such large data, several considerations must be taken into account: The total data adds up to 1,440,000 measures and a 4K screen shows a maximum of 4,096 pixels horizontally, so if a good resolution is needed, adequate ways of processing data must be applied.

As expected, raw data had inconsistencies, which had to be corrected. Once the cleaning and refining of the data were completed, categories were added in a grouped way to it: *Vehicles*; sounds that come from any means of transport whether having an engine or not; *Works*; construction work-related sounds; *City Life*; general sounds that occur in urban areas and do not fall into the other categories; *People*; any sound that comes from people; and an extra category for calling it somehow, *Cmplx*; corresponds to all those sounds that the team of collaborating researchers was unable to identify.

Among the problems to process the information, the following should be highlighted: There was a large amount of data, the values should not lose sequentiality, a record that only appears once is considered as important as those that appear several times; we solved this through label-preserving non-linear data aggregation. The algorithm preserves all events regardless of their duration. For this reason, some events do not appear linearly, but it is guaranteed that no event is lost. By these means, it has been possible to create data sets that maintain their integrity, and allow values with less incidence not to be underestimated. The result of this process are files of tab-separated values on (.tsv) format, of n/25 number of events; the column headings have been kept to perform the reversion process; a starting date and an ending date have been considered; an initial identifier too, which refers to the first event happening, and a final identifier, that corresponds to the last event.

5. VISUALIZATION APPLICATION

To solve the abovementioned problems, we developed a multi-view application that follows the visualization mantra: Overview first, zoom and filter, details-on-demand. Thus, an initial view will provide a summary of the captured data, both in form of a timeline (one for each location) and a cumulative bar chart, as shown in Figure 1. Then, a set of views let the users access to the details and inspect fine-grained data. We now proceed to describe all the components, starting with the initial view.

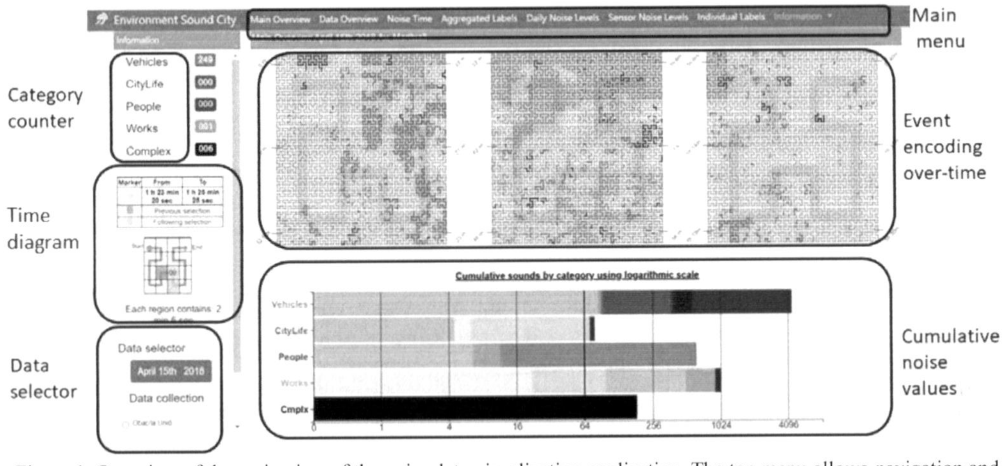

Figure 1. Overview of the main view of the noise data visualization application. The top menu allows navigation and selection among the various views, the Category counter depicts interactively the number of events that exist in the area where the cursor is pointing, also the Time diagram shows which section of the SFC we are at, while the data selector allows selecting data by day and location, finally, the lower chart depicts the values of accumulated noise data grouped by categories and labels in a logarithmic scale

To deploy a large number of events in such a small space, we decided to use the Space-Filling Curve (SFC) coding that depicts the total number of events per day and location, which we call *Event encoding over time*. The reason for choosing a Hilbert curve for the noise landscape is that it enables the possibility of taking advantage of two dimensions without losing continuity. This permits a better use of screen space and allows us to show up to three of these charts at the same time (thus solving R1). SFC has been previously used to display visual comparisons and has proven that it can depict more data than most of the other chart types in terms of metrics while preserving an understandable order (Uher et al., 2019). A stack bar chart, at the bottom, is used to show the hierarchy of categories. Since some of the categories are much larger than the others, we decided to use a logarithmic scale, since we thought its advantages overcome its potential shortcomings.

The fractal nature of the curve serves to define a hierarchical reading order, whereby, a section of the fractal to each event is assigned, the dimension being 2, were H_n is the ***nth*** approximation to the limit of the curve. The Euclidean length of: H_n is $2^n \frac{1}{2^n}$. The data representation for these types of charts, is of a discrete order, for example, we must display orders of type 32×32, 64×64, and so on. After empirical tests, we found that lesser values would not be enough, while higher values created clutter. On the left, we have a control panel (see Figure 2) with three sections, which are also linked views. The top region provides visual feedback on the number of linear events of each category in the region of the SFC where the user is pointing. The second section provides a higher-level illustration of the curve, and interactively highlights the regions pointed by the user, and gives details on the time range. It also serves as legend that indicates the previous and posterior regions in the timeline; finally, the bottom area lets the user select the data to be displayed on the charts.

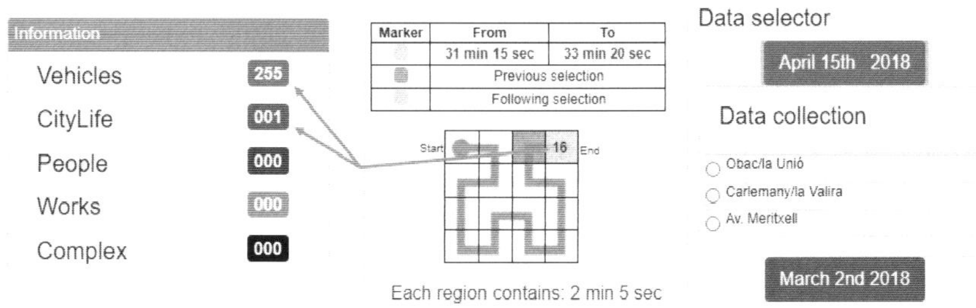

Figure 2. The three sections of the side menu interact with the charts to obtain all perspectives of position, time, and sounds' predominance

The reminder of the views that give access to fine-grained details of the data are described next:

Data Overview: It provides a visual comparison between both days (working day and weekend) in terms of sequentiality and category predominance, making use of the SFC. The side menu is used to provide further details. Upon click a new view pops up, with a sequential histogram containing each sound and its properties, such as decibels and corresponding labels, of the region, selected. This solves R5.

Aggregated Labels: This allows the inspection of the overall data, separated by days, and grouped by categories. It is important to note an important decrease that exists between the sounds coming from vehicles during the weekday, and the weekend, as well as the great increase that occurs in the category of people as can be seen on Figure 3. This addresses R3 for domain experts.

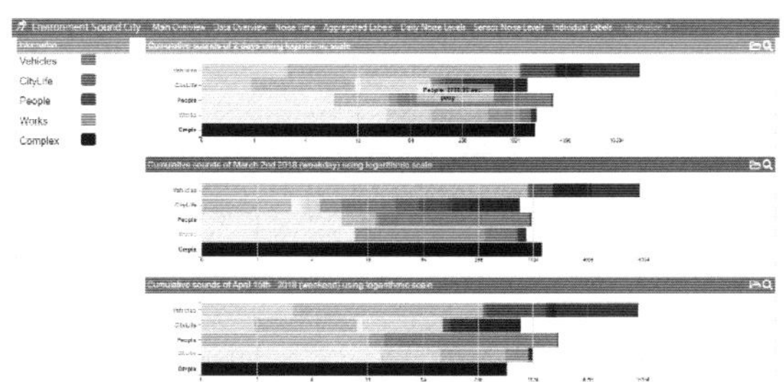

Figure 3. Cumulative sound categories using a logarithmic scale, the top chart will serve as a reference, while the middle and bottom ones serve to compare between days

Noise Time: this view allows comparisons as per day, and by recording locations at a certain time of the day; the menu shows all the possible data sources (60), and that all combinations are possible; a check button allows to hide or display categories on the SFC to customize visualization. When clicking on any section of the SFC chart, a sequential data histogram is shown, to which the corresponding value of the signal-noise ratio (SNR) has been incorporated, as shown on Figure 4. This enables user to solve R3 for city planners.

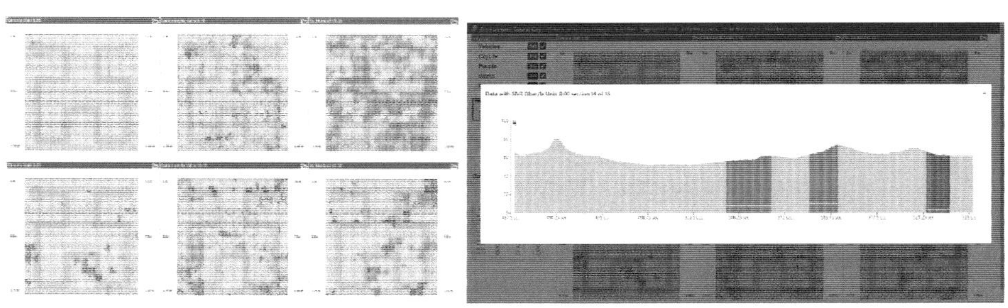

Figure 4. Noise time visualization, on the left side, the SFC comparison as per location and time; on the right side a detailed inspection of section 14 at the first location

Daily Noise Levels: this view allows comparisons to be made on linear histograms that show the intensity of each sound. At the upper part, a lens-shaped icon allows visualizing the same presentation of the data, but without the aggregation process, that is, the original data, which although may present blurring, can also be useful for the user, as seen on Figure 5. This is useful for solving requirement R2 for domain experts.

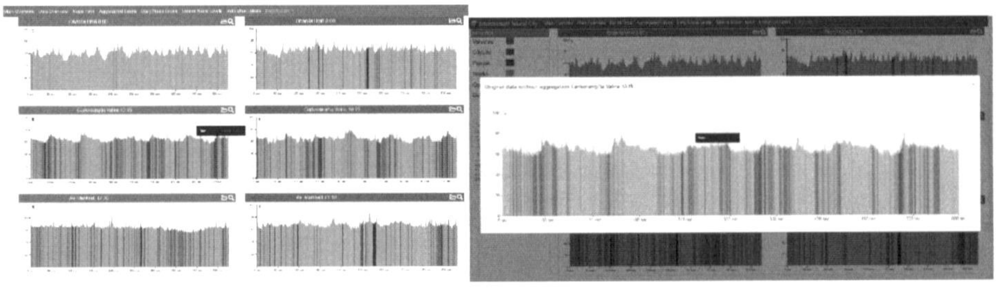

Figure 5. Daily noise levels comparison, on the left side the aggregated data, on the right side the original data of one location for detailed analysis

Sensor Noise Levels: another option to analyze noise levels is given as a histogram: the graph and the data has been divided into 25 non-visible sections; by clicking on each area of the chart it is possible to view that section in the original form, providing better details and avoiding blurring (also addresses R2 for domain experts).

Individual Levels: this view allows to oversee the total time-length of each label for a certain location, at a time, these charts consist of vertical histograms with percentages by category. Also useful for R2.

The web application was developed almost entirely using JavaScript and D3 libraries; the application works under the client-server architecture; the additional applications for data preprocessing were developed at visual development environments; all the tools were developed and tested on a Dell MSI notebook computer with a core I7 processor and 8GB RAM. To ensure that technical requirements were met, the loading time for the application was tested over the internet, using WebPageTest by catchpoint. The observed metrics for the index were as follows: First Byte: 1.425sec, Start Render: 2.700sec, First Contentful Paint: 2.512sec, Speed Index: 4.078sec, Largest Contentful Paint: 2.871sec, Cumulative Layout Shift: 0.007, Total Blocking Time ≥ 0.843sec, Total Bytes: 430KB. This demonstrates that neither the algorithms nor the system represents a heavy load, even for a commodity machine and a standard internet connection.

6. EVALUATION

This research has been carried out with the help of a domain expert, who is also the co-author of this article. In order to rate the usefulness of our system, besides the continuous inputs of our colleagues, we also performed a User's Study, with domain experts and common users. Three individuals, two from the URL Department of Engineering, as well as a Policymaker from Escaldes d'Engordany, Andorra, (where the data was collected), who is also responsible for urban planning, took part. Three other persons, with engineering degrees, formerly associated to teaching and not forming part of the project, also joined in. We proceeded the following way:

We gave the users a small tutorial with the description of the application and asked them to complete a series of tasks using the application. Then, a questionnaire was provided with several usability questions to be answered. This initial evaluation gave rise to some inconveniences. The most worrying one was that some users had failed to understand the SFC's sequentiality. In order to solve this, we changed some aspects of the interaction, we added visual support elements (on the left control panel) and prepared some training materials in the form of a tutorial, which ended with some exercises. These exercises asked concrete questions, such as identifying when exactly certain sound events had taken place, but also some general ones, such as which one of a pair of locations seemed noisier, or what was the dominant noise at a certain period of time. The results were encouraging: seven identical answers on nine different exercises were given, with minimal failures; only one of them being below average, since it consisted of a drawing, and the users expressed unwillingness to do it. The final User's Study consisted of a new set of exercises, and it is being performed at this time. At the moment of this writing, three users (non-experts) have answered using the web application, besides answering a set of exercises, which were carried out with most of them being correct; we asked them seven qualitative questions, that helped us measure up the efficiency and usefulness of the application. The users for the assigned tasks (7 out of 7) express the following on the application: it allows identifying easily, the time proportion of the different labels on each category; identifying easily, variations of the prevailing noise at each location throughout the day; identifying easily, the locations where most labels of a certain type were found; identifying easily, which one of those two days was noisier, and, whether the noise types changed throughout the day; identifying easily, the main noise at a certain location, and distinguishing the differences among various noise levels at distinct locations.

The results so far show that the participants found the application capable to convey the noise differences at different places. Thus, we have determined that the improvements made were significant, and made a positive difference in the results; we are still waiting for the answers from the domain experts, and will report them as soon as we get them.

7. CONCLUSIONS AND FUTURE WORK

We have designed and implemented a multi-view visualization system, which solves problems associated with the analysis of noise pollution in urban environments, helping the users to determine which days are noisier, the times of the day where the greatest amount of noise takes place, and where and why it is originated. It should also be interesting to know whether the rules for reducing noise have been followed or broken. The resulting web application can answer these questions, without effort. Since the users were not familiar with SFC curves, we prepared a tutorial that helps them to understand how these curves represent sequences. According to what the users expressed in the final tests of the web application, they also stated that the usefulness of this tool is highly significant because it allows making comparisons, as it views data generally as well as individually. Currently, our application is limited to data from 3 locations. However, it can be easily seen that 6 sequence charts are shown in some views, so scaling for a larger number of locations is feasible. On the other hand, for comparisons of 8 or 10 locations, some redesign would be necessary. Moreover, although we have two levels of labelling, a single event is detected per instant of time. In the future, we want to explore how to represent multi-labelled data that encodes information of more than a single label. This is quite challenging because adding more than two or three labels will likely derive into clutter very quickly.

ACKNOWLEDGEMENTS

Partially supported by project TIN2017-88515-C2-1-R(GEN3DLIVE), from the Spanish Ministerio de Economía y Competitividad, by 839 FEDER (EU) funds. Juan José Franco Moreno is supported by Consejo Nacional de Ciencia y Tecnología (CONACYT, Mexico). Thanks to Carlos Francisco Pérez-Vela y Dominick, Yuritzi Monrroy Ávila, and Marco Antonio González Silva, for their collaboration in the usability tests and overall support.

REFERENCES

A.L.Brown, & K.C.Lam. (1987). Urban noise surveys. *Applied Acoustics*, *20*(1), 23–29. https://doi.org/10.1016/0003-682X(87)90081-8

Aigner, W., Miksch, S., Müller, W., Schumann, H., & Tominski, C. (2011). Visualizing time-oriented data-A systematic view. *Computers and Graphics (Pergamon)*, *31*(3), 401–409. https://doi.org/10.1016/j.cag.2007.01.030

Alsina-Pagès, R. M., Almazán, R. G., Vilella, M., & Pons, M. (2019). Noise events monitoring for urban and mobility planning in Andorra la vella and escaldes-engordany. *Environments - MDPI*, *6*(2), 1–17. https://doi.org/10.3390/environments6020024

Bach, B., Shi, C., Heulot, N., Madhyastha, T., Grabowski, T., & Dragicevic, P. (2016). Time Curves: Folding Time to Visualize Patterns of Temporal Evolution in Data. *IEEE Transactions on Visualization and Computer Graphics*, *22*(1), 559–568. https://doi.org/10.1109/TVCG.2015.2467851

Bell, M. C., & Galatioto, F. (2013). Novel wireless pervasive sensor network to improve the understanding of noise in street canyons. *Applied Acoustics*, *74*(1), 169–180. https://doi.org/10.1016/j.apacoust.2012.07.007

Bello, J. P., Silva, C., Nov, O., Dubois, R. L., Arora, A., Salamon, J., Mydlarz, C., & Doraiswamy, H. (2019). Sonyc. *Communications of the ACM*, *62*(2), 68–77. https://doi.org/10.1145/3224204

Berry, L., & Munzner, T. (2005). *BinX: Dynamic Exploration of Time Series Datasets Across Aggregation Levels*. p2–p2. https://doi.org/10.1109/infvis.2004.11

Bocher, E., Guillaume, G., Picaut, J., Petit, G., & Fortin, N. (2019). Noisemodelling: An open source GIS based tool to produce environmental noise maps. *ISPRS International Journal of Geo-Information*, *8*(3). https://doi.org/10.3390/ijgi8030130

Botteldooren, D., De Coensel, B., Oldoni, D., Van Renterghem, T., & Dauwe, S. (2011). Sound monitoring networks new style. *Australian Acoustical SocietyConference 2011, Acoustics 2011: Breaking New Ground*, *93*, 626–630. https://biblio.ugent.be/publication/2043684/file/2043686

Cao, X., Wang, M., & Liu, X. (2020). Application of Big Data Visualization in Urban Planning. *IOP Conference Series: Earth and Environmental Science*, *440*(4), 042066. https://doi.org/10.1088/1755-1315/440/4/042066

Cartwright, M., Elisa, A., Mendez, M., Cramer, J., Lostanlen, V., Dove, G., Wu, H., Salamon, J., Nov, O., & Bello, J. P. (2019). Sonyc Urban Sound Tagging (Sonyc-Ust): A Multilabel Dataset From An Urban Acoustic Sensor Network Center for Urban Science and Progress , New York University , NY , USA Department of Computer Science and Engineering , New York University , NY , USA Corn. *Detection and Classification of Acoustic Scenes and Events 2019*, *October*, 35–39.

Doraiswamy, H., Zacharatou, E. T., Miranda, F., Lage, M., Ailamaki, A., Silva, C. T., & Freire, J. (2018). Interactive visual exploration of spatio-temporal urban data sets using urbane. *Proceedings of the ACM SIGMOD International Conference on Management of Data*, 1693–1696. https://doi.org/10.1145/3183713.3193559

Gleicher, M., Albers, D., Walker, R., Jusufi, I., Hansen, C. D., & Roberts, J. C. (2011). Visual comparison for information visualization. *Information Visualization*, *10*(4), 289–309. https://doi.org/10.1177/1473871611416549

Kaliski, K., Duncan, E., & Cowan, J. (2007). Community and regional noise mapping in the United States. *Sound and Vibration*, *41*(9), 14–19. http://www.sandv.com/downloads/0709kali.pdf

Keim, D. A. (1996). Pixel-Oriented Visualization Techniques for Exploring Very Large Data Bases. *Journal of Computational and Graphical Statistics*, *5*(1), 58–77. https://doi.org/10.1080/10618600.1996.10474695

Martinelli, L. (2016). *Global Noise Pollution Map*. http://lukasmartinelli.ch/gis/2016/04/03/openstreetmap-noise-pollution-map.html

Organization, W. H. (2011). *Burden of Disease from Environmental Noise*. 128.

Preto Paulo, J., Fazenda, P., Oliveira, T., & Casaleiro, J. (2016). Continuos Sound Analysis in Urban Environments Supported By Fiware Platform. *EuroRegio 2016, Portuguese Acoustical Societies*. http://ftp.sea-acustica.es/fileadmin/publicaciones/234.pdf

Rind, A., Miksch, S., Aigner, W., Turic, T., & Pohl, M. (2010). VisuExplore: gaining new medical insights from visual exploration. In Proc. Int. Workshop on Interactive Systems in Healthcare (WISH@ CHI2010) (pp. 149-152).

Santini, S., Ostermaier, B., & Vitaletti, A. (2008). First experiences using wireless sensor networks for noise pollution monitoring. *REALWSN 2008 - Proceedings of the 2008 Workshop on Real-World Wireless Sensor Networks*, *December*, 61–65. https://doi.org/10.1145/1435473.1435490

Socoró, J. C., Alías, F., & Alsina-Pagès, R. M. (2017). An anomalous noise events detector for dynamic road traffic noise mapping in real-life urban and suburban environments. *Sensors (Switzerland)*, *17*(10). https://doi.org/10.3390/s17102323

Zhou, L., Johnson, C. R., & Weiskopf, D. (2021). *Data-Driven Space-Filling Curves*. *27*(2), 1591–1600.

USING REORDERABLE HEATMAPS AS A SUPPORT FOR DATA ASSIMILATION IN PETROLEUM RESERVOIR MANAGEMENT AND DEVELOPMENT PROCESSES

Gabriel Paulo Turato[1], João Gabriel Nogueira Duarte de Oliveira[1], Antonio Alberto S. Santos[2], Denis José Schiozer[3] and Celmar Guimarães da Silva[1]

[1]*School of Technology - University of Campinas, Limeira, São Paulo, Brazil*

[2]*Center for Petroleum Studies - University of Campinas, Campinas, São Paulo, Brazil*

[3]*School of Mechanical Engineering - University of Campinas, Campinas, São Paulo, Brazil*

ABSTRACT

Petroleum exploration activities demand the creation of lots of models to represent the uncertainties of a given reservoir, aiming to guide decision-making regarding exploration strategies. As part of these activities, a data assimilation process may refine the model set and discard models that do not honor the history data of the reservoir, given an error tolerance level. Reservoir engineers may use visualizations to analyze the partial results of iterative data assimilation processes and make decisions such as accepting the models selected in an iteration or refining the model set. Among a set of available visualizations for this process, we did not find in the literature the use of interactive heatmaps based on reorderable matrices. In this paper, we propose to add this kind of visualization to the analysis toolset for data assimilation, aiming to help engineers to better overview data assimilation datasets and how their models honor the history data of a reservoir. The proposed visual mappings use a set of heatmaps that enable the engineers to analyze a misfit measure (NQDS) for a given iteration, regarding models, wells, and their dynamic attributes. Users may reorder and filter these heatmaps according to their needs. We implemented our proposal in a web-based prototype that was submitted to a preliminary evaluation with real users in a synthetic scenario. This evaluation revealed positive opinions about the potential of the tool, which may be used to complement other approaches, and provided some opportunities for improvement.

KEYWORDS

Reservoir Engineering, Data Assimilation, History Matching, Reorderable Matrix, Heatmap.

1. INTRODUCTION

Forecasting the behavior of an oil reservoir demands modeling its attributes (e.g. permeability, porosity, and oil saturation per reservoir block), so that dynamic attributes can be calculated by oil, gas, and liquid flow simulations, such as oil production along time. As the result of a modeling task, a reservoir model is usually represented as a tridimensional matrix whose dimensions refer to three orthogonal axes in the real world. Each cell of this matrix has attributes of the real-world block that it represents (commonly corresponding to a hexahedron), such as estimated values for oil, water, and gas saturation, as well as permeability and porosity. These values are uncertain, and therefore a multidisciplinary team (which includes engineers, geophysicists, geologists, and computing professionals – we will call them "reservoir engineers", for short) generally create a set with hundreds of models of the same reservoir to represent these uncertainties. Based on these models and on one or more exploitation strategies (which include positioning of production and injection wells, among other variables), this team can run flow simulations to discover the most probable values of dynamic attributes of interest for it, such as oil and gas production or net present value in a given reservoir exploration time.

One possible way to refine the forecast of a reservoir is to consider its historical data. In other words, the reservoir engineers may know data about the behavior of a given reservoir (e.g. production rate of oil, gas, and liquid) which were obtained until a given exploration time with a set of production and injection wells. This historical data can be used to discard models whose behavior (i.e. the values of the production data) differs from the historical one, or to guide adjusts in the model set so that their behavior approximates the historical behavior. This process, named *data assimilation*, aims to "reduce the geological and reservoir engineering uncertainties in simulation models by tuning them against the field responses" (Mirzaei-Paiaman et al., 2021). The process is also called history matching, parameter estimation, or computer-assisted history matching, among other names (Mirzaei-Paiaman et al., 2021). We have a special interest in iterative data assimilation methods whose goal is to choose the best fitting models that reduce uncertainty (Maschio et al., 2022). After such kind of method selects a suitable set of models, these selected models can be used in a production optimization study, such as in the methodology proposed by Schiozer et al. (2019).

The role of reservoir engineers in an iterative data assimilation process comprises at least the following tasks (Canceliere et al., 2011): (a) the selection of an objective function that will represent the misfit between the historical production data and the production data provided by the simulated models; (b) the choice, tuning, and execution of a suitable optimization algorithm to select models (from a large set of models representing the uncertainties of the reservoir) based on this function; and (c) a decision-making step, based on an analysis of the selected models. In this last step, the engineers should inspect the values of the misfit function per model, well, and dynamic attributes (e.g. bottom-hole pressure, and oil and water production rate) for one or more iterations of the data assimilation process. After that, the engineers must decide whether to end the data assimilation phase or whether to start a reparameterization of the models, so that the set of models could be adjusted to better fit the historical data. This decision can take into consideration factors such as the possible adherence of the misfit values to predefined tolerance levels, the misfit values from previous iterations of the ongoing data assimilation process, and also engineers' own experience and know-how. In summary, it is an iterative and assisted process of model selection and refinement, flow simulation, and misfit analysis.

Different visualizations are currently used to help engineers to make a good decision in this decision-making step, varying from line charts with temporal series to parallel coordinate plots and phylogenetic trees. In this paper, we propose to add a simple (yet powerful) visualization to this decision-making toolset for data assimilation processes: a heatmap of misfit values, based on reorderable matrices (or just "reorderable matrices" or "heatmap", for short) and supported by filtering resources. Reorderable matrices (Bertin, 2010) are matrices that support the permutation of its rows and columns without losing data. Suitable permutations may reveal visual patterns that are useful for data interpretation. The current literature presents a large set of matrix reordering algorithms (Behrisch et al., 2016), which are used in areas such as reservoir engineering, psychology, archaeology, anthropology, sociology, and biology (Liiv, 2012; Silva et al., 2020).

We hypothesize that heatmaps may provide a good overview of a data assimilation dataset, showing two of three independent variables per time (models, wells, and attributes) and misfit values related to them. Heatmaps are also scalable enough to provide an overview of a large set of models (e.g. 500 models) and wells (e.g. 50 wells) in a delimited space of the screen, without scrolling; this scalability may also be a differential regarding other visualization approaches for data assimilation.

In this work, we present a visualization prototype that uses three heatmaps to show misfit values in data assimilation processes. We exemplify these heatmaps with a data assimilation dataset and discuss their reordering and filtering resources. We also present petroleum reservoir engineers' opinions about this tool and suggestions for enhancing it.

This paper is organized as follows. Section 2 presents which kinds of visualizations are used for data assimilation processes in the literature. Our methodology for defining and implementing our visualization prototype is presented in Section 3. Section 4 shows the implemented prototype and highlights its resources. It also presents the opinions and suggestions of a set of reservoir engineers about the tool. Section 5 concludes our paper and points out future work.

2. RELATED WORK

Regarding the use of visualization techniques to present data assimilation datasets, we could observe that using line charts is a very common practice. *Line charts* can represent time series of a given reservoir attribute, where each series corresponds to the values of a model (or the values of the historical data). Historical data is commonly highlighted with distinct colors or formats. Tolerance levels can also be represented by colored regions or dashed series. Examples of this approach can be seen in the Petrel[1] and CMG[2] software as well as in the works of Evensen (2009), Maschio et al. (2022), and Tripoppoom et al. (2021). However, we found works that employ other types of visualizations, such as parallel coordinate plots and phylogenetic trees.

Parallel coordinate plots (PCP) may be used to show multidimensional data of a model set. As an example, Tripoppoom et al. (2020) present a PCP whose axes represent attributes from the reservoir and its fractures. Each model is represented as a polyline, whose color indicates if the model provided a non-history matching solution, a history matching solution, or the best solution from the history matching ones.

Scatterplots may also help to reveal similarities and misfits. Maschio and Schiozer (2008) use a scatterplot (a.k.a. cross-plot) to compare simulated and observed water rates, mapping these rates to the Y and X axes, respectively. The marks (black circles) of this chart represent data from six wells; they represent all times in a production period. Despite some areas with high superposition of marks, this chart enables the user to understand the matching (and non-matching) results.

When a normalized misfit measure is available, it is possible to combine the data of a set of attributes in a single chart or use side-by-side charts for each attribute. Using this last approach, Maschio and Schiozer (2018) use 4 (four) scatterplots to represent the misfit values (Y-axis) of a set of models for a given reservoir attribute (X-axis) related to a set of wells. These values are represented not only for the original set of models but also for two other sets provided by data assimilation algorithms; each set receives a distinct color and is also mapped to the X-axis. Despite being useful to analyze the distribution of misfit values for each well and attribute, the main critique of this visualization is that it does not help engineers to find out the behavior of any single model in particular. Besides, it may suffer from scalability problems if a large set of attributes must be visualized.

In the presence of a set of misfit functions, overview visualizations may be helpful. Soriano-Vargas et al. (2020) proposed the use of *phylogenetic trees* to overview how a set of models honor the historical data according to a set of misfit-related objective functions. Each model is considered as a node of a phylogenetic tree, and edges connect pairs of nodes according to the similarity of the water saturation maps of the models they represent. The tree is depicted in a node-link diagram, where each model is shown as a circle. The tree layout places circles of similar models (regarding their saturation maps) closer to each other. The color of each circle represents the number of objective functions whose misfit values are inside an acceptance interval.

Some works also provide *dashboards* with coordinated visualizations to help reservoir engineers to inspect the quality of the results of a data assimilation process. Maučec et al. (2013) and Carvahal et al. (2014) present dashboards that combine a set of visualizations. A first dashboard combines: (a) a 2D map of a selected reservoir attribute; (b) three pie charts showing the number of history-matched models for some reservoir attributes, (c) a line chart that shows the behavior of two indexes (a mismatch index and a convergence one) over history matching iterations; and (d) a table called "mismatch index summary". This table is a *heatmap* whose Y and X axes are respectively mapped to wells and attributes. The color of each cell (w, a) indicates if the well w has an acceptable (green), moderate (yellow), or poor (red) match for the attribute a. A second dashboard still uses the 2D map of a given attribute but uses other charts: two bar charts represent the misfit values of the attributes bottom-hole pressure and water cut for the iterations of the data assimilation process; and three line charts show series related to oil rate, water cut and flowing bottom-hole pressure. All these charts may present data related either to the entire reservoir or to a single well selected by the user. A third dashboard uses a small multiples layout to compare 2D maps of pessimist, intermediate and optimistic models before and after the model parametrization guided by the results of the data assimilation process.

Among the presented works, we observed that the "mismatch index summary" table (Carvahal et al., 2014) has some similarities to our proposal. However, it seems to be not scalable regarding the number of attributes and wells, and not reorderable. Besides, our proposal represents other combinations of attributes instead of only "attributes per wells", as we present in the following section.

---

[1]https://www.software.slb.com/products/petrel/petrel-reservoir-engineering/history-matching-production (March 7th, 2022)
[2]https://www.cmgl.ca/software (March 7th, 2022)

3. METHODOLOGY

Our methodology comprised the following steps: (1) brainstorming with stakeholders about the data assimilation process and new visualization proposals; (2) characterizing data assimilation datasets; (3) prototyping a visualization to meet users' needs; and (4) validating the prototype. In our initial step, we met two experts in reservoir engineering from our research team; one of them works directly with data assimilation algorithms. These experts helped us to understand their needs of overviewing the data assimilation datasets. They also sketched with us three visualizations of misfit values, based on reorderable heatmaps: attributes by wells; attributes by models; and models by wells. They also provided a representative data assimilation dataset that we used in the prototype development.

The second step consisted of understanding data assimilation datasets in general, and particularly the dataset the experts provided to us. In general, these datasets must provide data about a set of models and also historical data. The historical data has time series related to each attribute and well of a reservoir. Each model also has similar time series per attribute and well, which were generated by the flow simulation in the model. The misfit between a model and the historical data may also be available in the dataset. Each model's time series and misfit values are related to a single iteration of the data assimilation process.

The dataset provided by the experts comprises four independent variables (iterations, models, attributes, and wells), and one dependent variable – the misfit value. The attribute set may change among iterations of the same data assimilation process so that engineers can include attributes that they started to consider relevant in a given iteration (Avansi et al., 2016). The misfit value is called NQDS (normalized quadratic deviation with signal). It measures a quadratic deviation between a historical time series and the time series from a model, regarding a given attribute and well. This value is normalized according to an acceptable quadratic deviation, whose calculation depends on an acceptance level defined by reservoir engineers for each attribute and well (Avansi et al., 2016). This normalized value is further classified into six classes: excellent, very good, good, regular, bad, and very bad (or unsatisfactory) (Cavalcante et al., 2017; Cavalcante et al., 2019).

We split the prototyping phase into two parts. First, we used a visualization software to generate a proof of concept for the three visualizations proposed in the initial step. Next, we built a web prototype based on JavaScript visualization libraries (D3.js (Bostock, 2021) and reorder.js (Fekete, 2015)) on the client-side, and on PHP and MariaDB on the server-side. This tool groups the three proposed visualizations and also provides interactive filters and reordering resources for the users.

Last but not least, in the validation phase, we invited a team of researchers to test our prototype and provide opinions about it. The requirement for being invited was to have experience with oil reservoir management and development processes. Having expertise in data assimilation processes was desired but not required. We made available a version of our prototype for the researchers so that they could interact with the visualizations for a set of pre-loaded iterations of a data assimilation process. After this experimentation step, we asked the researchers to answer a brief profile questionnaire about their experience in petroleum engineering and particularly in data assimilation processes. Next, we asked them to answer the validation questionnaire itself, in which they should point out the highlights and drawbacks of the prototype. The questionnaire ended with researchers' suggestions to enhance the prototype.

4. RESULTS

In this section, we present the developed prototype (NQDS Heatmap) and the results of our validation questionnaire. In the initial screen of the NQDS Heatmap, the users can import a dataset related to a single iteration of a data assimilation process, or they can select an already imported one. After loading this dataset, the system shows its main window, which enables users to select one of three possible visualizations defined in the brainstorming activities. Figures 1 and 2 present these visualizations, and Table 1 depicts their visual mapping.

We used a synthetic dataset (obtained from the UNISIM-II-H Benchmark, available at www.unisim.cepetro.unicamp.br/benchmarks), to exemplify the proposed visualizations, the prototype interaction resources, and the potential they have to help engineers to overview a data assimilation dataset. This dataset comprises data from 20 wells (9 injection wells, named INJ1 to INJ9; and 11 production wells, named PROJ1 to PROJ10 and WILDCAT); 500 models, and five attributes (BHP – bottom-hole pressure, QO

– oil rate, QW – water rate, QL – liquid rate, and QWI – water injection rate) for a set of five iterations. The dataset provides a misfit value (NQDS) for each iteration, well, model, and attribute.

To prepare the dataset that each visualization will show, the prototype calculates a *worst misfit value* $\delta(v_x,v_y)$ which is the maximum value of NQDS (in absolute value) for the values of each pair of variables v_x and v_y mapped to the X and Y axes, respectively. The cell colors follow a diverging scale from green (low misfit) to red (high misfit), representing the classes of NQDS values. A grey cell is shown in the absence of data. It is worth noting that each visualization focuses on a single iteration at a time.

Figure 1 presents a *Wells* × *Models* visualization of a given iteration. The initial order of models and wells is similar to their order in the dataset, in which injection wells are grouped together, as are production wells. Given that the cell color represents the *worst* misfit value for a given model and well in that iteration, we may consider that a cell with the brighter green of the color scale ("excellent") means that all attributes have an excellent misfit value for that well and model. On the other hand, a brighter red cell indicates that at least one of the attributes has an unsatisfactory misfit value. As a consequence, the greenish region of the heatmap in Figure 1 points out that the misfit values vary mostly between excellent and very good. However, the production wells seem to have not this behavior, whose values should be further inspected. Exceptions should be made to PROD5 and INJ7, whose behavior differs from the other production and injection wells, respectively. This figure exemplifies how the visualization scales for a large set of models, given that all the 500 models are represented.

The *Attributes* × *Models* heatmap in Figure 2 (top) depicts the misfit for each attribute, in a filtered subset of the models. We highlight that the liquid rate (QL) has only excellent values for these models and their wells. Besides, the water injection rate (QWI) has excellent values for most of these models. However, the remaining attributes do not present good "worst case" misfit values and may need further analysis.

The visualization in Figure 2 (bottom) (the "*Attributes* × *Wells*" heatmap) shows misfit values related to bottom-hole pressure for production and injection wells; oil, gas, and liquid rates for production wells; and water injection rate for injection wells. NQDS values for liquid rate are excellent for all models, as already shown in Figure 2. However, this visualization highlights that the worst misfit values for every well (except INJ9 and INJ2) are far from the desired "excellent" or "very good" values.

Table 1. Visualizations available at the NQDS heatmap tool

Visualization name	*Visual mapping*		
	X-axis	*Y-axis*	*Color*
Wells × *Models*	Models	Wells	Maximum absolute NQDS value for a model *m* and a well *w*.
Attributes × *Models*	Models	Attributes	Maximum absolute NQDS value for a model *m* and an attribute *a*.
Attributes × *Wells*	Wells	Attributes	Maximum absolute NQDS value for a well *w* and an attribute *a*.

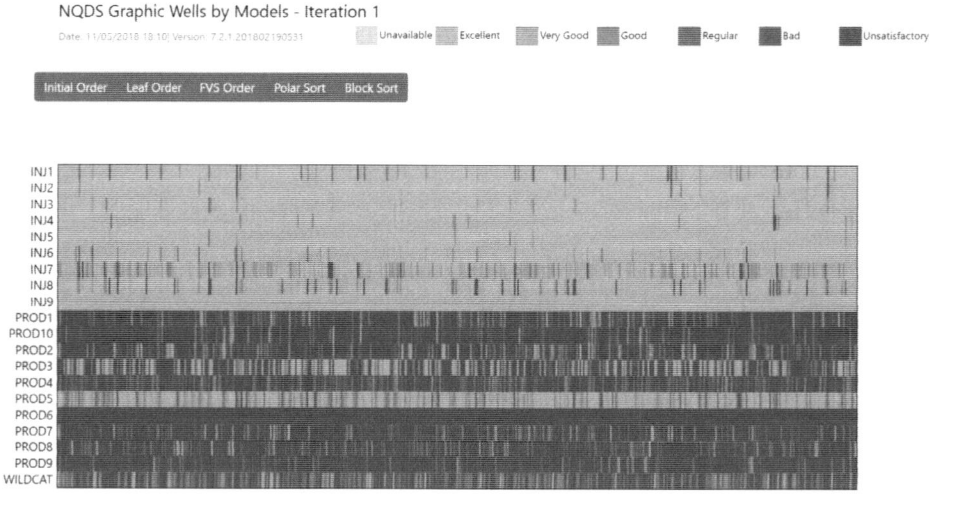

Figure 1. "Wells × Models" heatmap, without reordering

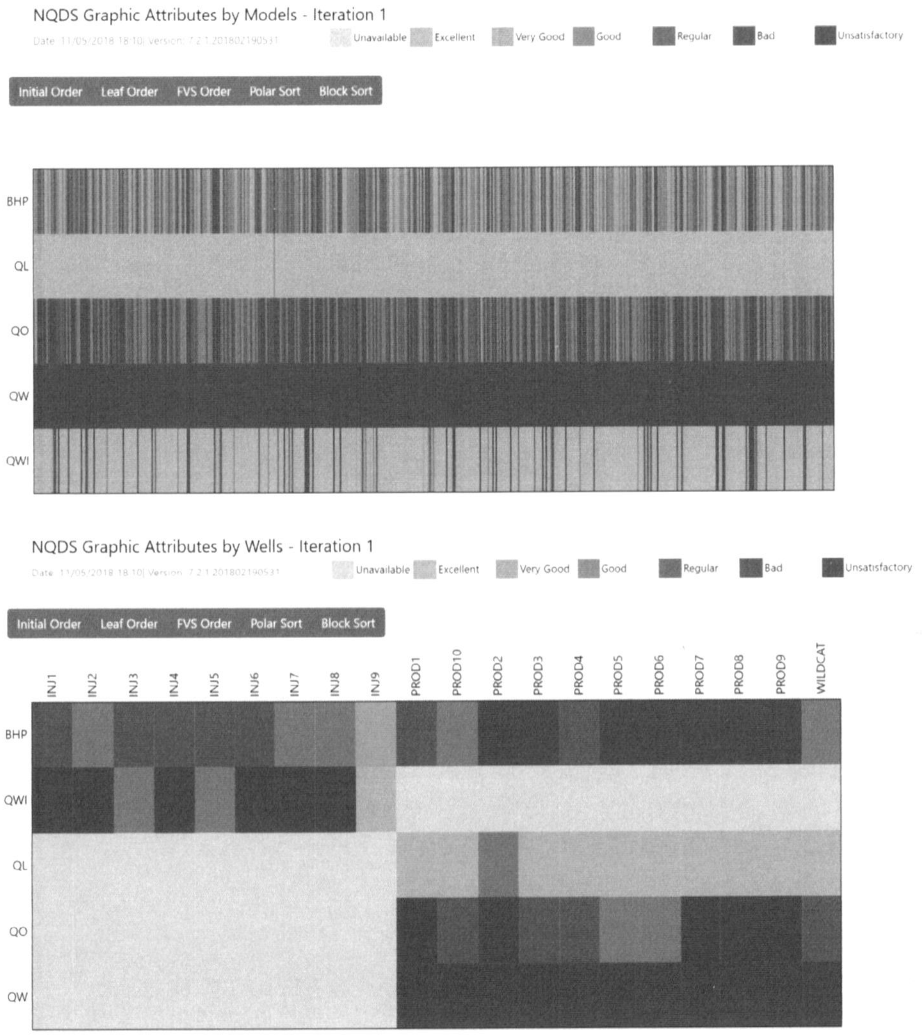

Figure 2. "Attributes × Models" (top) and "Attributes × Wells" (bottom) heatmaps, without reordering

Figure 3 presents the main window view of our tool. At the top, the figure shows checkboxes for filtering wells and attributes, and a slider to select a set of models. The Attributes × Models heatmap of this figure has only 100 models and shows only production wells (the injection ones were unchecked in the filters). Despite all five attributes having been checked, the heatmap does not show the water injection rate (QWI) because all injection wells were filtered out.

The prototype also provides reordering methods to group similar rows and columns in the heatmaps (e. g. columns whose models behave in a similar way regarding δ). The methods available in the prototype are optimal leaf ordering (Bar-Joseph et al., 2021), FVS (Silva et al., 2017), Polar Sort (Silva, 2019), and Block Reordering (Santos et al., 2016). Figure 3 exemplifies the use of FVS to reorder the matrix presented in Figure 2. Given that FVS reorder rows (columns) according to the average values of each row (column), we may state that the models on the left side have better misfit values than those on the right.

Regarding the validation of our proposal, seven researchers used the prototype and answered our questionnaires. According to their answers to the profile questionnaire, they have been working for 12 years (on average) with reservoir engineering in academic and/or professional activities. Three of them work directly with data assimilation. The main positive points they cited about NQDS Heatmap are related to its ease of use and the flexibility of its visualizations. As the main drawback, they pointed out that the position of the filters should be closer to the visualization and not in a separated area, which may force the use of scrolling. Among the suggestions about how to improve the tool, the researchers pointed out that it would be useful to provide a reordering algorithm that ranks models from the "best" to the "worst" one, and a filtering resource to show only a subset of this ordered list of models. A resource for exporting selected models would also be useful for the data assimilation process. They also suggested a side-by-side visualization of iterations, so that they would be able to compare datasets of subsequent iterations. Besides, they highlighted the need for shortcuts to select all injection (or all production) wells, a resource for changing color scale, and basic descriptions (with hints) about the reordering algorithms. Last but not least, small changes in the terminology would be helpful for the engineers, such as replacing "attributes" with "data series" (given that they already use the word "attributes" to properties of reservoir cells, such as porosity and permeability).

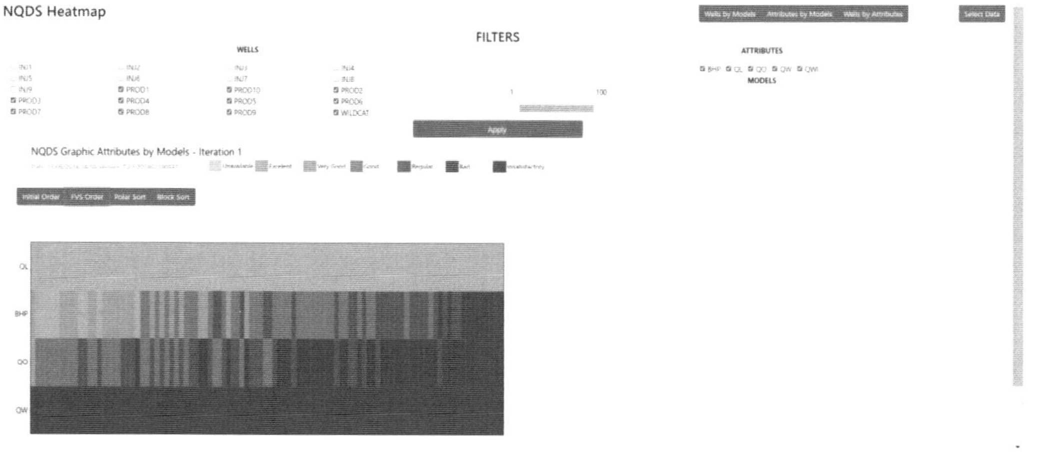

Figure 3. The main screen of prototype showing the "Attributes × Models" heatmap, ordered by the FVS algorithm. Only production wells (PROD* and WILDCAT) and only the models 1 to 100 were selected

5. CONCLUSION

In this work, we proposed the use of a set of filterable and reorderable heatmaps to provide an overview of misfit values in iterative data assimilation datasets, aiming to help reservoir engineers to understand these data and to make better decisions in each iteration of the assimilation process. We implemented these heatmaps in a prototype (NQDS Heatmap) which was used by a team of researchers in the petroleum engineering area. These engineers pointed out that the tool is intuitive, easy to use, and flexible to their needs. Future work will include (1) the connection of these visualizations to spatial visualizations of the models of a reservoir so that engineers can identify not only which models do not present the historical behavior, but also where these models fail on representing their reservoir; (2) enhancement suggestions made by reservoir engineers, such as an improved layout of controls, configurable color scales, and other reordering and filtering resources they identified as useful for decision-making in data assimilation; and (3) a more formal evaluation of the solution.

ACKNOWLEDGEMENT

We gratefully acknowledge the support of EPIC (Energy Production Innovation Center), hosted by the University of Campinas (UNICAMP) and sponsored by Equinor Brazil and by FAPESP (São Paulo Research Foundation; grant number 2017/15736-3). We acknowledge the support of ANP (Brazil's National Agency of Oil, Natural Gas, and Biofuels) through the R&D levy regulation. Acknowledgments are extended to the School of Technology (FT), Center for Petroleum Studies (CEPETRO), and School of Mechanical Engineering (FEM) at UNICAMP. We also acknowledge the funding from Energi Simulation and thank the Computer Modelling Group Ltd. (CMG) for software licenses and technical support.

REFERENCES

Bar-Joseph, Z. et al. (2001). Fast optimal leaf ordering for hierarchical clustering. *Bioinformatics* (Oxford, England). 17 Suppl 1. S22-9. DOI: https://doi.org/10.1093/bioinformatics/17.suppl_1.S22.

Behrisch, M. et al., 2016. Matrix reordering methods for table and network visualization. *Computer Graphics Forum 35*(3), pp. 693–716. DOI: https://doi.org/10.1111/cgf.12935.

Bertin J., 2010. Semiology of graphics: Diagrams, networks, maps. USA: Esri Press, 2010.

Bostock, M. 2021. *D3: Data-Driven Documents*. https://d3js.org/.

Cancelliere, M. et al. (2011). Benefits and Limitations of Assisted History Matching. *SPE Offshore Europe Oil and Gas Conference and Exhibition*, Aberdeen, UK, September 2011. DOI: https://doi.org/10.2118/146278-MS

Carvahal, G.A. et al. (2014). Next Generation Workflow for Multilevel Assisted History Matching: Visualization and Collaboration. *Int. Petroleum Technology Conf.* Doha, Qatar, 2014. DOI: https://doi.org/10.2523/IPTC-17667-MS.

Cavalcante, C.C.B. et al. (2017). History matching through dynamic decision-making. *PLoS ONE 12*(6): e0178507. DOI: https://doi.org/10.1371/journal.pone.0178507.

Cavalcante, C.C.B. et al. (2019). A continuous learning algorithm for history matching. *Engineering Applications of Artificial Intelligence 85*, pp.543–568. DOI: https://doi.org/10.1016/j.engappai.2019.07.012.

Evensen, G. (2009). Estimation in an oil reservoir simulator. In: *Data Assimilation: The Ensemble Kalman filter*. 2nd edition. Springer. DOI: https://doi.org/10.1007/978-3-642-03711-5_17.

Fekete, J.-D. Reorder.js: A JavaScript Library to Reorder Tables and Networks. *IEEE VIS 2015*, United States, 2015.

Liiv, I. (2010). Seriation and Matrix Reordering Methods: An Historical Overview. *Statistical Analysis and Data Mining, 3*(2), pp. 70-91. DOI: https://doi.org/10.1002/sam.10071.

Maschio, C. and Schiozer, D.J. (2008). A New Methodology for Assisted History Matching Using Independent Objective Functions. *Petroleum Science and Technology 26*:1047–1062. Taylor & Francis Group. DOI: https://doi.org/10.1080/10916460701208389.

Maschio, C. and Schiozer, D.J. (2018). A new methodology for history matching combining iterative discrete Latin Hypercube with multi-start simulated annealing. *Journal of Petroleum Science and Engineering 169*, pp. 560–577. DOI: https://doi.org/10.1016/j.petrol.2018.06.004.

Maschio, C. et al. (2022). Data assimilation for uncertainty reduction using different fidelity numerical models. *Journal of Petroleum Science and Engineering* 209, 109851. DOI: https://doi.org/10.1016/j.petrol.2021.109851

Maučec, M. et al. (2013). Next Generation of Workflows for Multilevel Assisted History Matching and Production Forecasting: Concept, Implementation and Visualization. *SPE Kuwait Oil and Gas Show and Conference*, Mishref, Kuwait, October 2013. DOI: https://doi.org/10.2118/167340-MS.

Mirzaei-Paiaman, A. et al. (2021). A review on closed-loop field development and management. *Journal of Petroleum Science and Engineering 201*, 108457. DOI: https://doi.org/10.1016/j.petrol.2021.108457

Santos, A. M. et al. (2016). Block Reordering: Um algoritmo para evidenciar padrão Block em matrizes reordenáveis. Workshop of Undergraduate Works (WUW) in the *29th Conference on Graphics, Patterns and Images,* Brazil.

Schiozer, D. J. et al. (2019). Model-based decision analysis applied to petroleum field development and management. *Oil Gas Sci. Technol. 74*, pp. 1–20. DOI: https://dx.doi.org/10.2516/ogst/2019019.

Silva, C. G. (2019). Polar Sort: combining multidimensional scaling and polar coordinates for matrix reordering. *Proc. Int. Conf. Interfaces and Human Computer Interaction 2019; Game and Entertainment Technologies 2019; and Computer Graphics, Visualization, Computer Vision and Image Processing 2019*, Porto, Portugal, pp. 239–243. https://doi.org/10.33965/cgv2019_201906L030.

Silva, C. G. et al. (2017). A fast feature vector approach for revealing simplex and equi-correlation data patterns in reorderable matrices. *Information Visualization 16*(4), pp. 261-274. DOI: https://doi.org/10.1177/1473871616666392.

Silva, C. G. et al. (2020). Using reorderable matrices to compare risk curves of representative models in oil reservoir development and management activities. *Proc. Int. Conf. Computer Graphics, Visualization, Computer Vision and Image Processing, 2020; Big Data Analytics, Data Mining and Computational Intelligence, 2020; and Theory and Practice in Modern Computing, 2020*. DOI: http://dx.doi.org/10.33965/cgv2020_202011L003.

Soriano-Vargas, A. et al. (2020). Leveraging Phylogenetic Trees to Assess Variability of Reservoir Models. *SPE Latin American and Caribbean Petroleum Engineering Conference*. DOI: https://doi.org/10.2118/199099-MS.

Tripoppoom, S. et al. (2020). Investigation of different production performances in shale gas wells using assisted history matching: Hydraulic fractures and reservoir characterization from production data. *Fuel 267*, 117097. DOI: https://doi.org/10.1016/j.fuel.2020.117097.

Tripoppoom, S. et al. (2021). *Assisted History Matching for Unconventional Reservoirs*. Elsevier. DOI: https://doi.org/10.1016/B978-0-12-822242-3.00011-0.

DETECTION OF FASHION LANDMARKS BASED ON POSE ESTIMATION AND HUMAN PARSING

Honghong He[1,2], Yanghong Zhou[1], Jin-tu Fan[1,2] and P. Y. Mok[1,2]
[1]*Institute of Textiles and Clothing, The Hong Kong Polytechnic University, Hunghom, Hong Kong*
[2]*Laboratory for Artificial Intelligence in Design, Hong Kong Special Administrative Region, Hong Kong*

ABSTRACT

Locating fashion items on any input images is referred as 'fashion image understanding', which is often a preliminary or initial step that supports various other visions tasks. The study of fashion image understanding has been widely benefited from the rapid advancements in deep learning-based new models and the availability of large datasets covering real-world fashion images. However, the real value of these datasets is in doubt, because different annotation strategies have been adopted in these datasets, resulting in different landmarks for different clothing styles and low compatibility of these datasets. In this paper, we propose a pose-aware segmentation-based method to locate key points of fashion items on fashion images by taking advantage of clear correspondence between clothing and human body, that can be applied to locate key points of fashion items and to re-annotate existing datasets for cross dataset learning. The validity of the method was validated on a subset of the DeepFashion2 dataset.

KEYWORDS

Fashion Landmarks Localization, Pose Estimation, Human Parsing, Graph-based Clothing Structure.

1. INTRODUCTION

Locating fashion items on any input images is often a preliminary or initial step that supports various other visions tasks, such as clothing image retrieval (Wang *et al*., Kuang *et al*., 2019), clothing category classification (He et al., 2016), attribute recognition (Sun *et al*., 2015, Fu *et al*., 2013), clothing segmentation (Chen *et al*., 2016b, Li *et al*., 2021), and clothing generation (Nakamura and Goto, 2018).

These image-based vision tasks in fashion domain are also referred as 'fashion image understanding', an active research field in recent years. Understanding fashion images has extended practical advantages and can be applied in enormous applications in fashion and other domains. The study of fashion image understanding has been widely benefited from the rapid advancements in deep learning-based new models and the availability of large datasets covering real-world fashion images. However, the real value of these datasets is in doubt, because different annotation strategies have been adopted in these datasets, resulting in different landmarks for different clothing styles and low compatibility of these datasets. For example, Ge *et al*. (2019) only created a data-richer dataset-DeepFashion2 (Ge *et al*., 2019) to solve problems, after he refutes the existing problems, such as single clothing-item per image, sparse landmarks (4~8 only), and no per-pixel masks, in DeepFashion (Liu *et al*., 2016a). Data annotation is incompatible between these two datasets serving similar problems, which results in a drain on financial resources and computing power.

In this paper, we propose an automatic method to locate key points of fashion items on fashion images by taking advantage of clear correspondence between clothing and human body. Our method consists of the initial mask extraction, the clothing mask completion, coarse clothing key-point sampling and a refined clothing key-point detector. Specifically, since most clothing key points are along edges/outline of the garment, coarse corners detector and morphology algorithm are developed to localize possible corner points on the clothing mask based on human parsing results. However, the initial points detected may not be valid corners along clothing boundary but points inside the clothing mask because of possible occlusions, the clothing mask completer (CMC) is therefore designed to help automatically complete occluded regions in the phase of the clothing mask completion. Finally, the graph-based clothing feature lines, human pose information as a priori and inherent clothing-body location constraint are used in conjunction to refine the location of detected clothing key points. Coarse points are divided into 6 groups in this paper, they are the collar part points, the clothing shoulder part points, the armpit part points, the waist points, the clothing hem points and the sleeve points. Figure 1 and Table 1 give the definition and naming of our fashion landmarks.

Figure 1. Illustration of our landmark's definition

Table 1. Naming of our landmarks

Index	Landmark Name
0	neckline_left
1	neckline_center
2	neckline_right
3	shoulder_left
4	shoulder_right
5	armpit_left
6	armpit_right
7	waistline_left
8	waistline_right
9	hem_left
10	hem_center
11	hem_right
12	sleeve_left_out
13	sleeve_right_out
14	sleeve_left_in
15	sleeve_right_in

2. RELATED WORK

The purpose of landmarks is to locate the neckline points, shoulder points and other functional areas of the clothing, helping to effectively identify the layout and extensive attributes of fashion items. Recent years, thanks to the public release of the large dataset (Ge *et al.*, 2019, Liu *et al.*, 2016a, Zou *et al.*, 2019) for accelerating the research on landmark detection task. Different methods are proposed by researchers in succession based on task dependencies. For example,(Liu *et al.*, 2016a) first proposed FashionNet to predict clothing attributes and landmarks to understand fashion images, and they introduced a richly annotated dataset named DeepFashion as a benchmark dataset for multiple tasks. Following FashionNet, (Liu *et al.*, 2016b) proposed a framework of cascading to improve fashion landmarks estimation accuracy while reducing the amount of computation. It's a three-stage structure that uses VGG-16 (Simonyan and Zisserman, 2014) to predict landmarks, estimating fashion landmark offsets and output contextual landmark offsets in each stage. These methods treat Fashion Landmarks Localization as the regression problems by training deep neural networks and using regression functions to minimize the mean square error of all N samples. Besides the regression-based model, attention mechanism is a widely used method in landmarks detection. For example, (Liu and Lu, 2018) introduced an attention mechanism, called 'landmark heatmaps' to produce a unified attention. Their proposed network adds two branches based on VGG-16 to capture attention and localize landmarks. (Li *et al.*, 2019) proposed a Spatial-Aware Non-Local model to detect fashion landmarks. This model can accept high-level semantic knowledge in the way of encoding the prior knowledge by the spatial attention map. Following this, (Lee *et al.*, 2019) detected landmarks by utilizing a global-local embedding model that contains a global procedure and a convolutional procedure to obtain long-range dependencies and local information in fashion images respectively. The above methods are deep learning based in a large number of data-driven way for feature extraction. The learned feature interpretability is weak, and some unusual landmarks are predicted to be incomprehensible although their overall performance is very good. We argue that the task of human pose estimation is similar to fashion key points localization but differs in the location and number of points. Unlike the above methods, we propose a pose-aware segmentation-based method to locate fashion landmarks by taking advantage of clear correspondence between clothing and human body inspired by(Cao *et al.*, 2017, Hu *et al.*, 2018). The segmented image is leveraged to extract the clothing mask and the joint points of human pose estimation are used as prior knowledge in our methods to roughly locate the different functional areas of the clothing.

3. METHOD

In this paper, we propose an automatic method to locate key points of fashion items on fashion images, and the method consists of four phases, including initial mask extraction, clothing mask completion, coarse clothing key-points sampling and clothing key-points refinement.

3.1 Initial Mask Exaction

Since the fashion landmarks are along the edge/outline of the garment, it is an important step to quickly and accurately detect the edge lines of each fashion item for our initial key points sampling. Considering the mixture of foreground and background of the input image, and each fashion item is difficult to be automatically distinguished, we thus extract the clothing and torso areas separately based on the segmentation method. These two areas are clothing masks (CM) and torsos masks (TM) as initial masks to be used by next step. By comparing image segmentation methods (Zheng *et al*., 2018, Gong *et al*., 2017, Chen *et al*., 2016a, Li *et al*., 2020) that have performed well in recent years, we end up using SCHP (Li et al., 2020) because this model can iteratively aggregate the current learned model and the previous optimal model in an online manner, thereby inferring more reliable pseudo masks, and the corresponding corrected labels can further improve the performance of the model. However, the predicted segmented area is not the 100% ground truth because of the blurred boundaries and similar pixel values between different semantic parts, which can cause confusion between the semantics of the image as well as the unexpected noise that can be generated in the predicted mask. So, the initial mask was constructed by the morphological closing operator based on the preservation of their critical geometry and topology.

3.2 Clothing Mask Completion

The problem of occlusion is often encountered in the fashion landmarks detection. If the clothing mask is occluded, the contour points inside the clothing will be recognized as edge points. A discriminator is then designed to determine if the initial masks are occluded or not. If the mask is not occluded, our system will continue with the process of initial coarse key-points sampling (section 3.3). Conversely, Clothing Mask Completer (CMC) is designed to automatically locate and complete occluded regions. It includes three modules 1). Pose-aware joints information, 2). Clothing feature line self-defined according to human body proportion and clothing structure, 3). The new mask created in the occluded area.

3.2.1 Discriminator

The discriminator is designed to determine if the clothing mask obtained is occluded. We count the number of connected components in the image, defined as n, $n \in Z+$. Figure 2 shows the number of connected components in different fashion pose.

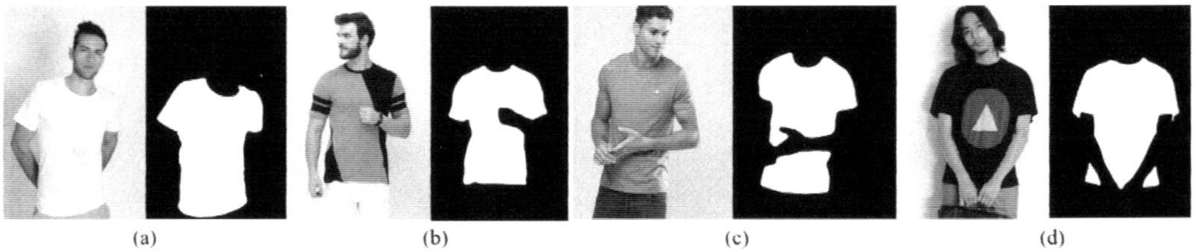

Figure 2. Examples of connected components with different poses: n=1 in (a) and (b), n=2 in (c), n=3 in (d)

If N>1, the clothing mask is occluded. At N=1, we calculated the minimum external rectangle of the clothing mask, and found the position coordinates of the midpoints M and N in the width direction of the rectangle, the line L_{MN} divide the rectangle into A and B. Calculate the area difference of A and B, $S_C = |S_A - S_B|$, and then compare S_C with the threshold T. If $S_C > T$, we think the clothing mask is occluded and vice versa.

3.2.2 Clothing Mask Completer (CMC)

CMC is designed to complete these covered areas, which includes 3 modules.

Modules1. Pose-aware joints information. Pose gives better global information in the form of connecting joints that can provide a reference standard for locating fashion landmarks. We use a state-of-the-arts pose estimation method (Cao et al., 2017) in this module of CMC to obtain the joints information. Figure 3 shows the output format of anatomical key-points or joints and their definitions.

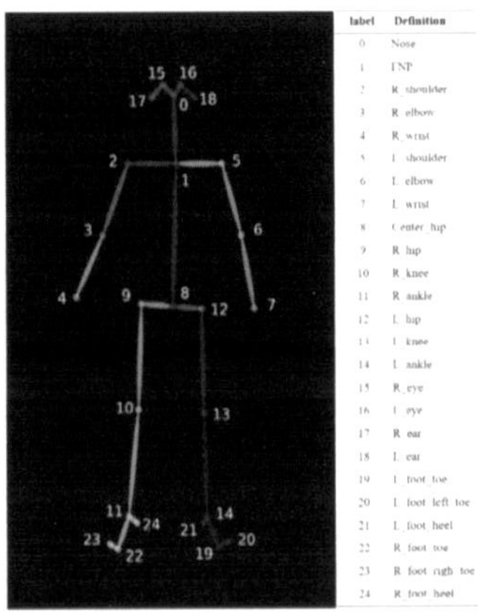

Figure 3. Joints definition of pose estimation

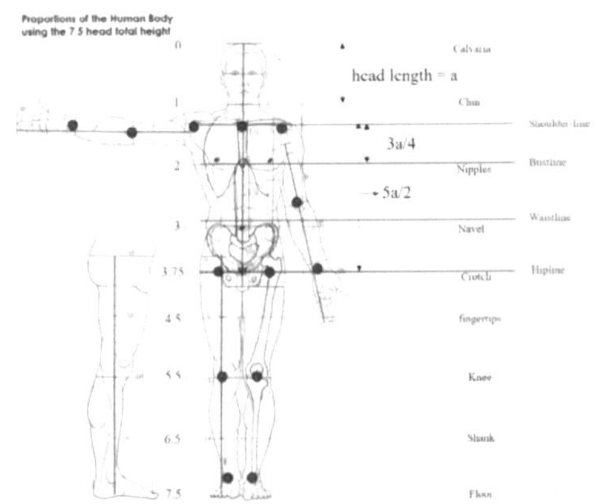

Figure 4. Illustration of self-defined clothing feature line

Modules2. Clothing feature line self-defined according to human body proportion and clothing structure. Based on the results of pose estimation, define the shoulder-line, hipline by connecting point R_shoulder, point L_shoulder and point R_hip, L_hip respectively. The position of the bustline and waistline is then estimated based on the 'head-to-body ratio'. The distance between the point FNP and point Center_hip is defined as Dsh. If the head length is a, Dsp = 2.5a. The approximate position of the shoulder-line, bustline, waistline, and hipline is shown in Figure 4. In addition, the width of the clothing is constrained according to the shoulder-waist ratio (SWR), bust-waist ratio (BWR)and the waist-hip ratio (WHR).

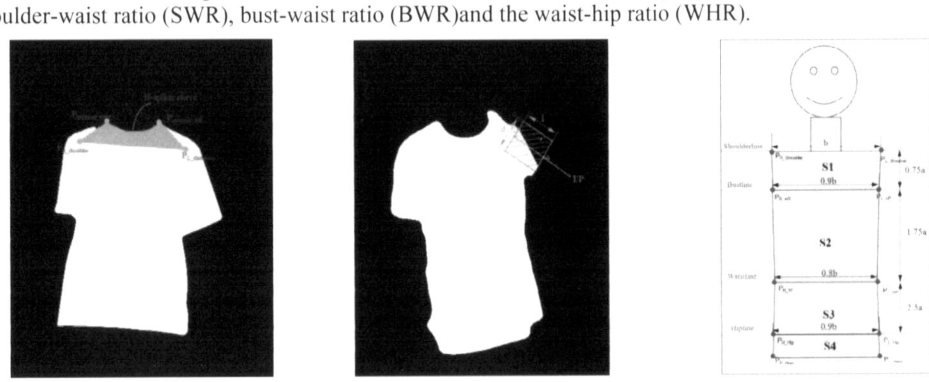

(a) (b) (c)

Figure 5. Illustration of the new mask created in the occluded area: (a) Collar area's new mask; (b) Sleeve area's new mask; (c) Main torso area's new mask

Modules3. The new mask created in the occluded area. According to the common fashion poses, the clothing mask patches (occluded areas) in this paper are distributed in the area of hair, limbs and decorations (e.g., bags). Hair usually covers the collar and shoulder area of the clothing, and limbs and ornaments usually cover the sleeves and large body area of the clothing. Modules 3 of CMC is used to complete these occluded areas, including the collar area, the sleeve area, and the main torso area.

Collar Area. B-spline curves and V-shaped polylines are used to fit collar arc according to the shape of the collar (round neck, V-neck). These curves or lines connect the left and right shoulder joints to create a mask called a collar patch mask, shown in Figure 5(a).

Sleeve Area. Create a new rectangular mask at the sleeve to complete the occluded clothing sleeve area. The length and width of the rectangular mask are constrained by the length of the clothing sleeves and the width of the human arm respectively, shown in the blue area of Figure 5(b).

Main Torso Area. The S1, S2, S3, and S4 areas shown in Figure 5(c) are used to complete the occluded clothing main torso area. We first calculate the European distance, defined as b, between the left and right shoulder joints. The SWR, BWR, WHR are used to roughly constrains the width of the clothing. The 'head-to-body ratio' is used to constrain the length of the clothing.

3.3 Coarse Clothing Key-Points Sampling

In this phase, our purpose is to sample key-points based on clothing masks obtained in section 3.2. The required clothing key-points are distributed on the contour line of the clothing mask. Considering that one of the properties of 'corners' is that the movement in any direction is large, the Corner Detection Algorithm is our priority. After comparing several classical corner detection algorithms, Shi-Tomasi corner detection is used for the following reasons: 1. Our task needs to return the fixed N best corners and set the Euclidean distance between the N corners. 2. The Shi-Tomasi corner detection operator is an improvement of the Harris corner detection operator, which is suitable for processing cloth masks in terms of stability, anti-noise capability and complexity. Define the S_{CKP} is the set of n coarse key-points, where $S_{CKP} = \{s_1, s_2, \ldots, s_n\}$, $s_i = (x,y)$.

3.4 Clothing Key-Points Refinement

First, we take 25 joints as the reference points and self-defined clothing feature lines as reference lines. With these coarse clothing key-points in hands, we group them into 6 subsets according to the human joints and clothing feature lines that they belong to. Specifically, we first define 4 subsets, denoted by S_{collar}, $S_{shoulder}$, S_{sleeve} and S_{hem}, which are located around the *Front Neck Point*, *Shoulder Point*, *Elbow Point* and *Hip Point*. S_{collar}, $S_{shoulder}$, S_{sleeve} and S_{hem} represent the set of clothing collar region points (N_{CP}), shoulder region points (N_{SHP}), sleeve region points (N_{SLP}), and hem region points (N_{HP}) respectively, where S_{collar}, $S_{shoulder}$, S_{sleeve}, $S_{hem} \in S_{CKP}$. In addition, other 2 sunsets denoted by S_{armpit}, S_{waist}, which are located around the *clothing bustline*, and *waistline* respectively. S_{armpit}, S_{waist} represent the set of clothing armpit region points (N_{AP}) and waist region points (N_{WP}) respectively, where S_{armpit}, $S_{waist} \in S_{CKP}$.

Collar Points Determination

input : set $S_{CKP} = \{s_1, s_2, \ldots, s_n\}$ of n coarse key points, where $s_i = (x, y)$
human key points of neck P_n and left shoulder P_{ls}
output: middle, left, and right key points of collar P_m, P_l, and P_r

Determine set S_{collar} for representing collar region points
for $s_i \in S_{CKP}$ **do**
  if $\|s_i - P_n\|_2 <= \|P_{ls} - P_n\|_2$ **then**
    $s_i \in S_{collar}$
  end
end
Determine the middle point of collar: $P_m \leftarrow \min_{s_i} \|s_i - P_n\|_2, s_i \in S_{collar}$;
Determine the rotation angle: $\theta \leftarrow - \arccos \frac{<\overrightarrow{P_{ls}}, \overrightarrow{P_n}> (1,0)}{\|<P_{ls}, P_n>\| * \|(1,0)\|}$;
Apply rotation transformation to S_{collar}
for $s_i \in S_{collar}$ **do**
  $s_i \leftarrow \begin{bmatrix} \cos\theta & -\sin\theta \\ \sin\theta & \cos\theta \end{bmatrix} s_i^T$
end
Split S_{collar} to left and right subset $S_{collarL}$ and $S_{collarR}$
for $s_i \in S_{collar}$ **do**
  if $s_i(x) <= P_n(x)$ **then**
    $s_i \in S_{collarL}$
  else
    $s_i \in S_{collarR}$
  end
end
Determine left collar point: $P_l \leftarrow \min_{s_i} s_i(y), s_i \in S_{collarL}$;
Determine right collar point: $P_r \leftarrow \min_{s_i} s_i(y), s_i \in S_{collarR}$;

Collar Landmarks Localization. First, we constrain S_{CKP} with the length of the L_shoulder and R_shoulder joints to identify S_{collar}. Then rotate the θ to do an angle regularization of the clothing mask according to the joint information. Next, determine the $P_{neckline\_center}$ by calculating the minimum Euclidean distance between $S_{crollar}$ and FNP. $P_{neckline\_left}$ or $P_{neckline\_right}$ is determined by calculating the minimum value of $s_i(y)$ in $S_{crollar}$. The collar landmarks localization algorithm is listed below.

Shoulder Landmarks Localization. Define $D_{SS(i)}$ as the Euclidean distance from $S_{shoulder}$ to L_shoulder and R_shoulder joints. Formula is as follows:

$$D_{SS}(i) = \| S_{shoulder}(i) - P_{R\_shoulder} \|_2 , \forall i \in \{1, 2, \cdots, N_{SHP}\} \quad (1)$$

$$D_{SS}(i) = \| S_{shoulder}(i) - P_{L\_shoulder} \|_2 , \forall i \in \{1, 2, \cdots, N_{SHP}\} \quad (2)$$

where $P_{shoulder\_left}$ and $P_{shoulder\_right}$ are simple to be located by calculating the minimum $D_{SS(i)}$.

Armpit & waist Landmarks Localization. The armpit and waist landmarks are respectively distributed on the bust and waist of self-defined clothing feature lines. And then the SBR and BWR of the human body are used as geometric constraints to locate the specific locations of armpit and waist landmarks. Due to the difference between SBR and BWR for men and women as well as the perspective problem of fashion images, geometric constraint parameters α are manually tuned in experiments based on clothing knowledge.

Hem & Sleeve Landmarks Localization. The Ramer-Douglas-Peucker Algorithm (Douglas and Peucker, 1973)was first used to handle a large number of redundant geometric data points on the basis of preserving the geometry skeleton of the clothing mask. In this way, the range of S_{hem} and S_{sleeve} are narrowed. Then L_hip, R_hip joints and L_elbow and R_elbow joints as spatial constraint priors to further narrowed the range of the S_{hem} and S_{sleeve} respectively. Finally, the gradient changes $f'(x_0)$ of N_{HP} and N_{SLP} to localize the hem and sleeve landmarks.

$$f'_{(x_0)} = \lim_{\Delta x \to 0} \frac{\Delta y}{\Delta x} = \lim_{\Delta x \to 0} \frac{f(x_0+\Delta_x)-f(x_0)}{\Delta_x} \quad (3)$$

4. EXPERIMENT

4.1 Data Preparation

Our approach can be extended to a variety of categories of clothing by changing the relative position of the clothing key points guided by the human joints. In this article, we picked one of the categories (e.g., T-shirts) for experimentation. Our dataset contains 1000 images from the DeepFashion2 dataset (Ge *et al.*, 2019) that contains 491K images of 13 clothing categories and 801K clothing items. Each item in an image is labeled with fashion landmarks annotations that can be the ground truth to examine the effectiveness of our proposed method. The fashion landmarks are predicted in DeepFashion2 with the KGDet model having 25 points in upper clothing. However, we suspect that some of these 25 points are redundant and don't reflect clothing functionality. We thus only used 16 points, as shown in Figure 1, to do qualitative and quantitative analysis.

4.2 Evaluation Metrics

We utilized the normalized error (NE) metric (Liu *et al.*, 2016b) as the criterion for evaluation of our proposed method and DeepFashion2 method. NE is the Euclidean distance between predicted and ground-truth landmarks, which formulated as:

$$\mathrm{NE} = \frac{1}{m}\sum_{i=1}^{m} \frac{|x_i-\hat{x}_i|_2}{h_i w_i} \quad (4)$$

where m denotes the number of points, x_i and $\hat{x}_i$ are the ground-truth and estimated landmarks respectively and h_i , w_i are the height and width of *i*-th point, $\frac{|x_i-\hat{x}_i|_2}{h_i w_i}$ was used to normalize the ground truth landmarks in coordinate space.

4.3 Result

We conduct experiments on the dataset in section 4.1 to compare the fashion landmarks located by our method with the landmarks predicted by (Ge *et al.*, 2019) method. The comparison results were shown in Table 2

(Hem Landmarks are not compared because different definitions). From the table, the accuracy of our proposed method was not as good as deepfashion2, the key-points in the collar and shoulder area are located more accurately. The purpose of our experiment is not to beat DL-based method in performance, but to verify the rationality of landmarks in our follow-up task (automatic annotation tool). Instead, we were surprised to find that the NE values of shoulder landmarks were 0.0127 and 0.0195, which were less than 0.0231 and 0.0249 of (Ge *et al.*, 2019) method. We also visualize landmark localization results in Figure 6. Our method can effectively eliminate the interference of other types of clothing textures because of the geometric constraints on clothing and body proportions, as shown in the first column of the fourth row of Figure 6, the prediction of point 10, Point 11, Point 12 are less accurate than our method. In addition, since Ge's method has a different definition of the hem landmarks from ours, we consider the hem landmarks should be along the edge of the upper clothing. But they believe that the hem landmarks should be invisible in this case shown in the first and third row of Figure 6, so there are no annotations for invisible hem landmarks. From the visualized results, even so, our method can still locate the reasonable hem landmarks. For example, at point 10 in the first row of Figure 6, Ge's method predicts on the trousers (unreasonable) and our method predicts on the upper clothing edge (reasonable)

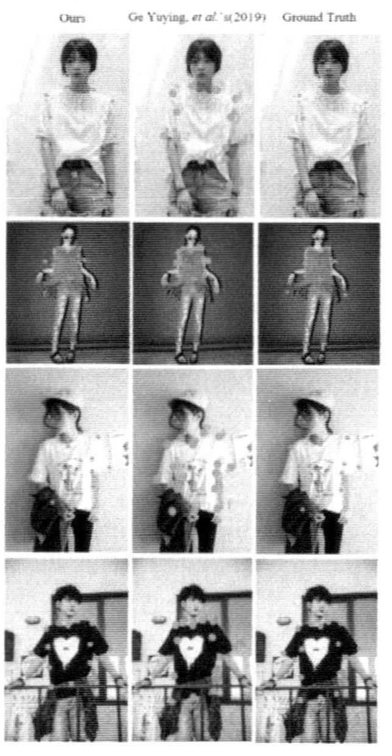

Figure 6. Examples of qualitative results

Table 2. Quantitative results

	DeepFashion2(2019)	Ours
neckline_right	0.031	**0.0261**
neckline_center	0.0291	**0.0253**
neckline_left	0.027	**0.0264**
shoulder_right	0.0231	**0.0127**
shoulder_left	0.0249	**0.0195**
armpit_right	0.0364	0.0564
armpit_left	0.0347	0.0541
waistline_right	0.0227	0.0347
waistline_left	0.0203	0.0331
sleeve_right_out	0.0316	0.0584
sleeve_right_in	0.0271	0.0632
sleeve_left_out	0.0261	0.0568
sleeve_left_in	0.0297	0.0694
Avg.	**0.028**	0.0412

5. CONCLUSION

This paper proposes a pose-aware segmentation-based method that can automatically locate key points even without Ground Truth. The proposed method can be applied to annotate fashion images and reannotate existing datasets for cross dataset learning. From the experimental results, our method has certain advantages compared with the state-of-the art method in locating clothing shoulder and collar landmarks. We will refine our algorithm to improve the overall accuracy of fashion landmark prediction.

ACKNOWLEDGEMENT

This research is funded by the Laboratory for Artificial Intelligence in Design (Project Code: RP1-1) under the InnoHK Research Clusters, Hong Kong Special Administrative Region Government.

REFERENCES

Cao, Z., Simon, T., Wei, S.-E. & Sheikh, Y. Realtime multi-person 2d pose estimation using part affinity fields. Proceedings of the IEEE conference on computer vision and pattern recognition, 2017. 7291-7299.

Chen, L.-C., Yang, Y., Wang, J., Xu, W. & Yuille, A. L. Proceedings of the IEEE conference on computer vision and pattern recognition, 2016a. 3640-3649.

Chen, L.-C., Yang, Y., Wang, J., Xu, W. & Yuille, A. L. Attention to scale: Scale-aware semantic image segmentation. Proceedings of the IEEE conference on computer vision and pattern recognition, 2016b. 3640-3649.

Douglas, D. H. & Peucker, T. K. 1973. Algorithms for the reduction of the number of points required to represent a digitized line or its caricature. Cartographica: the international journal for geographic information and geovisualization, 10, 112-122.

Fu, J., Wang, J., Li, Z., Xu, M. & Lu, H. 2013. Efficient Clothing Retrieval with Semantic-Preserving Visual Phrases. Springer Berlin Heidelberg.

Ge, Y., Zhang, R., Wang, X., Tang, X. & Luo, P. Deepfashion2: A versatile benchmark for detection, pose estimation, segmentation and re-identification of clothing images. Proceedings of the IEEE/CVF Conference on Computer Vision and Pattern Recognition, 2019. 5337-5345.

Gong, K., Liang, X., Zhang, D., Shen, X. & Lin, L. Look into person: Self-supervised structure-sensitive learning and a new benchmark for human parsing. Proceedings of the IEEE conference on computer vision and pattern recognition, 2017. 932-940.

He, K., Zhang, X., Ren, S. & Sun, J. 2016. Identity Mappings in Deep Residual Networks. Springer International Publishing.

Hu, Y., Xiao, L., Wang, Y. & Jin, Y. Fashion pose machine for fashion landmark detection. 2018 International Conference on Image and Video Processing, and Artificial Intelligence, 2018. SPIE, 186-190.

Kuang, Z., Gao, Y., Li, G., Luo, P., Chen, Y., Lin, L. & Zhang, W. Fashion retrieval via graph reasoning networks on a similarity pyramid. Proceedings of the IEEE/CVF International Conference on Computer Vision, 2019. 3066-3075.

Lee, S., Oh, S., Jung, C. & Kim, C. A global-local embedding module for fashion landmark detection. Proceedings of the IEEE/CVF International Conference on Computer Vision Workshops, 2019. 0-0.

Li, P., Xu, Y., Wei, Y. & Yang, Y. 2020. Self-correction for human parsing. IEEE Transactions on Pattern Analysis and Machine Intelligence.

Li, P., Xu, Y., Wei, Y. & Yang, Y. 2021. Self-Correction for Human Parsing. IEEE Transactions on Pattern Analysis and Machine Intelligence, 1-1.

Li, Y., Tang, S., Ye, Y. & Ma, J. Spatial-aware non-local attention for fashion landmark detection. 2019 IEEE International Conference on Multimedia and Expo (ICME), 2019. IEEE, 820-825.

Liu, J. & Lu, H. Deep fashion analysis with feature map upsampling and landmark-driven attention. Proceedings of the European Conference on Computer Vision (ECCV) Workshops, 2018. 0-0.

Liu, Z., Luo, P., Qiu, S., Wang, X. & Tang, X. Deepfashion: Powering robust clothes recognition and retrieval with rich annotations. Proceedings of the IEEE conference on computer vision and pattern recognition, 2016a. 1096-1104.

Liu, Z., Yan, S., Luo, P., Wang, X. & Tang, X. Fashion landmark detection in the wild. European Conference on Computer Vision, 2016b. Springer, 229-245.

Nakamura, T. & Goto, R. 2018. Outfit generation and style extraction via bidirectional lstm and autoencoder. arXiv preprint arXiv:1807.03133.

Qian, S., Lian, D., Zhao, B., Liu, T., Zhu, B., Li, H. & Gao, S. Kgdet: Keypoint-guided fashion detection. Proc. AAAI Conference on Artificial Intelligence, 2021. 2449-2457.

Simonyan, K. & Zisserman, A. 2014. Very deep convolutional networks for large-scale image recognition. arXiv preprint arXiv:1409.1556.

Sun, G.-L., Wu, X., Chen, H.-H. & Peng, Q. 2015. Clothing Style Recognition using Fashion Attribute Detection. Proceedings of the 8th International Conference on Mobile Multimedia Communications.

Wang, Z., Gu, Y., Zhang, Y., Zhou, J. & Gu, X. Clothing retrieval with visual attention model. 2017. IEEE.

Zheng, S., Yang, F., Kiapour, M. H. & Piramuthu, R. Modanet: A large-scale street fashion dataset with polygon annotations. Proceedings of the 26th ACM international conference on Multimedia, 2018. 1670-1678.

Zou, X., Kong, X., Wong, W., Wang, C., Liu, Y. & Cao, Y. Fashionai: A hierarchical dataset for fashion understanding. Proceedings of the IEEE/CVF Conference on Computer Vision and Pattern Recognition Workshops, 2019. 0-0.

AR IN VR: AUGMENTED REALITY CUES IN 360-DEGREE STEREOSCOPIC TELEPRESENCE FOR REMOTE COLLABORATION AND MAINTENANCE

Furkan Kaynar[1], Markus Hofbauer[1], Asa MacWilliams[2], Joseph Newman[2], Andreas Hutter[2] and Eckehard Steinbach[1]

[1]*Chair of Media Technology and Munich Institute of Robotics and Machine Intelligence, Technical University of Munich, Germany*

[2]*Siemens Technology, Munich, Germany*

ABSTRACT

Remote maintenance and collaboration applications are getting more interest with the development of mixed reality technologies. The combination of 360-degree telepresence and augmented reality (AR) cues have been shown to be an effective way of remote collaboration. However, most existing methods do not provide depth perception which can improve the remote inspection. Also, many methods that use holograms for live collaboration are limited with only pointing functionality. In this paper, we present a 360-degree telepresence system interacting with an AR backend to create an immersive mixed reality interface for remote collaboration. The proposed camera system does not need to be carried by any on-site person, but can be controlled by the remote operator intuitively. We deploy network delay compensation methods and propose novel projection strategies for a correct and efficient rendering. A comparative analysis shows advantages of the proposed system over previous work and that it is a promising approach for improving remote collaboration and maintenance.

KEYWORDS

Remote Collaboration, Remote Maintenance, Augmented Reality, Virtual Reality, 360-degree Telepresence.

Figure 1. Overview of the proposed telepresence system with Augmented Reality (AR) cues. The camera unit on the left mimics the head motion of the user. The user is provided with stereo views in all directions (360°) augmented with the AR cues (on the right). Some of the holograms are highlighted with orange circles for better visibility

1. INTRODUCTION

With the increasing availability of Augmented Reality (AR) and Virtual Reality (VR) systems, different remote inspection and collaboration systems have been developed based on AR and telepresence (Lee et al., 2018; Speicher et al., 2018).

The design of the telepresence system defines the capabilities and limitations of the remote session and hence determines what the operator perceives. Among different systems, 360° stereoscopic vision systems provide the strong experience with a high level of immersion and a natural 3D perception, which can improve the task performance for indoor applications greatly (Aykut et al., 2019). On the other hand, capturing a live stereoscopic 360° view of the environment is challenging due to problems like computational complexity, limited stereoscopic budget (the level of flexibility of changing the inter-pupillary distance), and constrained 3D impression due to unequal depth perception in different orientations (Aykut et al., 2019).

AR can be used for augmenting the scene with important technical details or auxiliary information, increasing the effectiveness of a remote inspection or collaboration session. The vast majority of the AR-based live collaboration systems either use a 2D view or a monoscopic panorama of the remote environment. A 2D view often leads to a limited field-of-view (FoV) and situational awareness, while a monoscopic panorama lacks the depth information.

In this paper, we present a remote AR system combined with a 360° stereoscopic telepresence system to improve real-time remote inspection and collaboration applications. The operator can freely observe the remote environment without depending on any other person, and with the depth perception due to omnistereoscopic vision. In addition, we deploy a state-of-the-art network delay compensation method (Aykut et al., 2019), to allow a natural and smooth Mixed Reality (MR) experience.

The proposed system uses an AR backend which provides hologram poses with respect to the anchor points initially defined for indoor localization. Any client device can add or modify the AR components, consisting of images, text information, web-content, or the live sensory data of an industrial environment. The holograms reappear at the saved 6-DOF poses once a client device revisits the same environment. This allows for an effective live collaboration as well as the generation of an information database improving the remote inspection in the long-term. We propose a novel system to efficiently map the hologram imagery onto the spherical VR scene created with fisheye lenses.

The rest of the paper is structured as follows. In Section 2, we summarize the related work in the field of mixed-reality telepresence systems. In Section 3, we introduce the architecture of the proposed 360° telepresence system interacting with an AR backend. We present a comparative analysis in Section 4. Section 5 concludes the paper.

2. RELATED WORK

In this section, we summarize existing systems proposed for 360° telepresence with AR overlays. Druta et al. (2021) provide a general overview on remote collaboration. Pretlove (1998) presented a mobile robotic platform equipped with an actuated stereo system synchronized with the operator's head-mounted display (HMD). The scene is overlayed with computer graphics to help the operator while navigating the remote robot in low visibility cases. While this system only focuses on navigation by teleoperation, it does not allow live manipulation of holograms for collaboration.

Wang et al. (2012) proposed a pan-tilt stereo camera unit and AR overlays of objects. They estimate the user's head orientation from the camera view attached to the head using visual processing. To avoid the slow response of the actuated system, the authors warp the video shown to the user to mitigate the inconsistency between the user's and the remote camera's orientations. However, this can lead to incomplete visualization of the remote environment and visual discomfort.

Speicher et al. (2018) proposed a system with a static 360° monoscopic camera and a projector for creating AR cues in a room for remote collaboration. The application scenarios are limited to putting markers on a straight wall and visualizing them with a projector.

Lee et al. (2018) proposed a live panorama system where the remote user views the panoramic video stream captured by the head-mounted 360° monoscopic camera carried by the local host. AR cues and hand gestures are used for non-verbal collaboration. The users reported motion sickness triggered in the dependent mode where they observe the viewport of the local host. Furthermore, the users reported arising discomfort due to the jittery motion introduced by the head-mounted device during the independent mode. Since this system only provides a monoscopic view, no 3D perception of the remote environment is available.

Teo et al. (2019) proposed a system with two modes. The first mode is 360° monoscopic view obtained by a head-mounted camera carried by the local host. The second mode provides a 3D model of the room for an independent viewing experience. While the second method addresses the problem of dependency to the host, it requires a 3D reconstruction of the room in advance.

Kasahara et al. (2016) proposed a head-mounted multi-camera arrangement that creates the 360° view of the environment and stabilizes the view to allow independent remote inspection by the second user. This system does not only bring high computational cost for combining multi-camera frames, but also results in severe stitching errors as viewed in the demonstration videos.

Most of the methods discussed in this section create and transmit a full 360° monoscopic video, which typically requires a high bandwidth. This can be problematic for many cases where the networks are limited or time-varying. The bandwidth limitations are an even more severe problem for transmitting a 360° stereoscopic video.

The head-mounted perception systems do not only cause a viewing discomfort and motion sickness by the remote viewer, but they also add the burden to the local host to carry the system on the head in addition to the maintenance task. For an efficient video transmission and processing, head-mounted camera systems are typically connected to the workstations via cables, which further limits the freedom of movement. Many works use AR cues for pointing at different objects, but they do not build a long-term information base which can be used in further telemaintenance sessions.

Our proposed system addresses all of the problems mentioned above. Our actuated camera system has a steady basis, eliminating the need for carrying the setup. The fisheye-based delay compensation is deployed to avoid motion sickness. We do not transmit the entire FoV per eye, but only the 180° FoV around the desired viewport, leading to less bandwidth usage. Finally, our AR backend brings a lot of flexibility for short term and also long term development of a remote AR system.

3. 360° TELEPRESENCE SYSTEM WITH AR BACKEND

In this section, we introduce the 360° telepresence system interacting with an AR backend. Figure 2 summarizes the architecture of the proposed framework.

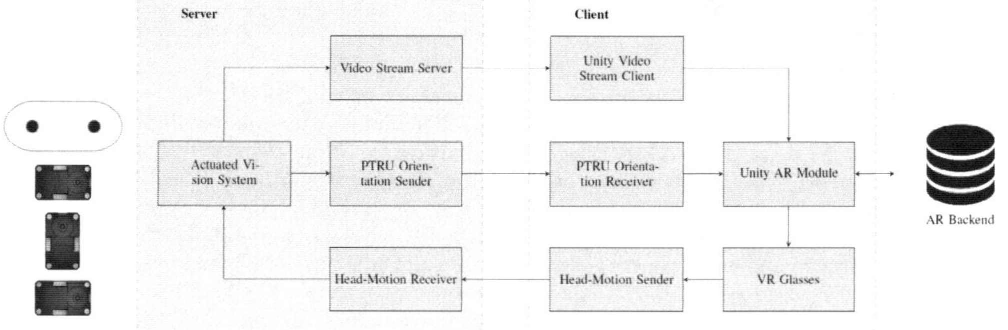

Figure 2. Overview of the proposed stereoscopic 360° AR/VR system

The server side includes an actuated camera unit, video streaming server, and modules for sending and receiving orientation data. To create a modular and scalable system, we designed each module on the server side as a separate ROS node. The client side uses Unity for the interaction with the HMD and rendering of the remote scene. The Unity system includes a video streaming client, an AR module communicating with the AR backend, as well as orientation sender and receiver modules. The user observes the remote scene enriched with holograms intuitively through VR glasses.

In the following sections, we discuss the individual modules of the proposed framework in detail.

3.1 Telepresence Server

The telepresence server provides the functionality of acquiring and streaming the desired viewport of the remote environment. We use a stereo fisheye camera system with network delay compensation, to avoid visual discomfort and motion sickness. We introduce each module in detail in the following sections.

3.1.1 Actuated Vision System

Acquiring live omnistereoscopic view of the environment is challenging. Many vision systems with multiple cameras and mirrors suffer from stitching errors, being not real-time capable, having a limited stereoscopic budget, and constrained depth perception (Aykut et al., 2019). To overcome these challenges, we use an actuated stereo vision system that allows the remote operator to control the stereo camera system with their head movement. Using an actuated system inevitably introduces a network delay. Since humans are very sensitive to delays in visual response of the system, we deploy a state-of-the-art network delay compensation method using fisheye lenses (Aykut et al., 2019).

For the hardware system, we deploy three fast servo motors for pan-tilt-roll rotation of the camera system. The resulting pan-tilt-roll unit (PTRU) is depicted in Figure 1 and Figure 2 on the left. The servo motors communicate with the server workstation via a serializer, which allows communication over USB. The motors follow the target pan-tilt-roll angles as received from the head-motion data of the user. Further, the motors provide their current orientation as sensed by their encoders to be used by the client for rendering the FoV of the fisheye view. The stereoscopic camera publishes the stereo frames as a single frame that is obtained through a USB interface. Since we use USB communication for both the servo motors and cameras, the system can be plug and play.

The fisheye lens-based network delay compensation has been shown to be effective in the literature (Aykut et al., 2019). Our stereoscopic camera has fisheye lenses to acquire a 180° FoV of the remote environment for each eye. We do not acquire and transmit the entire 360° FoV for each eye, but only a 180° FoV around the desired viewport for each eye. This yields a sufficiently larger image available for rendering than the viewport shown to the user wearing HMD. We leverage the extra image region around user's viewport in each eye for network delay compensation. This image buffer region allows for providing an immediate rendering of the environment when the user rotates the head before the PTRU moves to the new orientation and the new image is captured and transmitted back to the viewer. For usual head rotation speeds, this scheme can compensate network delays up to few seconds. This delay compensation mitigates the visual discomfort due to rendering delays during remote collaboration or maintenance tasks.

3.1.2 Video Streaming

The video stream captured by the cameras are encoded by the x264 software video encoder (VideoLAN) and transmitted to the client using the Real Time Streaming Protocol (RTSP). The stereo camera outputs a single frame with the two frames coming from the two cameras combined. We configure the encoder for ultrafast and low-delay encoding. Additionally, we integrated the video streaming system of TELECARLA (Hofbauer et al., 2020) to enable a dynamic video stream adaptation based on the available network transmission rate. The TELECARLA streaming system together with a multi-dimensional adaptation scheme such as deployed in the work of Hofbauer et al. (2022) enables an optimized spatio-temporal video stream adaptation.

3.1.3 Orientation Communication

For orientation data transmission, we use the ROS# package of Bischoff (2019), providing a WebSocket communication between ROS and Unity implemented in C#. The server subscribes to the ROS topics showing the HMD orientation published by the client. The PTRU follows the target angles to mimic the HMD motion. We use the HMD's motion tracking system and do not require any additional hardware.

We also transmit the current PTRU orientation back to the client side via ROS#. This information is used to place the remote scene in the correct 3D orientation for rendering in the HMD.

3.2 Telepresence Client with AR

The telepresence client consists of the client workstation and the HMD worn by the user inspecting the remote environment. We do not use any additional hardware other than the HMD's own base stations to capture the orientation. No training for the user is necessary, because of the intuitive usage of HMD. We use Unity as our main rendering framework, due to its compatibility with a wide range of devices such as HMDs. The modules of the proposed client system are explained in the following.

3.2.1 Scene Rendering

In this section, we detail how we created our rendering pipeline for a smooth and efficient visualization. Our aim is visualizing the remote scene in an immersive way and overlaying the holograms -which were created in world coordinates- at the correct image locations.

By designing our pipeline, we must consider the following points: The stereo camera outputs two images with fisheye projection. The viewport of the camera and the user can be at different orientations at a given time. The obtained scene must be placed to the exact orientation of the PTRU to depict the correct part of the remote environment. The hologram poses are saved in cartesian space and they must be transformed properly to the fisheye projected scene.

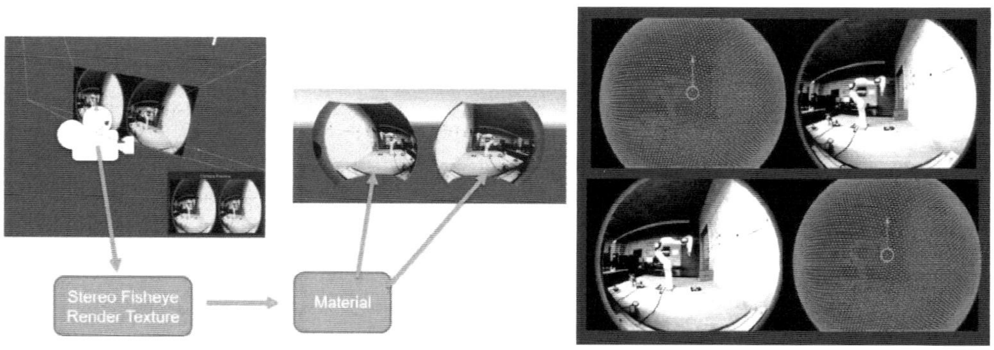

Figure 3. Projection from the stereo frame to hemispheres (on left). UV mapping from the stereo frame (on right)

We start our pipeline with the video acquisition. The client application connects to the RTSP server on the server side, and starts to receive the video stream using UDP. The video stream is then decoded and rendered in Unity scene. Since the camera system provides a single image that contains both camera views, we cannot directly render the image to each eye of the user. We first render the decoded stereo frame on a Quad object in Unity, as shown in Figure 3 on the left. To render the remote scene correctly, we must project the spherical images properly, and place them at the correct 3D orientation. In addition, we want to benefit from the image buffer-based delay compensation with the fisheye cameras.

The stereo images contain the fisheye projected view of the remote environment, each eye covering a horizontal FoV of 180°. We project each fisheye image onto a hemispherical shape, covering the half of the entire FoV. Hence, the stereo frame yields two hemispheres with the scene content after the mapping step as shown in Figure 3 in the middle.

We create 3D hemisphere models with a custom UV mapping from the stereo frame, assuming an equidistant fisheye projection, by which the radial distance from the center on the image plane is proportional to the angle of incidence (Hughes et al., 2010). This mapping is shown in Figure 3 on the right. The hemispherical models are cut from top and bottom since those parts are not covered by the camera frame. This mapping projects each pixel onto a point on the hemisphere. We define the UV mapping on the stereo frame such that each hemisphere receives pixel values from the respective part of the frame. This brings the advantage of being able to decode the frame only once, but render it twice on two hemispheres as shown in Figure 3 on the right. This decreases the computational load, which is of importance for having a smoothly running Unity application on a computer with decent graphical computation resources.

The hemisphere orientations in the scene must be the same as the fisheye lenses on the PTRU to show the correct portion of the remote environment. The two hemispheres are placed to have the same distance between each other as the physical cameras have. Note that we show the hemispheres separately in Figure 3 (in the middle) for better visibility.

Each hemisphere is observed by a Unity camera at its center, that renders to the left or right display of the HMD. Thereby, we create a spherical surrounding that the user can freely observe by rotating the head. We keep the two hemispheres in separate rendering layers, and each Unity camera observes only one layer. These Unity cameras follow the HMD orientation to let the user look at any desired orientation, while the hemisphere orientations are following the current orientation of the PTRU. Since the FoV of each eye is smaller than the available FoV, we can compensate the delayed response of the PTRU and visual feedback due to network and system delays. When the user rotates the head, we have an available image region to render, until the PTRU receives the new head orientation and transmits the new frame at the new orientation.

3.2.2 AR Backend

The holograms show technical information about the scene, and are kept on our AR backend. The AR backend holds the previously recorded holograms and their 6-DOF poses with respect to the defined anchor points in the corresponding room. The holograms can be modified at any time with a mobile device visiting the same place or via a web-based editor. This makes it possible to communicate between an on-site worker and remote collaborator.

Rendering of holograms. Upon fetching the holograms from the AR backend, they are loaded into the Unity scene at the locations as the real world locations in the room. The holograms live in a separate Unity layer and are rendered on top of the hemisphere layers. As a result, they are always visible to the Unity cameras rendering the scene on the HMD. The separation between these cameras creates the depth effect on the holograms.

If the holograms are simply rendered on top of the hemispheres as seen by the Unity cameras, the locations of them will be wrong on the spherical scene. This is because of the remote scene being acquired through fisheye projection and mapped on a hemisphere. In contrast, the holograms are just placed in the world coordinates and observed by a perspective camera in Unity.

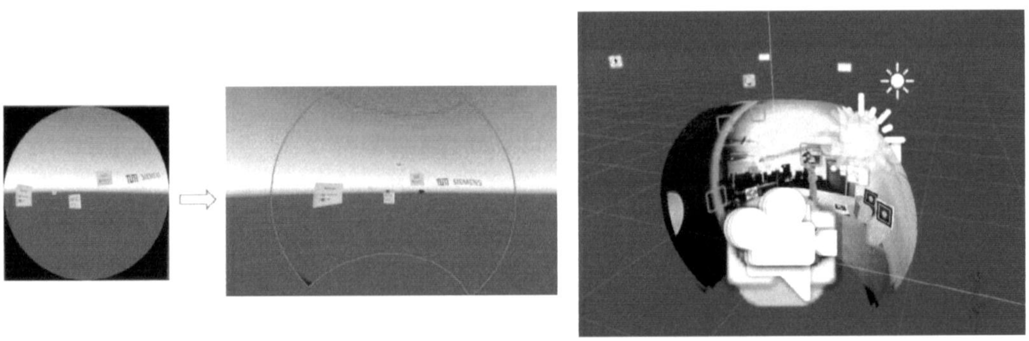

Figure 4. Fisheye warping of holograms (on left), an example scene with VR and AR components (on right)

We solve this problem by adding a fisheye projection step in Unity, only for warping the holograms, for them to be in accordance with the remote scene projected on the hemispheres. The fisheye warping of holograms is shown in Figure 4, on the left. We use a shader performing fisheye projection and add a fisheye camera in Unity that only observes the hologram layer. Then we render the view on a hemisphere model with transparent texture, resulting in the warping of holograms as if they were observed by a fisheye camera. We then place the transparent hemisphere in front of the other hemispheres, with its center at the middle of two hemispheres. Thereby, we create spherical view for both the remote scene, and the holograms. The holograms are static in their positions, but the optical effect of AR-warping changes when the hemispheres move, because of the fisheye projection.

PTRU Modeling for Correct Pose of Hemispheres. The PTRU has separate joints for pan, tilt, and roll. The two cameras are placed at a specific distance to each other. Ideally, the hemispheres should follow the rotation of the cameras realistically, rather than rotating around a single point using the pan-tilt-roll angles of the motors. For a realistic geometrical representation of the PTRU, we measure the distances between the joints and model the physical PTRU. We create three hinge (revolute) joints in Unity, combine these joints with links of specific sizes, and center the hemispheres at the positions of the real cameras. This mimics the real setup by size and motion and ensures that we are moving the hemispheres in the scene in the same way as the physical cameras move on the PTRU.

Figure 4 shows an exemplary scene with VR and AR components on the right. The AR components are placed in the world coordinates (visible behind the hemispheres), and they are projected on the hemispheres with AR-warping (visible on the hemispheres). Note that the both hemispheres are shown in the scene, however they are hardly separated due to the small distance between them.

3.2.3 Orientation Communication

ROS# is used for receiving and transmitting the orientation data. We create a custom joint state publisher in Unity, read the HMD orientation in Unity, and publish it to a ROS topic available to the server.

Secondly, the client subscribes to respective ROS topics showing the current orientation of the pan-tilt-roll motors. We mimic this current orientation by the joints of the PTRU model in Unity. These Unity joints move the hemispheres to the same pose as the real cameras have at the moment.

4. ANALYSIS AND DISCUSSION

In this section, we compare our method to previous works, by contrasting important system properties. Table 1 shows a comparison of our system against alternative systems.

Table 1. Comparison of 360° remote collaboration systems

Method	Camera	Depth percep-tion	Stitching required	Delay com-pen-sation	Entire FoV trans-mitted	Type of AR cues	3D recon-struction required	Camera carried by person	Image stabi-liza-tion re-quired	Orien-tation
Ours	Stereo fisheye	Yes	No	Yes	No	6-DOF static & modifi-able	No	No	No	3-DOF
Pretlove, 1998	Stereo	Yes	No	No	No	Static	No	No	No	3-DOF
Wang et al., 2012	Stereo	Yes	No	No	No	Static	No	No	No	2-DOF
Speicher et al., 2018	360° mono	No	No (in-camera)	No	Yes	Pointing cues	No	No	No	3-DOF
Lee et al., 2018	360° mono	No	No (in-camera)	No	Yes	Pointing cues	No	Yes	Yes	3-DOF
Teo et al., 2019	360° mono	Partial	No (in-camera)	No	Yes	Pointing cues	Yes	Yes	No	3-DOF
Kasahara et al., 2016	6 mono cameras	No	Yes	No	Yes	Pointing cues	No	Yes	Yes	3-DOF

We tested our system at 2560 x 920 resolution for two eyes up to 60 Hz frame rate and observed a smooth video transmission with a hardly noticeable motion-to-photon latency. As opposed to many other remote collaboration works, our camera setup is independent of a person on-site. This brings several advantages. Firstly, the remote user can observe the environment in a completely free way, rather than having to be dependent on another person's viewport on-site. Secondly, the person on-site does not have to carry a sensor setup which can be bulky and limiting the motions, hence the work efficiency is increased. Furthermore, we do not need to use image stabilization techniques to create an independent view for the remote observer, and thereby decrease the computational complexity and avoid possible visual defects. As opposed to methods using multi-camera stitching approaches, we use an actuated stereo camera with the vision-on-demand approach and thereby we eliminate the issues of stitching and visual defects that can be uncomfortable or misleading for the remote collaborator. We know where the camera setup is placed in the room and do not require any 3D reconstruction or digital twin of the remote environment. Since our AR system is based on the AR backend, the holograms can be created, modified and saved at any time from any client device. This brings a lot of flexibility for remote collaboration with non-verbal cues. In addition, holograms which stay in a given position and show important information can improve the remote maintenance not only for the moment, but also in the long term. The holograms are transmitted from the backend to the client, and the transmission is unaffected by the network quality between the server and the client. Even though the quality of the video content is decreased, the holograms can still be viewed in high quality by the client.

5. CONCLUSION

In this paper, we presented a system realizing "AR in VR" in real time. The proposed system can be used for remote collaboration and maintenance tasks. An actuated stereoscopic camera unit following the head-motion of the viewer captures the remote view. We use fisheye lenses for network delay compensation. Additionally, we present a novel scene rendering with UV mapping from a stereo frame for efficient video rendering. Holograms are fetched from a backend and warped with fisheye projection to be placed at the correct positions in the frame.

The resulting system has a low delay, low computational complexity and does not face any stitching problems. Our system runs at high resolution and high frame rates, thanks to low computational complexity. The depth perception quality is unaffected by the viewing orientation, since the stereo acquisition is the same in all directions.

Our system can be used in many remote collaboration scenarios. Both the on-site person and the remote collaborator can add or modify the holograms, sharing and saving important technical information. The remote person can discover the scene independently of the on-site person.

Extending the system with translation capabilities in addition to orientation can be an interesting future work direction. This can be done using virtual rendering techniques or adding more actuation units for translating the camera system.

REFERENCES

Aykut, T. et al., 2019, Realtime 3D 360-degree telepresence with deep-learning-based head-motion prediction. *IEEE Journal on Emerging and Selected Topics in Circuits and Systems*, *9*(1), pp. 231-244.

Bischoff, M., 2019, Ros#.

Druta, R. et al., 2021, A Review on Methods and Systems for Remote Collaboration. Applied Sciences: 10035.

Hofbauer, M. et al., 2022, Traffic-Aware Multi-View Video Stream Adaptation for Teleoperated Driving. *2022 IEEE 95th Vehicular Technology Conference: VTC2022-Spring*.

Hofbauer, M. et al., 2020, Telecarla: An open source extension of the carla simulator for teleoperated driving research using off-the-shelf components. In *2020 IEEE Intelligent Vehicles Symposium (IV)*, pp. 335-340.

Hughes, C. et al., 2010, Accuracy of fish-eye lens models. *Applied optics*, *49*(17), pp. 3338-3347.

Kasahara, S. et al., 2016, Jackin head: Immersive visual telepresence system with omnidirectional wearable camera. *IEEE transactions on visualization and computer graphics*, *23*(3), pp. 1222-1234.

Lee, G. A. et al., 2018, A user study on mr remote collaboration using live 360 video. *In 2018 IEEE International Symposium on Mixed and Augmented Reality (ISMAR)*, pp. 153-164.

Pretlove, J., 1998, Augmenting reality for telerobotics: unifying real and virtual worlds. *Industrial Robot: An International Journal*.

Speicher, M. et al., 2018, 360anywhere: Mobile ad-hoc collaboration in any environment using 360 video and augmented reality. *Proceedings of the ACM on Human-Computer Interaction*, *2*(EICS), pp. 1-20.

Teo, T. et al., 2019, Mixed reality remote collaboration combining 360 video and 3d reconstruction. In *Proceedings of the 2019 CHI conference on human factors in computing systems*, pp. 1-14.

Wang, Y. et al., 2012, Tele-ar system based on real-time camera tracking. In *2012 International Conference on Virtual Reality and Visualization*, pp. 19-26.

DESIGN ELEMENTS EXTRACTION BASED ON UNSUPERVISED SEGMENTATION AND COMPACT VECTORIZATION

Hong Qu, Yanghong Zhou, K. P. Chau and P. Y. Mok
Institute of Textiles and Clothing, The Hong Kong Polytechnic University, Hunghom, Hong Kong

ABSTRACT

Repeated design elements are abundant and ubiquitous in decorative patterns, which are now widely used in the process of design for objects, artworks and images found in our living environment. Extraction of repeated design elements from images of existing decorative patterns benefits understanding design, extracting compressed information for subsequent operation, e.g., design generation and vectorization. The early methods based on hand-crafted features were computationally inefficient and less accurate. Most deep learning (DL) based methods focus on natural environment images and are difficult to generalize to decorative images. Besides, DL-based methods require massive datasets with instance-level annotations, which are labor-intensive and hard to get. This paper proposes a novel scheme for design element extraction and vectorization. First of all, unsupervised segmentation is proposed to extract repeated design elements from images of unknown artworks without human assistance. We then distill the color information of the extracted repeated element based on statistics reflected in the color histogram of the input artwork. We develop an algorithm to remove redundant information extracted from images in order to get a compact vectorization result, reusable design element in vector format, at the end. To validate the proposed scheme, we conducted several experiments and the result demonstrated the effectiveness of our scheme and its potential for design generation application.

KEYWORDS

Image Understanding, Localization, Unsupervised Segmentation, Vectorization.

1. INTRODUCTION

Artist-drawn patterns with distinctly colored regions and sharp, independent boundaries are widely used in the fashion industry, wrapping paper, and other digital media (Hoshyari et al., 2018, Dominici et al., 2020). A pattern is composed of discrete numbers of recurring elements called repeated elements, often arranged in regular or near-regular layouts over a solid background layer. Since the artist-drawn pattern has powerful decorative and communication functions, creating a pattern is popular in both professional and amateur. Many patterns are created in vector format for wide applications, which are scalable, reusable, and easily adjusted to fit new requirements (Zhang et al., 2009). Unfortunately, designing a completely new pattern requires substantial time and effort, particularly for the amateur. It will be wonderful to extract and vectorize repeated elements from existing patterns to support and release workload for people who want to create their graphics.

Object detection is a task to localize instances of particular object classes in an image (Inoue et al., 2018, Zou et al., 2019). Best-performing object detection methods are supervised learning-based and typically learned from natural images. Compared to natural images, the content of patterns is more straightforward and more abstract. The domain difference stops us from applying object detection methods to extract repeated elements.

Image segmentation algorithms also aim to partition an image into multiple segments and distinguish the different objects or regions of interest inside (Vitale et al., 2016). Since a labeled pattern dataset cannot be obtained in a short time and high cost, we consider using traditional segmentation algorithms or unsupervised segmentation algorithms. The traditional ones assign image pixels to a specific segment by analyzing low-level image features, such as color and texture, or based on graph theory and multivariate image analysis (Vitale et al., 2016, Felzenszwalb and Huttenlocher, 2004). They tend to generate an over-segmentation result with too many regions with flat shading and meaningless shape (Zhang et al., 2009). However, unsupervised segmentation methods aim at partitioning an arbitrary input image into more general labels, such as foreground and background (Kanezaki, 2018, Kim et al., 2020). Kanezaki (2018) treated convolutional neural network (CNN) as a multi-level feature extractor, and she proposed a novel method alternately iterate segment images and network parameter learning. However, experiment results show the method still tends to suffer from over-segmentation over foreground content and occasionally fail in under segmentation. To overcome these problems, we repeatedly segment an input image three times and extract the stable background mask for subsequent application.

Image vectorization, also known as image tracing, of a raster image is the process of converting a raster image into a vector image. Learning-based image vectorization methods are still restricted to fonts and simple icons domains (Reddy et al., 2021, Lopes et al., 2019). Most classic methods use closed Bezier curves (Bezigons) to describe intermediate representations generated by boundary detection or segmentation in image vectorization results. Since raster images are composed of square pixels, they naturally have jagged edges and are even more apparent when zooming in. Consequently, the resultant Bezigons are sometimes imperfect due to accumulated errors, inaccurate segmentation, and a lack of curve priors, especially for low-resolution images. Yang et al. (2015) focus on this problem proposes a new method that directly optimizes the Bezigons rather than using intermediate representations. However, their method assumes discontinuity and corner points are given. Besides, commercial software, such as Adobe Illustrator (2017), prefers generating many small Bezigons for ambiguous border areas to ensure fidelity. Even so, the function is not widely used at work, as it is tedious to remove the meaningless Bezigons before subsequent operations. Recently, Dominici et al. (2020) and Hoshyari et al. (2018) proposed schemes to generate vector images consistent with viewer expectations, and learning-based corner points algorithms were embedded. However, their methods assume the input image only contains a single closed region, which means color separation or segmentation approaches should be processed in advance. Our goal is to prepare vector repeated elements for design generation. Compared with high quality, efficiency and compactness are prior considering factors. Therefore, we propose to get compact vectorized results based on optimizing Potrace (Selinger, 2003).

The paper proposes a novel framework for repeated elements extraction and compact vectorization from existing patterns without any manual intervention. After analyzing the character of design patterns, we improve an existing unsupervised segmentation algorithm to first separate foreground elements and background layers. Later, we extract the repeated elements by removing the duplicate and incomplete elements. We assume the input image is an image containing many colorful elements. Since Potrace focuses on vectorizing black-on-white images, we combine color histogram results and the K-means algorithm to separate the image into independent color masks at first. Then, we delete redundant Bezigons and combine residual Bezigons ordered by area for compactness.

The rest of the paper is organized as follows. Section 2 describes the framework. Section 3 contains experimental results and quantitative analysis, and section 4 contains the concluding remarks.

2. FRAMEWORK

2.1 Overview

The input to our system is a set of design pattern images with distinctly colored regions. In this case, each image is created as a planar composition of two main layers: background and foreground. Typically, the foreground layer consists of more complicated shapes and color information, while the background layer usually contains one homogeneous region. We aim to vectorize repeated elements in the foreground for future design generation.

The first stage in our framework is repeated elements extraction jointly by an improved unsupervised segmentation method and a Canny edge detector (Canny, 1986). A redundant elements removal operation follows. Afterward, the system separates the image into different, independent color masks. Finally, a compact vector file is obtained after filtering and reordering all the Bezigons generated from the Potrace algorithm. The overall framework is shown in Figure 1.

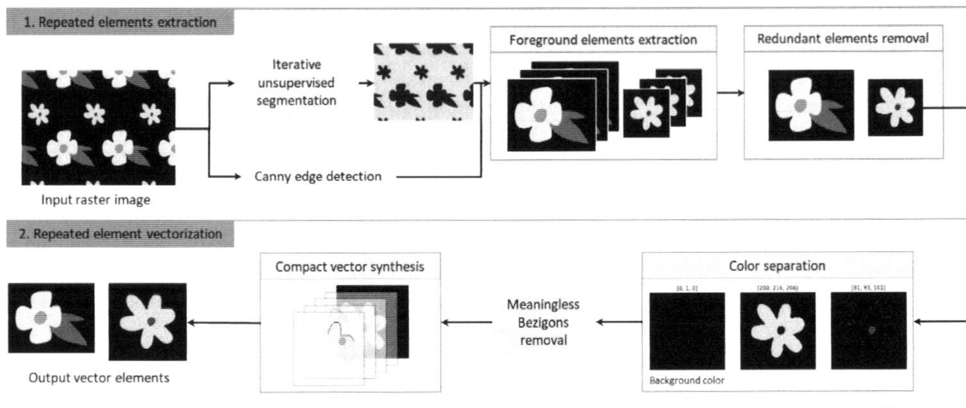

Figure 1. Framework overview: the framework consists of two stages. The top stage is repeated elements extraction, and the bottom stage is repeated element vectorization. The input of the framework is a raster pattern image, and the output is several vector elements

2.2 Repeated Elements Extraction

2.2.1 Foreground Elements Extraction

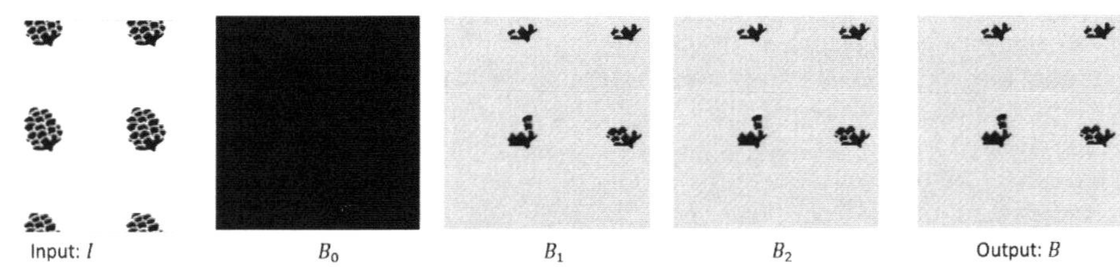

Figure 2. Iterative unsupervised segmentation

In order to separate the original image I into many foreground elements and a background layer, we adopt an unsupervised segmentation approach first presented in (Kanezaki, 2018) and later refined in (Kim et al., 2020). The approach can handle arbitrary images as the essence of the method is a clustering of image features. Ignoring the over-segmentation of the foreground, we find that the background mask is usually accurate. Therefore, instead extract foreground elements directly, we extract the background mask beforehand. To avoid occasional under-segmentation results (see B_0 in Figure 2), we first repeat the operation three times, getting a background mask $B_n, n \in [0, 1, 2]$ each time, then obtain the final background mask B by:

$$B' = \frac{1}{3} \cdot \sum B_n \tag{1}$$

$$B = \begin{cases} 1 \; if \; B'_{i,j} \geq 2 \\ 0 \; if \; B'_{i,j} < 2 \end{cases} \tag{2}$$

$$B_{i,j} \in B \tag{3}$$

where $B'_{i,j}$ and $B_{i,j}$ is the pixel value of B' and B, respectively. Here, when $B_{i,j}$ equals one means the corresponding pixel on I is the background, and the rest of I is foreground content. Later, we extract foreground elements following the bounding boxes obtained by OpenCV (Bradski, 2000). In case all extracted elements are incomplete, we do the same for the edge detection result of the original image. Then we collect all the extracted elements E as the input for the next operation. Besides, the RGB value C_{bk} of the original image's background is obtained by

$$C_{bk} = Mean(B \cdot I) \tag{4}$$

2.2.2 Redundant Elements Removal

A pattern consists of many highly similar elements, and it is unnecessary to vectorize each one. Therefore, before vectorization, we remove the redundant elements based on their similarity. Most element has an abstract and straightforward shape in which the local image feature descriptors, such as SIFT and DoG, fail to detect their key points and thus cannot compare the similarity between elements. The perceptual hashing algorithm encodes the result of the discrete cosine transform of the image to a snippet. Researchers can quickly compare the similarity between images by calculating the distance of their snippets.

Given all the elements E, for each pair of elements $e_i, e_j \in E$, we use a Perceptual Hashing algorithm (pHash) (Zauner, 2010) to encode and measure the similarity between them by calculating the distance $d_{i,j}$ and form all the distance to a set $D = \{d_{i,j}: |\, pHash(e_i) - pHash(e_j)\, |, \forall\, e_i, e_j \in E, i \neq j\}$. When the distance of a pair of elements is longer than the threshold $\theta = 0.8 * \max(D)$, we treat the smaller one as a redundant element and remove it. The procedure loops recursively until no pairs of elements satisfy the condition.

2.3 Repeated Element Vectorization

2.3.1 Color Separation

Before we vectorize all the extracted repeated elements, we separate a multi-color repeated element image into independent color masks. k-means clustering is a classical image segmentation algorithm where k is the number of clusters and should be given in advance (Jain, 2008). A color histogram represents the number of pixels with colors in each fixed list of color ranges. We calculate k through statistics the number of color ranges higher than a fixed threshold τ, in its color histogram after grayscale processing (see Figure 3). After this, we operate color separation by k-means clustering and successfully separate a multi-color image into k color masks. The nearest cluster center with C_{bk} is the final background color, we replace the value of C_{bk} to it and remove the corresponding color mask for computation reduction. Finally, we get a set of color masks denoted as $M_n, n \in \{1, \dots, k-1\}$ and their corresponding color values C_n and the background color C_{bk}.

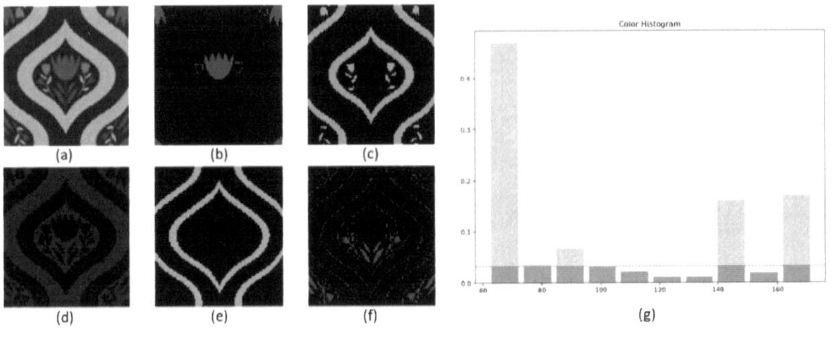

Figure 3. An example of color separation. (a) the input element image, (b)-(f) color masks after color separation, (g) color histogram, and in this image k equals five

2.3.2 Redundant Bezigons Removal

We first vectorize each color mask M_n by Potrace to V_n. Since raster images are composed of pixels with different density values, there are many redundant small Bezigons whose area is a small fraction of the overall image (see Figure 4). Therefore, the region V_n^i whose area a_n^i far less than the area of the whole image A will be removed, and a new Bezigon set Z can be obtained by $Z = \{Z_n: \frac{a_n^i}{A} \geq \omega\}$. In this paper, we used the value of $\omega = 0.05$.

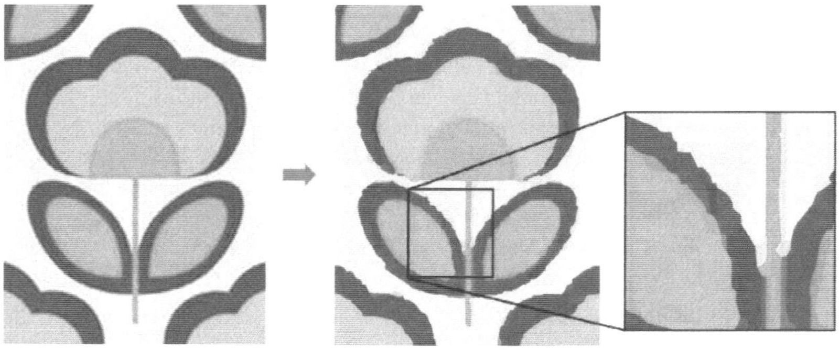

Figure 4. An example of Redundant small Bezigons

2.3.3 Compact Vector Synthesis

A vector image is a multi-layer composition of Bezigons, and each Bezigon exists in a separate layer. A Bezigon can be wholly determined by its geometric and color parameters in the final vector image. When we get the Bezigons set Z, we first order all the Bezigons by area to avoid occlusion between Bezigons. And then synthesize them together, filling them with their corresponding color. Moreover, we add a background rectangular filled with color value C_{bk} to the last layer of the vector image. An example is shown in Figure 5.

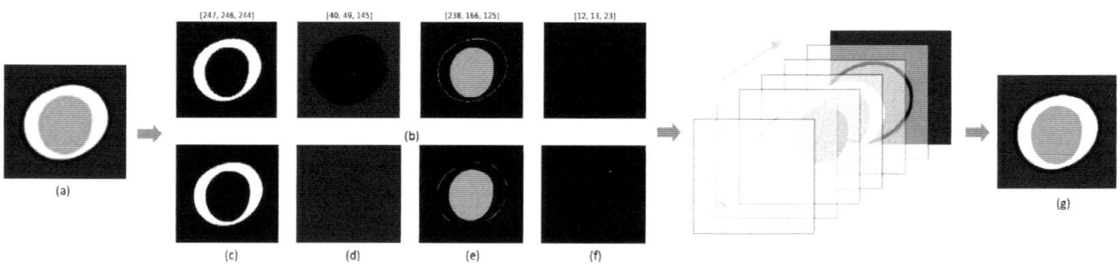

Figure 5. (a) is the input element image, (b) is its color separation results, (c)-(f) are the corresponding vectorization results by Potrace, and (g) is the final vector image our algorithm gets

3. EXPERIMENTAL RESULTS

We evaluated the proposed framework using 46 images downloaded online. Each image is different in size contains more than two repeated patterns. Meanwhile, each pattern has one or more repeated elements random layout on the planar. We first extracted the repeated patterns through our previous work (Qu et al., 2020) and then input them into our proposed framework. During the experiment, our method requires no additional operations. The experimental results demonstrate that our framework can successfully extract repeated elements and vectorize them into a compact form. Figure 6 shows part of our results, our framework can successfully extract almost all the elements inside and vectorize them (column (a) to (d)). The images here are of different sizes, proving that our method can handle input images of any size. Besides, some failed cases are shown in Figure 6. In column (e), our framework fails to detect elements with a triangular appearance, and in column (f), our compact vectorization algorithm misses the flower heart.

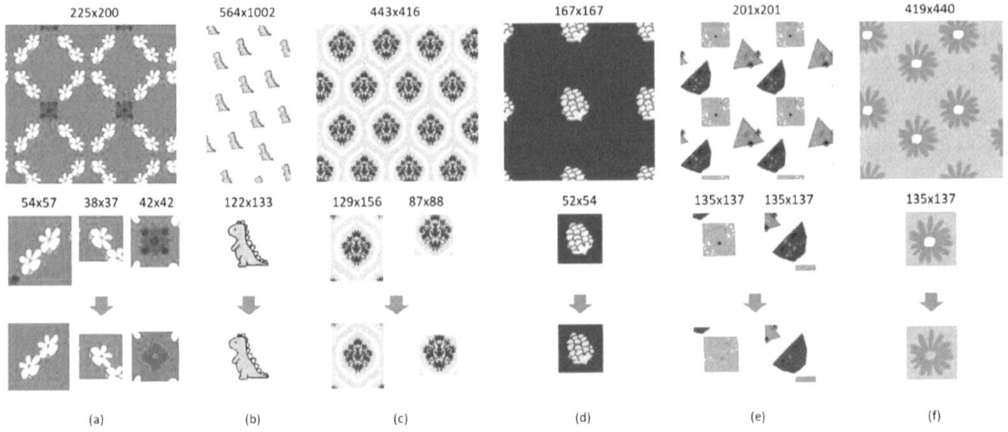

Figure 6. Part of the results of our framework

To analyze the efficiency of our method, we record the processing time of each step and summarize them in Table 1. From Nonetheless, the efficiency of our method is still within acceptable limits.

Table 1, we found that most of the time is spent on extracting repeated elements. The reason is the unsupervised segmentation network has no fixed parameters, and each time needs to be retrained to get the segmentation results. Nonetheless, the efficiency of our method is still within acceptable limits.

Table 1. Time cost record

	Repeated elements extraction	Repeated elements vectorization	Overall
Time cost (s)	22	4	26

To prove the compactness of our results, we counted the number of Bezigons in our vector images, and the average number of our results is less than 30. However, the number of commercial software is more than 50. To further prove that our method is suitable for reuse and re-creation, we randomly process the vectorized images obtained (see Figure 7). The experimental results prove that our method has the potential to assist design generation.

Figure 7. Random processing of the vector elements of our framework to generate new designs

4. CONCLUSION AND FUTURE WORK

This paper proposes a novel framework for repeated elements extraction and compact vectorization aiming to serve design generation. The repeated elements extraction phase creatively applies an unsupervised segmentation method to extract a pattern image's foreground elements and background color information. In addition, after noting that commercial vectorization software tends to produce many meaningless Bezigons to ensure the fidelity of vector results, we propose an optimization method. The proposed method first counts the number of primary colors by analyzing the color histogram result of the image, then separates the image into the given number of color masks. In the subsequent vectorization, the method removed redundant Bezigons and sorted the remaining Bezigons in order of area to synthesize the final compact vector image. Although these operations will lose details in some images, they do not affect subsequent reuse and recreation. In the future, we plan to add supplementary information to the unsupervised segmentation algorithm to accelerate its convergence and replace our compact vectorization algorithm with a learning-based one.

ACKNOWLEDGEMENT

The work described in this paper was supported by grants from the Research Grants Council of the Hong Kong Special Administrative Region, China (Project No. 152161/17E and 152112/19E).

REFERENCES

Adobe. 2017. *Adobe Illustrator*.

Bradski, G. 2000 The OpenCV Library. *Dr. Dobb's Journal of Software Tools*.

Canny, J. 1986. A computational approach to edge detection. *IEEE Transactions on pattern analysis machine intelligence*, 679-698.

Dominici, E. A., et al. 2020. Polyfit: Perception-aligned vectorization of raster clip-art via intermediate polygonal fitting. *ACM Transactions on Graphics (TOG),* 39, 77: 1-77: 16.

Felzenszwalb, P. F.andHuttenlocher, D. P. 2004. Efficient graph-based image segmentation. *International journal of computer vision,* 59, 167-181.

Hoshyari, S., et al. 2018. Perception-driven semi-structured boundary vectorization. *ACM Transactions on Graphics (TOG),* 37, 1-14.

Inoue, N., et al. Cross-domain weakly-supervised object detection through progressive domain adaptation. *Proceedings of the IEEE conference on computer vision and pattern recognition*, 2018. 5001-5009.

Jain, A. K. Data clustering: 50 years beyond k-means. *Joint European Conference on Machine Learning and Knowledge Discovery in Databases*, 2008. Springer, 3-4.

Kanezaki, A. Unsupervised image segmentation by backpropagation. *2018 IEEE international conference on acoustics, speech and signal processing (ICASSP)*, 2018. IEEE, 1543-1547.

Kim, W., et al. 2020. Unsupervised learning of image segmentation based on differentiable feature clustering. *IEEE Transactions on Image Processing,* 29, 8055-8068.

Lopes, R. G., et al. A learned representation for scalable vector graphics. *Proceedings of the IEEE/CVF International Conference on Computer Vision*, 2019. 7930-7939.

Qu, H., et al. 2020. Repeated pattern extraction with knowledge-based attention and semantic embeddings. *14th International Conference on Computer Graphics, Visualization, Computer Vision and Image Processing.*

Reddy, P., et al. Im2vec: Synthesizing vector graphics without vector supervision. *Proceedings of the IEEE/CVF Conference on Computer Vision and Pattern Recognition*, 2021. 7342-7351.

Selinger, P. 2003. Potrace: a polygon-based tracing algorithm. *Potrace (online), http://potrace. sourceforge. net/potrace. pdf (2009-07-01),* 2.

Vitale, R., et al. 2016. Segmentation techniques in image analysis: A comparative study. *Journal of Chemometrics,* 30, 749-758.

Yang, M., et al. 2015. Effective clipart image vectorization through direct optimization of bezigons. *IEEE Transactions on Visualization and Computer Graphics,* 22, 1063-1075.

Zauner, C. 2010. Implementation and benchmarking of perceptual image hash functions.

Zhang, S.-H., et al. 2009. Vectorizing cartoon animations. *IEEE Transactions on Visualization and Computer Graphics,* 15, 618-629.

Zou, Z., et al. 2019. Object detection in 20 years: A survey. *arXiv preprint arXiv:1905.05055.*

DOMAIN ADAPTATION IN IMAGE DEHAZING: EXPLORING THE USAGE OF IMAGES FROM VIRTUAL SCENARIOS

Angel D. Sappa[1,2], Patricia L. Suárez[1], Henry O. Velesaca[1] and Darío Carpio[1]
[1]Escuela Superior Politécnica del Litoral, ESPOL,Campus Gustavo Galindo Km. 30.5 Vía Perimetral, P.O. Box 09-01-5863, Ecuador
[2]Computer Vision Center, Campus UAB, 08193 Bellaterra, Barcelona, Spain

ABSTRACT

This work presents a novel domain adaptation strategy for deep learning-based approaches to solve the image haze removal problem. Firstly, a large set of synthetic images is generated by using a realistic 3D graphic simulator; these synthetic images contain different densities of haze, which are used for training the model that is later adapted to any real scenario. The adaptation process requires just a few images to fine-tune the model parameters. The proposed strategy allows overcoming the limitation of training a given model with few images. In other words, the proposed strategy implements the adaptation of a haze removal model trained with synthetic images to real scenarios. It should be noticed that it is quite difficult, if not impossible, to have large sets of pairs of real-world images (with and without haze) to train in a supervised way haze removal algorithms. Experimental results are provided showing the validity of the proposed domain adaptation strategy.

KEYWORDS

Domain Adaptation, Synthetic Hazed Dataset, Dehazing.

1. INTRODUCTION

Images captured by sensors sensitive to the visible spectrum are affected by natural phenomena such as fog, dust, mist, rain, snow, etc. This considerably reduces their quality, so processes such as detection, segmentation and classification of objects, among others, are considerably affected, for which they will not be able to obtain results that meet the required objectives. The effect of haze on image quality is the result of random light scattering and therefore affects all pixels in the image. There are several methods to enhance images by removing haze, one of them is the estimation of the optical transmission in blurred scenes given a single input image (Fattal et al., 2008). In another approach, presented in (Wang et al., 2017), a fast algorithm for removing haze from a single image based on linear transformation is proposed. It assumes that there is a linear relationship in the minimum channel between the blurred image and the dehazed image. Ju et al. (2017) propose an algorithm to address the inherent weaknesses of the atmospheric dispersion model to develop a way to smoothly remove haze using an adaptive method to adjust the transmission of the scene based on the characteristics of the scene.

In recent years, different convolutional neural networks (CNN) based approaches for haze removal have been proposed; these approaches achieve the best results in the haze removal problem. for example, Suárez et al. (2018) propose a stacked generative adversarial network (GAN) that has achieved outstanding results. There are other CCN-based approaches for haze removal that relies on unpaired images for training a generative model (Anvari et al., 2020); it could be also mentioned the Cycle GAN-based approach from Engin et al. (2018). Despite the promising results of convolutional networks, it is evident that each of the approaches mentioned above needs a set of haze & clear image data for training, which is not very easy given the complexity of obtaining them. There are just a few datasets available in the literature with real haze and the corresponding clear real-world images (see Figure 1).

Figure 1. Pairs of real-world clear/haze images from the dataset presented in (Lüthen et al., 2017)

Some of the techniques based on CNN have been trained with pairs of real-world images (clear) together with the corresponding synthesized haze images; an example of this strategy is the OTS RESIDE Beta dataset 2021 (Li et al. 2018), which has 2D synthesized haze images for each of the given real clear images. Unfortunately, haze images are obtained without depth information, hence obtained haze images do not follow real-world haze scenarios. In order to overcome the limitation of obtaining real-world images with haze, 3D models of different scenarios are required in order to simulate realistic haze image datasets. It should be mentioned that the usage of 3D virtual environments to generate a dataset of synthetic images has already been considered for tackling different computer vision problems for instance object recognition (e.g., pedestrians (Fabbri et al., 2021), vehicles (Tang et al., 2019)), camera calibration (Charco et al., 2018; Charco et al., 2020; Charco et al., 2021), just to mention a few. In the current work, a similar strategy is followed to address the problem of image haze removal. The main contributions are summarized below:

1) Datasets generation: a dataset with pairs of synthetic hazy/clear images has been generated using a realistic 3D scene simulator; multiple scenarios and different levels of haze are considered.
2) Training strategy: the dataset with synthetic haze/clear images is used to train the network and then transfer the learned knowledge to real environments where maybe just a few samples of real images are available.
3) Empirical analysis: results obtained from the proposed domain adaptation strategy (i.e., training with synthetic images and then fined tuned with real images) are analyzed for the model that solves the problem. Comparisons with and without the proposed transfer learning are provided.

The manuscript is organized as follows. Section 2 briefly presents work related to the haze removal problem, as well as the basic concepts of domain adaptation strategies. Then, in Section 3, the proposed strategy is detailed. Experimental results with a set of synthetic and real-world images are presented in Section 4 together with a comparison and analysis of obtained results. Conclusions are given in Section 5.

2. RELATED WORKS

Image dehazing is a well-known method to remove haze, smoke, dust, or fog from single images without any prior knowledge about the camera, calibration data, scene content, 3D structure, or environmental conditions. A quite old but still very popular formulation of the problem is given in (McCartney, 1976), where haze effects are formulated using the atmospheric scattering model. During the last two decades, several approaches have been proposed in the literature, starting with the use of global or local image information techniques, as well as non-local pre-processing to remove haze from images (Berman et al., 2016). This technique is based on counting the different colors present in the images, assuming that the variety of the color range is sufficient to achieve a good representation of the images. Following the traditional techniques, Wang et al. (2017) proposes the estimation of the effective transmission using an atmospheric luminous value to guarantee the chromatic authenticity and the contrast of the images. A novel technique based on the fusion of the result of two energy functions is proposed by (Galdran et al., 2016). Recently, several convolutional neural networks (CNN) based approaches have been proposed achieving outstanding results compared to those obtained by traditional techniques. We can start by reviewing the approach presented by Wu et al. (2021), where the authors propose a contrastive regularization based on learning both information from blurred images and clear images as negative and positive samples, respectively. The technique applies an adaptive combination and the expansion of the receptive field to improve the learning of the network called AECR-Net. Continuing with the deep learning-based methods, in (Wang et al. 2021) a technique is presented that consists of training an adaptive model of haze concentration from end to end, whose layers include a pyramidal feature extractor and a multi-scaling attention mechanism to help the generalization of the trained model. Also, in Zhao et al. (2021), a two-stage haze removal model is proposed, the first in charge of processing a haze removal framework to restore visibility and the second stage in charge of enhancing reality with contradictory learning using unpaired clear and blurred images, ending with a perceptual fusion.

As mentioned above, the haze removal task is quite challenging, not only because of the complexity of the problem, but also due to the lack of large datasets with pairs of clear and haze images to train models. This lack of images is because this is a natural phenomenon of distortion produced by nature, which depends on specific climatic conditions. There are a few datasets available in the literature with real haze and the corresponding clear real-world images; for instance, in (Lüthen et al., 2017) the authors acquire clear images in indoor scenarios and later produce haze, at different densities, and acquire a new set of images (see Figure 1). The main problem with this dataset is the limited number of pairs of images. Another strategy followed for tackling the limitation on datasets, consists of using synthesized haze images, which are obtained by adding haze to real clear images (Li et al., 2018). This dataset is referred to as RESIDE beta dataset. The main problem with this dataset lies in the lack of realism on the added haze, since 3D information is missed the same density of haze is added all over the clear images.

The problem mentioned above, the lack of a large dataset for training deep learning based approaches, is a common problem in different image processing and computer vision approaches. This problem has been tackled by using images acquired in virtual 3D scenarios (e.g., (Fabbri et al., 2021; Tang et al., 2019; Charco et al., 2018). Images from these virtual scenarios, generally referred to as synthetic images, are used for training deep learning models. Then, trained models are adapted (e.g., fine-tuned) to work with real images. Some issues between feature space and layout could arise in real-world applications due to factors like lighting change, image quality and scale, just to name a few. To solve this, a process called Domain Adaptation can be used, where data labeled in one or more relevant source domains is applied to new tasks in a destination domain. Some superficial DA methods have been proposed to solve a domain switching problem between two domains. These can be divided into two classes: instance-based DA (Bruzzone et al., 2010; Chu et al., 2013) and function-based DA (Pan et al., 2011; Marzieh et al., 2018). Both classes of DA reduce the discrepancy between domains. The first select certain pieces of data from the auxiliary datasets to compose the intermediate domains to train the deep network. These auxiliary datasets could be obtained by combining certain parts of the source and target data. For the second, the shared space is learned to match the distributions of both domains (i.e., source and destination). Some methods based on deep learning have recently been proposed, in which different DA strategies are integrated into the learning process (Wang et al., 2018). Depending on the relationship between the source and destination domains, knowledge transfer can be performed in a single or multi-step DA. In the first case, when both domains (source and destination) are directly related, that is, the feature space is the same, it is known as homogeneous DA, which is divided into three types, such as supervised DA with labeled data, semi-supervised DA with labeled and unlabeled data and unsupervised DA with unlabeled data; on the contrary, in the second case, when the feature spaces between the source and destination domains are not equivalent, it is known as heterogeneous DA.

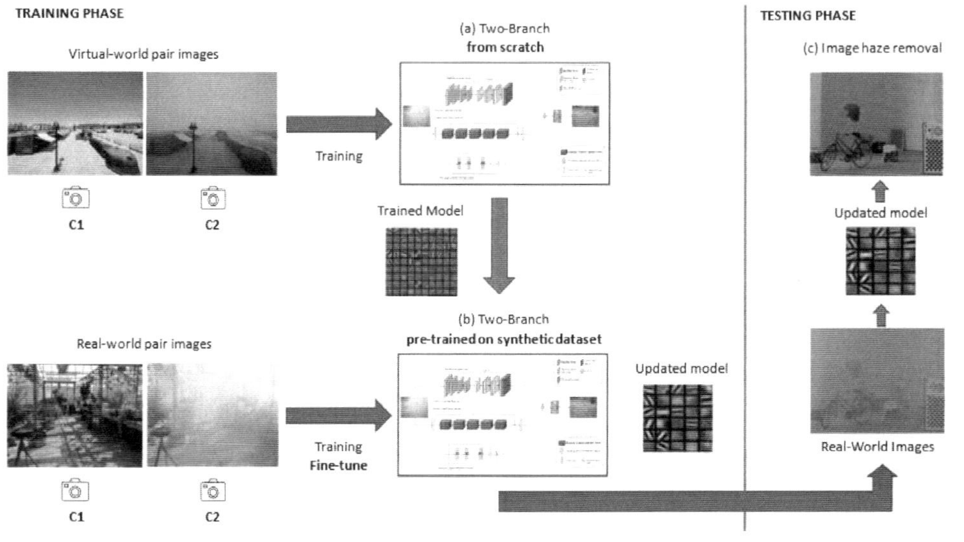

Figure 2. (a) Architecture trained using synthetic images. (b) Knowledge from the synthetic domain is adapted to be used with real-world images. (c) Updated weights after DA strategy used to evaluate image haze removal

3. PROPOSED APPROACH

This section describes the strategy proposed for training haze removal approaches when few real pairs of (clear/haze) images are provided. This section stars by providing details on the CNN architecture selected to carry out the haze removal. Additionally, the synthetic image dataset generation, which is acquired from virtual 3D outdoor environments, is presented. The CNN architecture is first trained with the synthetic dataset and then adapted to real-world by means of a domain adaptation approach. It should be noted that the proposed strategy is valid not only for the network architecture used in this work, but it can be considered during the training of any model based on CNN. Figure 2 shows an illustration of the strategy proposed for training the CNN model in the current work (the Two-Branch (Yu et al., 2021) network has been selected).

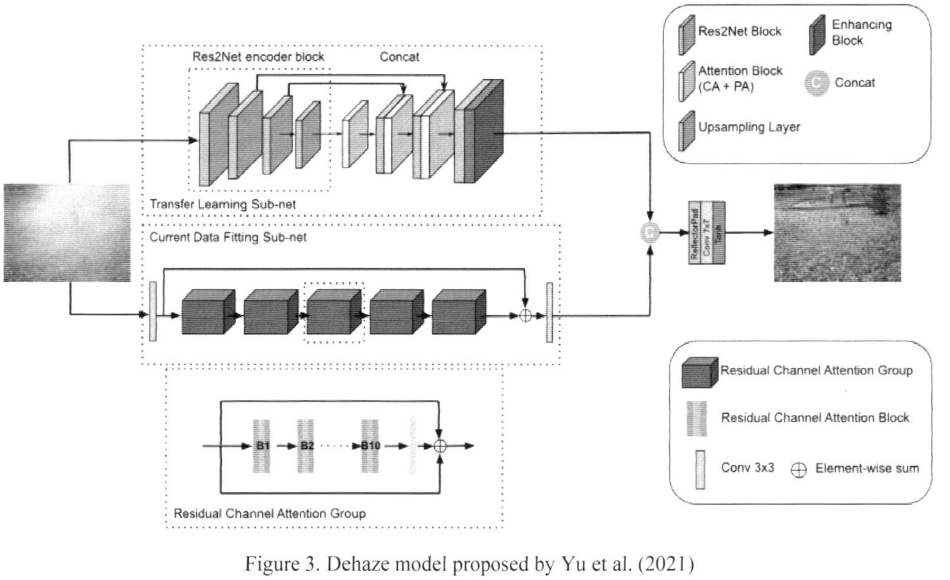

Figure 3. Dehaze model proposed by Yu et al. (2021)

3.1 Network Architecture

This section presents details of the network architecture used as a benchmark to evaluate the proposed Domain Adaptation (DA) strategy. The architecture selected after analyzing a variety of state-of-the-art haze removal techniques has been the one proposed by Yu et al. (2021) since it has been designed with two branches, one that contains data-specific learning techniques (attention per channel blocks) and attention per pixel and the other branch that focuses on learning transfer. Because of the focused learning, the haze can be removed in a more adaptive way to its spatial representation. An illustration of the architecture is presented in Figure 3; the model consists of two learning branches, specializing in the removal of the haze present in the images, with a very limited dataset. The model performs a mapping of the most relevant characteristics and at the same time learns a domain transfer representation of another trained network, to facilitate the convergence of the model. In order to validate the results of this model, the authors have used real-world and synthesized haze images. It is worth mentioning that this model has also validated the removal of non-homogeneous haze, which allows us to evaluate this type of scenario in the future with our DA strategy.

Figure 4. Examples of pairs of images (clear and haze) captured from the different 3D scenarios proposed in the current work; these pairs of images are used during the training, testing and evaluation stages

3.2 Synthetic Dataset Generation

This section presents the steps followed to generate the datasets with synthetic images, which are used to train the CNN architecture. The synthetic images are obtained from one of the virtual worlds configured by default in CARLA Simulator (Dosovitskiy et al., 2017). Among the different options available in the CARLA simulator is that of modifying the climate settings, this option was used to generate a climate with different intensities of haze in the virtual scenes. In addition, to obtain a dataset with greater variability of structures, shapes, colors and textures, different scenarios of the virtual worlds available by default in CARLA were explored. The different synthetic images used in this work are generated from the CARLA simulator, as detailed below. As a first task, the trajectory to be followed within the scenarios of the virtual world is defined. Two virtual cameras are defined which move synchronously around the scene. The attributes of both cameras are defined as follows: width = 1600, height = 1200 and FOV = 100. The difference between both cameras is that camera #1 is used to obtain the (clear) ground truth images in RGB format while camera #2 adds a haze density percentage that varies from 20% to 60% in steps of 10%. For each camera and step, 50 images are generated. The sequence is executed to generate 6 synthetic datasets with 250 image pairs (i.e., GT and haze image) for each one. At the same time that the configured cameras follow the predefined trajectory, their pose randomly varies at each instant of time (i.e., on the translation the X coordinate could take random values in between [−2, 2]m, the Y coordinate [− 2, 2]m, while the Z coordinate [−1, 1]m; regarding the orientations, the pitch angle could take random values in between [0, 7] degrees, yaw angle [−7, 7] degrees while roll angle [−7, 7] degrees). These values were defined according to the characteristics of each scene. Figure 4 shows examples of images of the synthetic dataset generated from 6 3D virtual scenarios and different haze intensity levels.

4. EXPERIMENTAL RESULTS

As described above, this work addresses the problem of haze removal in different real-world scenarios when the required number of images needed to train the model based on deep learning is not available. This problem of lack of data is addressed through a DA strategy. This section first presents details of results obtained when just a set with few pairs of real images is considered; then, experimental results with the proposed DA strategy are presented. In short, this strategy consists of first training with synthetic images, obtained from the CARLA simulator, and then transferring this learned knowledge to a real-world training process. The architecture evaluated in this work has been implemented in TensorFlow-Keras and trained with an NVIDIA Titan XP GPU and an Intel Core I9 3.3GHz CPU. As mentioned above, the Two Branch architecture is firstly trained from scratch with the dataset presented in (Lüthen et al., 2017), Figure 5 shows illustrations of results obtained by the Two Branch network for qualitative evaluation; PSNR and SSIM are provided in Table 1 for a quantitative evaluation.

Figure 5. (*left*) Real clear image; (*middle*) Real haze image; (*right*) Result from the Two Branch network trained from scratch with Lüthen et al. dataset

As can be appreciated from Figure 5 and Table 1, having just a few sets of pairs of images for training the CNN architecture constrains the quality of results. In order to overcome this limitation, in this work, a DA strategy is proposed. It consists of training the Two Branch network from scratch but with the acquired synthetic (clear/haze) images; then the resulting trained network is fine-tuned with images from the dataset presented in (Lüthen et al., 2017). Figure 6 shows the illustration of the results with the synthetic images (Figure 6 (*bottom-left*)) as well as after the DA strategy (Figure 6 (*bottom-right*)). It can be appreciated that the result from the proposed DA is considerably better than the one presented in Figure 5(*right*); quantitative results presented in Table 1 confirm this improvement. In order to appreciate the need for fine-tuning the model, results obtained by using the model just trained with synthetic images, no DA applied, are presented in Figure 5 *(right)* and Table 1 *(4th row)*. Finally, in order to complement the analysis, the Two Branch network has been also trained from scratch but with the synthesized dataset RESIDE (Li et al., 2018). As can be seen in Table 1 (*2nd row*), the results do not overcome those obtained with the synthetic dataset (*4th row*). This is mainly caused by the lack of realism in the generation of the haze. Finally, the network trained with RESIDE is also used with the proposed DA strategy; in other words, the weights of the network are used as initialization to fine-tune them with the dataset presented in (Lüthen et al., 2017), and quantitative results are depicted in Table 1 (*3rd row*). The lack of realism in RESIDE does not help to converge the training of the DA process.

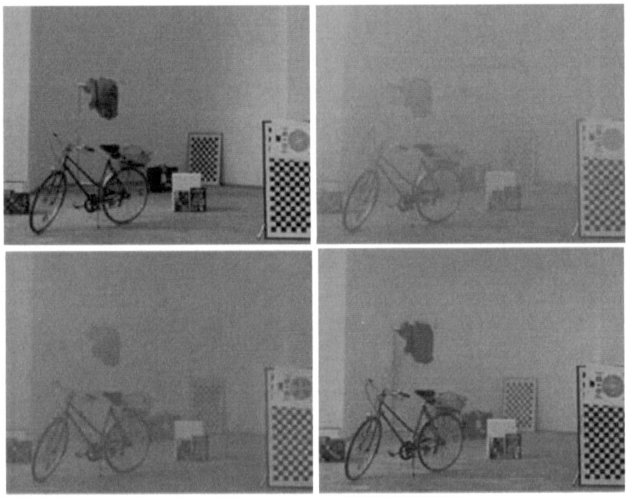

Figure 6. (*top-left*) Real clear image; (*top-right*) Real haze image; (*bottom-left*) Result from the Two Branch trained with our synthetic dataset. (*bottom-right*) Result from the Two Branch trained with our synthetic dataset and fine-tuned with Lüthen et al. dataset

Illustrations in Figure 6 and the results shown in Table I confirm that training with more data, even if it is synthetic, favors the convergence of the model and its corresponding generalization. It can be evidenced that the DA strategy applied in the training of few data of the real world, has helped to improve the convergence and avoid the excessive fit of the model when performing the haze removal. Undoubtedly, the features that are relevant to solve the problem have been transferred from the synthetic domain to the real world.

Table 1. Results from the Two Branch network trained with different strategies

Strategy	PSNR	SSIM
Trained from scratch with Lüthen et al.	18,303	0,749
Trained with RESIDE dataset and validated with Lüthen et al.	18,216	0,264
DA from RESIDE (trained with RESIDE images and fine-tuned with Lüthen et al.)	15,826	0,816
Trained with our synthetic images and validated with Lüthen et al.	21,624	0,867
Proposed DA (trained with our synthetic images and fine-tuned with Lüthen et al.)	**24,067**	**0,922**

5. CONCLUSION

This paper addresses the challenging problem of haze removal of real images with few labeled samples. This problem is addressed through a domain adaptation strategy, which avoids the need to have a large dataset of real-world images for training. The proposed DA strategy overcomes the approaches presented in the literature, which usually use synthesized images that do not represent the atmospheric haze model that is dependent on the distance and depth of the objects present in the scene. The proposed strategy consists of first training with synthetic images and then transferring this knowledge to real image scenarios. The knowledge transfer is performed with a DA strategy that fine-tuned the network parameters with a few samples of real-world (clear/haze) images. As future work, we will consider exploring DA strategy by analyzing the model behavior results between the different percentages of haze on the images.

REFERENCES

Anvari, Z., and Athitsos, V., 2020. Dehaze-GLCGAN: unpaired single image de-hazing via adversarial training. *arXiv preprint arXiv:2008.06632.*

Bruzzone, L., and Marconcini, M., 2010. Domain Adaptation Problems: A DASVM Classification Technique and a Circular Validation Strategy. *IEEE Transactions on Pattern Analysis and Machine Intelligence.* Vol 32, No. 5, pp. 770-787.

Charco, J. L., Vintimilla, B. X., and Sappa, A. D., 2018. Deep Learning Based Camera Pose Estimation in Multi-view Environment. *14th Int. Conf. on Signal-Image Technology & Internet-Based Systems*, 2018, pp. 224-228.

Charco, J. L., Sappa, A. D., Vintimilla, B. X., and Velesaca, H. O. 2020. Transfer Learning from Synthetic Data in the Camera Pose Estimation Problem. *15th Int. Joint Conf. on Computer Vision, Imaging and Computer Graphics Theory and Applications*, pp. 498-505.

Charco, J. L., Sappa, A. D., Vintimilla, B. X., and Velesaca, H. O. 2021. Camera pose estimation in multi-view environments: From virtual scenarios to the real world. *Image and Vision Computing*, Vol. 110, pp. 1-12.

Chu, W., De la Torre, F., and Cohn, J. F., 2013. Selective Transfer Machine for Personalized Facial Action Unit Detection. *Proceedings of the Conference on Computer Vision and Pattern Recognition*. pp. 3515-3522.

Dosovitskiy, A., Ros, G., Codevilla, F., Lopez, A., and Koltun, V., 2017. CARLA: An Open Urban Driving Simulator. *Proceedings of the 1st Annual Conference on Robot Learning. pp. 1-16.*

Engin, D., Genç, A., and Kemal Ekenel, H., 2018. Cycle-dehaze: Enhanced cyclegan for single image dehazing. *Int. Conf. on Computer Vision and Pattern Recognition Workshops*, pp. 825-833.

Fabbri, M., Brasó, G., Maugeri, G., Cetintas, O., Gasparini, R., Ošep, A., and Cucchiara, R., 2021. MOTSynth: How Can Synthetic Data Help Pedestrian Detection and Tracking?. *Int. Conf. on Computer Vision*, pp. 10849-10859.

Fattal, R., 2008. Single image dehazing. *ACM transactions on graphics*, Vol. 27, No. 3, pp. 1-9.

Galdran, A., Vazquez-Corral, J., Pardo, D., and Bertalmio, M., 2016. Fusion-based variational image dehazing. *IEEE Signal Processing Letters*, Vol. 24, No. 2, pp. 151-155.

Ju, M., Zhang, D., and Wang, X., 2017. Single image dehazing via an improved atmospheric scattering model. *The Visual Computer*, Vol. 33, No. 12, pp. 1613-1625.

Li, B., Ren, W., Fu, D., Tao, D., Feng, D., Zeng, W., and Wang, Z. 2018. Benchmarking single-image dehazing and beyond. *IEEE Transactions on Image Processing,* Vol. 28, No. 1, pp. 492-505.

Lüthen, J., Wörmann, J., Kleinsteuber, M., and Steurer, J., 2017. A RGB/NIR data set for evaluating dehazing algorithms. *Electronic Imaging*, Vol. 12, pp. 79-87.

McCartney, E., 1976. Optics of the atmosphere: scattering by molecules and particles. *New York, John Wiley and Sons.*

Marzieh, G., and Mahdieh Soleymani, B., 2015, Unsupervised domain adaptation via representation learning and adaptive classifier learning, *Neurocomputing*, Vol. 165, pp. 300-311.

Pan, S. J., Tsang, I. W., Kwok, J. T., and Yang, Q., 2011, Domain Adaptation via Transfer Component Analysis. *IEEE Transactions on Neural Networks*. Vol 22, No 2, pp. 199-210.

Suárez, P. L., Sappa, A. D., Vintimilla, B. X., and Hammoud, R. I., 2018. Deep learning based single image dehazing. *Int. Conf. on Computer Vision and Pattern Recognition Workshops*, pp. 1169-1176.

Tang, Z., Naphade, M., Birchfield, S., Tremblay, J., Hodge, W., Kumar, R., and Yang, X. 2019. Pamtri: Pose-aware multi-task learning for vehicle re-identification using highly randomized synthetic data. *Int. Conf. on Computer Vision*, pp. 211-220.

Wang, W., Yuan, X., Wu, X., and Liu, Y., 2017. Fast image dehazing method based on linear transformation. *IEEE Transactions on Multimedia*, Vol. 19, No. 6, pp. 1142-1155.

Wang, M. and Deng, W., 2018. Deep visual domain adaptation: A survey, *Neurocomputing*, Vol. 312, pp. 135-153.

Wu, H., Qu, Y., Lin, S., Zhou, J., Qiao, R., Zhang, Z., and Ma, L., 2021. Contrastive learning for compact single image dehazing. *Int. Conf. on Computer Vision and Pattern Recognition*, pp. 10551-10560.

Yu, Y., Liu, H., Fu, M., Chen, J., Wang, X., and Wang, K., 2021. A two-branch neural network for non-homogeneous dehazing via ensemble learning. *Int. Conf. on Computer Vision and Pattern Recognition,* pp. 193-202.

Zhao, S., Zhang, L., Shen, Y., and Zhou, Y., 2021. RefineDNet: a weakly supervised refinement framework for single image dehazing. *IEEE Transactions on Image Processing*, Vol. 30, pp. 3391-3404.

INTERPOLATION AND CONTEXT MAGNIFICATION FRAMEWORK FOR CLASSIFICATION OF SCENE IMAGES

Anas Tukur Balarabe and Ivan Jordanov
School of Computing, University of Portsmouth, United Kingdom

ABSTRACT

Recently, there has been an upsurge in publicly available remote sensing image classification datasets. Standard CNNs and pre-trained architectures have been applied for scene classification tasks. However, transfer learning models accept specific image dimensions as the minimum required size for their respective image input layers. Depending on the size of the input image, the final feature map might not contain the discriminative information needed for accurately classifying the dataset categories. The proposed technique effectively enables and enhances a transfer learning model (*Xception*) to be applied to scene classification tasks. The model works on an adaptive framework that interpolates images and selects an appropriate dilation layer to enhance the quality of extracted features for improved classification. This approach is evaluated on the *EuroSAT,* a dataset with images of 64x64 pixels, *UCM* and *AID* datasets, respectively. We recorded 98.55%, 99.22%, and 96.15% accuracy for the *EuroSAT*, *UCM*, and *AID* datasets, respectively. Our model and the reported results have opened the potential of the *Xception*, which in our view, has not been given its fair share of attention, despite its efficient parameter utilisation.

KEYWORDS

Deep Learning, Image Interpolation, Scene classification, Transfer Learning.

1. INTRODUCTION

Public access to high-resolution remote sensing images has become a reality thanks to the technological advancements recorded in recent years (Helber *et al.*, 2019). Access to satellite images for commercial and research purposes has fuelled interest and innovation in remote sensing and associated fields (Balarabe and Jordanov, 2021). This availability, in turn, triggered an avalanche of applications in domains such as agriculture, environment monitoring, disaster risk analysis, climate change, urban development, surveillance, land mapping, and land use and land cover classification (*LULC*) (Bi *et al.*, 2020; Z. Li *et al.*, 2020; Balarabe and Jordanov, 2021; Broni-Bediako *et al.*, 2021). Interestingly, most of these datasets used for the research and training scene classification systems have images with varying resolutions and dimensions. For example, the *EuroSAT* dataset (Helber *et al.*, 2019) has images of 64x64 pixels, while the *AID* dataset (Xia *et al.*, 2017) has images with dimensions up to 600x600 pixels. Generally, the accuracy of image classification models mostly depends on image representations such as image size, colour, shape, texture, and other properties (Bi *et al.*, 2020). More recently, researchers have proven that deep learning classifiers pre-trained on natural images can be repurposed for the task of scene classification (Hu *et al.*, 2015; Bi *et al.*, 2020). However, no one-size-fits-all transfer learning model can work with all the scene classification datasets (Liu and Huang, 2018). The quality of the discriminative features extracted by a transfer learning model could depend on the input data size because the feature maps are generated from the raw image data and fed into the classification layer for inference (Bi *et al.*, 2020). Depending on the dataset image dimensions, resizing or scaling up is often needed to reduce or increase the size of the images to an appropriate level that can produce feature maps containing enough discriminative information. For datasets with relatively larger samples, such as the *AID* dataset (Xia *et al.*, 2017), the images are usually resized to a moderately smaller dimension without throwing away any vital information. In other datasets, the images are either fed into the CNNs models in their original form or resized to reduce the model training time (Broni-Bediako *et al.*, 2021). Other datasets, notably the *EuroSAT* (Helber *et al.*, 2019), have images with a tiny dimension of 64x64 pixels, which cannot fit into the first layer of some transfer learning models. To experiment on this dataset with transfer learning models, such as the *Xception* (Chollet, 2017), images must reach at least the minimum size that the input layer of the architectures accepts.

Figure 1. Images of three different datasets: a) *EuroSAT*; b) *UCM*; and c) *AID*

This model, the most advanced evolution of the Inception models variants, has not received its fair share of attention from computer vision researchers. Therefore, this paper investigates the effectiveness of this transfer learning architecture on scene classification problems. This work repurposed a pre-trained *Xception* (Chollet, 2017) to perform scene classification tasks on the *EuroSAT*, *UCM*, and *AID* datasets. For the *EuroSAT* dataset, we employed the *LANCZOS* image interpolation algorithm to scale up the images of the *EuroSAT* dataset from 64x64 to 71x71 pixels, which is the minimum that the image input layer of the *Xception* model accepts. The *UCM* images were left in their original form, while the samples of the *AID* dataset were resized to 256x256 pixels. In each case, the proposed framework chooses an appropriate context magnifying module to improve the quality of the extracted features before feeding them into the final classification layer for inference.

2. RELATED WORKS

Several research articles have been published on scene classification tasks using the traditional convolutional neural networks as the core models, while others were implemented using repurposed transfer learning architectures (Yuan *et al.*, 2020; Balarabe and Jordanov, 2021). As a rule of thumb, CNNs, traditional or pretrained, downsample images as they traverse a model from the input to the classification layer. This downsampling could cause the suppression of local discriminative information, impacting the overall performance (Z. Li *et al.*, 2020). Some researchers proposed a feature fusion approach to address the challenge by combining two models into a single unit to improve classification efficiency (Wang and Yu, 2020). In contrast, others used inference aggregation to obtain the average classification results of different model streams (F. Li *et al.*, 2020). Li *et al.* embedded context enhancement modules within the repurposed pre-trained models to extract more robust features for better discrimination and improved classification accuracy (Z. Li *et al.*, 2020). In most standard CNNs, an image's low-level and mid-level discriminative features tend to be lost as the depth of a model increases. Bi *et al.* developed a model that learns the feature representations in an image using a multiple instance learning framework that categorises labels by highlighting the semantics relevance of each category and generating a probability value for its prediction (Bi *et al.*, 2020). Unlike in natural images, where the critical discriminative feature is the most dominant aspect, a scene classification image contains the discriminatory features of other images, which could lead to one scene being confused with another by a classifier (Alhichri *et al.*, 2021). Alchiri *et al.* proposed a technique to address misclassifications by paying attention to sections of an image that uniquely identify it (Alhichri *et al.*, 2021).

Another challenge in remote sensing image classification is the discriminative information occlusion due to fused boundaries among objects in an image. Often, the discriminating features are mixed-up with the non-discriminative features. As a result, some authors developed a feature fusion framework that uses an entropy-based technique to fuse selected layers of some pre-trained models into a unified hierarchical scene classification framework (A. *et al.*, 2018). Despite the successes recorded by transfer learning models in scene classification, within-class variability and between-class similarity still need further attention (Balarabe and Jordanov, 2021). Xie *et al.* in (Xie *et al.*, 2019) highlighted that indiscriminate resizing of images could degrade the part of an image containing the information vital for its classification. As a result, the authors proposed a framework that accepts arbitrary image size and effectively extracts quality feature representation for improved classification. Wang *et al.* also developed a technique that extracts and combines local and global discriminative information in an image to increase the classification performance. The method proposed by the authors has two branches for the feature extraction, connected by a structured key area localisation mechanism (SKAL) (Wang *et al.*, 2020).

3. PROBLEM STATEMENT AND METHODOLOGY

3.1 Problem Statement

There are many publicly available scene classification datasets (F. Li *et al.*, 2020), such as *UCM*, *AID*, and *OPTIMAL-31*, each with its inherent uniqueness: meter(s) per pixel, image dimension, and the number of samples per category are a few of the underlined differences among these datasets. There is a strong link between a CNNs classifier's accuracy and the size and quality of the input images (Bi *et al.*, 2020). The traditional CNNs and the pre-trained models use either local or global discriminative features for the classification unless engineered to combine the two to improve the outcome. Depending on image size, resizing or scaling up to an appropriate dimension is often needed to produce feature maps containing sufficient discriminative information. For datasets with large enough samples, such as the *AID* dataset (Xia *et al.*, 2017), the images are usually scaled down to a relatively smaller dimension without losing the essential information. In other datasets, such as the *UCM* and *OPTIMAL-31*, there is the choice of resizing the images or passing them into the CNNs models in their original form (Xie *et al.*, 2019). Other datasets, for example, particularly the *EuroSAT* (Helber *et al.*, 2019), have images with a small dimension of 64x64 pixels. To use this dataset with some transfer learning models, such as the *Xception* model (Chollet, 2017), the images must be interpolated to reach at least the minimum acceptable size for the model input layer. This paper investigates the impact of image interpolation and feature enhancement on the accuracy of the *Xception* model. Section 3.2 briefly describes the overall model architecture, section 3.3 highlights the datasets used, 3.4 explains the training strategy, and 3.5 summarises the metric employed to evaluate the model.

3.2 Model Architecture

The overall model architecture (Figure 2) consists of four components: the image interpolation module, the feature extraction module, the feature magnification module, and other additional layers for performance enhancement. The backbone of the feature extraction component comprises the *Xception* model's bottom layers, from the image input layer to the last convolutional layer. The dimension of the input image is first checked to ascertain whether interpolation is needed or not. If the image size is below 71x71, then the *LANCZOS* algorithm resizes it from its original dimension to 71x71 pixels; otherwise, it is forwarded to the feature extraction part of the framework. The reason for choosing *LANCZOS* is its ability to scale up an image without compromising its quality. Considering the impact that fused boundaries could have on a classifier's performance, we added a dilation layer and a few fully connected layers to preserve the extracted features as they go further down the pipeline. We included dropout layers with values from 0.25 to 0.5 to mitigate the effect of overfitting before the *softmax* layer. In addition, each fully connected layer has an *l2* regulariser with a 0.001 regularisation value. The output of the feature extraction component goes through one of the context magnifiers, depending on the size of the input from which these features have been extracted. Extractions from images with 71x71 dimensions are fed into a feature magnifier with a 2x2 dilation rate, and for a larger image, a 4x4 dilation rate is used. Then they are fed into the *GlobalAveragePooling 2D* layer, which processes the spatial information therein. Although LeakyReLU has been proposed recently in several deep learning-based applications (Goceri, 2021) to overcome the biasing issue caused by ReLU, we used the ReLU due to its efficiency in the structure of the proposed network with our datasets. The primary motivation behind choosing this model for this research work is that it is lightweight compared to some frequent transfer learning models, such as *VGG-Net, ResNet* and *GoogleNet*. Also, from the articles we have reviewed, it is evident that researchers have neglected this pre-trained architecture despite its efficiency and ease of use.

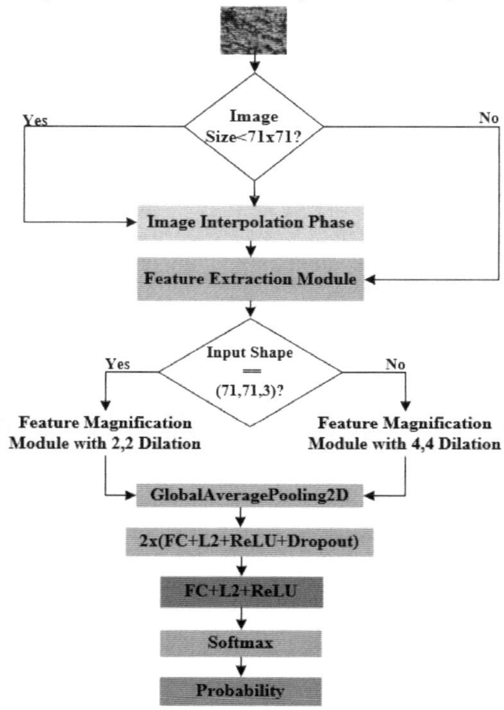

Figure 2. The overall architecture of the proposed model (*FC* – fully connected, *L2* – regularisation function, *ReLU* – transfer function; *Softmax* – output transfer function)

3.3 Datasets

EuroSAT dataset was released in 2019 by (Helber *et al.*, 2019). It consists of 13 classes of land use and land cover (*LULC*) images extracted across 34 European countries using Sentinel-2 satellite images containing 13 categories of 2000 to 3000 samples. *Annual crops, forests, herbaceous vegetation*, and *residential and sea lakes* have 3000 scene representations. In contrast, *highway, industrial, permanent crop, and river* have 2500, and *pasture* has the smallest number (200 instances), making 27000 64x64 pixels images for the entire dataset.

The *UCM* dataset (Yang and Newsam, 2010) has 21 categories containing 2100 images of different land use and cover types, with a uniform size of 256x256 pixels. The images in this dataset have a resolution of approximately 0.3m.

AID Dataset (Xia *et al.*, 2017) is one of the most extensive scene classification datasets, with 30 categories containing images with 600x600 pixels. This dataset includes the following categories: *airport, baseball field, bare land, bridge, beach, centre, commercial, church, dense residential, farmland, desert, industrial, forest, meadow, mountain, medium residential, parking, playground, park, pond, railway station, port, river, resort, sparse residential school, square storage tanks, viaduct, stadium, and football field*. Each category comprises 240 to 420 images.

3.4 Training Strategy

We used an adaptive training strategy to train the proposed model on the *EuroSAT*, *UCM*, and *AID* datasets. For the *EuroSAT* dataset, the main difference is in the dilation rate used to enhance the quality of the extracted features. After scaling up the images of the *EuroSAT* dataset from 64x64 pixels to 71x71 pixels, some data augmentation techniques were used to bolster the training dataset size from 21600 to 151200 samples, 20% of which was reserved for validation and the remaining 20% from the initial split for testing. For the second part of the experiment, which involves the *UCM* and the *AID* datasets, no image interpolation was used since the dimension of these images satisfies the requirement of the image input layer of the backbone model. The images in the *UCM* datasets were left in their original dimension of 256x256 pixels, while the *AID* dataset images were resized to 256x256 pixels. The model was trained for 350 epochs using a *batch size* of 32 *Adam* optimiser with a *learning rate* of 0.0001 and decay value of 10-e5. Also, an *early stopping* was added to monitor the model's training progress and avoid overfitting. For *UCM* and *AID* images, the framework chooses the dilation rate of 4,4. All experiments were carried out using Keras and TensorFlow in the Google Collab environment.

3.5 Evaluation Strategy

The proposed model's performance has been evaluated using some of the most popular deep learning performance evaluation metrics by following the performance evaluation strategy used by the baseline models for ease of comparison. In addition to the *confusion matrix*, *precision*, *recall*, and *F1 score*, we also incorporated the *balance accuracy* metric to evaluate our model further, having split the datasets randomly into the train, validation and test subsets as in (Wang *et al.*, 2019; Zheng, Yuan and Lu, 2019; Z. Li *et al.*, 2020).

4. EXPERIMENTAL RESULTS

Table 1 compares the results from the first experiment on the *EuroSAT* dataset with the other two methods. The result produced by our model is competitive with what has been published by (Helber *et al.*, 2019).

Table 1. Performance comparison between our model and other approaches on the *EuroSAT* dataset

Model	OA%	Epochs	Training Time	Backbone	Source
EuroSAT	98.57	-	-	*ResNet* -50	(Helber *et al.*, 2019)
SLGE-CNN	99.76	600	9.6GPU days	*EfficientNet*	(Broni-Bediako *et al.*, 2021)
Ours	**98.55**	**400**	**1h 15min**	***Xception***	

ResNet -50, which has nearly 3 million more parameters than the *Xception,* produced the best result in the baseline paper. However, the marginal difference of 0.02% between the performance of our model and the state-of-the-arts means the proposed architecture would demand much fewer computing resources than *ResNet* -50. Therefore, the tradeoff is between the margin of 0.02% in classification accuracy and the extra computing power needed to manage an additional 3 million parameters. The *SLGE-CNN* architecture (Broni-Bediako *et al.*, 2021) is 1.21% more accurate than our method. However, it took 9.6 GPU days for *SLGE-CNN* to achieve 600 training epochs compared to the 1h 15mins and 350 epochs it took to train the framework we proposed in this paper. Two classes with very high outer-class similarity affected the performance of our method, as can be observed in Figure 3. Out of the test set, 13 images belonging to the *herbaceous vegetation* class were misclassified as instances of the *permanent crop* class, and 11 images of the *permanent crop* class were misclassified as *herbaceous vegetation*. This misclassification stemmed from the high spatial similarity between the two categories. Table 4 gives the other evaluation metrics monitored in the proposed framework. Table 2 shows that our model performed remarkably well on this dataset compared to other techniques. The *VGG-Net*, the backbone used in most baseline models in Table 2, has nearly 120 million more parameters than the *Xception*, making it more computationally costly to run than the proposed architecture's backbone. Our approach outperformed all the models compared in the table despite having only one dilation layer. For example, the *CNN+MIL* (Z. Li et al., 2020) incorporated a context enhancement module that uses many layers with varying dilation rates and a summing function to concatenate all the features into a single block and feeds it into a multiple instant learning module.

Table 2. Performance comparison between our model and other approaches on the *UCM* dataset

Model	OA%	Epochs	Training Time	Backbone	Source
MSCP-Net	96.56±0.18	-	-	*VGG-Net*	(He, Member, *et al.*, 2018)
EuroSAT Paper	94.38		-	*GoogleNet*-50	(Helber *et al.*, 2019)
ARCNet	93.10±0.55	50	-	*VGG-Net*	(Wang *et al.*, 2019)
CNN+FV	93.9	-	-	*VGG-Net*	(Zheng, Yuan and Lu, 2019)
MIDC-Net_CS	92.95±0.17	-	-	Dense-Net	(Bi *et al.*, 2020)
CNN+MIL	99.26	90		*VGG-Net*	(Li, Z. *et al.*, 2020)
Ours	**99.22**	**400**	**80 min 47 sec**	***Xception***	

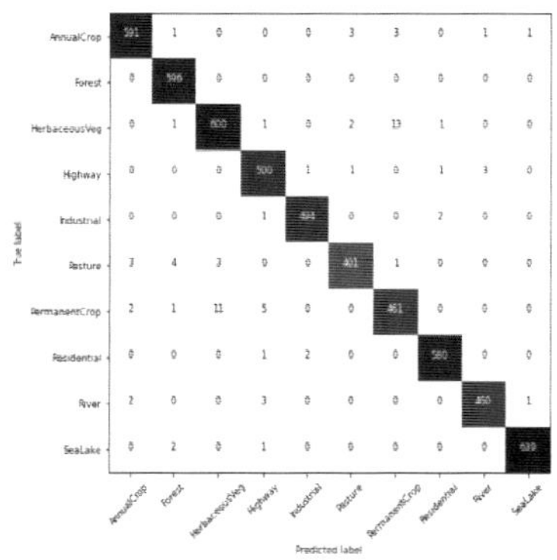

Figure 3. Confusion matrix for the *EuroSAT* dataset

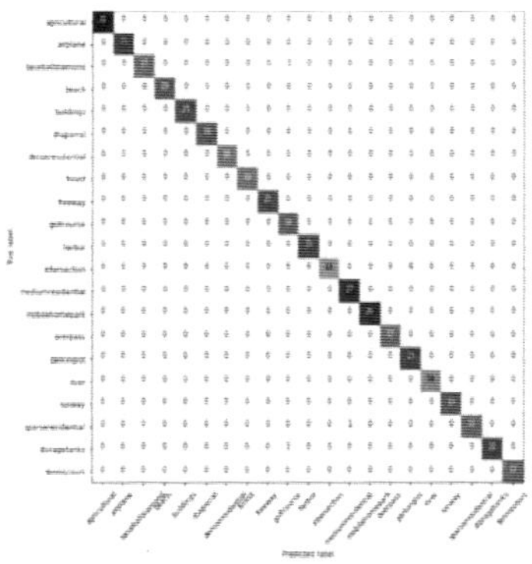

Figure 4. Confusion Matrix for the *UCM* dataset

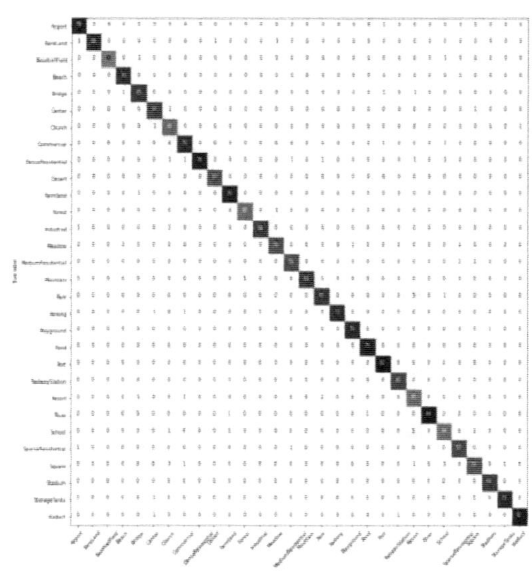

Figure 5. Confusion matrix for the *AID* dataset

However, the proposed architecture used only one dilation layer and outperformed the model presented in (Z. Li *et al.*, 2020). This performance proves that the *Xception* is as effective as other transfer learning models and even better in some areas. Our model classified the *UCM* dataset with very high accuracy, recording only 3 misclassifications, as shown in Figure 4. Table 4 shows that the other performance metrics we monitored to evaluate this framework corroborate the overall test accuracy result. We resized the images of the *AID* dataset from 600x600 pixels to 256x256 pixels, as was done to the *UCM* dataset images.

Table 3. Performance comparison between our model and other approaches on the *AID* dataset

Model	OA%	Epochs	Training Time	Backbone	Sources
MSCP-Net	96.56±0.18	-	-	*VGG-Net*	(He, N, *et al.*, 2018)
EuroSAT Paper	94.38		-	*GoogleNet-50*	(Helber *et al.*, 2019)
ARCNet	93.10±0.55	50	-	*VGG-Net*	(Wang *et al.*, 2019)
CNN+FV	93.9	-	-	*VGG-Net*	(Zheng, Yuan and Lu, 2019)
MIDC-Net_CS	92.95±0.17	-	-	*Dense-Net*	(Bi *et al.*, 2020)
Ours	**96.15**	**400**	**3hrs 57min**	***Xception***	

Table 4. Other Performance evaluation metrics on *EuroSAT*, *UCM* and *AID* Datasets

Metrics	Precision	Recall	F1 Score	Kappa	Balance Accuracy
EuroSAT	0.9852	0.9849	0.9851	0.9839	0.9849
UCM	0.9935	0.9926	0.9931	0.9925	0.9926
AID	0.9558	0.95689	0.9563	0.9601	0.9607

The idea is to utilise memory by reducing the resources needed to process the images at 600x600 pixels. The proposed model performed remarkably well on the *AID* dataset, producing competitive results with the state-of-the-art significantly better than many baseline papers. Table 3 shows the performance of our approach on the *AID* dataset compared to other state-of-the-arts. The *VGG-Net* is also the predominantly used pre-trained backbone for feature extraction, as shown in the table. The *Xception* model is more lightweight, despite having more layers deeper than the *VGG-Net*. The latter has more parameters than the former and has more efficient parameter utilisation. Looking at the result published by (He, N *et al.*, 2018), it is evident that *MSCP-Net* is slightly more accurate than the model; however, it is at the expense of using a pre-trained architecture that has nearly 120 more million parameters, and much bigger images compared the 256x256 pixels we used in our experiment. Overall, our model produced a result on this dataset that is competitive and even better than many of the state-of-the-art methods, as shown in Table 3. The values of other evaluation metrics monitored on the model's performance on the *AID* dataset are given in Table 4.

5. CONCLUSION

This paper proposes a framework for classifying remote sensing images using a hitherto unused pre-trained model. We experimented on the *EuroSAT* dataset, one of the most extensive publicly available datasets for scene classification. It equally has images with the smallest dimension among the remote sensing (RS) datasets. We scaled up the dataset images from 64x64 pixels to 71x71 pixels using the *LANCZOS* image interpolation algorithm to meet the minimum input size requirement of the backbone model. In the second experiment, the performance of the proposed approach on some of the most popular satellite image classification datasets (*UCM* and *AID*) was further evaluated. Our framework produced competitive results with state-of-the-art and better accuracy and computational efficiency in each case. The performance of the proposed model shows that *Xception* can also be efficiently utilised for tasks of satellite image classification. It also shows that a careful selection of dilation rate and hyperparameters can significantly reduce the impact of misclassification by CNNs classifiers. Despite the computational efficiency of the proposed framework, we believe there is still room for improvements with respect to reducing the training time and increasing the accuracy. As part of future work, we intend to enhance the model by incorporating an adaptive hybrid dilation approach using *Xception* and *EfficientNet,* which will help to achieve these objectives.

ACKNOWLEDGEMENT

This work is part of a PhD research sponsored by the Petroleum Technology Development Fund (PTDF), Nigeria.

REFERENCES

A., F. K. G. *et al.* (2018) 'A deep heterogeneous feature fusion approach for automatic land-use classification', *Information Sciences*. Elsevier Inc., 467, pp. 199–218. doi: 10.1016/j.ins.2018.07.074.

Alhichri, H. *et al.* (2021) 'Classification of Remote Sensing Images Using EfficientNet-B3 CNN Model with Attention', *IEEE Access*, 9, pp. 14078–14094. doi: 10.1109/ACCESS.2021.3051085.

Balarabe, A. T. and Jordanov, I. (2021) '*LULC* IMAGE CLASSIFICATION WITH CONVOLUTIONAL NEURAL NETWORK Anas Tukur Balarabe and Ivan Jordanov School of Computing , University of Portsmouth , UK', *International Geoscience and Remote Sensing Symposium (IGARSS)*. IEEE, pp. 5985–5988.

Bi, Q. *et al.* (2020) 'A Multiple-Instance Densely-Connected ConvNet for Aerial Scene Classification', *IEEE Transactions on Image Processing*, 29, pp. 4911–4926. doi: 10.1109/TIP.2020.2975718.

Broni-Bediako, C. *et al.* (2021) 'Searching for CNN Architectures for Remote Sensing Scene Classification', *IEEE Transactions on Geoscience and Remote Sensing*. IEEE, pp. 1–13. doi: 10.1109/tgrs.2021.3097938.

Chollet, F. (2017) '*Xception*: Deep learning with depthwise separable convolutions', *Proceedings - 30th IEEE Conference on Computer Vision and Pattern Recognition, CVPR 2017*, 2017-Janua, pp. 1800–1807. doi: 10.1109/CVPR.2017.195.

Goceri, E. (2021) 'Diagnosis of skin diseases in the era of deep learning and mobile technology', *Computers in Biology and Medicine*. Elsevier Ltd, 134(January), p. 104458. doi: 10.1016/j.compbiomed.2021.104458.

He, N., Fang, L., *et al.* (2018) 'Remote sensing scene classification using multilayer stacked covariance pooling', *IEEE Transactions on Geoscience and Remote Sensing*. IEEE, 56(12), pp. 6899–6910. doi: 10.1109/TGRS.2018.2845668.

Helber, P. *et al.* (2019) '*EuroSAT*: A novel dataset and deep learning benchmark for land use and land cover classification', *IEEE Journal of Selected Topics in Applied Earth Observations and Remote Sensing*, 12(7), pp. 2217–2226. doi: 10.1109/JSTARS.2019.2918242.

Hu, F. *et al.* (2015) 'Transferring deep convolutional neural networks for the scene classification of high-resolution remote sensing imagery', *Remote Sensing*, 7(11), pp. 14680–14707. doi: 10.3390/rs71114680.

Li, F. *et al.* (2020) 'High-Resolution Remote Sensing Image Scene Classification via Key Filter Bank Based on Convolutional Neural Network', *IEEE Transactions on Geoscience and Remote Sensing*, (Cv), pp. 1–16. doi: 10.1109/tgrs.2020.2987060.

Li, Z. *et al.* (2020) 'Deep Multiple Instance Convolutional Neural Networks for Learning Robust Scene Representations', *IEEE Transactions on Geoscience and Remote Sensing*, 58(5), pp. 3685–3702. doi: 10.1109/TGRS.2019.2960889.

Liu, Y. and Huang, C. (2018) 'Scene classification via triplet networks', *IEEE Journal of Selected Topics in Applied Earth Observations and Remote Sensing*. IEEE, 11(1), pp. 220–237. doi: 10.1109/JSTARS.2017.2761800.

Wang, H. and Yu, Y. (2020) 'Deep Feature Fusion for High-Resolution Aerial Scene Classification', *Neural Processing Letters*. Springer US, 51(1), pp. 853–865. doi: 10.1007/s11063-019-10119-4.

Wang, Q. *et al.* (2019) 'Scene classification with recurrent attention of VHR remote sensing images', *IEEE Transactions on Geoscience and Remote Sensing*. IEEE, 57(2), pp. 1155–1167. doi: 10.1109/TGRS.2018.2864987.

Xia, G. S. *et al.* (2017) '*AID*: A benchmark data set for performance evaluation of aerial scene classification', *IEEE Transactions on Geoscience and Remote Sensing*. IEEE, 55(7), pp. 3965–3981. doi: 10.1109/TGRS.2017.2685945.

Xie, J. *et al.* (2019) 'Scale-Free Convolutional Neural Network for', *IEEE Transactions on Geoscience and Remote Sensing*. IEEE, PP(9), pp. 1–13. doi: 10.1109/TGRS.2019.2909695.

Yang, Y. and Newsam, S. (2010) 'Bag-of-visual-words and spatial extensions for land-use classification', *GIS: Proceedings of the ACM International Symposium on Advances in Geographic Information Systems*, pp. 270–279. doi: 10.1145/1869790.1869829.

Yuan, B. *et al.* (2020) 'Multi-deep features fusion for high-resolution remote sensing image scene classification', *Neural Computing and Applications*. Springer London, 7, pp. 49–51. doi: 10.1007/s00521-020-05071-7.

Zheng, X., Yuan, Y. and Lu, X. (2019) 'A Deep Scene Representation for Aerial Scene Classification', *IEEE Transactions on Geoscience and Remote Sensing*. IEEE, 57(7), pp. 4799–4809. doi: 10.1109/TGRS.2019.2893115.

MULTI-MODALITY IMAGE SUPER-RESOLUTION USING GENERATIVE ADVERSARIAL NETWORKS

Aref Abedjooy and Mehran Ebrahimi
Faculty of Science, Ontario Tech University
Oshawa, Ontario, Canada

ABSTRACT

Over the past few years deep learning-based techniques such as Generative Adversarial Networks (GANs) have significantly improved solutions to image super-resolution and image-to-image translation problems. In this paper, we propose a solution to the joint problem of image super-resolution and multi-modality image-to-image translation. The problem can be stated as the recovery of a high-resolution image in a modality, given a low-resolution observation of the same image in an alternative modality.
Our paper offers two models to address this problem and will be evaluated on the recovery of high-resolution day images given low-resolution night images of the same scene. Promising qualitative and quantitative results will be presented for each model.

KEYWORDS

Image Super-Resolution, Image-to-Image Translation, Generative Adversarial Networks, Deep Learning.

1. INTRODUCTION

Super-Resolution (SR) refers to the process of creating High-Resolution (HR) images from a corresponding Low-Resolution (LR) image. In computer vision, image resolution enhancement or super-resolution has been explored for decades, yet it remains a challenging task (Wang, Z. et al, 2020).

In image-to-image translation, images are transferred from a source domain or modality to a target domain while maintaining their content representations. Its wide range of applications in many computer vision and image processing problems, such as image synthesis, segmentation, style transfer, restoration, and pose estimation have attracted increasing attention and tremendous progress in recent years (Pang, Y. et al, 2021), (Choi, Y. et al, 2020), (Fu, Y. et al, 2021).

The generative adversarial networks (GANs) are deep learning-based generative models for both semi-supervised as well as unsupervised learning that outperform state-of-the-art methods for many image-to-image translation and super-resolution tasks (Wang, Z. et al, 2020), (Alotaibi, A., 2020).

Translation and up-sampling of images simultaneously would be an interesting challenge. It is important that any model should produce realistic results in both tasks. An example would be to produce a high-resolution daytime image of a scene given a low-resolution nighttime image of the same scene. When combining super-resolution with image-to-image translation, it can be more difficult to create a realistic image, since more unknown quantities have to be recovered.

Our paper presents GAN-based solutions to the problem of combining image-to-image translation with image super-resolution. The problem is addressed via two models using Real-ESRGAN (Wang, X. et al, 2021) for image super-resolution and CUT (Park, T. et al, 2020) for image-to-image translation. The models will be evaluated both qualitatively and quantitatively.

2. RELATED WORK

To best of our knowledge, no studies have been conducted on the use of GANs to combine image super-resolution with image-to-image translation.

The idea of image-to-image translation dates back to Hertzmann et al.'s image analogies (Hertzmann, A. et al, 2001), a non-parametric model that uses a pair of images to generate image transformations (Zhu, J.Y. et al, 2017). There are many problems relating to computer vision and computer graphics applications that are instances of the image-to-image translation problem. Image-to-image translation involves mapping of an image given in a domain to a copy of the image in a different target domain. An example of the translation problem could be the mapping of grayscale images to RGB. In order to learn how to map one visual representation to another, it is necessary to understand the underlying features that are shared among these representations, such features can be either domain independent or domain-specific (Pang, Y. et al, 2021).

During translation, domain-independent features represent the underlying spatial structure and should be preserved (e.g., the content should be preserved when translating a natural image to Van Gogh's style), whereas domain-specific features relate to the rendering of the structure and may need to be changed during translation (e.g., if the style needs to be changed when translating the image to Van Gogh's style) (Alotaibi, A., 2020).

It is challenging to learn the mapping between two or more domains. It is sometimes difficult to collect a pair of images or the relevant images may not exist. Another challenge is where one input image can be mapped to multiple outputs. The development and use of GANs and their variants in image-to-image translation have provided state-of-the-art solutions in recent years (Alotaibi, A., 2020), (Park, T. et al, 2020), (Emami, H. et al, 2020).

Over the past few decades, researchers have been exploring image super-resolution, a technique for reconstructing images from low-resolution observations into higher resolution images. In particular, deep learning-based SR approaches have attracted much attention and have significantly improved reconstruction accuracy on synthetic data (Bashir, S.M.A. et al, 2021). GANs can be used to enhance lower quality images by reducing noise and enhancing sharpness and contrast along with the resolution (Gupta, R. et al, 2020), (Nazeri, K. et al, 2019). A super-resolution GAN combines a deep network with an adversary network to create higher resolution images (Wang, X. et al, 2021).

3. METHODOLOGY

The problem description and a possible methodology are presented in this Section.

3.1 Problem Description

It is possible to formalize the task of combining super-resolution and image-to-image translation in the following way. While this paper presents the problem in the context of daytime and nighttime images, our approach can be generalized to any arbitrary multi-modality super-resolution scenario.

A LR input image in nighttime mode of a scene N_{LR} is provided to the model. The model will generate a corresponding HR daytime image of the same scene D_{HR} such that A. Its contents are meaningful and coherent with N_{LR} so that human eye would accept it as a HR daytime image of N_{LR}. B. It is similar to ground truth image $D_{HR_{gt}}$, when it is available. C. Based on a daytime image, it has a realistic-looking texture and color spectrum.

3.2 System Overview

To address this problem, we propose and investigate two different two-stage models based on GANs.

3.2.1 M1: SR-First Model

First stage in this model would be to generate N_{HR} using Real-ESRGAN (Wang, X. et al, 2021). N_{HR} is the generated HR version of N_{LR}. Then, CUT (Park, T. et al, 2020), which is a newer version of CycleGAN (Zhu, J.Y. et al, 2017), is fed by NHR as an input image. N_{HR} would be translated to HR daytime image D_{HR} in the second stage. Both Real-ESRGAN and CUT are GAN-based models and have to be trained and tuned. This approach is depicted in Figure 1.

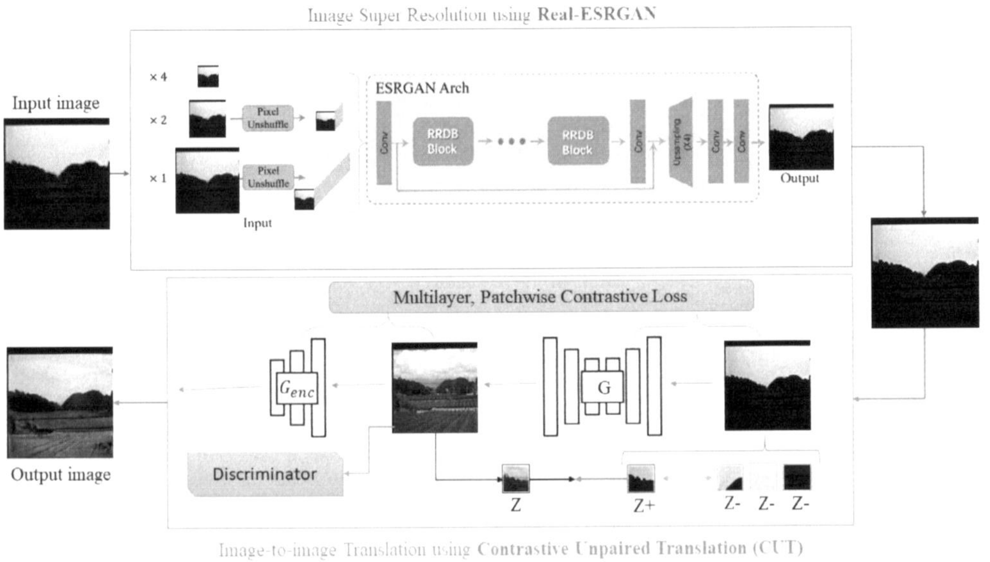

Figure 1. SR-first Model (M1); Super-resolution module followed by an image-to-image translation module

3.2.2 M2: Translation-First Model

This model examines the opposite order of the operations of the SR-first model. It means that the CUT (Park, T. et al, 2020) is used in the first stage to translate N_{LR} into LR daytime image D_{LR} followed by the second stage which is using the Real-ESRGAN (Wang, X. et al, 2021) to generate HR version of daytime image D_{HR}. Dimensions of input images and dimensions of output images in the CUT (Park, T. et al, 2020) are the same. Therefore, the zooming factor could be set in Real-ESRGAN (Wang, X. et al, 2021). Figure 2 illustrates how this approach works.

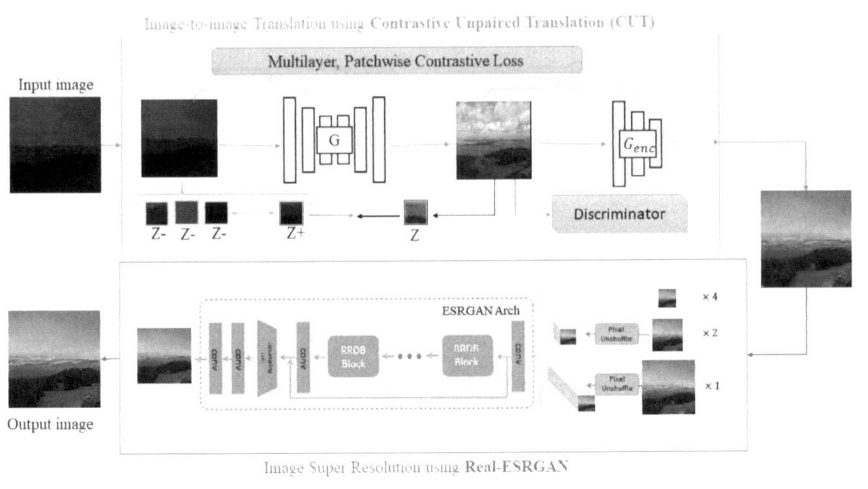

Figure 2. Translation-first Model (M2); An image-to-image translation module followed by a super-resolution module

4. EXPERIMENTS AND RESULTS

In this Section, the proposed models are assessed quantitatively and qualitatively. We will also explain the dataset and setup.

4.1 Dataset

The Transient Attributes dataset (Laffont, P.Y. et al, 2014) was used to create the night2day dataset. Each original sample is of size 256 × 512 containing two 256 × 256 images, i.e., one day image along with its corresponding night image. These images have been divided into 20,110 night images and 20,110 corresponding day images. The dataset was then randomly split into training, validation, and test subsets for each night and day categories. More precisely, 2,011 or 10% for testing, 2,011 or 10% for validation, and 16,088 or 80% for training phases.

In SR, down-sampling is the basic operation for synthesizing LR images. In general, we consider both down-sampling and up-sampling as resizing. In addition to the nearest neighbor interpolation algorithm, there are also bilinear interpolation and bicubic interpolation algorithms. A resize operation can produce a variety of effects; some produce blurry results, whereas others may produce overly-sharp images.

In this study, the bilinear interpolation is used to convert dataset into LR images. To resize an image, OpenCV's "cv2.resize()" function can be used. This function which uses the bilinear interpolation (INTER LINEAR) as its default interpolation method, is used to produce low-resolution version (64×64) of each sample data.

Considering zooming factor of 4 in each direction, after creating a low-resolution version of each image, we have 80% or 16,088 LR night images (64×64) and 80% or 16,088 LR day images (64 × 64) for training, 10% or 2,011 LR night images (64×64) and 10% or 2,011 LR day (64×64) images for validation, and 10% or 2,011 LR night images (64×64) and 10% or 2,011 LR day images (64×64) for testing. The nearest-neighbor interpolation was used to up-sample the LR images when comparing it to the HR image.

4.2 Training

There are two stages of training for each model. To start the training for the first stage of the *M1 model*, a pre-trained Real-ESRGAN (Wang, X. et al, 2021) was used. Real-ESRGAN uses only HR images (256×256) for training and validation. Thus, there is no need to use the resized training data and the resized validation data at this stage. The pre-trained model is trained for 300 epochs on the *night2day* dataset. It is optimized using the Adam optimizer using an initial learning rate of 0.0002.

In the second stage of the *M1 model*, we follow the setting of the CUT (Park, T. et al, 2020). For training parameters, the number of epochs is 200. The Adam optimizer (Kingma, D.P. and Ba, J., 2014) with $\beta_1 = 0.5$ and $\beta_2 = 0.999$ is used to optimize the model. The Initial learning rate for Adam optimizer is 0.0002. The type of GAN objective is LSGAN (Mao, X. et al, 2017). Size of image buffer that stores previously generated images is 50.

In the *M2 model*, first stage is translation of the LR night image of size (64×64) into the LR day image (64×64). The CUT (Park, T. et al, 2020) input image and output image sizes are changed from 256×256 to 64×64 by adjusting the scaling factor. Therefore, LR night images and LR day images are used to train the translation module. In order to keep consistency, the *CUT*'s settings from the previous approach were used. In the second stage of the *M2 model*, a trained Real-ESRGAN (Wang, X. et al, 2021) model was used with the same settings as the first stage of the *M2 model*.

We conducted all experiments using the Linux Ubuntu operating system and the NVIDIA GeForce GTX TITAN X GPU.

4.3 SR-First Model (M1) Evaluation

A model evaluation is performed using 2,011 LR nighttime images (64×64). Three evaluation phases have been defined for a better quantitative evaluation of the M1 model.

- M1-Pre: Comparing *the LR night image (*64 × 64*) (Input)* VS *Real day image i.e. Day Ground truth image*.
- M1-Intermediate: Comparing the generated HR night image with 256×256 resolution (After SR) VS Real day image i.e. Day ground truth image.
- M1-Post: Comparing the generated HR day image with 256×256 resolution (Output) VS Real day image i.e. Day ground truth image.

By comparing M1-Pre with M1-Intermediate and M1Post, the overall performance of the M1 model can be assessed. Root Mean Square Error (RMSE), Mean Absolute Error (MAE), Structural Similarity Index Measure (SSIM), Normalized Cross-Correlation (NCC), and Fréchet inception distance (FID) are calculated for each phase and histograms of these similarity measures over the test data are provided. The comparisons are shown in Figure 3.

Figure 3 shows that the RMSE (top-left) and the MAE (top-right) are shifted to the left from the "M1-Pre" state to the "M1-Post" state. Lower value of these measures for final results in "M1-Post" indicates better performance. Similarly, the "M1-Post" phase provides higher values for SSIM (bottom-left), and the NCC (bottom-right) in comparison with the "M1-Intermediate" and the "M1-Pre" states. Table I presents the mean and the standard deviation of these measures for Pre, Intermediate, and Post. The FID metric for each phase is computed as well. Based on all these measures, Table 1 suggests that final results from the model are more consistent with ground truth.

Table 1. Comparing final results M1-Pre vs M1-Intermediate vs M1-Post of the SR-first model (M1) using different measures

	M1-Pre	M1-Intermediate	M1-Post
RMSE (↓)	0.48±0.14	0.36±0.10	**0.23±0.08**
MAE (↓)	0.43±0.14	0.30±0.09	**0.06±0.04**
SSIM (↑)	0.34±0.14	0.36±0.14	**0.43±0.14**
NCC (↑)	0.81±0.14	0.83±0.13	**0.91±0.08**
FID (↓)	173.95	146.76	**90.47**

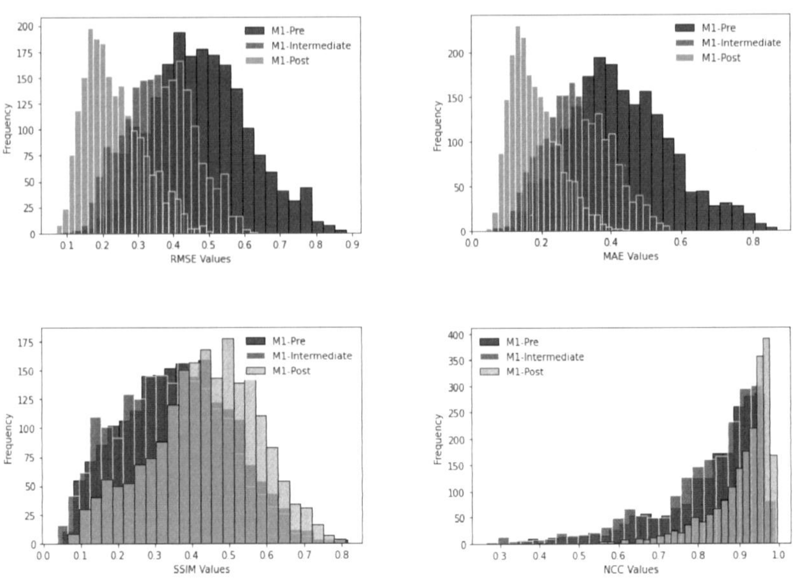

Figure 3. Comparison of final results (Pre vs Intermediate vs Post) of the SR-first model (M1) using different measures

Some examples of images for different stages of the M1 model is provided in Figure 4 for qualitative evaluation. From left to right, each column shows the following: a) Input image (LR night image), b) The generated HR night image (after super-resolution), c) Real night image (night ground truth image), d) Output (generated HR day), and e) Real day image (day ground truth image).

Figure 4. Qualitative evaluation of M1 model; from left to right; (a) Input image, (b) Generated HR night image, (c) Night ground truth, (d) Output image, (e) Day ground truth

4.4 Translation-First Model (M2) Evaluation

LR nighttime images (64×64) are used to evaluate the model. For a more quantitative analysis of the M2 model, two phases have been defined.

• M2-Pre: Comparing the LR night image (64 × 64) (Input) VS Real day image i.e. Day ground truth image.

• M2-Post: Comparing the generated HR day image with 256×256 resolution (Output) VS Real day image i.e. Day ground truth image.

In addition, M2-Intermediate phase could have also been defined as comparing the generated LR day image (64×64) (after translation) VS Real day image i.e. day ground truth image. However, the output size of the translation module in the M2 model would be different from that of the first stage if it had been up-sampled. As a result, this evaluation phase was not considered and the total performance of the M2 model is evaluated only by comparing M2-Pre with M2-Post.

For RMSE, MAE, SSIM, NCC, and FID, we compare the results of these evaluation phases. Figure 5 illustrates these comparisons.

In Figure 5, it can be seen that the RMSE (top-left) and the MAE (top-right) are shifted to the left significantly from the "Pre" to the "Post". Therefore, lower values of these measures for final results in M2-Post indicate better performance. The SSIM (bottom-left) and NCC (bottom-right) are shifted to the right in the "Post", which means that the generated images are more similar to the desired output.

In Table 2, these measures are listed along with their means and standard deviations for M2-Pre, and M2-Post. Furthermore, FID metrics for each phase are calculated. There is a ↓ sign next to each measure indicates that a lower value is "better", and similarly, a ↑ sign means a higher value is "better".

Some examples of images for different stages of the M2 model is provided in Figure 6 for qualitative evaluation. From left to right, each column shows the following: a) Input image (LR night image), b) The generated LR day image (after translation), c) Output (generated HR day), and d) Real day image (day ground truth image).

Table 2. Comparing final results M2-Pre vs M2-Post of the Translation-first model (M2) using different measures

	M2-Pre	**M2-Post**
RMSE (↓)	0.48±0.14	**0.24±0.08**
MAE (↓)	0.43±0.14	**0.07±0.07**
SSIM (↑)	0.34±0.14	**0.44±0.14**
NCC (↑)	0.81±0.14	**0.90±0.08**
FID (↓)	173.95	**96.56**

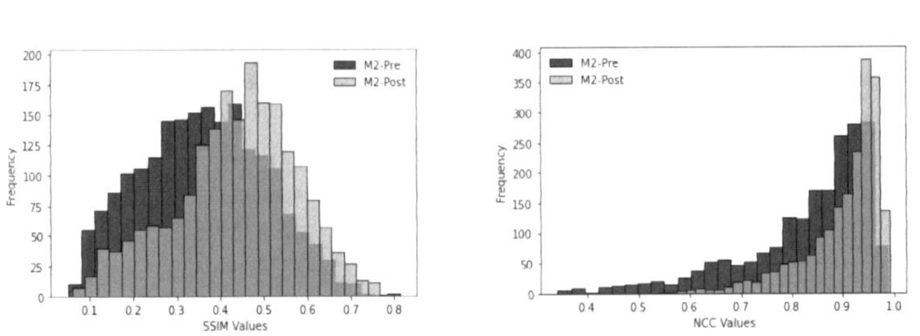

Figure 5. Comparison of final results (Pre vs Post) of the Translation-first model (M2) using different measures

Figure 6. Qualitative evaluation of the translation-first model (M2) model; from left to right; (a) Input (LR night image), (b) The generated LR day (after translation), (c) Output (generated HR day), and (d) Real day image (day ground truth)

4.5 SR-First Model (M1) VS Translation-First Model (M2)

Comparing the **M1-Post** and **M2-Post** results will enable us to compare the M1 and M2 models' performance. In both models, the Post phase is comparing the generated HR day image (Output) VS Real day image or day ground truth image. This comparison using the RMSE (top-left), the MAE (top-right), the SSIM (bottom-left), and the NCC (bottom-right) is depicted in Figure 7. Table 3 summarizes these comparisons.

Table 3. Comparing final results of the **M1: SR-first** with **M2: Translation-first** models using different measures

	M2	M1
RMSE (↓)	0.24±0.08	**0.23±0.08**
MAE (↓)	0.07±0.07	**0.06±0.04**
SSIM (↑)	**0.44±0.14**	0.43±0.14
NCC (↑)	0.90±0.08	**0.91±0.08**
FID (↓)	96.56	**90.47**

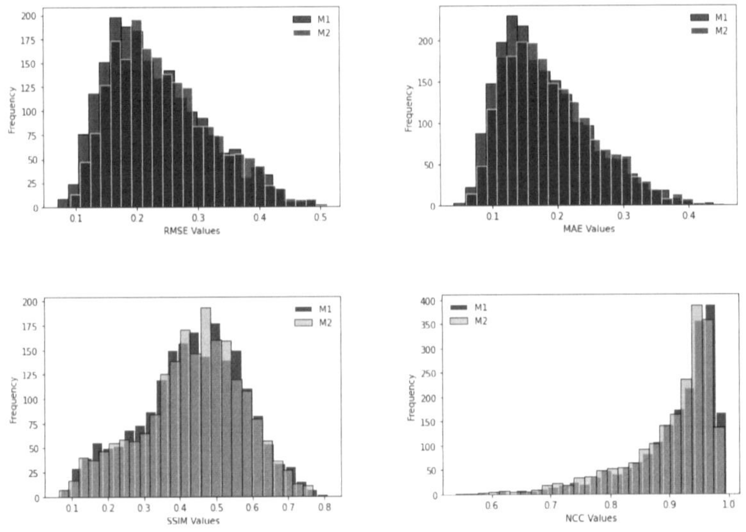

Figure 7. Comparison of final results of the **M1: SR-first** with **M2: Translation-first** models using different metrics

The models can be assessed qualitatively using figures 4 and 6. The quantitative and qualitative results indicate that the two models perform similarly and that there is no significant difference between them.

5. CONCLUSION

The problem of combining the image-to-image translation with the image super-resolution was proposed and addressed by concatenating two existing modules and rigorously evaluating the performance of both models after training. This paper describes the steps involved in preparing the selected dataset for the defined problem. In addition, a variety of evaluation phases are used to evaluate M1 and M2 models. Qualitative and quantitative analysis indicate that both models perform similarly.

By performing both tasks simultaneously, an end-to-end generative network may provide more accurate results. Our study focuses on the night-to-day image super-resolution and provides promising results.

In many image enhancement tasks including medical imaging, a similar approach can be used to generates realistic high-resolution image of a desired modality based on a given low resolution image in a different modality.

ACKNOWLEDGEMENT

This work was supported in part by the Natural Sciences and Engineering Research Council of Canada (NSERC).

REFERENCES

Alotaibi, A., 2020. Deep generative adversarial networks for image-to-image translation: A review. *Symmetry*, *12*(10), p.1705.

Bashir, S.M.A., Wang, Y., Khan, M. and Niu, Y., 2021. A comprehensive review of deep learning-based single image super-resolution. *PeerJ Computer Science*, *7*, pp. 621.

Choi, Y., Uh, Y., Yoo, J. and Ha, J.W., 2020. Stargan v2: Diverse image synthesis for multiple domains. In *Proceedings of the IEEE/CVF conference on computer vision and pattern recognition* (pp. 8188-8197).

Emami, H., Aliabadi, M.M., Dong, M. and Chinnam, R.B., 2020. Spa-GAN: Spatial attention GAN for image-to-image translation. *IEEE Transactions on Multimedia*, *23*, pp.391-401.

Fu, Y., Ma, J. and Guo, X., 2021. Unsupervised Exemplar-Domain Aware Image-to-Image Translation. *Entropy*, *23*(5), p.565.

Gupta, R., Sharma, A. and Kumar, A., 2020. Super-resolution using GANs for medical imaging. *Procedia Computer Science*, *173*, pp.28-35.

Hertzmann, A., Jacobs, C.E., Oliver, N., Curless, B. and Salesin, D.H., 2001, August. Image analogies. In *Proceedings of the 28th annual conference on Computer graphics and interactive techniques* (pp. 327-340).

Kingma, D.P. and Ba, J., 2014. Adam: A method for stochastic optimization. *arXiv preprint arXiv:1412.6980*.

Laffont, P.Y., Ren, Z., Tao, X., Qian, C. and Hays, J., 2014. Transient attributes for high-level understanding and editing of outdoor scenes. *ACM Transactions on graphics (TOG)*, *33*(4), pp.1-11.

Mao, X., Li, Q., Xie, H., Lau, R.Y., Wang, Z. and Paul Smolley, S., 2017. Least squares generative adversarial networks. In *Proceedings of the IEEE international conference on computer vision* (pp. 2794-2802).

Nazeri, K., Thasarathan, H. and Ebrahimi, M., 2019. Edge-informed single image super-resolution. In *Proceedings of the IEEE/CVF International Conference on Computer Vision Workshops* (pp. 0-0).

Pang, Y., Lin, J., Qin, T. and Chen, Z., 2021. Image-to-image translation: Methods and applications. *IEEE Transactions on Multimedia*.

Park, T., Efros, A.A., Zhang, R. and Zhu, J.Y., 2020, August. Contrastive learning for unpaired image-to-image translation. In *European Conference on Computer Vision* (pp. 319-345). Springer, Cham.

Wang, X., Xie, L., Dong, C. and Shan, Y., 2021. Real-ESRGAN: Training real-world blind super-resolution with pure synthetic data. In *Proceedings of the IEEE/CVF International Conference on Computer Vision* (pp. 1905-1914).

Wang, Z., Chen, J. and Hoi, S.C., 2020. Deep learning for image super-resolution: A survey. *IEEE transactions on pattern analysis and machine intelligence*, *43*(10), pp.3365-3387.

Zhu, J.Y., Park, T., Isola, P. and Efros, A.A., 2017. Unpaired image-to-image translation using cycle-consistent adversarial networks. In *Proceedings of the IEEE international conference on computer vision* (pp. 2223-2232).

Zhu, J.Y., Park, T., Isola, P. and Efros, A.A., 2017. Unpaired image-to-image translation using cycle-consistent adversarial networks. In *Proceedings of the IEEE international conference on computer vision* (pp. 2223-2232).

WSSL: WEIGHTED SELF-SUPERVISED LEARNING FRAMEWORK FOR IMAGE-INPAINTING

Shubham Gupta, Rahul Kunigal Ravishankar, Madhoolika Gangaraju, Poojasree Dwarkanath and Natarajan Subramanyam
PES University
100 Feet Ring Road, Banashankari Stage III, Bengaluru, Karnataka, India

ABSTRACT

Image inpainting is the process of regenerating lost parts of the image. Supervised algorithm-based methods have shown excellent results but have two significant drawbacks. They do not perform well when tested with unseen data. They fail to capture the global context of the image, resulting in a visually unappealing result. We propose a novel self-supervised learning framework for image-inpainting: Weighted Self-Supervised Learning (WSSL) to tackle these problems. We designed WSSL to learn features from multiple weighted pretext tasks. These features are then utilized for the downstream task, image-inpainting. To improve the performance of our framework and produce more visually appealing images, we also present a novel loss function for image inpainting. The loss function takes advantage of both reconstruction loss and perceptual loss functions to regenerate the image. Our experimentation shows WSSL outperforms previous methods, and our loss function helps produce better results.

KEYWORDS

Image Inpainting, Self-Supervised Learning, Weighted Pretext Task, Loss Functions, WSSL.

1. INTRODUCTION

Image Inpainting involves reconstructing scratches, splotches, blurred or discolored regions of an image using precise algorithms. Several Image inpainting methods based on sequential algorithms (Anitha & S Natarajan 2008), Convolutional Neural Networks (CNNs) (Wang 2018), and Generative Adversarial Networks (GANs) (Demir, U. & Unal, G. 2018) have been utilized in the past to perform image inpainting. However, these methods produce unsatisfactory results when the regions are too big, as seen in (Anitha and S Natarajan 2008), (Wang 2018), or require access to expensive resources (Demir, U. & Unal, G. 2018). A common factor among these methods is that they are fully supervised algorithms.

Self-supervised learning (SSL) algorithms have recently surpassed supervised algorithms in Computer Vision tasks like object classification and detection (Chen et al 2020), (Grill et al 2020). Taking inspiration from their success in learning feature representations without manually annotated data, we employ self-supervised learning for image-inpainting. A self-supervised algorithm has a pretext training phase and a downstream training phase. During the pretext training, the model learns the general feature representations such as texture, boundaries, and shape of the subjects present in the image. It does so by learning pseudo-labels for very simple tasks like rotation prediction (Gidaris, S., Singh, P. & Komodakis, N. 2018), and image-colorization (Zhang, R., Isola, P. & Efros, A.A. 2017), etc.

We study the effectiveness of single and combined pretext tasks in our work. We also vary the weights of pretext tasks in combinations to find a trend. To study the effectiveness of different weighted combinations, we build an SSL framework called Weighted Self-supervised Learning (WSSL). We can train on multiple pretext tasks and assign weights to each of the individual tasks through our framework. Assigning weights to the pretext tasks helps vary the importance given to different features learned by the individual pretext tasks. While the features learned during training are essential, the loss function we optimize while training is often overlooked (H. Zhao, O. Gallo, I. Frosio & J. Kautz, 2017). For this reason, we study multiple reconstruction loss functions. These loss functions may achieve an acceptable score quantitatively, but it fails to reconstruct visually appealing images (H. Zhao, O. Gallo, I. Frosio & J. Kautz, 2017). We also explore perceptual loss functions in combination with reconstruction loss to create a balanced novel loss function. Our results show that the presented loss function significantly improves the performance of our SSL framework. To summarize our contributions in this paper:

1. We present a novel self-supervised learning framework for image inpainting, Weighted Self-supervised Learning (WSSL).
2. We compare the performance of various pretext tasks under different weighted configurations.
3. We present a novel loss function that utilizes both reconstruction and perceptual loss. The resulting function, when optimized, significantly boosts the performance of our framework.

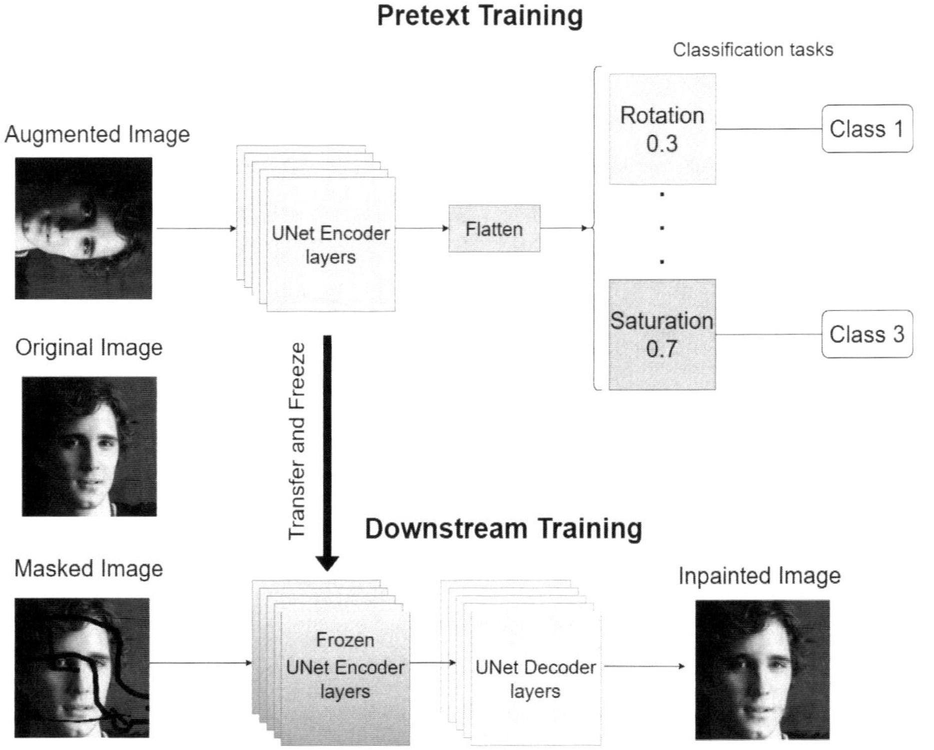

Figure 1. The proposed architecture of the Weighted Self-Supervised Learning (WSSL) framework demonstrates a weighted double pretext task. The Rotation classification task has a loss weight of 0.3 and the Saturation classification task has a loss weight of 0.7

2. LITERATURE SURVEY

(Elharrouss et al 2020) elaborates on several Sequential algorithms, methods that use CNNs, and methods that use GANs. The two categories of sequential algorithms include patch-based algorithms and diffusion-based algorithms. In patch-based methods, the missing regions are filled patch-wise with the best match (Ruzic, Tijana & Aleksandra Pižurica, 2015), (K. H. Jin & J. C. Ye 2015) from the known regions of the image. In diffusion-based methods, the image content is smoothly propagated from the boundary of the missing region to its interior (Li, Haodong, Weiqi Luo & Jiwu Huang 2017) (Kangshun et al 2014).

The global structure of the image can be captured using CNNs or encoder-decoder networks. (Pathak et al 2016) proposed a network called Context Encoders that has an encoder-decoder based architecture with the encoder being able to learn the semantically meaningful representation of the images and the decoder being able to synthesize high-level features for image inpainting. GANs have a contextual attention module that is helpful for inpainting. Although the GAN-based methods perform better than CNNs in many cases (Shin, Y.G.

et al 2020), (Vitoria, P.; Sintes, J. & Ballester, C 2019), it is computationally expensive, and the training time is high.

(H. Zhao, O. Gallo, I. Frosio & J. Kautz 2017) discuss the variety of loss functions that are overlooked when solving the image restoration problem. Their work shows the shortcomings of the L2 loss function, which only penalizes enormous errors and assumes the pixels follow a gaussian distribution. This behaviour is highly ideal and very unlikely. Instead, they look into perceptual loss functions such as the Structural Similarity Index (SSIM) and Multiscale Structural Similarity Index (MS-SSIM). Their results show that using L1 and MS-SSIM loss results in a consistent image reconstruction with minimal colour blemishes.

(Gidaris, S., Singh, P. & Komodakis, N. 2018) proposed a simple yet effective way of learning image representation by predicting image rotations. (S. Yenamandra et al 2020) proposed a DNN framework that can learn both in self-supervised and semi-supervised modes that leverage the information available within the incomplete images. Removing some of the known regions and aiding the DNN framework to learn to inpaint the removed region enables the DNN framework to learn to inpaint even without corresponding uncorrupted images.

Inpainting involves the extraction and generalization of the structural characteristics of images, such as texture and border. (Shin, Y.G. et al 2020), (Yamaguchi, S.Y. et al 2021) propose a network that captures information regarding the shape and texture of objects in images by predicting the rotation, sharpness, and saturation of the images simultaneously. Rotation, sharpness, and saturation capture the object's general shape, edges, and colour patterns respectively.

Furthermore, self-supervised learning on multiple pretext tasks has shown to be robust to out-of-domain samples (Albuquerque, I. et al 2020). Their work proposes a two-stage network for predicting the output for the Gabor filter (Fogel, I. & Sagi, D. 1989) on an image using either a single or multiple tasks. The result obtained easily competes against supervised methods on domain generalization and outperforms in localization. Through this, we are inspired to build WSSL's two-stage architecture with variations in pretext tasks.

3. METHODOLOGY

3.1 Data

We use the CelebA HQ dataset (Karras, T. et al 2017) which contains 30,000 high-resolution images of celebrities, each of 1024x1024 pixel resolution. We resize the images to 256 x 256 pixels and then obtain a random crop of size 224 x 224 pixels. We use a predefined dataset of masks, Quick Draw Irregular Mask (QD-IMD) (Iskakov, K. et al 2018) dataset. We filtered the masks such that the percentage of missing pixels is within 30 - 50%. The masks and images from the dataset are paired randomly during the training phase.

3.2 Weighted Pretext Tasks

The augmentations considered in this paper are rotation, saturation, and sharpness. The combination of pretext tasks used for testing our framework includes rotation, saturation, sharpness, rotation-saturation, rotation-sharpness, saturation-sharpness, and rotation-saturation-sharpness. In the case of multiple pretext tasks, intuitively, the features learned by one of the tasks might give a better semantic representation of the image than the other. Assigning weightage to each of these tasks based on their performance can help distribute the importance of the features that these tasks have identified. The weightage would, in turn, lead to much better feature representations. Hence, we experiment with combinations of pretext tasks, with different weights assigned to each pretext task. The image is discretized into four rotations of 0, 90, 180, and 270 degrees. The sharpness and saturation of the image are discretized into 0, 0.25, 0.75, and 1.0.

3.3 Loss Function for Downstream Task

3.3.1 SSIM

SSIM stands for Structural Similarity Index Measure and is used as a metric to measure the similarity between two given images using a value between 0 and 1. SSIM incorporates critical perceptual phenomena such as luminance and contrast masking and is a perception-based model (Zhou et al 2004).

$$SSIM = \frac{(2\mu_x\mu_y + c_1).(2\alpha_{xy} + c_2)}{(\mu_x^2 + \mu_y^2 + c_1).(\alpha_x + \alpha_y + c_2)}$$

$$L_{SSIM} = 1.0 - SSIM$$

3.3.2 Log(cosh)

Log(cosh) is the logarithm of the hyperbolic cosine of the prediction error. It is a reconstruction loss function. Log(cosh(x)) is approximately equivalent to $\frac{x^2}{2}$ for small values of x and $|x| - \log(2)$ for larger values of x. log(cosh), therefore, works mostly like the mean squared error, but will not be so strongly affected by the occasional wildly incorrect prediction (Moshagen, T., Adde, N.A. & Rajgopal, A.N. 2021). This is the advantage of log(cosh) over mean squared error. The log(cosh) function behaves as the L1 loss for small values and like L2 loss for larger values, giving us the best of both worlds.

$$L_{log(cosh(a,t))} = \frac{1}{a} log(\frac{e^{at} + e^{-at}}{2})$$

3.3.3 Novelty

Reconstruction losses perform well quantitatively but fail to regenerate a visually pleasing image. A metric like SSIM, however, will help produce a less aberrated image. For this reason, we implement a weighted sum of SSIM and log(cosh). The novel loss function is a weighted sum of SSIM and log(cosh). The weight α, is a free parameter that varies based on the application. $\alpha = 0.84$ gave us optimal results for Image Inpainting.

$$L_{total} = \alpha . L_{log(cosh)} + (1 - \alpha) . L_{SSIM}$$

where, $\alpha = 0.84$

4. IMPLEMENTATION DETAILS

Our entire codebase is written in Python 3.9 using Tensorflow 2.0 framework. We utilize a vanilla UNet architecture (Ronneberger, O., Fischer, P. & Brox, T. 2015) which consists of five encoders and five decoders. The architecture is designed to regenerate images of size 224 x 224 pixels. The pretext model consists of UNet encoders, followed by different branches of classification layers depending on the number of pretext tasks used. For example, if a combination of two pretext tasks is being used, there would be two different branches, each with its classification layers. The pretext model was trained for 40 epochs using an Adam optimizer with a learning rate of $1e - 4$, a batch size of 64. For the downstream model, the first 16 layers of the pretext model are frozen to keep the learned feature representations, and the classification layers are replaced with the decoder layers of the UNet model to perform image-inpainting. The downstream model uses the same settings for 20 epochs. The models were trained using Nvidia's K80 GPU. Our best model, further discussed in Section 5, took 4 hours to train including pretext and downstream tasks.

5. RESULTS AND DISCUSSION

In this section, we compare our image inpainting method with other methods that have been proposed recently such as ShiftNet (Yan, Z. et al 2018) and PIC (Zheng, C., Cham, T.J. and Cai, J., 2019). We evaluate all methods quantitatively and qualitatively using Structural Similarity Index Measure (SSIM) and Peak Signal to Noise Ratio (PSNR) metrics.

Table 1. Results using WSSL with a single pretext task

Pretext task	SSIM	PSNR
Sharpness	0.9281	25.84
Saturation	0.9596	29.90
Rotation	**0.9608**	**29.89**

We have used simple pretext tasks such as Rotation, Saturation, and Sharpness to perform our experiments. Rotation forces the model to learn the general shape of the objects within the image. Altering the sharpness of the image changes the emphasis put on the edges of the images' objects. Altering the saturation of the images will force the model to look for patterns and correlate colour with the objects present within the image. In Table 1, we can see that the network can learn to extract a good set of features with the pretext task Rotation. We can see that just identifying the edges or colours and patterns within the image is not sufficient to inpaint the image.

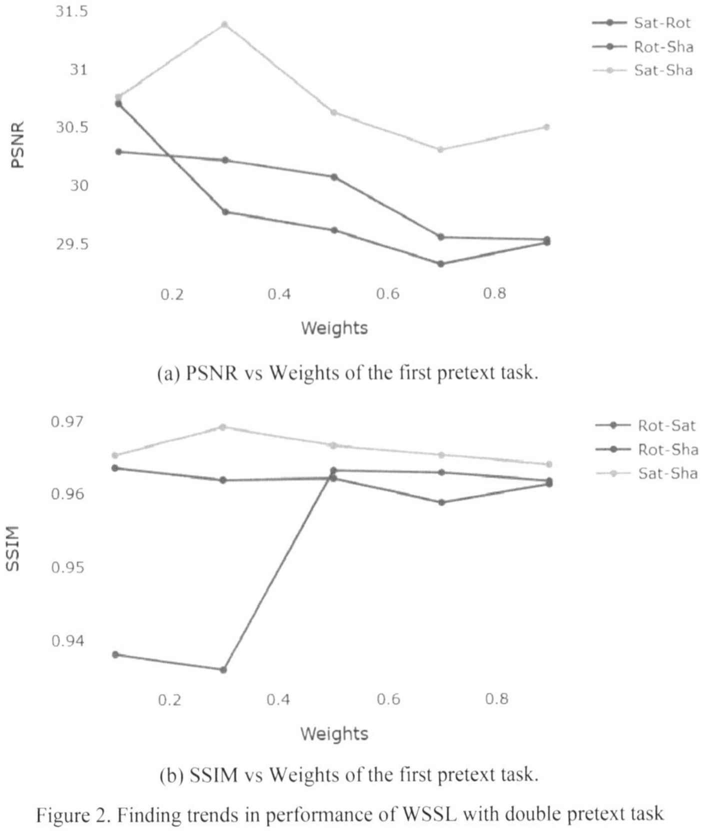

(a) PSNR vs Weights of the first pretext task.

(b) SSIM vs Weights of the first pretext task.

Figure 2. Finding trends in performance of WSSL with double pretext task

We have used combinations of two or more pretext tasks and weighted each pretext task, thereby varying the importance of identifying shapes, edges, and colour patterns. In Table 2, when using a combination of Rotation and Saturation, we can see that the network performs better with a higher weightage given to the Rotation pretext task and a lower weightage given to saturation, as shown in Figure 2.

Table 2. Results using WSSL with double pretext task

Pretext task	Loss weights		SSIM	PSNR
Rotation - Sharpness	0.9	0.1	0.9612	29.50
	0.7	0.3	0.9587	29.31
	0.5	0.5	0.9621	29.61
	0.3	0.7	0.9619	29.77
	0.1	**0.9**	**0.9636**	**30.70**
Rotation - Saturation	0.9	0.1	0.9616	30.29
	0.7	0.3	0.9628	30.21
	0.5	**0.5**	**0.9631**	**30.06**
	0.3	0.7	0.9359	29.55
	0.1	0.9	0.9380	29.52
Saturation - Sharpness	0.9	0.1	0.9639	30.49
	0.7	0.3	0.9651	30.30
	0.5	0.5	0.9665	30.62
	0.3	**0.7**	**0.9692**	**31.38**
	0.1	0.9	0.9653	30.76

Table 3. Results using WSSL with triple pretext task

Pretext task	Loss weights			SSIM	PSNR
Saturation - Sharpness -	0.6	0.2	0.2	0.9667	31.03
Rotation	0.2	0.2	0.6	0.9634	30.23
	0.2	0.6	0.2	0.9662	30.74
	0.3	**0.4**	**0.3**	**0.9685**	**31.04**

On the other hand, we can see that the network performs better with a lower weightage given to the Rotation pretext task when a combination of Rotation and Sharpness pretext tasks are used. Nevertheless, the network performs better when a higher weightage is given to the sharpness pretext task when using a combination of saturation and sharpness. Therefore, the weight given for each pretext task is a free parameter that depends on the combination of pretext tasks used.

In Figure 4, we can see that the mean of the SSIM obtained with a combination of two pretext tasks is much higher than the individual pretext tasks. By combining all three pretext tasks, we can see that the SSIM further increases. We can also see that the standard deviation of the SSIM decreases, and the results are more consistent with an increase in the number of pretext tasks (Table 3). Therefore, combining the pretext tasks would span a broader feature space, leading to a better feature representation of the images.

As shown in Table 4, WSSL with the custom loss function performs better when compared to using only SSIM or only log(cosh) as loss functions. It can also be observed from the PSNR and SSIM values, and Figure 3, that our model outperforms Shiftnet and PIC models. PIC generates a semantically meaningful result whereas our framework generates an optimal result using a single ground-truth image. Hence, a higher SSIM value is obtained through our framework although the results from PIC look more realistic.

Table 4. Performance of models on CelebA dataset.

Method	SSIM	PSNR
ShiftNet	0.7878	20.88
WSSL + log(cosh) loss function (ours)	0.9338	29.46
PIC	0.9434	31.27
WSSL + SSIM loss function (ours)	0.9629	28.90
WSSL + Novel loss function (ours)	**0.9692**	**31.38**

Figure 3. (a) Masked image (b) Shiftnet (Yan, Z. et al 2018) (c) PIC (Zheng, C., Cham, T.J. and Cai, J., 2019) (d) WSSL + log(cosh) loss function (e) WSSL + SSIM loss function (f) WSSL + novel loss function (g) Original image

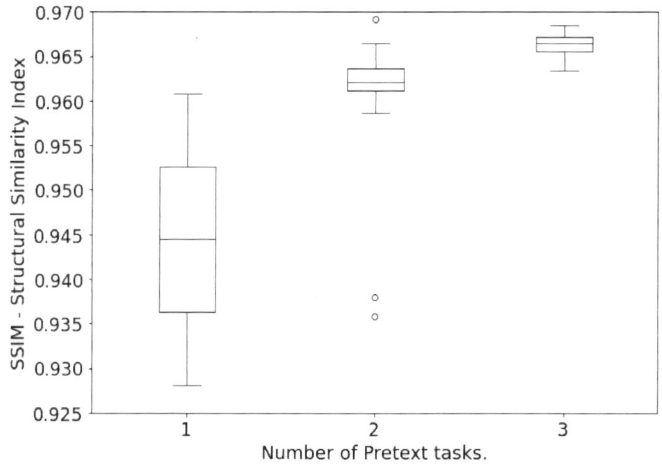

Figure 4. Plot comparing SSIM obtained from networks trained with single, double, and triple pretext tasks

6. CONCLUSION

In this paper, we have demonstrated the advantages of Self-supervised learning, such as improving robustness, better image feature representation, domain generalization, and transfer learning. Our experiments show that simple augmentations provide good feature representations of the images. We demonstrated the effectiveness of our novel framework, Weighted Self-supervised Learning (WSSL), through different weighted combinations of pretext tasks for Image Inpainting. Providing weights to the pretext tasks helps guide the framework to learn better feature representations of an image. Using multiple pretext tasks reduces the variation in the downstream results. The analysis of the compatibility of different pretext tasks and how they improve performance when utilized together can be a part of future work.

We also study the performance of different loss functions for image-inpainting. Our observation is that a weighted combination of reconstruction and perceptual loss functions is best suited to produce a visually appealing result. WSSL combined with our novel loss function significantly boosts the inpainting performance. We observe that our loss function's inpainted results have more recovered structures and colour than the other loss functions. We could further test the efficacy of WSSL on other image generation tasks in the future, such as image segmentation, object detection, and image super-resolution.

REFERENCES

Albuquerque, I., Naik, N., Li, J., Keskar, N. and Socher, R., 2020. Improving out-of-distribution generalization via multi-task self-supervised pretraining. arXiv preprint arXiv:2003.13525.

Anitha and S Natarajan, 2008. Image inpainting based on weighted similarity and pair matching. *International Conference for Signal and Image Processing.* Germany.

Chen, T., Kornblith, S., Swersky, K., Norouzi, M. and Hinton, G.E., 2020. Big self-supervised models are strong semi-supervised learners. *Advances in neural information processing systems*, 33, pp.22243-22255.

Demir, U. and Unal, G., 2018. Patch-based image inpainting with generative adversarial networks. arXiv preprint arXiv:1803.07422.

Elharrouss, O., Almaadeed, N., Al-Maadeed, S. and Akbari, Y., 2020. Image inpainting: A review. Neural Processing Letters, 51(2), pp.2007-2028.

Fogel, I., Sagi, D., 1989. Gabor filters as texture discriminator. *Biological cybernetics*, 61, pp.103–113.

Gidaris, S., Singh, P. and Komodakis, N., 2018. Unsupervised representation learning by predicting image rotations. arXiv preprint arXiv:1803.07728.

Grill, J.B., Strub, F., Altché, F., Tallec, C., Richemond, P., Buchatskaya, E., Doersch, C., Avila Pires, B., Guo, Z., Gheshlaghi Azar, M. and Piot, B., 2020. Bootstrap your own latent-a new approach to self-supervised learning. Advances in Neural Information Processing Systems, 33, pp.21271-21284.

H. Zhao, O. Gallo, I. Frosio and J. Kautz, 2017. Loss Functions for Image Restoration with Neural Networks. IEEE Transactions on Computational Imaging, vol. 3, no. 1, pp. 47-57.

Iskakov, K., 2018. Semi-parametric image inpainting. In Proceedings of the IEEE/CVF Conference on Computer Vision and Pattern Recognition (CVPR) 2018.

K. H. Jin and J. C. Ye, 2015. Annihilating Filter-Based Low-Rank Hankel Matrix Approach for Image Inpainting. IEEE Transactions on Image Processing, vol. 24, no. 11, pp. 3498-3511.

Kangshun Li, Yunshan Wei, Zhen Yang, Wenhua Wei, 2014. Image inpainting algorithm based on TV model and evolutionary algorithm. In Soft Computing, Vol 20, Issue 3, pp 885-893.

Karras, T., Aila, T., Laine, S. and Lehtinen, J., 2017. Progressive growing of gans for improved quality, stability, and variation. International Conference on Learning Representations (ICLR) 2018.

Li, Haodong, Weiqi Luo and Jiwu Huang, 2017. Localization of Diffusion-Based Inpainting in Digital Images. IEEE Transactions on Information Forensics and Security 12, pp.3050-3064.

Moshagen, T., Adde, N.A. and Rajgopal, A.N., 2021. Finding hidden-feature depending laws inside a data set and classifying it using Neural Network. arXiv preprint arXiv:2101.10427.

Pathak, D., Krahenbuhl, P., Donahue, J., Darrell, T. and Efros, A.A., 2016. Context encoders: Feature learning by inpainting. In Proceedings of the IEEE conference on computer vision and pattern recognition, pp. 2536-2544.

Ronneberger, O., Fischer, P. and Brox, T., 2015, October. U-net: Convolutional networks for biomedical image segmentation. In International Conference on Medical image computing and computer-assisted intervention, pp. 234-241.

Ruzic, Tijana and Aleksandra Pižurica, 2015. Context-Aware Patch-Based Image Inpainting Using Markov Random Field Modeling. IEEE Transactions on Image Processing 24, pp.444-456.

S. Yenamandra, A. Khurana, R. Jena and S. P. Awate, 2020, "Learning Image Inpainting from Incomplete Images using Self-Supervision," 2020. 25th International Conference on Pattern Recognition (ICPR) 2021, pp. 10390-10397.

Shin, Y.G., Sagong, M.C., Yeo, Y.J., Kim, S.W. and Ko, S.J., 2020. Pepsi++: Fast and lightweight network for image inpainting. IEEE transactions on neural networks and learning systems, 32(1), pp.252-265.

Vitoria, Patricia & Sintes, Joan & Ballester, C., 2019. Semantic Image Inpainting through Improved Wasserstein Generative Adversarial Networks. 14th International Conference on Computer Vision Theory and Applications, 249-260.

Wang, Y., Tao, X., Qi, X., Shen, X. and Jia, J., 2018. Image inpainting via generative multi-column convolutional neural networks. Advances in neural information processing systems, 31.

Yamaguchi, S.Y., Kanai, S., Shioda, T. and Takeda, S., 2021. Image enhanced rotation prediction for self-supervised learning. In 2021 IEEE International Conference on Image Processing (ICIP), pp. 489-493.

Yan, Z., Li, X., Li, M., Zuo, W. and Shan, S., 2018. Shift-net: Image inpainting via deep feature rearrangement. In Proceedings of the European conference on computer vision (ECCV), pp. 1-17.

Zhang, R., Isola, P. and Efros, A.A., 2017. Split-brain autoencoders: Unsupervised learning by cross-channel prediction. In Proceedings of the IEEE Conference on Computer Vision and Pattern Recognition, pp. 1058-1067.

Zheng, C., Cham, T.J. and Cai, J., 2019. Pluralistic image completion. In Proceedings of the IEEE/CVF Conference on Computer Vision and Pattern Recognition, pp. 1438-1447.

Zhou Wang, A. C. Bovik, H. R. Sheikh and E. P. Simoncelli, 2004. Image quality assessment: from error visibility to structural similarity, in IEEE Transactions on Image Processing, vol. 13, no. 4, pp. 600-612.

A METHOD OF ESTIMATION OF MOBILITY OPERATIONAL SERVICES FORMING PASSENGERS' TRAVEL TRAJECTORIES BASED ON EXCLUSIVE MAP MATCHING

Shuichiro Sakikawa[1], Takahito Ikuhara[2], Norihisa Komoda[3] and Toru Fujiwara[3]

[1] R&D Group, Hitachi, Ltd., 292, Yoshida-cho, Totsuka-ku, Yokohamashi, Kanagawa 244-0817, Japan

[2]Social Business Unit, Hitachi, Ltd, 6-27-18 Minami-oi,Shinagawa-ku, Tokyo 140-8572, Japan

[3]Osaka-University, 1-1 Yamadaoka, Suita, Osaka 565-0871, Japan

ABSTRACT

Public transportation demand has increased with an increasing expectation of a sustainable and decarbonised society. MaaS (Mobility as a Service) is one of the representative concepts in this field that integrates several mobility services and provides them as a single service. For the management of such mobility services effectively, continuous feedback by analysing the gap between passengers' actual journey and mobility services provided by multiple mobility operators is critical, and estimation of passengers' travel trajectory is essential to interpreting the gap. In this paper, we propose a method of estimating mobility services forming passengers' travel trajectories based on exclusive map matching technology. We show the method's efficiency by some numerical simulation assuming traffic disruption.

KEYWORDS

MaaS, Operational Service Estimation, Passenger Travel Trajectory, Exclusive Map Matching.

1. INTRODUCTION

Public transportation demand has increased with an increasing expectation of a sustainable and decarbonised society. MaaS (Mobility as a Service) is a concept that bundles the services of multiple transportation organisations to provide seamless door-to-door transportation services that respond to passenger travel demand. Under the MaaS concept, some practical mobility services have become feasible recently (MaaS Alliance., 2017; Hidaka et al., 2019; Hidaka, 2019). To manage this transportation service efficiently, operation plans should be synchronised even though different organisations work on these plans. Each organisation should continue improving its service quality by adjusting its operation plan to fit passengers' demands. Congestion rate with operational delay is a primary indicator to evaluate service quality. The connection between passengers' travel trajectories and operational services must be identified to measure the indicator accurately enough to consider adjusting the operation plan. Passenger travel trajectories data can be captured over transportation by passengers' intelligent devices such as GPS location data or sensing data. On the other hand, some pf operational service-related data is managed closely by each operator. For example, dynamic data such as operational result data is still managed closely by each organisation. To provide a monitoring method of congestion rate quickly for various types of transportation organisations equally, the method must be designed based on typical usage data such as smart device data and open data.

In this paper, we propose a method for estimating a set of mobility services that form passengers' travel trajectories, which we named "exclusive map matching", using common usage data.

2. OPERATIONAL SERVICE ESTIMATION

2.1 Operational Service

Operational service is the minimum management unit of mobility service provided by a transportation operator such as a railway operator or a bus operator. Each operational service is identified by its unique id, consisting of departure time, arrival time and locations where a mobility vehicle runs and stops. The operation plan is the bundle of operational services within 1days in the planning phase. Figure 1 shows an example of operational services and operation plan. In figure 1, the vertical axis means location, the horizontal axis represents time, and a shaded line corresponds to operational service. The solid lines show the planned time, and the dotted lines show historical time with delays. In addition, this figure shows operation plans of two different service routes (Line X and Line Y) side by side, and shaded lines connected with curved lines show passenger travel trajectories over the two service routes. For example, line "xa", line "ya", and curve "p" show a passenger travel trajectory starting from operational service "xa" in-service route X, walking from location M to location M', and transferring to active service "ya" in-service route Y. In this paper, the term "passenger travel trajectory" means actual/historical passenger's travel trajectory, not planned one, and time values containing the passenger travel trajectory reflect the actual time of operational services that passenger took. For example, a passenger travel trajectory composed of the line "xb", curve "q", and line "yb" reflects an actual time of operational service "xb" and operational service "yb" with some amount of delay.

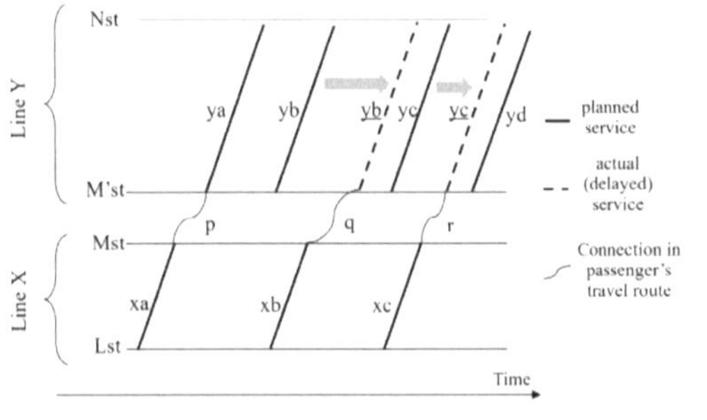

Figure 1. Operational Service

2.2 Operational Service Estimation

Operational service estimation (OSE) is a technology which combines passengers' travel trajectories and operational services. OSE performs based on various data provided by mobility service operators and passengers (Kusakabe et al., 2009; Zhang et al., 2016; Stenneth et al., 2011; Nemoto et al., 2020). Representative data used in OSE is as follows:

(1) Operation plan

This data means operational service for a day at the planned phase. The information is available to passengers and mobility operators before the working day.

(2) Operation result

This data means results of operational services. When there are no delays, the values are like the value of the operation plan. When operation delays, each operational service's time values show different values. The maturity of management of operation results data is other in each mobility service operator. Whether the data can be utilised for operational service estimation depends on the maturity condition of mobility service operators.

(3) OD (Origin and Destination)

This data means origin, destination location, and time when passengers passed on the areas of passengers with a unique ID for each passenger. The data can be gathered by the station gate system and onboard ticketing system. Railway operators can obtain OD data from their station gate systems. On the other hand. Bus operators with fixed fares operation can get departure location data only.

(4) Passenger travel trajectory

The data means passenger travel history consisting of passenger ID, start location, end location and intermediate locations with passed time. The data is obtained from smart devices owned by passengers.

(5) Vehicle location information

This data means running the history of mobility vehicles. The information consists of Vehicle ID, start/end and intermediate location and time at each location.

2.3 Aim of this Research

Public transportation services are moving toward the realisation of seamless door-to-door services that combine multiple transportation modes following the MaaS concept. Therefore, OSE must apply not only to passenger movement on the railways but also to passenger movement combined with other transportation modes such as buses. In addition, OSE should be constructed from data that can be provided by many transport operators equally.

In this paper, we propose an OSE method that can cover passengers' travel on railways and buses using operation plan data and passenger travel trajectory. In addition, our proposed method can apply to the situation when there is a discrepancy between the operation plan and the actual operation time due to operational delay.

3. EXCLUSIVE MAP MATCHING METHOD

3.1 Overview

Conventional approaches to OSE find the possible operational service to each passenger travel trajectory repeatedly until all passenger travel trajectories are combined with operation services (Kusakabe et al., 2009; Zhang et al., 2016; Stenneth et al., 2011; Nemoto et al., 2020). These approaches can fit when operation service results and passenger travel trajectory data show similar value enough to be evaluated. Aiming to support situations where operation plan and passenger travel trajectory are different values due to operational delay, our OSE approach applying the combination optimisation method can simultaneously confirm multiple combinations of passenger travel trajectories and operation services. Figure 2 shows the overview of our approach. Passenger travel trajectories are transferred to nodes, which we call passenger nodes in this paper. A passenger node consists of passenger ID, origin location, destination location, departure time of origin location and arrival time of destination location. In addition, passenger travel trajectories allocated on the same operational service are shown as the same node. Operational services on the operation plan are transferred nodes, which we call operational nodes in this paper. An operational node consists of operation ID, origin location, destination location, departure time of origin location and arrival time of destination location. A matching process, the relationship between passenger nodes and operational nodes is expressed as a network model with links connecting passenger nodes and operational nodes. Each connection between a passenger node and an operational node is evaluated whether constraints related to geolocation and time are satisfied. When all constraints are satisfied, the link can be valid. In addition, each passenger node and operational node must be connected by only a connection and to optimise the entire objective value, the links are calculated as a combination optimisation problem. Our approach must satisfy the above two types of constraints; we call the method as "Exclusive Map Matching Method".

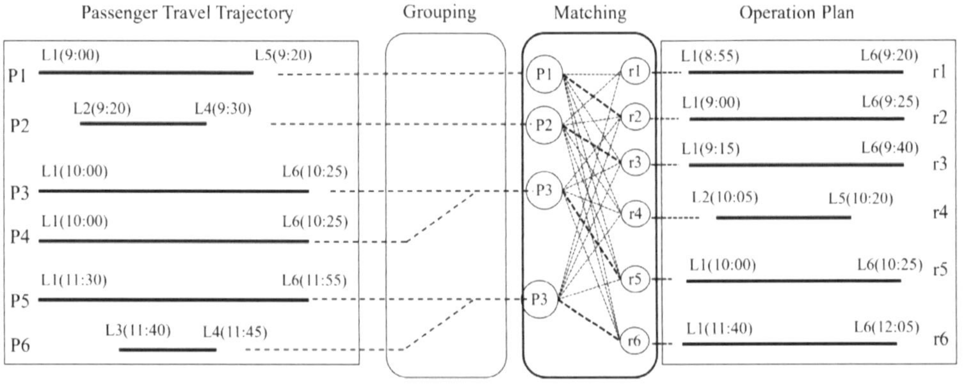

Figure 2. Overview of Exclusive Map Matching

3.2 Constraints of Combination

Each link must satisfy constraints to combine passenger and operation nodes by network links. One category of the constraint is time-based, and the other is location-based.

(1) Time-based constraint

✓ Departure time of operational node is equal to or earlier then a departure time of passenger node. -(a)

Mobility service operators aim to work following their operation plan, and departure time earlier than the operation plan is prohibited. The departure time of passenger node reflects departure time on actual operational result and departure time of operation node reflects departure time on operation plan. For this reason, constraint(a) must be satisfied. Figure 3(a) shows time-based constraint, and (r1),(r2) and (r3) are valid for the condition in this case.

(2) Location-based constraint

✓ Section between an origin location and destination location of operation node covers the section of passenger node. ---(b)

Passengers can get on vehicles from the start of the operation service location or intermediate locations and get off places where passengers aim to do so until the terminated location. For this reason, constraint(b) must be satisfied. Figure 3(b) shows location-based constraints and (r1) and (r2) are valid for the constraint.

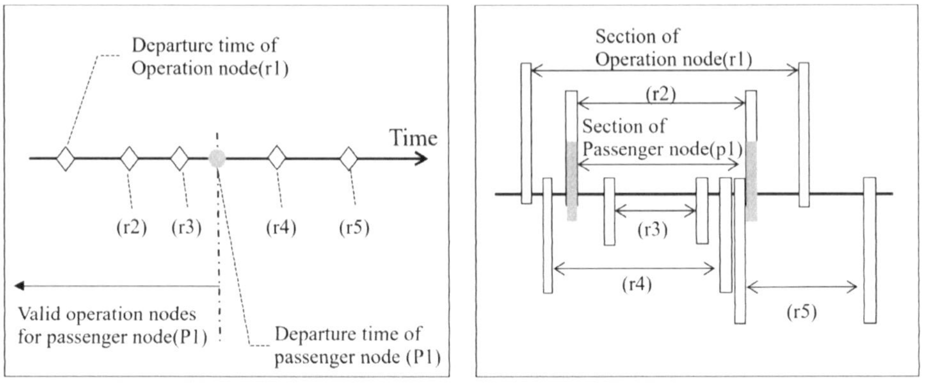

(a) Time-based constraint (b)Location based constraint

Figure 3. Constraints of Combination

3.3 Mathematical Model for Combination Optimization Problem

As we explained in Section 3.1, combinations between passenger and operational nodes are expressed as a network model with links representing constraints between passenger and operational nodes. To find appropriate combinations for the mathematical optimisation problem, we defined the network model as the below mathematical model.

(1) Variable

We define variables as below. The variable(a) means validity of a link between a passenger node(p) and operational node(r). If the link is valid, the value of the variable shows "1".

$$x(p,r) = \{0,1\} \quad \text{............(a)}$$

(2) Expression

We define three constraints below (b)(c)(d).

(b)All passenger nodes have a valid link with operational nodes, and each has only one valid link to an operation node. This constraint is represented below the expression.

$$\sum_{r=1}^{r=R} x(p,r) = 1 \quad \text{............(b)}$$

(c) Each operational node has up to one valid link to a passenger node because some operational nodes might have no connection passenger nodes due to the possibility that no one gets on the operation services. This constraint is represented below the expression.

$$\sum_{p=1}^{p=P} x(p,r) \leq 1 \quad \text{............(c)}$$

(d) Order of operational services is not changed from the operation plan even through disrupted cases. So, when a combination is fixed, order constraints between passenger nodes which show earlier departure time than the selected passenger node and operation nodes which show later departure time than the fixed operation nodes are occurred to keep the order of operational services as the same as order on operation plan. This constraint is represented below express.

$$if\ x(p_m, r_n) = 1, then \sum_{p=1}^{p=p_{m-1}} \sum_{r=r_{n+1}}^{r=R} x(p,r) = 0 \quad \text{............(d)}$$

(3) Objective Function

We define the sum of the difference between the departure/arrival time of the combined operational node and passenger node as an objective function so that the mathematical model can choose se result of combinations closer to the operation plan.

$$\sum_{r=1}^{r=R} \sum_{p=1}^{p=P} \sum_{l=1}^{l=L} x(p,r) * (Pt(p,l) - Rt(r,l)) \quad \text{............(e)}$$

4. EVALUATION

4.1 Numerical Experiment

To evaluate our proposed OSE method, we developed a prototype system and conducted a numerical experiment. For the experiment, we prepared input data as below:

(1) Operation plan

As operation plan data, we used an accurate bus operation data in a city that publishes the operation data as open data. The data consists of two service roots, as fig.4, and these two have a duplicated section where shared bus stops are allocated. The number of operational services in these two service routes is around 140 in total a day.

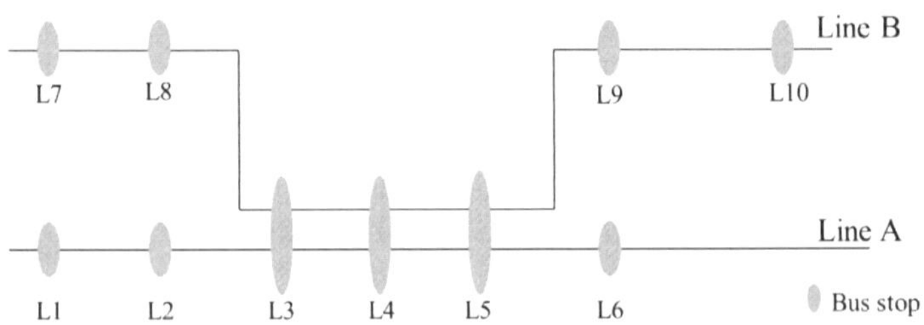

Figure 4. Service lines of bus operation

(2) Passenger travel trajectory

We prepared around 570 passenger travel data as simulation data for passenger travel trajectory data. The data consists of three groups. The first one is passengers who travel in Line A only, the second one is passengers who travel in Line B and the other one is passengers who travel within a duplicated section only. Each data has passenger ID, origin location, destinated location and travel time at each location.

4.2 Result of Numerical Experiment

To evaluate availability of the proposed method in disrupted operation cases, we prepared some set of data for disrupted patients by putting some delay on the operation plan. Before starting the numerical experiment, manually allocated the passenger travel trajectories on the delayed operation plan data ly utilise the result of manual allocation as correct combination data. In the numerical experiment, we evaluated how accurately our method can marightect combinations between the operation plan without delay and passenger travel trajectories in the delayed situation. Delay time is set on each operation service according to a normal distribution, and we conducted some tests changing the average delay and standard deviation. Table 1 shows the result.

Table 1. Result of Numerical Experiment

#	Disrupted Condition	Num of Passenger node	Num of Operation node	Num of Correct Combination	Error rate
1	Average Delay:300sec Standard Deviation:120sec	128	140	122	4.7%
2	AD:600sec, SD:180sec	128	140	115	10%
3	AD:900sec, SD:300sec	121	140	89	26%
4	AD:1200sec, SD:300sec	123	140	66	46%
5	AD:1500sec, SD:300sec	116	140	11	95%

In all of the five cases in Table 1, a number of operation nodes are equal because a number of operational services don't change according to the delay. On the other hand, number of passenger nodes slightly changes due to the amount of uncertainty even though a number of passenger travel trajectories does not change. As explained in Section 3.1, passenger travel trajectories are gathered as one passenger node if they could consider that they travel by the same operational service. Regarding the result, it shows that up to around 600sec delay, our proposed method works efficiently with under 10% miss combination. On the other hand, in the case of over 1200sec delay, the process can't work with a high error rate.

In the experiment, we assumed that any information about the operational delay on operation services is not notified by mobility service operators. However, in actual situations, it should be reasonable to think that some of the delay information, even far from the complete data set, can be notified. For that reason, we re-evaluated the accuracy of our proposed method with some rate of notified operation service delay. Table 2 shows the result. The error rate with 0% notification is the same as the result shown in Table 1. Table 2 shows that only 30% notification can be available to improve accuracy, especially for serious delay situations and 50% notification is enough to keep accuracy under 10% error even around1500sec delay situations.

In conclusion, our proposed method can be applicable under 600sec delay without any notification of operation service delay, and the process can be applied on even 1500sec delay if around 50% of operation service delay is notified.

Table 2. Result of Numerical Experiment (Delay notification)

#	Disrupted Condition	Error rate (0% notification)	Error rate (30% notification)	Error rate (50% notification)	Error rate (80% notification)
1	Average Delay:300sec Standard Deviation:120sec	4.7%	3%	0.7%	0%
2	AD:600sec, SD:180sec	10%	6%	3%	0%
3	AD:900sec, SD:300sec	26%	11.5%	6.6%	1.6%
4	AD:1200sec, SD:300sec	46%	16%	7.3%	1.6%
5	AD:1500sec, SD:300sec	95%	18%	8.6%	2.5%

5. CONCLUSION

This paper introduced an operation plan and passenger travel trajectory data method for Operation Service Estimation (OSE) in this paper. We regarded combinations between passenger travel trajectories and operation services as a network model which consists of passenger nodes, operation nodes and links to connect them and defined a numerical model to search for appropriate links as the combination by mathematical optimisation method. To confirm the availability of our proposed method, we developed a prototype and ran numerical experiments. The result shows that under a 600sec delay situation, the method works, and it works even around 1500sec delay under the condition where operation delay notification can be utilised.

REFERENCES

Hidaka Y. (2019). Possibility of MaaS Utilization for Sightseeing Industry. *IATSS Review* Vol.45, No.1, pp.23-27.

Hidaka Y., Abe A., Nagashima C. (2019). The Present Status of Mobility as a Service and Future Prospects of Service Design. *Society for Serviceology*, Vol.6, No.3, p.33-34.

Kusakabe T., Takagi Y., Iryo T., Asakura Y. (2009). Estimation of Passenger's Train Choice in Railway Network with Smart Card Ticket System. *Committee of Infrastructure Planning and Management*, vol.26, no.4, pp.655 - 662

MaaS Alliance. (2017). MaaS Alliance White Paper Guidelines and Recommendations to create the foundations for a thriving MaaS Ecosystem. *https://maas-alliance.eu/wp-content/uploads/sites/7/2017/09/MaaS-WhitePaper_final_040917-2.pdf.*

Nemoto , J., Toyama M. (2020). Evaluation of GPS-location-based Ride Detection for Gateless Railway Service. *IPSJ Transaction on Datbases(TOD)*, vol.13, No.1, pp.33-44(January)

Stenneth L., Wolfson O., Yu P.S., Xu B. (2011). Transportation mode detection using mobile phones and GIS information. *Proceedings of the 19th ACM SIGSPATIAL International Conference on Advances in Geographic Information Systems*, November 2011, pp.54-63

Zhang F., Zhao J., Tian C., Xu C., Liu X., Rao L. (2016). Spatiotemporal Segmentation of Metro Trips Using Smart Card Data. *IEEE Transactions on vehicular technology*, vol.65, no.3, March

DESIGN CHALLENGES FOR AN ENERGY EXCHANGE PLATFORM ENABLING A SUCCESSFUL ENERGY TRANSITION

Zeba Khanam and Aikaterini Bourazeri
University of Essex
School of Computer Science and Electronic Engineering
Colchester, United Kingdom

ABSTRACT

Improving energy efficiency and reducing CO_2 emissions are key strategic objectives for governments on an international level. Energy transition initiatives have been put in place to promote such measures and enhance decarbonisation efforts that can mitigate adverse climate change effects. Given that the energy transition equally focuses on the demand-side and is predicated on active consumer participation, we propose a new user infrastructure interface in which information visualisation and interface cues for energy consumption and efficiency are integrated within an Energy Exchange Platform. Following an innovate co-design methodology including a user survey for initial requirements, co-design workshops with end-users and usability testing, we aim to promote active consumer participation and other aspects of user engagement with critical infrastructure through information visualisation and interface cues.

KEYWORDS

Design Challenges, Energy Transition, Prosumer, User-Infrastructure Interface.

1. INTRODUCTION

Decarbonising the power sector, maintaining the energy resources and delivering cost-effective solutions for boosting the economy are key strategies both on national and international levels. The urgent need to address the rising levels of CO_2 emissions in the atmosphere requires new legislations and policies at various scales that will support a new decentralised and digitalised energy infrastructure for reduced fossil fuels consumption. Within this context, the world follows a pathway towards energy transition. Digitalisation along with smart control and operation can boost the energy transition by providing accurate information both to the grid and the end-users (Antikainen, M. et al., 2018).

This trend towards greater digitalisation of the energy sector has been enabled by advances in smart controllers, sensors, communication devices and data analytics (Del Rio, D. D. F. et al., 2021). These include increasing volumes of data, due to the declining cost of sensors and data storage; rapid progress in advanced analytics such as deep learning; greater connectivity of people and devices; and faster and cheaper data transmission (Verhoef, P.C. et al., 2021). Consumers and producers (i.e., prosumers) can now actively participate across energy system operations, enhancing the flexibility with which the system can cope with changes in supply and demand, and reduce the cost of integrating new technologies like distributed generation, energy storage or electric vehicles standalone in the network or even in the form of microgrids, local energy networks, etc. (Cozzi, L. et al., 2017).

The introduction of the new technologies is not a guaranteed panacea for active consumer participation, as energy consumers need to learn how to interact with the user-infrastructure interface, which is still largely neglected. Given that energy transition focuses on the demand-side and is predicated on active consumer participation, we propose a new user infrastructure interface, in which information visualisation and interface cues for energy consumption and efficiency are integrated within an Energy Exchange Platform. Accordingly, this paper is structured as follows. In Section 2, we introduce the energy transition concept, and we review similar approaches for flexible energy networks. Section 3 describes the design methodology that was followed for implementing the new user infrastructure interface, and Section 4 explores the design challenges that emerged as part of the user journey. We conclude in Section 5 with some remarks about how our approach can promote not just active consumer participation, but also other crucial aspects of user engagement with critical infrastructure.

2. BACKGROUND & MOTIVATION

A major theme of the low-carbon energy transition is the rise of the consumer. In the new, consumer-centric energy world, energy users are no longer just energy buyers at the end of power lines, they have an active involvement in energy services such as contributing to reduce costs and to enhance the system health. By 2030, local power plants (mostly solar and wind) will comprise nearly half of UK capacity, up from a quarter in 2018. Much will be traded peer-to-peer by a new class of energy "prosumers" offering a range of clean energy services locally, and to the grid operators. Advanced communication and information technologies are massively used to improve asset utilisation and provide full choice to the energy user. However, the introduction of these technologies to the grid alone is not a formula magically solving the issue as the energy system needs optimization and adjustment to the energy users' needs and preferences. Education and training are required for the energy users to learn how to interact with the new technologies and be aware of any changing conditions over different timescales, e.g., energy prices depend on the total consumption of the energy at a given moment, but investment decisions (e.g., home insulation) require many years to see a return on the investment. Moreover, information visualization provided through the 'user-infrastructure interface' is of critical importance (Bourazeri, A. et al., 2012).

2.1 The Energy Transition

The global energy sector is being transformed and transitioned from fossil-based to zero-carbon by 2050. At the heart of this transition is the urgent need to reduce CO_2 emissions in order to reverse climate change and its catastrophic effects. Worldwide, new regulations and policies have been introduced to encourage and promote energy transition, with the UK being the first major economy trying to eliminate carbon emissions. To achieve these goals, a significant transformation of the energy sector is required including a restructuring of the energy market and a new way of engaging with the wider public to make what is conceptually significant, perceptually prominent.

Within this context, new technologies (i.e., smart grids) have emerged to help with the decarbonization attempts while empowering prosumers to take action and become more active users of the network. For a successful implementation of the new technologies, social engagement and user acceptance are of critical importance (Bourazeri, A. and Pitt, J., 2018; Taherdoost, H., 2018). Prosumers still lack knowledge regarding efficient energy use, and they are not aware of the service options and pricing information in order to be able to make well informed and rational decisions. Real-time feedback is needed to increase prosumer awareness and explain all the changes and potential benefits associated with the electricity network (Bourazeri, A. et al., 2012), helping end-users to take part in energy markets and local generation. Empowering end-users will transform them from passive and inelastic consumers to active and conscious prosumers with the capability to indirectly determine how the energy sector is being operated in the 21st century (Gómez-Expósito, A. et a., 2018). A crucial component for uplifting active consumer participation is the 'user-infrastructure interface', which is often neglected by the new technologies. An advanced and smart user-infrastructure interface with integrated sensors, communication links, applied intelligence and real-time feedback can enable prosumers to make 'smart' and informed decisions leading to more responsive and sustainable energy use.

2.2 Existing Solutions

Over the years there have been many efforts and attempts on an international level to develop flexible energy solutions that could help to reverse the adverse effects of climate change. Cornwall Local Energy Market (Bray, R. et al., 2020) is one of the UK's biggest trials which managed in a three year's period to reduce greenhouse gas emissions by 10,000 tonnes per year. Even though the innovative approach adopted was used by more than 200 businesses and households, its user-infrastructure interface has complex functionality, and it is not very user-friendly, especially for an end-user who might not have technical knowledge or experience around power systems and energy bidding mechanisms.

Another initiative is the ReFLEX Orkney (Fell, M.J. et al., 2020), a low-carbon energy system which is only available to the residents of Orkney, UK. This initiative helps household and business users to get a better idea of the energy they use for heating, transport and electricity, and discover low-cost and low-carbon solutions that might work for their needs. In order to use the ReFLEX Orkney system, end-users have to complete an online questionnaire/carbon calculator and insert details about the amount of fuel they use in their home each year (i.e., kgs for solid fuel/bottled gas and litres for liquid fuels), or the emission factor for their electricity supply (i.e., Kg CO2e per kWh). However, these details are not usually available to end-users, and therefore it is impossible for them to use the service and make informed decisions based on their needs.

Sonnen Community (Harris, J., 2019) envisions clean, reliable and affordable energy for all. Members of the Sonnen community can check how much electricity they have consumed both on an individual and common level, and they can also observe the impact of their consumption on the environment (e.g., state of change in %). The available information to end-users is only limited to electricity consumption in kWh without providing any prompts or tips on how to reduce it. Another drawback of this service is that in order to become a member of the community, end-users will have to install a battery on their premises, and it is only available to residential users. Another successful innovation is the Brooklyn Microgrid (Mengelkamp, E. et al., 2018) whose objective is to develop a microgrid community in New York to support local users during extreme weather conditions or other emergencies. Focusing on reduced consumer costs and promoting clean and renewable electricity, energy resources are better distributed in times of power outages and emergencies to protect the local community and economy. Even though users are encouraged in taking part in community projects, their involvement is basically limited to investments.

Examining the different approaches and initiatives for flexible energy solutions, we found that the 'user-infrastructure interface' is being usually neglected, hampering thereby the active consumer participation. The 'user-infrastructure interface' of our proposed Energy Exchange Platform supports a more beneficial approach to the use of smart meters, sensors, and information visualization, and we are expecting that the platform will not be just used as a monitor for pricing and consumption, but also as a key enabler for direct action, feedback and incentivization. Specifically, the proposed Energy Exchange Platform with its intuitive user interfaces will provide prosumers with access to an exhaustive array of services for understanding energy consumption and production, making it the most comprehensive local energy service for smart towns/cities.

3. DESIGN METHODOLOGY

Embracing the notion of energy democratization and focusing on prosumers' empowerment, a user-centric approach was followed for the design, development and evaluation of our proposed Energy Exchange Platform. Over the course of twelve months, we undertook the following steps: i) a user survey for initial requirements' gathering, ii) a series of three co-design workshops, and iii) a user testing. Over the years, co-design has been widely used in software development, as active involvement of users can ensure the successful adoption of the new technology which can further lead to greater empowerment of end-users (Greenhalgh, T. et al., 2016). Co-design means not only asking users what they want, but treating them on a par in co-creation as researchers and having equal creative input as designers in developing the solutions (Sanders, E.B.N. and Stappers, P.J., 2008).

3.1 User Survey

A mix of 365 residential participants (i.e., different household types), geographically located across the UK, took part in the user survey, and answered questions regarding energy decisions in their households. The survey provided an insight on customer preferences and current amenities, as it largely focused on the alignment of the user interface design with the consumer wants and needs. The questions were split into four main categories: i) household information (i.e., type of property, age of property, ownership, etc.); ii) costing (i.e., energy bills, energy reduction initiatives, etc.); iii) equipment (i.e., smart appliances, smart metering, type of heating, electric vehicles, etc.); and iv) energy behaviour (i.e., energy transition initiatives). Analysing the data, we discovered that the majority of the participants live in owned properties (80.3%) with control over energy decisions and choice of energy supplier, however only half of them had considered switching energy supplier to reduce their energy bills. Another important finding was that almost 1/3 of the participants use smart appliances such as washing machine, fridge, light bulbs, etc., but only 17 participants out of 365 have an electric vehicle. Another very interesting finding was that even though the majority of the participants were aware of the energy transition and had given much thought on how to save energy in their property, only a very small percentage (3.6%) of participants were aware of energy transition initiatives in their local region, despite the mass advertising regarding the UK government's plans to decarbonize the UK power system by 2030. Finally, almost all participants would like to be involved in decisions regarding energy limit, electricity prices and consumption, and they would welcome a new technology that would help them have a more active role in their household. All these findings helped us refine the requirements of our proposed Energy Exchange Platform to ensure that the highest priority is given to the platform's functionality, appearance and value.

3.2 Co-designing the Energy Exchange Platform

After gathering the initial requirements, three co-design workshops were held about two months apart over the course of six months, focusing on exploration, design and evaluation. 12 residential, commercial and institutional participants were recruited based on inclusion/exclusion criteria (e.g., having an interest in efficient use of energy resources, better managing energy consumption, changing energy patterns and so on). Different group activities and discussions were set up, and participants were asked to comment on their energy patterns, electricity bills and their interest in locally produced energy. Specifically:

- Workshop 1: exploring the energy use of end-users (i.e., explore energy use, patterns and behaviour in households, commercial properties (i.e., offices) and institutional premises (i.e., universities and local councils), and introducing sensors and smart meters for better energy monitoring);
- Workshop 2: designing the Energy Exchange Platform interface using low-fidelity prototyping (i.e., explore possible ways of monitoring energy use through paper prototyping – using paper to create possible user interface designs);
- Workshop 3: evaluating the Energy Exchange Platform interface using a series of specific tasks and questions focusing on the end-users' perspective.

3.2.1 Exploring Energy Use

In the first workshop we explored the energy use and patterns of our participants, focusing also on any technology they might currently interact with in their premises such as smart appliances or smart metering. We examined different ways on how a new technology and energy services can help them change their energy patterns to achieve their own priorities related to cost, sustainability and so on, and introduced different designs of smart metering to help them better understand how they can monitor the full array of flexible resources at a local level: distributed heat and power resources, demand side response, energy storage, electric vehicles (EV), power-to-gas, domestic appliances, commercial loads, etc. We concluded the first workshop with an analysis of demand pattern alignment to production patterns of low-carbon technologies and an introduction to different demand profiles (e.g., EV uptake, charging profiles and travel patterns).

3.2.2 Designing the Energy Exchange Platform

The second workshop was mainly dedicated to co-designing the user interface of the Energy Exchange Platform using low-fidelity prototyping with post-its, pens, different UI elements such as buttons, checkboxes, dropdown lists, text fields, date field, and blank A3 "screens". We focused on the main design concepts for monitoring energy consumption and billing. Participants were mainly left to their own devices, starting from a blank page. The resulting low-fidelity prototypes were simple but indicated important functionality that the technology had to achieve. Low-fidelity prototyping is often used in co-design and works well when exploring the required functionality. After completing the co-design workshop, we integrated the feedback and participants' designs into final designs using a dedicated software (Figure 1).

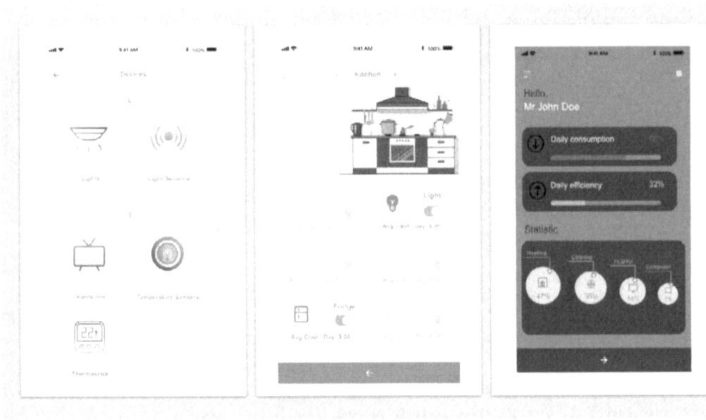

Figure 1. Initial Designs (2nd Workshop)

3.2.3 Evaluating the User Interface

Our aim in the final co-design workshop was to evaluate the refined prototypes using a cognitive walkthrough (Rieman, J. et al., 2015), focusing on the usability of the interface designs. Even though participants were overall happy with the functionality of the interface, they felt that more low-level information regarding energy consumption would help them to better monitor their energy use. Particularly, they asked for a 'Tips' screen with a focus on CO_2 emissions and money savings which will give them feedback and advice on how they can save energy and money. They also said that a personalised report at the end of the day could help them better understand their energy performance and how they can set objectives for their premises; energy efficiency rating and how to achieve it. This feedback was integrated into a new version of designs (Figure 2).

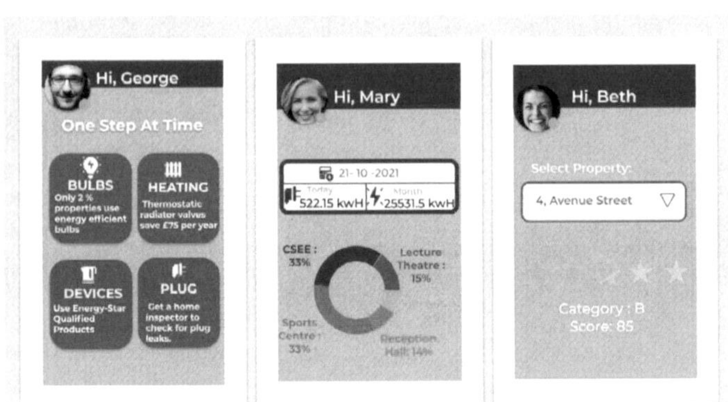

Figure 2. Refined Designs (3rd Workshop)

3.3 User Testing

After completing all co-design workshops and integrating participants' feedback into the final designs, we ran a user testing session with the same participants as the ones who took part in the co-design workshops. The interface designs were tested on a tablet focusing on different tasks such as checking energy consumption and efficiency of a specific property, monitoring progress and achievements regarding energy consumption, and checking the energy demand of an institutional property (i.e., university building). This approach was chosen in order to help us identify potential problems that might arise when end-users start using the Energy Exchange Platform at their premises and ensure that the produced interface designs are indeed usable by a wider sample of the population (i.e., residential, commercial and institutional users).

During the user testing, participants were asked to "think aloud" and describe what they were looking at, what they were thinking, and anything else that came to their mind including questions and opinions about the screens, content, layout, language, and anything else they noticed during their interaction with the clickable interface designs. This usability approach through free response ensured that validity and objectivity were achieved, instead of using specific questions or rating scales such as System Usability Scale (SUS) that only focus on the most salient features without considering the big picture. Upon completion of all tasks, participants were given a chance to comment on the screen navigation, the information provided, and their overall impression of the Energy Exchange Platform.

4. DESIGN CHALLENGES

A thematic analysis on the data captured was undertaken to explore and investigate the design challenges of the proposed Energy Exchange Platform. The analysis began with a bottom-up investigation of headline data from the co-design workshops. An initial set of 'super-codes' was created and 'emergent' codes were added when necessary. This code-set was then re-applied to the data iteratively to understand its main themes and develop the design framework. Data were coded based on conversational turn, and saturation was considered to have occurred when no more codes emerged, which (Aldiabat, K.M. and Le Navenec, C.L., 2018) describe as "code saturation". Both authors created and applied the codes ensuring consistency and accuracy. Table 1 presents the codes that arose from the data analysis. Several overarching themes emerged as a result of this analysis. In this section, we report and describe these themes and how they relate to our data in the context of our codes.

Table 1. Emerged Design Challenges from Bottom-Up Data Investigation

SUPER-CODE	*CODE*	*DEFINITION*	*DESIGN CHALLENGE*
Interface Design	*Simplicity*	A simple and neat user interface that will empower users to monitor their energy consumption.	A simple user interface displaying both high-level and low-level information about energy consumption.
Information Visualisation	*Data Info & Suggestions*	Data representation in a meaningful way so that users can fully understand their energy consumption.	Include different interface cues to guide the user interface interaction and communicate important information to users.
Scheduling & Monitoring	*Empowerment*	The Energy Exchange Platform should enable users to monitor their consumption and schedule the operation of their electrical appliances and assets.	Design and develop a platform for tracking energy consumption in real-time and giving appropriate suggestions for energy efficiency.

Technology	*Choice of Platform*	A platform that is compatible with any device or platform. No need for a specific software to be downloaded, installed, updated or managed, which is accessible anytime anywhere.	Design and develop a platform that can be accessed by any device regardless of software or hardware restrictions.
Privacy	*User Access*	Depending on authorisation credentials, users will see only the app's layers applicable to them.	Defining different roles with different access rights.

Interface Design: The interface design of the proposed Energy Exchange Platform is very important to ensure that our users will actually use it in the long term. Our participants mentioned that the interface design should be flexible to accommodate the needs and requirements of the different users depending on their expertise and interest in further monitoring energy consumption. The proposed platform has a simple but intuitive user interface that allows users to track their energy consumption and check their premise's performance at the end of the day.

Information Visualisation: The proposed Energy Exchange Platform should provide appropriate presentation and representation of data, making what is conceptually significant, perceptually prominent. Users usually prefer data visualisation (e.g., statistical graphics, plots, etc.) over text. The use of graphs is common for monitoring or tracking energy consumption in a more pleasant and understandable way.

Scheduling & Monitoring: The proposed Energy Exchange Platform becomes a personalised application by simply completing a few steps. The platform's objective is to optimise support to the users and their energy consumption, while the suggestions and tips are tailored to their needs and preferences. Users can set up the platform with some basic information about the electrical appliances they have at their premises, when they want to operate them (e.g., scheduling their operation for specific times per day) and the objectives they want to achieve (e.g., reduce energy consumption by 20% in comparison to last year's consumption). Using this platform, energy users are in the centre of decision-making regarding their energy consumption and efficiency.

Technology: New technologies can encourage energy users to have a more active role on how they consume energy and make informed decisions regarding their plans and goals for energy efficiency. The proposed Energy Exchange Platform is a web-based application compatible with any device. There are no requirements for a specific software to be downloaded, installed, or updated, and it can be accessible anytime anywhere.

Privacy: Users of web-based applications generally expect that different levels of security or privacy will be embedded into those applications according to the degree of information sensitivity. Energy users are usually very concerned about who receives details about their energy consumption and how these details are being handled. The majority of web applications, regardless of their use, include a 'User Privacy Profile' with a set of privacy preferences that users can set up. All participants highlighted that depending on the authorisation credentials, they will only get access to the app's layers that should be seeing.

5. CONCLUSIONS

The main contribution of this paper is to propose a user infrastructure interface for energy systems, in which information visualisation and interface cues are integrated in an Energy Exchange Platform. Providing an appropriate user interface for active consumer participation will enable long-term user engagement with the grid and offer both consumers and producers a deeper insight into decision-making, resource allocation and energy efficiency. Making consumers active participants in the network requires exploration and identification of their needs and preferences, taking always into consideration any concerns they might have, or any barriers imposed by the network providers. User acceptance and engagement can solve any socio-technical challenges that might affect the development and deployment of smart energy solutions. To conclude, our work presented a further step in developing methods and techniques for co-designing novel technologies for the energy sector.

REFERENCES

Aldiabat, K.M. and Le Navenec, C.L., 2018. Data saturation: The mysterious step in grounded theory methodology. *The qualitative report*, *23*(1), pp.245-261.

Antikainen, M., Uusitalo, T. and Kivikytö-Reponen, P., 2018. Digitalisation as an enabler of circular economy. *Procedia Cirp*, *73*, pp.45-49.

Bray, R., Woodman, B. and Judson, E., 2020. Future prospects for local energy markets: lessons from the Cornwall LEM.

Bourazeri, A., Pitt, J., Almajano, P., Rodríguez, I. and Lopez-Sanchez, M., 2012, September. Meet the meter: visualising smartgrids using self-organising electronic institutions and serious games. In 2012 IEEE Sixth International Conference on Self-Adaptive and Self-Organizing Systems Workshops (pp. 145-150). IEEE.

Bourazeri, A. and Pitt, J., 2018. Collective attention and active consumer participation in community energy systems. *International Journal of Human-Computer Studies*, *119*, pp. 1-11

Cozzi, L., Turk, D., Abergel, T., Bartos, J., Bellevrat, E., Bennett, S., Berly, T., Bouckaert, S., Dulac, J., Alvarez, C.F. and Pales, A.F., 2017. Digitalization and Energy. OECD.

Del Rio, D. D. F., Sovacool, B. K., & Griffiths, S. (2021). Culture, energy and climate sustainability, and smart home technologies: A mixed methods comparison of four countries. *Energy and Climate Change*, *2*, 100035.

Fell, M.J., Bray, R., Ford, R., Hardy, J. and Morris, M., 2020. Post-Pandemic Recovery: How Smart Local Energy Systems Can Contribute.

Greenhalgh, T., Jackson, C., Shaw, S. and Janamian, T., 2016. Achieving research impact through co-creation in community-based health services: literature review and case study. *The Milbank Quarterly*, *94*(2), pp. 392-429.

Gómez-Expósito, A., Arcos-Vargas, A., Maza-Ortega, J.M., Rosendo-Macías, J.A., Alvarez-Cordero, G., Carillo-Aparicio, S., González-Lara, J., Morales-Wagner, D. and González-García, T., 2018. City-friendly smart network technologies and infrastructures: The Spanish experience. Proceedings of the IEEE, 106(4), pp.626-660.

Harris, J., 2019. Power... With a little help from your friends. Electrical Connection, (Autumn 2019), pp.34-35.

Mengelkamp, E., Gärttner, J., Rock, K., Kessler, S., Orsini, L. and Weinhardt, C., 2018. Designing microgrid energy markets: A case study: The Brooklyn Microgrid. *Applied Energy*, *210*, pp.870-880.

Rieman, J., Franzke, M. and Redmiles, D., 1995, May. Usability evaluation with the cognitive walkthrough. In Conference companion on Human factors in computing systems (pp. 387-388).

Sanders, E.B.N. and Stappers, P.J., 2008. Co-creation and the new landscapes of design. *Co-design*, *4*(1), pp. 5-18.

Taherdoost, H. (2018). A review of technology acceptance and adoption models and theories. *Procedia manufacturing*, 22, 960-967

Verhoef, P.C., Broekhuizen, T., Bart, Y., Bhattacharya, A., Dong, J.Q., Fabian, N. and Haenlein, M., 2021. Digital transformation: A multidisciplinary reflection and research agenda. *Journal of Business Research*, *122*, pp.889-901.

SMART CITY DISTRICT SIMULATOR – HOW WE MADE A VIRTUAL SMART CITY DISTRICT COME ALIVE

Arian Ajdari, Philipp Neuschwander, Frank Elberzhager and Patrick Mennig
Fraunhofer IESE
Fraunhofer Platz 1, 67663 Kaiserslautern, Germany

ABSTRACT

More and more cities are striving to becoming more digital, offering their citizens, for instance, digital services aimed at supporting their daily lives. Another urgent trend that cities have to address is climate friendliness. In the EnStadt:Pfaff research project, we are developing a climate-neutral city district. One aspect is to examine how digital services might support climate topics. As the district is currently under construction, resulting in the challenge that only a very limited number of future citizens and further stakeholders are currently known, we have to find new ways of evaluating new ideas for digital services. As we assume that the foundation of digital services will be a future digital ecosystem – which, however, currently does not exist yet, we need an alternative mechanism to mock such a digital environment. We do this via a mock platform that supports fast evaluation of new ideas for digital services. In order to be able to evaluate connected and environmentally sensitive services, in particular, we developed a simulator that is able to simulate several different actors and sensors. This enables us to check how concrete digital services behave when, for example, citizens, cars, or other objects run inside the district. In this paper, we provide concepts regarding the simulator and describe how we realized an initial version of it, followed by a discussion on the benefits of our solution.

KEYWORDS

Smart City, City District, Digital Ecosystem, Platform, Simulator, Digital Services.

1. INTRODUCTION

Two of the current megatrends are the digital transformation and climate change. These megatrends affect all parts of our daily lives, and also have several interconnections. One concrete application case are cities. Many cities have transformed during the last decade, becoming more digital, for example by offering digital services supporting citizens in administrative tasks, or by installing traffic control systems [Hendy et al.]. New services supporting climate-friendly behavior can also be observed, such as bike rental and corresponding apps. Furthermore, this trend is expected to continue, and new digital ecosystems are likely to emerge with greater density of the connected digital services [Neirotti et al.].

In the EnStadt:Pfaff research project, we are supporting the development of a climate-neutral city district. This city district is currently being developed, i.e., we are in an early development process. This means that only a very small number of future stakeholders and citizens are already known. Consequently, we are unable to speak to residents from this future city district and, as we are responsible for developing digital solutions, in particular, we have no real stakeholders with whom to elaborate requirements for a future digital ecosystem and corresponding digital services.

This leads to the challenge of how we can evaluate new ideas for digital services that support, among others, citizens in behaving in a more climate-friendly manner. Our idea is a so-called mock platform whose focus is on offering a technical environment where digital prototypes can be tested. In such an environment, we neglect requirements such as high security or strong performance, rather concentrating on making prototypes available early to test the idea, the usability, and the initial functionality. As we have no real users or "objects" such as cars in the real district to test the interaction of the digital services and the environment, we developed a simulator for the mock platform environment. With this simulator, we are able to test many more interactions and have some kind of test bed for sensors and state-based solutions. This enables us to get early feedback about how our digital services will interact in the future real city district, and have much more realistic feedback to observe what works, which ideas for digital services are interesting, and where potential problems occur.

In this paper, we present details about the simulator, how it is being developed, and what we can currently simulate (Section 3). Section 2 provides some background about our environment, and briefly presents some related work. Section 4 discusses the current results and demonstrates the simulator's applicability. Section 5 concludes our paper with a short summary and an outlook on future work.

2. RELATED WORK AND BACKGROUND

Smart cities present an environment where inhabitants benefit from digital, interconnected services [Lea 21]. Furthermore, one of the objectives of smart cities is to address problems related to the environment, such as climate change, with the help of digital services. Santana et al. surveyed the state of the art in software platforms for smart cities and analyzed 23 platforms [Santana et al. 2017]. They identified technologies, which serve to realize the concept of smart cities. Relevant in this context are also Digital Twins. Digital Twin is an approach of continuously learning a digital copy of real-world assets in order to allow experts to bring in policies and updates which would improve life in the city. One concrete implementation of the Digital Twin concepts is DUET, which spans one region and two cities [Fuller et al. 2020, Duet 2022]. Since no complete smart city concept has been realized anywhere yet, we developed components that model certain aspects of a smart city in order to understand how digital services cooperate with each other and make the concept of a smart city possible [Elberzhager et al. 21 (2)].

To support developers in experiencing connected services, we developed a mock platform where they can create, prototype, and test their ideas for connected services [Elberzhager et al. 21 (1)]. To connect services, we use an event broker, which relies on a publish-subscribe pattern. This allows connected services to publish information or events that may be relevant for others in the ecosystem. This enables the developers to experience the services as isolated units, or as one instance governing the smart city. By viewing the services as isolated units, developers can understand the impact of a particular service in the smart city and can make adjustments in order to increase the benefits as much as possible. Furthermore, by logically connecting different services, developers can help tackle challenges that may arise in smart cities.

Besides developers, we want to support other stakeholders as well. The realization of a smart city district requires innovative and mostly out-of-the-box thinking. Therefore, we organized four hackathons where participants were invited to prototype their ideas in the form of digital services that are useful for a smart city. Hackathon participants used the mock platform and developed digital services in order to grasp the general vision of smart city and test implemented ideas for digital services.

Digital services based on our mock platform and the hackathon events taught us valuable lessons about the future inhabitants of the smart city district. We learned about their potential needs, derived digital services that could be useful, and examined how much of an appeal the smart city would have for them. However, these digital services proved to be too specific, too isolated (i.e., no real interaction with people or other services), or impossible to test in a real environment. We could not answer the question of how the general public would feel and how it would experience living in the smart city district. We could not realize use cases when many digital services interact with each other. Furthermore, we could not predict any threats or opportunities arising from having many digital services interacting with each other. To overcome this problem, we developed the smart city district simulator to gain more insights into all these questions.

3. SMART CITY DISTRICT SIMULATOR

3.1 General Idea and Concept

The main idea of understanding how digital services are applied and what happens in a digital ecosystem is to have a virtual smart city district that can be used for simulations and quick prototyping. To address this idea, we worked out a concept that considers sensors, actuators, humans, and things as well as connected software solutions in a virtual world, which forms the foundation for a comprehensive smart city district simulator. Our concept for such a virtual world comprises six solution components, each addressing one specific concern:

world state storage, world visualization, actor engine, software-based sensors, control components, and environmentally sensitive services.

The **world state storage** component addresses the concern of keeping and managing the observable state of the virtual world. Therefore, it offers two primary functionalities. First, there is a functionality to obtain the current world state and second, there is a functionality to populate changes to the world state. By offering these two functionalities, the world state storage component takes the position of a single point of truth regarding the current state of the virtual world. Consistency can be named as one concrete example of the challenges that need to be addressed by realizations of this component.

The **world visualization** component provides a visualization of the virtual world by rendering the current world state in a way that is suitable for human observers. Therefore, the current world state is served by the world state storage component and the visualization component can render this state – for example – as a 2-dimensional world. When it comes to the realization of this component, one needs to make sure that changes to the world state are considered by the visualization so human observers can actually observe what is happening in the virtual world.

The **actor engine** component simulates humans and things in the virtual world by executing one or more scripts. We refer to those entities as actors because their behavior is scripted. The respective state changes are populated to the world state storage. Thus, the actors become part of – and enact their play in – the virtual world. For example, there could be a script for a pedestrian actor to walk along a walkway in the virtual world.

Software-based sensors generate sensor data by processing a perception of the world. Providing the world state as input to a software-based sensor, we can have sensors – analogous to those in the real world – in our virtual world, too. Depending on their implementation, such sensors can detect numerous types of circumstances in the virtual world and make information about them available as input to or trigger for other components in the system. For example, there could be a software-based sensor for detecting pedestrians in a specific location of the virtual world.

Control components manage controllable entities (e.g., actuators) and offer functionality to control them. In our concept, we stipulate that control components take care of managing the state and state transitions of the entities. Furthermore, it is a concern of the control component to populate the recent state of the entities it manages to the world state storage. Thus, the entities become part of the virtual world and their state can be observed by others. For example, there could be a control component for a lamp in our virtual world that offers functionality to turn the lamp on and off.

Environmentally sensitive services react to their environment. By utilizing the concepts of software-based sensors and control components, one can form environmentally sensitive services that react to the virtual world and can also cause an impact on this very world. For example, there could be a software-based sensor for detecting pedestrians in a specific location in the virtual world. This information can be consumed, e.g., by a smart lighting service that – depending on the sensed data – controls the lamps in a demand-actuated way by using their control components.

The solution components that we just introduced can be brought together and form the simulator we were aiming for: An actor engine executes scripts to simulate actors enacting their play and continuously populates their states to the world state storage. Software-based sensors can continuously interpret the world state and generate sensor data out of it. This sensor data can be used by environmentally sensitive services and serve as input to or trigger for them. Control components offer functionality to control entities and take care of populating the recent entity state to the world state storage. Environmentally sensitive services and other components can use this functionality provided by control components to impact the world (e.g., turn on a lamp). World visualization components can consume the world state provided by the world state storage and render a depiction of the world in a way that is suitable for human observers. Given that a world visualization component is implemented and integrated in such a way that changes to the world state can be considered, human observers can potentially continuously observe what is happening in the virtual world. This includes the plays enacted by actors as well as the impact of environmentally sensitive services on the world (potentially triggered by the actors' play).

Figure 1 depicts this as a big picture view and highlights the respective data flows between the different types of solution components (left), and their realization as implemented components and the data flow among them in our software architecture (right).

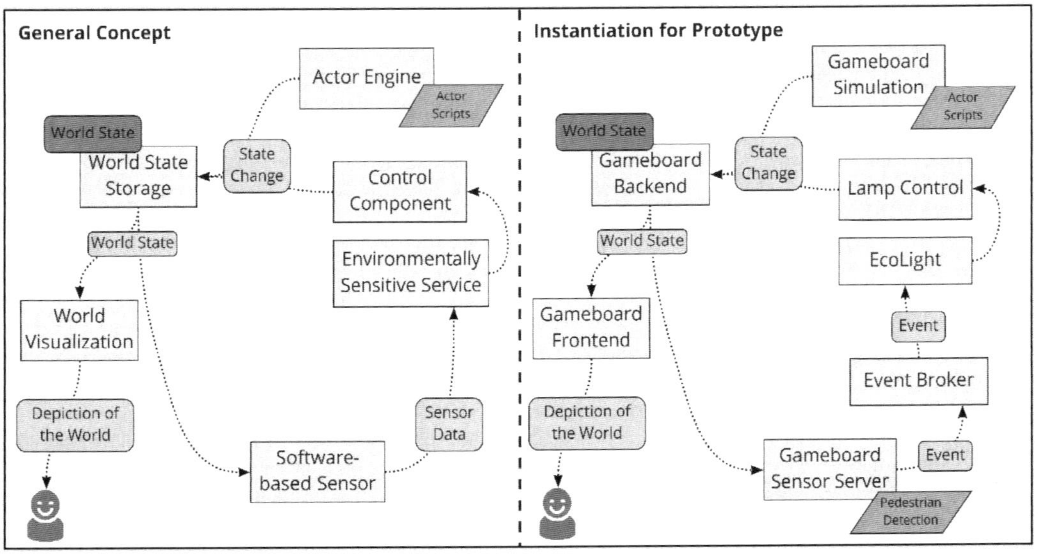

Figure 1. Smart city district simulator: general concept (left) and its instantiation for the prototype (right)

3.2 Architecture and Implementation

One of the topics we encountered in our research project is related to smart lamp posts, which can house various sensors and actuators. A simple scenario related to this is to sense for the presence of pedestrians in the range of the lamp post and control the lamp in a demand-actuated way in order to reduce light pollution and energy consumption in the planned city district while still providing illuminance, hence safety, to pedestrians. With this simple scenario in mind, we developed and applied the previously introduced concept in the context of the project and realized a prototype for a smart city district simulator. We decided to use this simple scenario as it is easy to understand for the developers of the simulator as well as for the people that will be using the simulator (e.g., hackathon participants) to realize their own more sophisticated scenarios and prototypes. It is essential to onboard the latter as easy and fast as possible so they can make the most out of it; choosing a simple sample scenario to illustrate the principles of the simulator supports this goal and should not limit its applicability.

The architecture of our smart city district simulator largely corresponds to the six solution components. Basically, we instantiated and realized the conceptional solution components according to our scenario: Besides the components for world state storage (which we called "Gameboard Backend") and world visualization ("Gameboard Frontend"), we implemented an actor engine ("Gameboard Simulation") with scripts for several types of actors (including pedestrians), software-based sensors for detecting those pedestrians (as part of the "Gameboard Sensor Server") and a control component offering control of some lamps ("Lamp Control"). The environmentally sensitive service for processing the pedestrian detection information and controlling the lamps accordingly is called "EcoLight".

To loosely connect EcoLight and pedestrian detection, we decided to integrate our existing mock platform, which provides an event broker and concepts on how to arrange information flows based on the publish-subscribe pattern in a prototypical smart city digital ecosystem [Elberzhager et al. (1)]. This architectural design decision enables easy distribution and consumption of the sensor data in the ecosystem. In addition, we prevent possible dependencies and assumptions related to the Gameboard Backend or Gameboard Sensor Server implementation in the EcoLight implementation. Thus, facilitating the usage of the EcoLight prototype in other environments (maybe even in the real world) as the underlying world implementation is just an implementation detail hidden by abstractions and loose coupling.

The **Gameboard Backend** (world state storage) is realized as a web service offering a web API that can be used to query the world state and to populate state changes. Internally, we differentiate between the world's map ("fields") and the things or humans that exist in the world ("tokens"). The positional correlation between fields and tokens is made by using a *position* attribute (x-y coordinates) in their respective data structures.

Besides that, there are attributes for *id*, *type*, and *properties*. For example, there could be fields with the *type* "street" or "walkway" or any other meaningful value. In the case of tokens, values could be "pedestrian" or "lamp" or any other meaningful type of thing or humans. In the *properties* attribute, arbitrary information related to the observable state of that entity can be stored. For example, for a lamp, one might want to store whether it is currently on or off. By choosing such a generic approach for realizing the world state, we empower developers to model whatever they want without the need to make changes to the Gameboard Backend. Tokens can be created, read, updated, and deleted via the offered web API. Thus, populating a state change corresponds to modifying a token and its attributes. A noteworthy detail in this regard is that we only allow the creator of a token to modify that token. We do this to nudge developers in the direction of using the simulator in a transparent and realistic way: In the real world, one does not have any kind of direct write access to the observable state of entities, e.g., we cannot turn off a lamp by just flipping a bit in a world state storage; instead, we need to interact with the entity itself or with some kind of control component (e.g., a switch) that manages the state of the entity. Therefore, only the creator of a token is allowed to manage that token and its properties.

The **Gameboard Frontend** (world visualization) is realized as a React web application that communicates with the Gameboard Backend to retrieve the world state and renders it in a way that is suitable for human observers. The fields are retrieved as they are stored in the Gameboard Backend and displayed as a two-dimensional map. Of particular interest is the actual depiction of the simulated environment, i.e., its resemblance to the world to be simulated. Currently, the chosen implementation of the world state storage (Gameboard Backend) uses fields with distinct x-y coordinates and unknown, but also unimportant, size. As the Gameboard Backend does not differentiate field orientation (e.g., whether x is horizontal or vertical), the Gameboard Frontend must choose one interpretation. To model a random environment, the orientation is arbitrary, but to represent a certain planned environment, the same choice must be made for entering the fields and displaying them. This example shows the decoupled nature of the Gameboard Backend and Gameboard Frontend. It is merely one way of visualizing the world state and intended for interaction with humans. The same principle thus applies to the representation of a certain type of field, which is not an implementation detail of the backend but rather of the frontend component. Hence, different world visualization components could be implemented that visualize the same world state in different ways in order to support different use cases. Tokens, such as actors (e.g., pedestrians or cars), are displayed on their respective fields and visualized to show their type. To support debugging activities, there are some other features for developers: In addition to the two-dimensional representation, the Gameboard Frontend offers a mode for listing the tokens and their attributes in a table. A similar feature is available for the fields, too. Furthermore, there is functionality to list invalid tokens. We consider a token as invalid if there is no field for its position.

The **Gameboard Simulation** (actor engine) executes actor scripts specified by developers and populates the related state changes continuously to the Gameboard Backend. By doing so, the actors become part of the simulated world (in the form of tokens) and their enacted play (in the form of token attribute changes) can be observed by others. To support developers in writing such actor scripts, we provide them with a development kit offering multiple ready-to-use constructs for specifying different types of actors and their behavior to be enacted (e.g., movement of a pedestrian). Gameboard Simulation consumes these constructs to initialize and execute the actors accordingly. Furthermore, developers can extend the provided constructs and realize their own types of actors. To control the speed of the script executions, developers can configure the Gameboard Simulation's global tick rate. This configuration determines how fast actors will transition to their subsequent state. To model slower actors, one can specify the actor's individual speed in the range (0,1), which is evaluated relative to the global tick rate. With this mechanism, we can differentiate between faster actors (e.g., cars that might move on each tick) and slower actors (e.g., pedestrians that might move on every second tick).

The **Gameboard Sensor Server** (software-based sensors) repeatedly queries the Gameboard Backend for the recent world state using a configurable sample rate. The world state is then propagated to the software-based sensor instances operated by the server for further evaluation. In case a sensor instance wants to publish information, it publishes a corresponding event at the event broker (see Figure 1). Software components interested in that information can easily subscribe to the respective topics at the event broker to receive and process those events. For our scenario, we realized a sensor implementation to detect pedestrians in a specific location. To do so, the world state is evaluated and checked for the presence of a token with the type "pedestrian" in the area being observed. The corresponding information is published to the respective topic at the event broker.

Lamp Control (control component) populates eight lamp instances and their state to the Gameboard Backend on startup. Additionally, Lamp Control offers a web API that can be used to control the eight lamp instances. State changes of the lamps are populated to the Gameboard Backend.

EcoLight (environmentally sensitive service) subscribes to the event broker to receive events related to pedestrian detection. In case the event contains the information that a pedestrian has been detected in a specific area, the lamp in that area will be turned on. In case the event contains information that there is no longer a pedestrian detected in a specific area, the lamp in that area will be turned off. To do so, EcoLight reaches out to the web API offered by Lamp Control and consumes its functionality to control the lamp instances.

Figure 2 depicts the visualization of a pedestrian and the lamps. The pedestrian walks along the walkway according to the actor script. Every time the pedestrian enters the range of a lamp, that lamp turns on; and every time the pedestrian leaves the range of a lamp, that lamp turns off. The end-to-end scenario that we wanted to realize is working as expected.

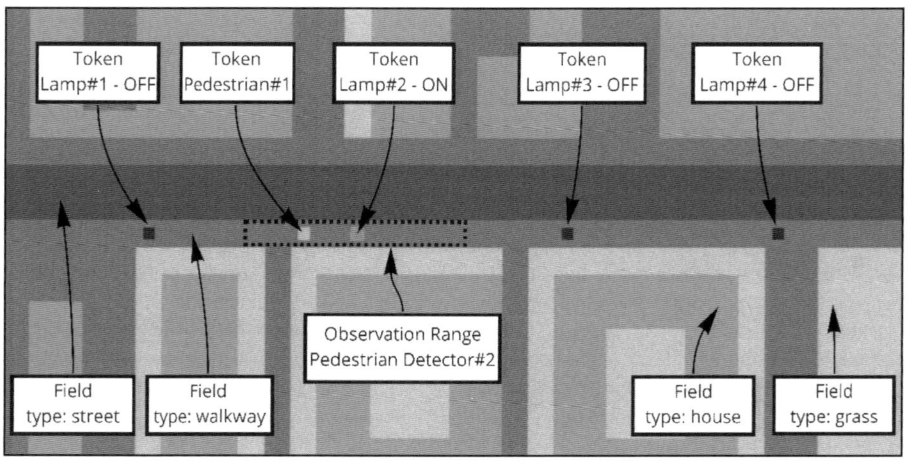

Figure 2. Visualization of the simulated smart city district with additional explanatory annotations.

4. APPLYING THE SMART CITY DISTRICT SIMULATOR TO IMPLEMENT PROTOTYPES

With our current implementation, we proved that the concept we developed works for creating a smart city district simulator that provides the support we were looking for. We can enact scenarios in the virtual world using scripted actors and visualize their play, hence make the city district come alive even if it does not exist yet. With this feature, we can facilitate communication with the stakeholders about the future way of living in the district, possible problems, and solutions. Human observers can observe the virtual world in a similar way to watching a film and empathize with the situation. Furthermore, we can have environmentally sensitive services that react to the virtual world. The enacted play can trigger the environmentally sensitive services, which may impact the simulated world. Of course, now everything is highly simplified and cannot keep up with on-site experiences in the real world. Nevertheless, we see a remarkable benefit and potential in the smart city district simulator as it fosters civic participation.

As discussed in Section 1, the goal is to enable users, i.e., the general public, including future citizens, to experience the possible impact of digital services (or prototypes thereof) on their future life. The emphasis here is on "experience". A precondition for "experiencing" is being able to empathize with an example situation. In our case, this refers to the simulated environment ("what will living in the smart city be like" as well as "what is the status of that environment") and the problem to be solved by the digital service. To experience the impact of the digital services, they must first understand the problem to be solved. One can tell users about the context and implications of a certain problem. When users are interacting with the simulator, they should be able to empathize more, as they also see what they are being told.

Developers, including tech-savvy citizens, can use the smart city district simulator to create environmentally sensitive solutions that react once certain criteria within an environment or states of an environment are met. In the simulated environment, such criteria and status can be brought about, visualized, and made understandable. This includes using the Gameboard Frontend to visualize the modeled city district (the fields) and its status (field types and their attributes relevant for the experience), and explaining and showing the current problems through actors (their movement and status) and potentially visualized sensors (their processing of field and actor data).

Then the digital service prototype can be presented to the users. As it is connected to the smart city district simulation, it reacts to the actors' play and the environment's status. Consider the example of the digital service prototype "EcoLight", which switches on streetlamps only when the presence of a pedestrian is detected. The smart city simulator's Gameboard Frontend and the actor scripts can be used to show scenarios where the lamps are passed only by cars, by cars and pedestrians, or only by pedestrians. "EcoLight" processes the environmental states and switches on the simulated lamps accordingly. Stakeholders can experience what it will be like to live in such a smart city district.

Furthermore, if such digital solutions offer direct interaction to users (e.g., through an app on their smartphone), they can interact with the interface based on the observable and understandable simulated environment state to solve the problem, create a new state in the simulated environment, and change the actors' play. This is opposed to using arbitrary test data, written scenarios, or stories as the origin of an interaction with a prototype. Our implementation supports actual prototypes interacting with the virtual world. One can easily prototype an environmentally sensitive service and make it come alive in our smart city district simulator before it is realized in the real world.

Moreover, after a digital solution prototype has been applied to a problem to be solved within the simulated environment, developers and users will expect change in actors' play. As we are dealing with a future smart city district and both, users and developers, must envision the "correct" change in play based on their experience and empathy with the situation. Such change could be co-created by users and developers. Through discussion and interaction, developers gain a deeper understanding of the users' needs and thoughts, and users gain a deeper understanding of the technical limitations and possibilities of the future smart city district from the developers. This co-creation process helps developers of future smart city solutions to understand today's users and potentially extrapolate into the future.

By developing the smart city district simulator, we have created a platform where a wide range of stakeholders, mainly the general public, future citizens, and developers can experience what it is like to live in a smart city. The smart city district simulator allows for easy testing of digital solutions and finding out how they work. It allows us to realize many use cases that arise while building a smart city and moving future citizens there. The smart city district simulator can be easily integrated with other services as well, due to its loosely coupled nature. As a side effect, it is easy to replace the simulation with the real world once it is available, as environmentally sensitive services – and partially control components – are decoupled from the simulated smart city district.

The capacity and scalability of our simulator is limited and at the moment, we cannot simulate a complete smart city in full scale with millions of actors, sensors, devices and services simultaneously. However, this is something that we intentionally neglected to accelerate ideation processes and prototyping. Prototypes for connected smart city solutions should be able to demonstrate in a small scale with just a few elements that do not imply relevant requirements related to capacity and scalability. The first step – and our focus – is to identify and evaluate ideas. Later, the transfer of the most promising ideas into reality is another challenge that needs to consider qualities such as scalability, performance, or security.

The presented smart city district simulator and our mock platform can, for example, be utilized in hackathon events to provide the participants with an environment facilitating prototypes for connected smart city solution innovations. Due to containerization of the components we developed, one can easily set up a new instance in significantly less than one day. Given that the participants have access to proper introduction material (e.g., documentation) and the source code of the components we developed, they are able to reuse many elements and make their own prototype come alive in less than one day.

5. CONCLUSION AND OUTLOOK

In this paper, we presented a software simulator for a smart city district. As the real city district is currently under construction, we needed an alternative way to evaluate new digital services already. In order to simulate the future digital ecosystem, we created a mock platform first with some basic functionality in order to have a technical environment for running different digital services. Furthermore, we developed a simulator that is able to simulate different kinds of entities, such as actuators and sensors, people, cars, and more. In this technical environment, we are currently testing different use cases and observing whether our digital services will be able to support citizens in the future smart city district, which is currently under construction. However, with our solution, we are already able to get first insights into the digitalization of the smart city district, the implications regarding climate-neutral behavior, and the question of how a digital ecosystem can support future stakeholders of the smart city district. Prototypical solutions can be developed in less than one day with our simulation environment.

As the current representation (i.e., the graphical user interface) is very simple, one of the next steps will be to enhance our implementation of the world visualization component. We plan to find more adequate representations of the different entities and make the interactions and simulations more adequate and easier to follow. Furthermore, we want to derive more use cases in order to be able to evaluate more digital services. As one of our main project goals is to address climate friendliness, our digital services should be checked in terms of how well they can provide support in this direction. This means that the identified use cases need to be implemented and then simulated. The results from the simulation will help us in the future development of the digital services and the platform.

ACKNOWLEDGMENT

The research described in this paper was performed in the EnStadt:Pfaff project (grant no. 03SBE112D and 03SBE112G) of the German Federal Ministry for Economic Affairs and Climate Action (BMWK) and the Federal Ministry of Education and Research (BMBF). We thank Sonnhild Namingha for proofreading.

REFERENCES

Duet, https://www.digitalurbantwins.com/, last accessed 22/04/20

El Hendy, M.; Miniaoui, S.; Fakhry, H. Towards strategic information & communication technology (ICT) framework for smart cities decision-makers. In Proceedings of the 2015 2nd Asia-Pacific World Congress on Computer Science and Engineering (APWC on CSE), Nadi, Fiji, 2–4 December 2015; pp. 1–7, doi:10.1109/apwccse.2015.7476218.

Elberzhager, F. (1); Mennig, P.; Stüpfert, P., On the road towards a smart Urban district supported by a mock platform, Connected Smart Cities 2021, pp. 138-142

Elberzhager, F. (2); Mennig, P.; Polst, S.; Scherr, S.; Stüpfert, P. Towards a Digital Ecosystem for a Smart City District: Procedure, Results, and Lessons Learned. Smart Cities 2021, 4, 686-716. https://doi.org/10.3390/smartcities4020035

Fuller, A., Fan, Z., Day, C. and Barlow, C., Digital Twin: Enabling Technologies, Challenges and Open Research, in IEEE Access, vol. 8, pp. 108952-108971, 2020, doi: 10.1109/ACCESS.2020.2998358

Lea, R.; Smart Cities: An Overview of the Technology Trends Driving Smart Cities, IEEE, available: https://www.ieee.org/content/dam/ieee-org/ieee/web/org/about/corporate/ieee-industry-advisory-board/ieee-smart-cities-trend-paper-2017.pdf

Neirotti, P.; De Marco, A.; Cagliano, A.C.; Mangano, G.; Scorrano, F. Current trends in Smart City initiatives: Some stylised facts. Cities 2014, 38, 25–36, doi:10.1016/j.cities.2013.12.010.

Santana, E. F. Z., Chaves, A. P., Gerosa, M. A., Kon, F., Milojicic, D. S.; Software platforms for smart cities: Concepts, requirements, challenges, and a unified reference architecture, ACM Comput. Surv. 50 (6) (Nov. 2017). https://doi.org/10.1145/3124391

ADVANCED DATA PROCESSING METHODS IN AN INTELLIGENT HEALTH GATEWAY

Mezui Eya'a Guy Lysmos and Mostafa Hanoune
Dept. of Computer Science, University Hassan II of Casablanca
Faculty of the Sciences Ben M'Sik Av Driss El Harti B.P 7955, Sidi Othmane, Casablanca, Morocco

ABSTRACT

In this article, we introduce advanced data processing methods in an intelligent gateway. These methods are techniques for optimizing, in a first stage, the storage space of the data of the system coming from the sensors in real time and, in a second stage, the bandwidth of the network for the transfer of the data from the local to the cloud or the remote server. Among these methods, we have first, centralized data processing that uses cyclical supervision at each detected data stream. This supervision is carried out thanks to a controller agent, which filters and segments the data according to their nature, their size and their sensitivity over regular time intervals. Second, random data processing, which consists of randomly processing the data sent by the sensors when the behavior of the compression node is stable. Third, dynamic targeted data processing that allows you to dynamically choose which node to query. During this approach, we used global variables to determine the limits of the volumes of data stored during a given period, to control the stopping and the resuming of data transfer. Finally, a comparative study of these methods has been highlighted to highlight the performance and efficiency of each.

KEYWORDS

Internet of Things, Healthcare, Data Processing, Data Compression, Smart Gateway, Lossless Algorithms.

1. INTRODUCTION

Nowadays, the volume of data generated by healthcare sensors and devices is growing exponentially, which is why healthcare IoT solutions must include a data processing strategy to properly manage large volumes of data (Dash, S & Shakyawar, 2019). This is the case of our intelligent gateway which has the ability to locally integrate an advanced information processing system to take corrective measures for storing and transmitting data (Mezui Eya'a & Hanoune, 2020). On the other hand, guarantee data integrity and optimize bandwidth.

In this article, we will present the various optimal data processing techniques in terms of reconnaissance, analysis of local storage and transmission of data to the cloud or the remote server.

The remainder of the article is organized as follows: Section 2 illustrates the sources of inspiration for this work that we have taken as references; Section 3 presents the overall architecture of the information system of our gateway; Section 4 explains the various advanced data processing methods; Section 5 reports the results obtained in our evaluation campaign and the comparison of the performance of the results on the real scenario; And finally section 6 which concludes the document with some future remarks.

2. RELATED WORKS

During this research work, we had the opportunity to approach several projects related to our work. We present them below according to the order of use in our project:

2.1 Distribution and Priority of Data to be Processed

We were inspired by the work of Roger Young, Sheila Fallon and Paul Jacob to find out how to distribute the processing of data according to their sensitivity. They created three types of data streams and the third one was considered the most urgent data that needs to be processed locally at all times. The first and second represented data that could be processed locally, but not with high demand on low latency. However, when CPU utilization exceeded the specified threshold, calculations that occurred on data streams 1 and 2 were pushed to the cloud.

2.2 Data Compression Mechanisms

This was our old work. The first is "the implementation of a hybrid data compression system in an intelligent E-Health gateway for medical monitoring applications" (Mezui Eya'a & Hanoune, 2020, P.578-584). The latter allowed us to distribute the data according to their original format. The second is "Data Compression mechanisms in an intelligent E-Health gateway for medical monitoring applications", to integrate data compression techniques (Cao et al 2012. P.365 – 376.).

2.3 Using Global Variables

The work of (Cao et al, 2012) in "Dynamic Control of Data Streaming and Processing in a Virtualized Environment" allowed us to use predefined global variables to control the transfer and the volume of data during a given session.

2.4 Centralized and Distributed Data Processing

(Krishnan, K, 2013) research on "data warehousing in the era of Big Data", has allowed us to use two fundamental styles of data processing and which are accepted as de facto standards (data processing centralized and distributed processing).

2.5 Random Data Processing

The solution of (Wei et al, 2018, P.347-364) in "A Two-Stage Data Processing Algorithm to Generate Random Sample Partitions for Big Data Analysis", allowed us to implement the random data processing technique. They present the processing of file blocks and a large data set distributed as random samples for big data analysis.

2.6 Dynamic Data Processing

The last was by (Chena et al, 2021) in "Service-Oriented Data Processing for Dynamic Schema" presented a new design of service-oriented data processing for dynamic schema to meet the need to bind to data storage, such as simulation data, measurement data, formulation data, component data and process data. We were inspired by this work to set up our method of dynamic data processing.

3. THE OVERALL ARCHITECTURE OF THE INFORMATION SYSTEM

3.1 Architecture of the Smart Gateway for Health

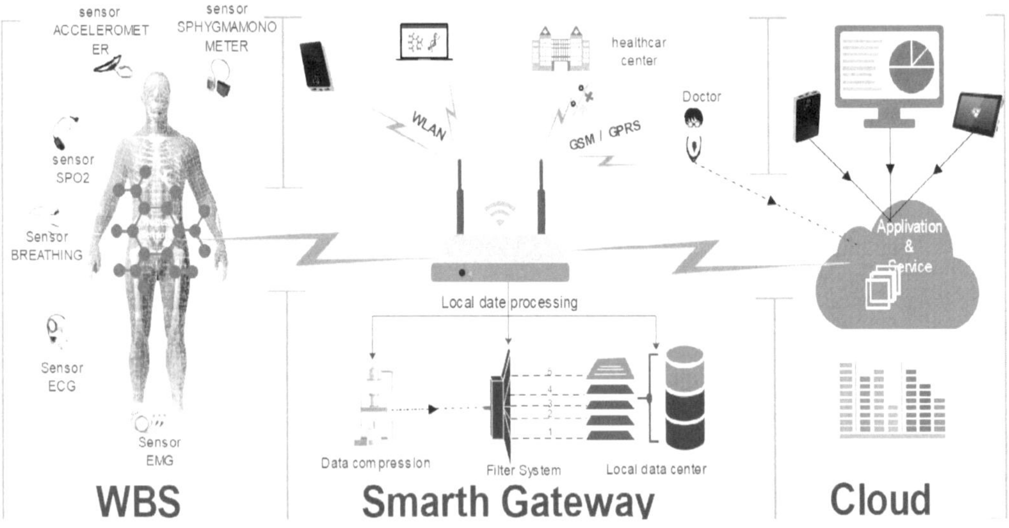

Figure 1. Architecture of the smart gateway for health

In Figure 1, the first part of the architecture is characterized by a biomedical sensor node with several physical devices. The second part of the architecture is a gateway that ensures the transmission of data from the sensor node to the remote or cloud server. However, if the gateway does not work properly or a bottleneck occurs, the whole system will be affected. The third part of the architecture is characterized by its backend. First, it is composed of a cloud server to store, process and serve data. Secondly, several services which differ according to the technologies of the system used. These services are responsible for representing the data in real time for the various analyzes and the medical follow-up by the doctor.

3.2 Data Source Recognition and Classification System

The data stream is subject to an efficient system of recognition and classification of data sources in relation to their original format. It is managed by a controller agent called a data flow analyzer. The agent analyzes the data and its formats by in-depth research on several existing data models. However, it does the comparison between the new data model and the existing models to establish the identity of the document.

4. PRESENTATION OF ADVANCED DATA PROCESSING

4.1 Centralized Data Processing

Cyclic data monitoring is carried out at each data flow detected, thanks to a controller agent, which filters and segments the data according to their nature, size and sensitivity over regular time intervals.

The first line of investigative research was to decrease the number of data sent as the behavior of the compression node is stable. This method is inspired by the method used by Trickle in the RPL protocol which decreases the number of routing messages as the routing becomes stable (Levis, P & Clausen, T.H, 2011). In addition, the data coming from the compression node is transmitted to the local processing unit called "CENTRAL CONTAINER". This data is managed by a central controller, i.e. a custom program consisting of a Thread-Local Storage (TLS) storage function. However, to properly evaluate the pattern of this dataset, we calculated the data reception frequency at a precise time interval of 500ms.

$$\text{F= Frequency} \qquad \text{with} \qquad F = \frac{received\ data\ size}{total\ obtained\ data\ size}$$

Also, if there is no missing data and no variance in the delay, a single peak is obtained for all data received at a sampling rate of 500 Ms. This is the ideal or stable situation for our compression node.

The total average size of the data obtained during our tests is 101750 bytes and the frequencies are rounded to the nearest thousandth. See the treatment method evaluation table below.

Table 1. Evaluation table of the treatment method

Number of sensors nodes connected	1	2	3
Data size (bytes)	17470	36540	47740
Frequency	0.172	0,359	0,469
Percentage (%)	17.2	35.9	46.9

This approach has two drawbacks: The first is the processing time which increases linearly with the number of nodes present in the WBAN network. It can be costly in terms of resources if the data reception frequency is too high. The second is the heavy reliance of bundled information processing on the stability of the compression node. However, as long as the measurements received from the sensors do not all have a constant value norm, the compression node cannot be considered stable to begin the data storage and transfer processing. If one of the sensors breaks down, the entire treatment procedure will be considered faulty.

4.2 Random Data Processing

A second line of research was to randomly process the data received from the sensors while the behavior of the compression node is stable. This method makes it possible to merge the data transmitted to the local processing unit according to their nature and their sources. This is done by a processor called "*ExecuteStreamCommand*" which uses a controller agent, i.e., a custom instance, to transform the entire data set into a single data block of limited size (Young et al., 2018). Moreover, we do not need to optimize the location of the data.

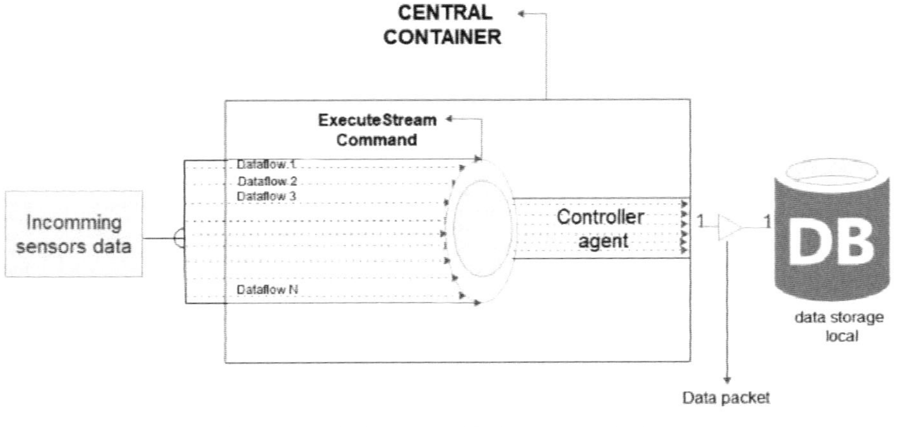

Figure 2. Evaluation table of the treatment method

In this process, data processing was performed in two steps, to convert the large dataset into a random sample partition. The first was not only to sequentially fragment the large data set into non-overlapping subsets of data, but also to distribute these subsets in the form of data block files for storage. The second step was to take a random sample from each subset without replacement to form a new subset stored as a data block file to be transferred to the cloud or remote server. This step is repeated until all data records in all subsets are used. The disadvantage of this method is that the instances are chosen randomly from the set of service instances located in the gateway.

This will create a problem of data processing priority. Furthermore, the bandwidth estimate of a random signal varies from one estimate to another each time a new data set is used (Hossain et al, 2020, V.20).

4.3 Dynamic Data Processing

This approach consists of dynamically choosing which node to query in order to improve data processing frequency and reduce local storage space. However, the gateway cannot know beforehand if the behavior of the compression node is stable before asking it. Thus, if a node is temporarily unstable it may periodically require a large gain of information if the gateway chooses. This may cause the gateway to request more regularly when the data gain was only temporary (Young et al, 2018). To overcome this problem, we used global variables (Krishnan, K, 2013).

The global variables Smax and Smin which are respectively the upper and lower values predefined to determine the limits of the volume of data stored during a given period. They allow you to control the pause and resume of data transfers. That is, when the volume of storage data reaches its upper limit, data transfer is stopped and when this volume reaches the lower limit, transfer is resumed.

The global variable Tmax is the predefined upper value for determining the size of packets that are sent. That is, if the size of the packet sent is greater than Tmax then the packet will be segmented into packets smaller than Tmax. This technique regulates the rate of data transfer in the network to optimize bandwidth.

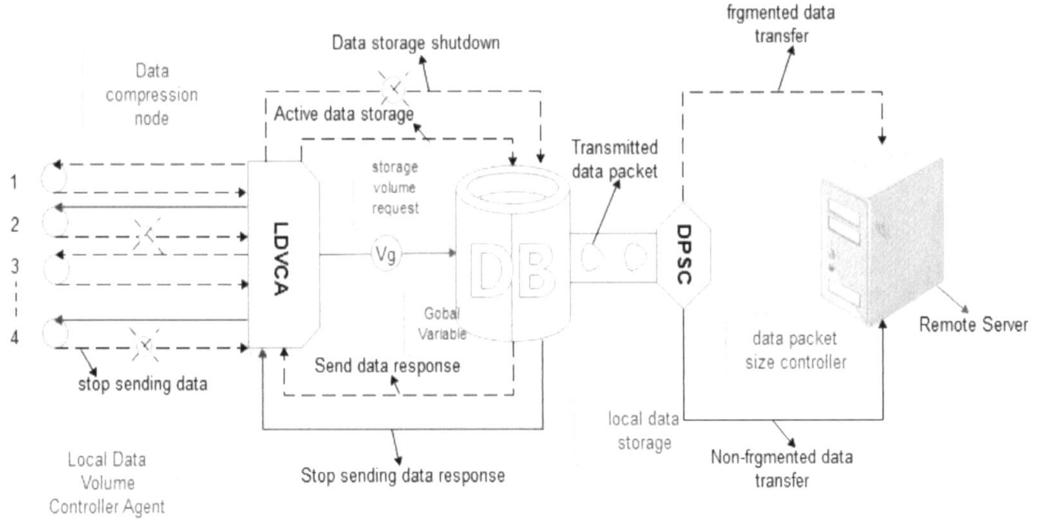

Figure 3. Dynamic data processing

In addition, we have implemented the asynchronous data transfer model to determine the start and end value of the transfer. A start value is designated as 0 and a stop value is detected when the threshold value (Smax) is reached. We have also defined a data transfer state to show that data processing is being carried out. And the value of this state is 1.

5. COMPARATIVE STUDY OF TREATMENT METHODS

In this section, we make comparisons between the different data processing techniques in our smart gateway to evaluate the effectiveness of each method over a 500ms time interval. See table below.

5.1 Table of Search Results

Table 2. Centralized Data Processing Performance Results

Number of sensors nodes connected	1	2	3
Volume of data processed (bytes)	17470	36540	47740
Data processing time (ms)	225	315	405
Data volume stored locally (bytes)	17470	36540	47740

Table 3. Random Data Processing Performance Results

Number of sensors nodes connected	1	2	3
Volume of data processed (bytes)	75360	163013	284220
Data processing time (ms)	197	260	380
Data volume stored locally (bytes)	75010	162633	283838

Table 4. Dynamic Data Processing Performance Results

Number of sensors nodes connected	1	2	3
Volume of data processed (bytes)	84220	172220	261225
Data processing time (ms)	325	405	500
Data volume stored locally (bytes)	83200	171197	260198

5.2 Analysis of Table Results

According to the table of results below, we can notice at first that the volume of data processing for the Centralized method is lower (47740 bytes) compared to the random method and the dynamic method. In addition, there is no data loss when processing and transferring data to the cloud or remote server. These results are explained by the behavior of the data compression node, which has a filter system that is very sensitive to the stability of the information coming from the sensors.

Secondly, the dynamic method has not only a high volume of processed data (261225 bytes) compared to the other two, but also, it takes more time (500ms) and has a slight loss of information (260198 bytes stored / 261225 bytes processed) during its processing and data transfer to the cloud.

Finally, in a third time, the random method takes less time to process all the data received (380 MS) compared to other methods. It has a high loss of information during its processing and transfer to the cloud.

5.3 Highlighting Performance

Table 3. Table of Advantages and Disadvantages

Data processing methods	Advantages	Disadvantages
Centralized data processing	✓ No data loss	✓ Volume of data to be processed is small. ✓ Data processing time is long.
Random data processing	• Data processing time is fast. • Volume of data to be processed is medium.	• A slight loss of data.
Dynamic targeted treatment	❖ Volume of data to be processed is large.	❖ Slight loss of data. ❖ Data processing time is long.

6. CONCLUSION AND PERSPECTIVE

In this work, we propose a new approach to data processing in a smart gateway. The first technique is based on centralized data processing which reduces the amount of data sent to the local processing unit called CENTRAL CONTAINER. The second technique is to randomly process the data sent when the behavior of the compression node is stable. Finally, dynamic targeted processing, which consists of dynamically choosing which node to query in order to improve the data processing rate. In addition, a comparative study of the processing methods allowed us to highlight the performance of each over a 500ms interval. For the centralized and random methods, the volume of data processing is not high and moreover, there is no data loss. Whereas for the dynamic method, the data processing volume is high and with some data loss.

REFERENCES

Cao, J., Zhang, W. and Tan, W. (2012). Dynamic Control of Data Streaming and Processing in a Virtualized Environment. *In IEEE Transactions on Automation Science and Engineering,* volume 9, page(s): 365 – 376.

Chena, M., Zhoua, H., Fan, Z., Wang,Y., Hong, D. and Dong, Q. (2021). Service-Oriented Data Processing for Dynamic Schema. *25th International Conference on Knowledge-Based and Intelligent Information & Engineering Systems*. Procedia Computer Science 192 (2021) 3856–3864.

Dash, S., Shakyawar, S., Sharma, M. and Kaushik, S. (19 June 2019). Big data in healthcare: management, analysis and future prospects. *Journal of Big Data,* volume 6, Article number: 54.

Edwards, R. (1994). *Processing of Random Data.* Springer, Boston, MA, Chemical Engineering Department Case Western Reserve University Cleveland, USA.

Hossain, T., Ahad, M. and Inoue, S. (2020). A Method for Sensor-Based Activity Recognition in Missing Data Scenario. *Sensors,* volume 20, Issue 14.

Krishnan, K. (2013). *Data Warehousing in the Age of Big Data.* Morgan Kaufmann Publishers, San Francisco, USA.

Levis, P, Clausen, T.H.; Gnawali (2011). The Trickle Algorithm; RFC 6206; IETF Secretariat: Fremont, CA, USA.

Lysmos, M. & Hanoune, M. (2020). Data Compression mechanisms in an intelligent E-Health gateway for medical monitoring applications. *By Procedia Computer Science Journal*, volume 175, Pages 578-584.

Lysmos, M. and Hanoune, M. (2020). Hybrid Data Compression System in Smart E-Health Gateway for Medical Monitoring Applications. *By SSRG - IJCSE Journal,* volume 7, Issue 1.

Rahmani, A.-M., Thanigaivelan, N., Gia, T., and Granado, J. (2015). Smart e-Health Gateway: Bringing Intelligence to Internet-of-Things Based Ubiquitous Healthcare Systems. *12th Annual IEEE Consumer. Communications and Networking Conference (CCNC)*, At USA, Volume: 826-834.

Wan, J., Al-awlaki, M., Li, M., O'Grady, M., Gu, X., Wang, J. & Cao, N. (2018). Wearable IoT enabled real-time health monitoring system. *EURASIP Journal on Wireless Communications and Networking.* Volume 2018, Article number: 298.

Wei, C., Salloum, S., Emara, T., Zhang, X., Huang, J., He, Y. (2018). *A Two-Stage Data Processing Algorithm to Generate Random Sample Partitions for Big Data Analysis.* Cloud Computing – CLOUD 2018, P.347-364.

Young, R., Fallon, S. and Jacob, P. (2018). Dynamic Collaboration of Centralized & Edge Processing for Coordinated Data Management in an IoT Paradigm. *IEEE 32nd International Conference on Advanced Information Networking and Applications (AINA).* Krakow, Poland. Electronic ISSN: 2332-5658.

A MEMETIC ALGORITHM FOR OPTIMIZING THE ASSIGNMENT OF TABLES ON RELATIONAL DATABASE STORAGE UNITS

Arturo Lucas, Rony Cueva and Manuel Tupia
Pontificia Universidad Católica del Perú
Avenida Universitaria 1801, San Miguel, Lima, Peru

ABSTRACT

Optimizing the storage of large volumes of information in relational databases has become an increasingly common need in modern organizations. Database management systems and load balancers aim to accomplish this and employ often inefficient or empirical table mapping protocols. Artificial Intelligence, through bio-inspired algorithms, has come to the aid of this optimization process and the present paper seeks to propose a memetic algorithm to perform the best allocations to tables in relational database storage units, seeking best configurations and accelerating the access to such data. This paper proposes the use of a Memetic Algorithm in the table assignment problem that works on two levels. First, optimizing the result of the best local search algorithm found in the literature, such as the Taboo Search Algorithm; and, secondly, the minimization of exchange processes between tables was achieved, as no other algorithm in the reviewed literature presents.

KEYWORDS

Memetic Algorithm, Assignment Problem, Tables, Relational Databases.

1. INTRODUCTION

Currently, data has a great value for organizations, it is for this reason that companies have sought ways to store it safely for later use. This objective has been achieved thanks to the creation of relational database systems which allow to store, organize and access data efficiently, which is why today, databases are considered as the main source to manage a company (Kamatkar *et al.*, 2018). However, due to the rapid development of information technologies, more and more information systems generate enormous amounts of data, making the task of organizing, storing and accessing them quickly highly challenging (Matalqa and Mustafa, 2016) and, since relational databases play a vital role in many information systems, the performance of these same systems depends directly on the performance of the database (Wijesiriwardana and Firdhous, 2019).

Every relational database system has the function of "reading" or "writing" data from or to secondary storage units and due to the inherent characteristics of these devices, compared to other resources, disk input/output is often the slowest resource in the database system. It is for this reason that it is essential to investigate how the design and configuration of the storage system can be optimized in order to achieve high database performance (Kamatkar *et al.*, 2018). Precisely in this context, table assignment strategy is proposed, which seeks to store the most "appropriate" database objects (tables, indexes, among others) in the most "appropriate" secondary storage units under a certain criteria, with the goal of improving database system performance by optimizing disk input/output (Wu, Huang and Chang, 2019).

However, many of the optimization tools offered by modern database systems do not support table assignment as an optimization method, leaving this task to be done manually by database administrators, who are usually based on their past experience or just a few variables to take a decision (Yoon et al., 2015).

At present and according to the state of the art review, the assignment problem is solved through a series of series methods proposed for the optimization of the object allocation to storage units, such as, for example, using different variations of *dynamic programming algorithms* (Canim *et al.*, 2009; Shi *et al.*, 2013) These methods are called *heuristics* and have the limitation that many of them have been designed for a specific problem without the possibility of generalization or application to similar problems (Martí, 2003). On the other hand, there is the use of empirical data prioritization methods and iterative algorithms (Lin *et al.*, 2011; Ou *et al.*, 2014; Wu, Huang and Chang, 2019), which, although they manage to have reasonable results (Lin *et al.*, 2011) they are based on calculations created by the authors themselves specifically for the cases raise in their studies.

Finally, we can find meta heuristic GRASP algorithm as in (Cueva and Tupia, 2008) , this method belongs to the category of metaheuristic algorithms, which are high-level mechanisms that can provide appropriate solutions to optimization problems using less computational effort than methods based on simple calculations or heuristics (Du and Swamy, 2016) , however, the GRASP algorithm is an already consolidated method, which has proven its effectiveness on a large collection of problems (Martí, 2003), including the table assignment problem. This does not happen with other metaheuristic algorithms such as, for example, the Memetic Algorithm, which, although it has been used successfully in problems of similar complexity (Neri *et al.*, 2012), was not directly applied to the problem of assigning tables to storage units. In summary, despite the fact that data allocation has been extensively studied in the literature, in most cases methods have been used that can provide results that are not optimal for the allocation of tables to storage units, since these are based on heuristics and simple calculations.

In that sense, what is sought in this paper is to implement a new proposal that allows optimizing the allocation of tables to storage units, this proposal is based on the use of a memetic algorithm, which has shown to have good results in tasks optimization of similar complexity (Neri *et al.*, 2012) , belongs to a class of high-level algorithms that can provide appropriate solutions to optimization problems using less computational effort than the methods proposed in the literature, and furthermore it has not been directly applied in the table assignment task. The paper is organized as follows: in section 1 we are presenting the introduction; section 2 deals with the problem to be solved; section 3 presents the proposed memetic algorithm; section 4 shows the numerical experimentation performed and section 5 ends with the conclusions of the research.

The main benefits of applying this algorithm in optimizing the allocation of tables to storage units are:

- It allows you to optimize the performance of relational database management systems, and thereby improve the performance of the information systems that use them.
- It supports database administrators in the task of assigning tables, making it less tedious and prone to errors, since it would be done automatically.
- It allows companies to better harness the potential of their current hardware, reducing unnecessary spending on hardware upgrades.

2. PROBLEM DEFINITION

Now, developing a bio-inspired algorithm not applied so far to solve the problem of table assignment in relational databases is motivated, on the one hand, to investigate the possibility of adapting this type of algorithm to optimization problems with or without multi-objective and, on the other hand, as a tool for improving algorithms that have already reached local optimal solutions for assignment and satisfiability problems (SAT).The table assignment task can be seen as a generalized assignment problem (GAP), this problem consists of minimizing the cost of assigning $n > 0$ jobs to $m > 0$ agents, such that each job is assigned to exactly one agent, subject to an available capacity of each agent (Kundakcioglu, 2009).

In the case of assigning tables to storage units, the "jobs" are the database tables, which have a certain size and frequency of use, and the "agents" are the storage units, which have a certain capacity to host tables and a speed or performance defined by the database administrator.

Likewise, since the table allocation process is carried out with the aim of adequately distributing the tables of a database in the available storage devices, should be ensured that: (i) the highest priority tables are deposited on the disks of higher performance and (ii) does not overload the disks, causing their performance to decrease. The proposed objective function must seek to meet these two requirements to have an optimal configuration of tables and disks.

Therefore, what is sought is to maximize the total benefit "***B***" of assigning all the tables to the available storage devices, understanding as "total benefit" the score obtained thanks to the distribution made. A higher total benefit translates into better database system performance. In this sense, the objective function is expressed as follows:

$$F = maximize(\sum_{i=1}^{n} B_{ij,S_i})$$

Where:

- n is the total number of tables.
- $B_{i,j}$ is the benefit of assigning table i to storage device j.
- S is a list of n elements where each index identifies a table and each element represents the storage unit to which said table was assigned.
- S_i represents the identifier of the storage unit in which the table i has been allocated.

The calculation of the expected benefit "$B_{i,j}$" of assigning a table i to a disk j is expressed as follows:

$$B_{i,j} = TablePriorScore^2{}_i * (DiscPerf_j * Penal_j)$$

Where:

- ***TablePriorScore$_i$*** is the total table prioritization score, that is, the score that is assigned to a table to determine its level of importance with respect to the other tables that you want to distribute in the storage system. This score is calculated as follows:

$$TablePriorScore_i = (CoefSize_i * TableSize_i) + (CoefFreq_i * TableFreq_i)$$

Where:

- ***CoefSize$_i$*** is the coefficient of importance of the size of table i.
- ***CoefFreq$_i$*** is the importance coefficient of the frequency of use of table i.

- ***DiscPerf$_j$*** represents the performance of the disk to which a certain table is assigned.
- ***Penal$_j$*** represents the penalty imposed on a given storage device j and is calculated as follows:

$$Penal_j = 1 - (\frac{DiscLoad_j}{TotalLoad})$$

Where:

- ***DiscLoad$_j$*** represents the current load that the disk "manages" in terms of frequency of use, this is calculated as the sum of the frequencies of use of the tables assigned to the disk.
- ***TotalLoad*** represents the total load that must be distributed among the different disks of the storage system, this is calculated as the sum of the frequencies of use of all the tables that are wanted to assign.

It is worth mentioning that since the ranges of existence of the variables used are between 0 and 1 for all cases, since a normalization process was applied to avoid that the great differences between these can negatively affect the calculations to be carried out in the objective function.

3. MEMETIC ALGORITHM

In this paper, the integration between two components is carried out: the first is called evolutionary, and is characterized by maintaining a population of agents with a constant size, which evolves by applying operations such as crossover, mutation and selection. The second component is that of "local search", which is the most distinctive feature of the memetic algorithm, since it is a method that allows further exploitation of the solutions found in the evolutionary phase (Neri *et al.*, 2012). This method consists of maintaining a "current" solution and exploring its "neighbors" for better quality solutions. Eventually one of them becomes better than the "current" solution and becomes the new "current" solution, with which the process is repeated until some termination criterion is met (Onwubolu and Babu, 2004). This component is used in two ways: first, a local search is applied to the initial population and then a local search is applied to an amount "N" of agents selected by the roulette method. This process is carried out every "M" generation, since it allows better control over when and on which agents to apply the local search process, which is considered useful to be able to find a balance between the behavior of the evolutionary algorithm and the local search algorithm. **Algorithm 1** shows a pseudocode of the memetic algorithm designed.

Algorithm 1 Memetic Algorithm

```
Initialize: Generate an initial population
Evaluate individuals in the population
Apply local search over the population
Select best solution in the population
While Stopping conditions are not satisfied do:
    Evolve new population using uniform crossover
    Apply random mutation over the offspring
    Evaluate individuals in the offspring population
    If Generation Nth was reached:
        Select M agents from offspring
        For each agent:
            Apply local search over the selected agent
    Apply elitist selection
    Update best solution
Return best solution
```

The choice of a suitable local search algorithm for the problem of assigning tables to storage units is carried out through an intensive process of tests over three algorithms selected considering the research by P. Thainiam entitled "The effects of memes on memetic algorithms for solving quadratic assignment problem" and the book by Ferrante Neri and others entitled "Handbook of Memetic Algorithms", in which various "sophisticated" and "popular" local search algorithms are proposed.

The reasons for applying an intensive testing process before making a decision are: (i) to make sure that the best performing local search algorithm is chosen to work together with the evolutionary algorithm and thus have a sufficiently supported implementation of the memetic algorithm, (ii) because there is no reference point to ensure that, in the case of the assignment problem, some local search method is better than another, and (iii) because it is known that one of the most important parts of memetic algorithms is local search, since it is the characteristic that differentiates them from typical evolutionary algorithms (Thainiam, 2019), therefore, special attention is made to both its design and its implementation and testing.

The algorithms evaluated are: (i) Simulated Annealing Algorithm, a probabilistic method that is inspired by thermodynamics and has the advantage that it can avoid local optima (Thainiam, 2019). (ii) Iterated Local Search Algorithm, a method that builds a sequence of solutions by iteratively applying a local search algorithm and a perturbation strategy (Thainiam, 2019). (iii) Tabu Search Algorithm, an algorithm that uses memory to store the "moves" or actions performed previously, which allows to guide searches towards more promising environments.

Table 1 below shows the results obtained in the tests performed on each of the local search algorithms evaluated.

Table 1. Test results made on each local Search algorithm

Nr.	Instance	TS		ILS		SA	
		Best	**Average**	**Best**	**Average**	**Best**	**Average**
1	20-5	4.93	4.91	4.72	4.64	4.64	4.50
2	30-10	4.64	4.61	4.98	4.89	4.47	4.33
3	40-10	10.20	10.17	9.01	8.75	8.09	7.63
4	80-20	22.97	22.94	19.83	19.56	19.22	18.60
5	100-20	24.05	24.01	19.61	19.30	19.97	19.52
6	100-25	25.47	25.42	18.80	18.45	19.06	18.05
7	120-40	29.29	29.24	26.27	25.77	24.91	24.56
8	150-30	30.52	30.47	27.07	26.75	25.29	24.83
9	150-50	36.69	36.65	29.21	28.85	28.56	27.80
10	160-40	39.43	39.39	34.40	33.58	31.11	30.34
11	165-55	41.04	41.01	36.34	35.97	33.93	33.45
12	200-40	47.18	47.13	38.71	38.11	38.18	37.62
13	225-45	56.03	55.94	42.78	42.06	47.43	46.82
14	240-60	60.49	60.37	49.42	48.83	48.26	46.08
15	250-50	69.95	69.88	56.95	55.86	53.93	53.40
Net Average		**33.52**	**33.48**	**27.87**	**27.42**	**27.14**	**26.50**

Conclusions and considerations for the set of tests carried out:

- The data used for the tests was randomly generated using an algorithm developed by the authors, these data are grouped into "Instances".
- Each "Instance" refers to the randomly generated data set on which the tests are performed. In the table, the name of each instance has two numbers separated by hyphens (50-10), the first of which refers to the number of simulated tables and the second to the number of simulated disks.
- Each result column in the table has titles that refer to the algorithm being tested:
    - TS: Tabu Search Algorithm
    - ILS: Iterated Local Search Algorithm
    - SA: Simulated Annealing Algorithm
- Each algorithm is executed ten times with each of the instances, for this reason two columns of results are shown, which are:
    - Best: it is the best result obtained in the ten repetitions
    - Average: it is the average of all the results obtained in each repetition
- The best performance recorded is that corresponding to the Tabu Search Algorithm; therefore, this algorithm is chosen to be used as part of the memetic algorithm.
- The average final result of all the tested local search algorithms increases considerably when applied in conjunction with the evolutionary algorithm. This shows that the strategy used by the memetic algorithm when combining these optimization methods is effective and provides a substantial improvement in the final results.

4. EXPERIMENTAL RESULTS

Once the Memetic Algorithm is defined, an experimentation process is carried out in order to verify that it provides good results and can be successfully applied in the table assignment task. To achieve this objective, the memetic algorithm designed in this paper will be compared with the GRASP algorithm proposed in the most relevant research found in the state of the art regarding the optimization of the allocation of tables to storage units. This research is entitled "Double relaxation - GRASP algorithm for solve the table assignment problem on database store devices" and is proposed by the authors R. Cueva and M. Tupia.

In order to compare both algorithms under equal conditions, we proceed to use those variables that give them their best performance for a given problem. That said, Table 2 shows the values of the variables used in the Memetic Algorithm, Table 3 shows the same for the GRASP Algorithm.

Table 2. Variables used by the Memetic Algorithm

Evolutive Algorithm variables	
Variable	**Value**
Maximum number of iterations	800
Maximum number of generations without improvement	200
Population size	200
Crossover rate	100%
Mutation rate	5%
Mutation probability	60%
Tabu Search Algorithm variables	
Variable	**Value**
Maximum number of iterations	500
Number of neighbors	20
Number of Tabu attributes	100
Each N generations	40
Over M agents	90

Table 3. Variables used by the GRASP Algorithm

GRASP Algorithm variables	
Variable	**Value**
Maximum number of iterations	100
Alfa parameter	0.25
Beta parameter	0.25

Likewise, in order to analyze the behavior of the proposed algorithms, a data set was randomly generated with the characteristics shown in Table 4.

Table 4. Randomly generated values

Name	Number of values	Range of values
Usage frequency of tables	120	[155.0, 975.0]
Table size	120	[45.0, 1055.0]
Disc performance	40	[255.0, 1055.0]
Disc capacity	40	[59169.0, 59760.0]

Then, having this number of randomly generated values, 40 samples are also randomly selected. With each of these samples, the algorithms are executed 20 times, registering the best result, the average result and the standard deviation, as shown in Table 5. Finally, the results are compared using statistical tests (F test, Z test, two-tailed test, and one-tailed test) to reach a proper conclusion.

Table 5. Experimental results

Sample	MEMÉTICO			GRASP		
	Best	**Average**	**Std. Dev.**	**Best**	**Average**	**Std. Dev.**
1	25.8018	25.7954	0.0049	24.9402	24.9002	0.0264
2	26.9714	26.9692	0.0018	26.0858	26.0244	0.0311
3	24.8545	24.8505	0.0031	23.6070	23.5447	0.0367
4	27.8194	27.8130	0.0043	27.2038	27.1648	0.0263
5	26.0893	26.0881	0.0010	24.7509	24.7150	0.0311
6	27.4689	27.4671	0.0021	26.6503	26.5270	0.0620
7	27.9787	27.9696	0.0091	27.3226	27.2613	0.0314
8	27.0776	27.0662	0.0075	26.4658	26.4197	0.0279
9	28.8920	28.8898	0.0026	28.1936	28.1540	0.0241
10	27.2752	27.2680	0.0049	26.7089	26.6746	0.0184

11	25.9797	25.9752	0.0023	25.4211	25.3722	0.0245
12	25.0477	25.0473	0.0006	23.4316	23.3728	0.0310
13	24.6244	24.6214	0.0024	23.6342	23.6038	0.0190
14	28.1421	28.1317	0.0077	27.6135	27.5479	0.0303
15	29.7722	29.7544	0.0119	29.2304	29.1912	0.0212
16	28.5919	28.5910	0.0010	27.7759	27.7421	0.0241
17	27.7411	27.7308	0.0054	27.0467	26.9934	0.0312
18	28.1294	28.1267	0.0021	27.4734	27.3884	0.0427
19	26.6800	26.6799	0.0001	25.7729	25.7436	0.0215
20	23.0409	23.0402	0.0008	22.0082	21.9446	0.0344
21	25.9856	25.9850	0.0011	24.7276	24.6729	0.0231
22	28.2026	28.1994	0.0014	27.3393	27.2540	0.0347
23	26.7061	26.7053	0.0007	25.8463	25.7909	0.0323
24	29.2515	29.2255	0.0177	28.7481	28.7066	0.0249
25	25.8858	25.8794	0.0048	25.2668	25.2410	0.0157
26	26.6465	26.6451	0.0011	25.6750	25.6274	0.0321
27	30.5315	30.5302	0.0018	29.9825	29.9414	0.0200
28	27.8055	27.8014	0.0031	27.2093	27.1213	0.0319
29	28.0225	28.0202	0.0019	27.1772	27.1067	0.0444
30	24.9482	24.9475	0.0009	23.7707	23.6988	0.0433
31	25.1226	25.1209	0.0028	23.9378	23.9130	0.0113
32	27.0665	27.0658	0.0012	25.8188	25.7843	0.0188
33	27.0723	27.0697	0.0014	25.8207	25.7727	0.0218
34	27.7610	27.7567	0.0062	26.6609	26.6381	0.0140
35	27.2876	27.2802	0.0052	26.7556	26.6844	0.0287
36	28.1687	28.1634	0.0045	27.5515	27.4732	0.0348
37	27.7712	27.7683	0.0024	27.1980	27.1564	0.0283
38	26.0574	26.0498	0.0092	25.4462	25.3560	0.0394
39	22.3179	22.3178	0.0001	19.7162	19.5978	0.0518
40	27.8456	27.8410	0.0026	27.0203	26.9849	0.0201
Net Average	**26.9609**	**26.9562**	**0.0036**	**26.0751**	**26.0202**	**0.0292**

5. CONCLUSION

This article proposes the use of a Memetic Algorithm in the table assignment problem, for which tests were carried out at two levels. First, the behavior of the algorithm was compared using three local search algorithms, concluding that the Taboo Search Algorithm is the most appropriate to use for the present problem. Second, the performance of the algorithm was compared against the most relevant proposal found in the state of the art, deriving, after analyzing the results through statistical tests, that the results provided by the Memetic Algorithm are superior to the results of the GRASP algorithm.

On the other hand, it is concluded that the objective of implementing a memetic algorithm to optimize the assignment of tables to storage units could be achieved, with which a solution is proposed that allows covering the problem of assigning tables and, due to which is an algorithm that was not previously applied to this specific problem, it is expected to be a contribution to the scientific community and to research related to database optimization.

Regarding the applicability of the design of the presented algorithm, since it is built based on a generalized assignment problem, it can be extended to be applied in the allocation of other database resources such as indexes and materialized views, which might have their own considerations and would help further improve the performance of the database system. Also, the Memetic Algorithm can be integrated as part of a business information system or as an extension of a database management system to be used directly by its administrators.

REFERENCES

Canim, M. *et al*, 2009. An Object Placement Advisor for DB2 Using Solid State Storage, *Proc. VLDB Endow.*, 2(2), pp. 1318–1329. doi:10.14778/1687553.1687557.

Cueva, R. and Tupia, M., 2008. Double Relaxation -- GRASP Algorithm for Solve the Table Assignment Problem on Data Base Store Devices, in *2008 Fourth International Conference on Networked Computing and Advanced Information Management*, pp. 418–421. doi:10.1109/NCM.2008.186.

Du, K.-L. and Swamy, M.N.S., 2016. *Search and optimization by metaheuristics techniques and algorithms inspired by nature*. Springer International Publishing. Available at: http://dx.doi.org/10.1007/978-3-319-41192-7 (Accessed: 4 July 2020).

Kamatkar, S.J. *et al*, 2018. Database performance tuning and query optimization, *Lecture Notes in Computer Science (including subseries Lecture Notes in Artificial Intelligence and Lecture Notes in Bioinformatics)*, pp. 3–11. doi:10.1007/978-3-319-93803-5_1.

Kundakcioglu, O.E., 2009. Encyclopedia of Optimization, *Encyclopedia of Optimization* [Preprint], (January 2008). doi:10.1007/978-0-387-74759-0.

Lin, L. *et al*, 2011. Hot random off-loading: A hybrid storage system with dynamic data migration, *IEEE International Workshop on Modeling, Analysis, and Simulation of Computer and Telecommunication Systems - Proceedings*, pp. 318–325. doi:10.1109/MASCOTS.2011.41.

Martí, R., 2003. Procedimientos Metaheurísticos en Optimización Combinatoria. Facultad de Matemáticas de la Universidad de Valencia, pp. 2–60. Available at: https://www.uv.es/rmarti/paper/docs/heur1.pdf.

Matalqa, S. and Mustafa, S., 2016. The effect of horizontal database table partitioning on query performance, *International Arab Journal of Information Technology*, 13(1A), pp. 184–189.

Neri, F. *et al*, 2012. *Handbook of memetic algorithms*. Berlin, Heidelberg: Springer Berlin Heidelberg (Studies in Computational Intelligence). doi:10.1007/978-3-642-23247-3.

Onwubolu, G.C. and Babu, B., 2004. *New Optimization Techniques in Engineering Springer-Verlag Berlin Heidelberg GmbH Studies in Fuzziness and Soft Computing, Volume 141.*

Ou, J. *et al*, 2014. EDM: An endurance-aware data migration scheme for load balancing in SSD storage clusters, *Proceedings of the International Parallel and Distributed Processing Symposium, IPDPS*, pp. 787–796. doi:10.1109/IPDPS.2014.86.

Shi, H. *et al*, 2013. Optimal disk storage allocation for multitier storage system, *IEEE Transactions on Magnetics*, 49(6), pp. 2603–2609. doi:10.1109/TMAG.2013.2250936.

Thainiam, P., 2019. The Effects of Memes on Memetic Algorithms for Solving Quadratic Assignment Problem, *IEEE International Conference on Industrial Engineering and Engineering Management*, pp. 1334–1338. doi:10.1109/IEEM44572.2019.8978780.

Wijesiriwardana, C. and Firdhous, M.F.M., 2019. An Innovative Query Tuning Scheme for Large Databases, *2019 International Conference on Data Science and Engineering, ICDSE 2019*, pp. 154–159. doi:10.1109/ICDSE47409.2019.8971483.

Wu, C.-H., Huang, C.-W. and Chang, C., 2019. A data management method for databases using hybrid storage systems, *ACM SIGAPP Applied Computing Review*, 19(1), pp. 34–47. doi:10.1145/3325061.3325064.

Yoon, D.Y., Mozafari, B. and Brown, D.P., 2015. DBSeer: Pain-free database administration through workload intelligence, *Proceedings of the VLDB Endowment*, (12), pp. 2036–2039. doi:10.14778/2824032.2824130.

FRAUD DETECTION IN AUTOMOTIVE INSURANCE DOMAIN USING MACHINE LEARNING

Md Abdul Masud Rana[1] and Ahmedul Kabir[2]
[1]*Department of Information and Communication Technology, Bangladesh University of Professionals, Dhaka, Bangladesh*
[2]*Department of Information Technology, University of Dhaka, Dhaka, Bangladesh*

ABSTRACT

The insurance industry is one of the most vital aspects of modern society, the economy, and people's lives. It brings peace and security to people by offsetting the financial risks of damage and loss. Fraud in the Automotive Insurance domain illustrates a scenario in which the client obtains money by providing falsified papers, demonstrating fake accidents or economic claims for early losses. One of the biggest harmful challenges here is an interaction between policyholders and the insurance industry which creates a possible situation for fraud claims. By keeping these in mind, in this research, fraud detection in the automotive insurance domain (AID) is performed using machine learning (ML) techniques. It is a binary classification problem that utilized the recursive feature elimination (RFE) method to uncover the most influential factors for detecting fraud. The significance of each attribute is also determined. Moreover, a comparative analysis of the ML models is performed. The experimental outcomes show that the multilayer perceptron model is quite robust and outperforms the other algorithms in detecting fraud.

KEYWORDS

Fraud Detection, Machine Learning, Feature Engineering.

1. INTRODUCTION

In the current era, the automotive insurance domain (AID) is developed and is used in providing smart and optimal services for the security and protection of cars (Itri, Mohmed, Y., Mohammed, Q., & Omar, B., 2019). It is a very complex business that involves millions of dollars which increases the possibility of fraudulent activities due to the significant amount of capital (Albashrawi, 2016). Fraud in AID is the USA's priciest white-collar offense that varies from generally honest individuals twisting the facts to huge amounts of money in organized criminal organizations (Agrecha, S., Johnson, R.A., & Chawla, N.V., 2018). An automotive insurance document is a legal contract made by both an insurance provider and the holder of an automobile to offer financial assistance in the event of an automotive accident or injury. Fraud in AID illustrates a scenario in which the client obtains money by providing falsified papers to the insurance corporation by demonstrating fake accidents or financial claims for early losses (Ngai, Hu, Y., Wong, Y.H., Chen, Y., & Sun, X., 2011). Such fraudulence may be done by anyone such as drivers, policyholders, garage technicians, attorneys, policemen, insurance employees, etc. (Bodaghi & Teimourpour, B., 2018). Previously, various researchers explored fraud detection in different domains like healthcare (Gupta, Mudigonda, S.S., Baruah, P.K., & Kandala, P.K., 2021), banking sector (Taha & Malebary, S.J., 2020), and network intrusion (Lei & Ghorbani, A.A., 2012) by implementing different Machine Learning (ML) techniques. Most of the prior studies only focus on the machine learning (ML) model's performance and did not find the most influential factors which are helpful to detect fraudulent activities. However, fraud detection in the automotive insurance domain (AID) gained huge attention from the insurance enterprises and society due to their terrific loss (Wang & Xu, W., 2018). So, there is a requirement to build a fraud detection model for AID to identify the deception activities and provides assistance to the insurance industry. To fill this gap, we proposed a solution to detect fraudulent activities in AID using machine learning (ML) techniques and find the most influential features from the dataset. Previously, Feature selection in fraud detection has been performed using topic modeling (Wang & Xu, W., 2018), tree-based method (Abdallah, A., Maarof, M.A., & Zainal, A., 2016), and filter method (Yadav & Sora, M., 2021) to find the most significant attributes from the dataset which are helpful for building a better prediction technique. In this research, features subset selection is performed using the recursive feature elimination (Wrapper method) on the CIF dataset to uncover the most significant attributes to build an effective ML technique for detecting fraudulent activities in AID. It is a very robust method that only wraps those attributes which are most important and discards the unimportant factors from the dataset. Car Insurance Fraud (CIF) dataset is utilized in this research to build a robust prediction model (supervised learning) for fraud identification (Gupta S. , 2019). The feature's importance is also determined to find their scores for detecting fraud and it is helpful to rank the features for better outcomes. The rest of this article is organized accordingly. Section 2 provides a background discussion of some items of this research. Section 3 provides a detailed overview of previous research. The technological basis is explained in Section 4 which includes the proposed methodology, dataset overview, and evaluation measures for ML techniques. Furthermore, Section 5 explains the details of the experiment which is consist of the feature extraction and their importance. The ML techniques comparison is also performed here. Section 6 describes the conclusion and future work in fraudulent detection for AID.

2. BACKGROUND

This section provides an overview of the different classification algorithms, feature selection techniques and evaluation metrics relevant to this research.

Machine Learning is a data analysis technique that teaches computer systems to do what's naturally comes to people and animals: studying from experience. Machine Learning algorithms use computational strategies to "learn" records at once from the data, without counting on a predefined equation as a model. (Abdallah, A., Maarof, M.A., & Zainal, A., 2016). Two types of Machine Learning techniques are Supervised learning (which develops a predictive model based on both input and output label) and Unsupervised learning (which group and expound data based only on input data) Classification and Regression techniques are used by Supervised Machine Learning to develop models. In this research, several supervised classification algorithms are used.

Random Forest is an ensemble learning method. This can be used to solve classification or regression types of problems. Here a sample of data from the dataset is taken randomly, and based on that sample data multiple decision trees are created. The final output is a combination of the outputs of the individual trees (Li Y., Ya C., Liu W, & Li M., 2018).

Gradient Boosted Tree (GBT) is a machine learning technique for regression, classification, and other tasks that creates a forecasting model as a set of weak forecasting models. When the decision tree is used as a weak learner, the resulting algorithm is called gradient trees, which usually outweigh a random forest (Dhieb, Ghazzai, H., Besbes, H., & Massoud, Y., 2019).

A multilayer perceptron or Neural network is a set of algorithms modeled after the human brain, designed to recognize patterns. They interpret sensory data through a type of machine perception, labeling, or grouping of raw inputs. (Lei & Ghorbani, A.A., 2012).

Decision trees extract predictive information in the form of human-understandable tree rules. Decision Tree is an algorithm useful for many classification problems that can help explain the model's logic using human-readable "If. . .. Then. . ." rules (Panigrahi & Palkar, B., 2018).

Support Vector Machine (SVM) is a discrimination technique that can be applied to both regression and classification problems. The strategy of this algorithm is to find the hyperplane with the limit of maximum separation in the three-dimensional feature space. (Dong, Yu, Z., Cao, W., Shi, Y., & Ma, Q., 2020).

Recursive feature elimination (RFE) is a feature selection method that fits a model and removes the weakest feature (or features) until the specified number of features is reached (Brownlee, 2021).

3. RELATED WORK

This study is set in the broad area of fraudulent activities in the financial sector which includes automotive insurance and is based on a large variety of machine learning scientific papers on the subject. The important factors for fraud detection that play a crucial part in increasing the effectiveness of the implemented framework are also discussed here. Throughout this section, we will discuss some of the most important research findings from this area of interest. (Bhowmik, 2011) proposed a solution to identify fraud from data using data mining. They utilized the Decision tree and Naive Bayes models to assess the performance of the algorithms on the dataset. The findings of this research show that the Decision tree model is more accurate to identify the fraud in auto insurance platforms as compared to Naive Bayes. Panigrahi et al. (Panigrahi & Palkar, B., 2018) conducted research for the automobile insurance industry on their claims dataset. It is a binary classification analysis by comparing the various ML models to detect fraud using the feature selection algorithms. Results of this research show that the Random Forest (RF) model is the best one and gets the highest accuracy to identify the fraud. A forecasting model for car insurance fraud was developed by Li et al. (Li Y., Ya C., Liu W, & Li M., 2018) utilizing Principal component analysis (PCA) and Random Forest (RF). The proposed solution is functional for detecting fraud in car insurance. A drawback of the research is that it only applies the method to a small number of entries in the database. Because of this, there is potential for testing this approach on a huge number of observations. Text analysis on the text of the fraudulent claim for car insurance is performed by Wang et al. (Wang & Xu, W., 2018) using the LDA (Latent Dirichlet allocation) method. It is a novel method to compute the attributes from claims text to detect fraud and helpful to build a framework on the publicly available datasets. A deep learning method is trained on the extracted factors from LDA. The outcome of this research depicts that the applied approach outperforms traditional ML models that include SVM and RF. To discover suitable methods to define the duty of insurance drivers and detect malicious claims, Derrig et al. (Weisberg & Derrig, R.A., 1991) examined a variety of fraud aspects linked to intentional build-ups in order to establish suitable ways to express the obligation of covered drivers. They argue that circumstances irrelevant to accidents and falsification of substances should be given special consideration when defining fraudulence indicators within the definition of fraud risk factors. In addition, Artis et al. divided the fraudulence indications into three main categories: incident info, insured drivers' details, and car details (Artís, M., Ayuso, M., & Guillén, M., 2002) (Artís, M., Ayuso, M., & Guillén, M., 2002). Researchers hypothesized that the timing and location of an event had a significant impact on the likelihood of fraud occurring. As per their findings, incidents that happened at nighttime, on weekends, or within non-urban regions have a disproportionately high likelihood of being fake. Subelj et al. (Šubelj, Furlan, S., & Bajec, M., 2011) propose a method where claim information may be expressed as a network, wherein vertices indicate individuals like drivers and cars, while edges imply relationships between objects. For each characteristic, they separate it into intrinsic and relational properties, with the structural attributes showing the relationships between individuals. The IAA (iterative assessment algorithm) detects fraud cases by using the two kinds of characteristics to provide a suspicious value to each incident victim. Another algorithmic fraud detection method for car insurance firms is proposed by Dheib et al. (Dhieb, Ghazzai, H., Besbes, H., & Massoud, Y., 2019) using the XGBoost ML technique. The intention is to intelligently identify and categorize fraudsters. Cleaning, exploring, and extracting important characteristics from data is done using methodological approaches. In the car insurance business, the suggested framework seeks to limit human involvement, provide warnings for dangerous claims, and decrease financial damage via the use of artificial intelligence (AI). Findings demonstrate that XGBoost outperforms other competing ML techniques when it comes to identifying and categorizing false claims. Hanafy et al. (Hanafy & Ming, R., 2021) developed innovative techniques for effectively handling the increasing quantity and complexity of vehicle insurance claims. They utilized the various types of ML techniques to forecast the analysis and processing of the big insurance dataset that increased their client service via a deeper knowledge of their requirements. Their experimental findings demonstrated the RF outperformed other techniques like SVM, and DT to identify fraudulent claims. They demonstrated in this research that data checking is required to remove duplicate variables throughout the preparations and cleanup phase, as well as how to manage an unbalanced database to avoid bias in a classification model.

4. PROPOSED METHODOLOGY

In this research, fraud detection in the automotive insurance domain (AID) is performed using machine learning (ML). It is a binary classification problem. Figure 1 shows the different steps which are followed in this research. A total of five ML techniques are considered here to detect the fraud by developing an effective predictive model. The important factors for fraud detection in AID are being uncovered using features engineering. Evaluation of the ML techniques is conducted on basis of several metrics and by analyzing the confusion matrix.

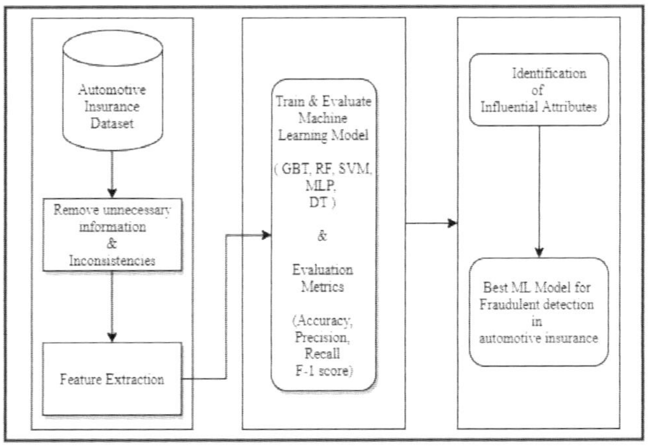

Figure. 1. Proposed Methodology for Fraudulent detection in AID

4.1 Dataset Description

The car Insurance Fraud (CIF) dataset is utilized here to build the prediction model for AID to detect fraud. It is an open-source dataset that can be obtained from Kaggle platform (Gupta S. , 2019). The reason for using an open-source dataset is to minimize the data collection cost and eliminate the security issues. There is a total of 34 variables in the dataset including the target class (Fraud Found/Reported). The name of each attribute is shown in Table 1 for a better understanding of the dataset.

Table 1. Detail of CIF dataset Attributes

Month	Week of Month	Day of Week
Make	Accident Area	Day of Week Claimed
Month Claimed	Week of Month Claimed	Sex
Marital Status	Age	Fault
Policy Type	Vehicle Category	Vehicle Price
Claim Size	Policy Number	Rep Number
Deductible	Driver Rating	Days Policy Incident
Days Policy Claim	Past No of Claims	Age of Vehicle
Age of Policy Holder	Police Reported File	Witness Present
Agent Type	No of Supplements	Address Change Claim
No of Cars	Base Policy	Fraud Found / Reported
Unnamed: 15	Year	

4.2 Dataset Preprocessing

The preprocessing of the CIF dataset is conducted to eliminate the unwanted variables and handle the missing values. The duplication in the dataset is also removed. Total '11' variables are dropped (Day of Week Claimed, Day of Week, Month Claimed, Week of Month Claimed, Week of Month, Year variables are dropped those they are related to time series analysis and there is no need for them. Month, Age of policyholder variables are dropped due to their duplication. Address Change Claim, Deductible, Rep Number variables are dropped due to irrelevance to this research). Two variables (age, driver rating) have missing values (which affect to 11 rows) which are handled to make the CIF dataset clean and ready for prediction.

4.3 Evaluation Measures and ML Techniques

Fraudulent detection is a supervised machine learning (binary classification) problem for the automotive insurance domain. For implementation purposes, Python script is implemented to train and test the ML techniques to identify the fraud for AID. The name of the ML models that are considered in this research is

Random Forest (RF), Gradient Boosted Tree (GBT), Multilayer perceptron (MLP), Decision Tree (DT), and Support Vector Machines (SVM). The significant features are utilized on these ML models to make a prediction model for fraud detection in AID. In this research, a 10-fold cross-validation process is applied to assess the robustness of ML techniques. The dataset is divided into 10 equal parts from which 9 parts are employed for training the model and 1 part is used to test it in the cross-validation process. This whole process is repeated 10 times and the mean accuracy score is calculated at the end as the final score. Four evaluation measures (accuracy, recall, precision, f1-score) are calculated using the confusion matrix to assess the performance of each ML technique.

5. RESULTS

Detailed experimental results are performed by implementing the ML techniques for the CIF dataset to evaluate the findings. Initially, feature engineering is conducted using the recursive feature elimination (RFE) method to find the most significant attributes. Besides, the feature importance is also uncovered to find the most useful features by calculating their scores for fraud detection. After that, the comparative analysis of the ML models using the significant features is performed to find the most robust ML model to detect fraud in AID. The evaluation of the ML techniques is conducted on the basis of the four evaluation measures. Finally, a best ML technique is recommended to detect the fraud in AID on the basis of their best scores which are calculated using the confusion matrix.

5.1 Features' Engineering

The features engineering is performed on the CIF dataset to find the most influential attributes for fraud detection in AID. The main objective of this step is to uncover the most correlated variables in the dataset that are useful to make a better prediction model. For this purpose, a recursive feature elimination (RFE) technique is employed on the CIF dataset to find the most suitable attributes using the RF model (Brownlee, 2021). RFE technique chooses the most influential subset of features by eliminating the insignificant features from the dataset. There are a total of 23 features that are selected after this step. Subsequently applying the RFE technique on the CIF dataset, it is observed that only 15 features are selected by RFE technique. The name of the feature is given in Table 2.

Table 2. A subset of the selected attributes

S. No	Name of the Attributes
1	Make
2	Accident Area
3	Marital Status
4	Age
5	Fault
6	Policy Type
7	Vehicle Price
8	Policy Number
9	Driver Rating
10	Past Number of Claims
11	Age of Vehicle
12	Number of Supplements
13	Number of Cars
14	Base Policy
15	Claim Size

It is inferred from the feature engineering process that only 15 features are highly correlated with the target variable using the RFE technique on the dataset. Therefore, the above subset of the selected features is being utilized to test and train the ML model to make a prediction model for Fraud detection in AID. Significant indicators unquestionably enable detection techniques and algorithms to enhance the efficiency of their detection system.

5.2 Features' Importance

This subsection presents the experiments to calculate the importance of each attribute that is selected by the feature engineering phase. The purpose of this step is to highlight the most significant attributes that take part to detect fraud in AID. There is a total ''15" attributes that are used to determine their feature importance score for fraudulent detection. For experiments, the RF model is implemented on the attributes to compute each features' importance score to detect the fraud for AID. RF classifier has a built-in function to calculate the feature importance using the 'Gini' method that is considered here (Nembrini, König, I.R., & Wright, M.N., 2018). Moreover, it is a very efficient and fast computation method and helps to uncover the significance score of each feature. Figure 2 demonstrates the standing of all attributes and provides the importance score of each feature. Findings of this experiment show that the 'Policy Number', 'Claim Size' and 'Age' attributes are the topmost attributes for detecting fraud in AID by achieving the 0.197, 0.188, and 0.143 scores respectively.

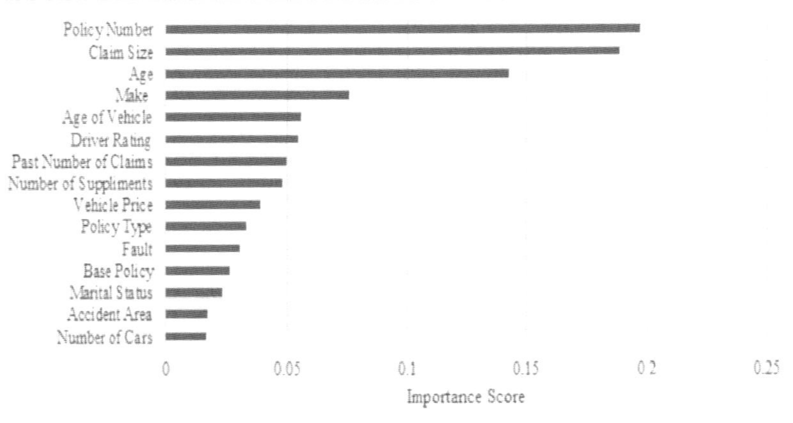

Figure 2. Features' Importance for Fraudulent detection in AID

In addition, the features' importance score for each attribute s listed and some attributes' score is very less. Some of the least important features from the bottom side are 'Accident Area', 'Number of cars' and 'Marital Status'. The outcome of this experiment shows that all attributes are significant for fraud detection in AID due to their non-zero feature importance score.

5.3 Comparative Analysis of ML Models

The prediction analysis for the fraudulent detection in AID is conducted in this subsection by implementing the five ML models (Random Forest, Neural Network, Gradient Boosted Tree, Decision Tree, Support Vector Machines). The subset of the selected features using the RFE method is considered to build the prediction model for fraudulent detection in AID. The five ML models are trained and tested using the 10- fold cross-validation process to find the most robust ML model among all of them. Initially, the ML models are trained and tested using the various hyperparameters and find the best model among them. In table 3, the ML model f-1 score is given against each ML model using their hyperparameters. Findings show that different types of hyperparameters are considered for each model to find the robust model and their scores are improved with the changing of their values. For RF and DT models 'gini' and 'entropy' are used by changing the depth of the tree. Besides, SVM various types of kernels (linear, rbf, poly) are utilized and linear kernel gets the best results. For MLP classifier, different activation functions (tanh, relu, logistics) are implemented with varying the size of the hidden layer and outcomes show that the relu function achieves the best results.

Table 3. ML models f-1 score using various hyperparameters

S.NO	Model Name	Hyperparameters	F-1 (%)	Hyperparameters	F-1 (%)	Hyperparameters	F-1 (%)
1	Random Forest	n_estimators=42, criterion='entropy', max_depth=10, min_samples_split=1	91.12	n_estimators=100, criterion='gini', max_depth=50, min_samples_split=2	90.68	n_estimators=100, criterion='gini', max_depth=10, min_samples_split=6	90.61
2	Multi-layer Perceptron	hidden_layer_sizes=100, activation='relu', solver='adam', alpha=0.0001, batch_size='auto', learning_rate='constant'	91.35	hidden_layer_sizes=80, activation='logistic', solver='sgd', alpha=0.0001, batch_size='auto', learning_rate='adaptive'	91.2	hidden_layer_sizes=80, activation='tanh', solver='adam', alpha=0.0001,batch_size='auto', learning_rate='constant'	91.2
3	Support Vector Machine	C=10, kernel='linear', degree=30, gamma=0.0011, coef0=0.0	91	C=20, kernel='poly', degree=50, gamma=0.0011, coef0=0.4	70	C=40, kernel='rbf', degree=20, gamma=0.0011, coef0=0.4	41
4	Decision Tree	criterion='entropy', splitter='random', max_depth=10, min_samples_split=2	89.5	criterion='gini', splitter='best', max_depth=200, min_samples_split=5	82.8	criterion='gini', splitter='random', max_depth=150, min_samples_split=15	90
5	Gradient Boosted Tree	loss='deviance', learning_rate=0.1, n_estimators=500, subsample=1.0, criterion='friedman_mse'	74.1	loss='exponential', learning_rate=0.13, n_estimators=200, subsample=1.0	81.88	loss='exponential', learning_rate=0.11, n_estimators=100, subsample=1.0	88.07

The comparative analysis is performed among the ML models using the highest f-1 score. The performance of each ML model is listed in figure 3. Four evaluation measures are used for the supervised learning that are accuracy, recall, precision, and f-1 score. The assessment of five ML models is measured on the basis of these four evaluation measures.

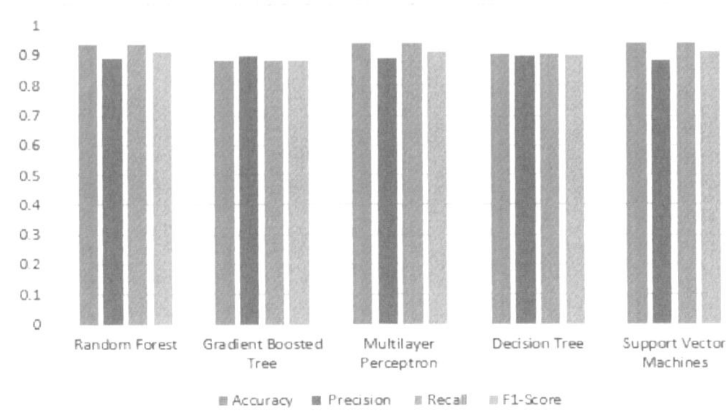

Figure 3. ML models' comparative analysis

The tunned hyperparameters from table 3 are utilized and each ML model with its optimum hyperparameters results are shown in figure 3. The RF classifier is tunned using the 'entropy' method with '42' number of tresses and the linear SVM kernel is implemented using the gamma'0.0011' and C '10' hyperparameters. Furthermore, hyperparameters for GBT model are 'loss' function, learning rate '0.11', and '100' number of trees. The MLP model is tunned using the 'relu' activation function, '100' hidden layers, 'adam' solver and with 'constant' learning rate. Finally, the DT model considered the 'gini' method, 'random' splitter and '15' minimum sample split for fraudulent detection in AID. The experimental findings depict that the Neural network outperforms to detect fraudulent detection in AID by achieving the highest f-1 score (91.35%) among all of them. The f-1 score for Support Vector Machines, Gradient Boosted Tree, Decision Tree and Random Forest are 91.2%, 88.07%, 90%, and 91.12% respectively. Moreover, the findings show that the Gradient Boosted Tree gets the lowest result and could not perform well for fraudulent detection of AID. The recall, precision, and accuracy scores are also presented as evidence. Finally, Neural Network is the more robust and effective ML model to predict the fraudulent detection in AID using the '15' selected subset of attributes on the CIF dataset.

6. CONCLUSION

In this study, the problem of fraud detection is investigated using five well-known machine learning models for the automotive insurance domain. A total of 15 features are selected in the feature engineering phase by utilizing the recursive feature elimination (RFE) method on the CIF dataset. Then, the most influential features from the dataset are uncovered using Random Forest for feature importance. Findings show that the 'Claim Size' and 'Policy Numbers' are the most significant attributes among all of them for fraud detection in the automotive insurance domain. Moreover, the comparative analysis shows that the Multilayer perceptron and random forest are the more robust ML technique to detect fraud in terms of the f1 score. The outcome of this research is very helpful for automotive insurance to detect and overcome fraudulent activities and enhance their revenue in the future by saving their consumers from fraud. In the future, this methodology can be used for various domains like frauds in credit cards and intrusion detection in networks. Moreover, further studies could utilize more feature engineering techniques along with deep learning and ensemble models.

REFERENCES

Abdallah, A., Maarof, M.A., & Zainal, A. (2016). Fraud detection system: A survey. *Journal of Network and Computer Applications, vol. 68*, pp. 90-113.

Agrecha, S., Johnson, R.A., & Chawla, N.V. (2018). FraudBuster: Reducing fraud in an auto insurance market. *Big data, vol. 6, no. 1*, pp. 3-12.

Albashrawi, M. (2016). Detecting financial fraud using data mining techniques: A decade review from 2004 to 2015. *Journal of Data Science, vol. 14, no. 3*, pp. 553-569.

Artís, M., Ayuso, M., & Guillén, M. (2002). Detection of automobile insurance fraud with discrete choice models and misclassified claims. *Journal of Risk and Insurance, vol. 69, no. 3*, pp. 325-340.

Bhowmik, R. (2011). Detecting auto insurance fraud by data mining techniques. *Journal of Emerging Trends in Computing and Information Sciences, vol. 2, no. 4*, pp. 156-162.

Bodaghi, A., & Teimourpour, B. (2018). Automobile insurance fraud detection using social network analysis. *In Applications of Data Management and Analysis*, pp. 11-16.

Brownlee, J. (2021). *Recursive Feature Elimination (RFE) for Feature Selection in Python*. Retrieved from Machine Learning Master: https://machinelearningmastery.com/rfe-feature-selection-in-python/

Dhieb, N., Ghazzai, H., Besbes, H., & Massoud, Y. (2019). Extreme gradient boosting machine learning algorithm for safe auto insurance operations. *2019 IEEE International Conference on Vehicular Electronics and Safety (ICVES)* (pp. 1-5). IEEE.

Dong, X., Yu, Z., Cao, W., Shi, Y., & Ma, Q. (2020). A survey on ensemble learning," Frontiers of Computer Science. pp. 241-258.

Gupta, R., Mudigonda, S.S., Baruah, P.K., & Kandala, P.K. (2021). Markov model with machine learning integration for fraud detection in health insurance. *arXiv preprint arXiv:2102.10978*.

Gupta, S. (2019). *Car_Insurance_Fraud*. Retrieved from Kaggle: https://www.kaggle.com/datasets/incarnyx/car-insurance-fraud

Hanafy, M., & Ming, R. (2021). Machine learning approaches for auto insurance big data. *Risks, vol. 9, no. 2*, p. 42.

Itri, B., Mohmed, Y., Mohammed, Q., & Omar, B. (2019). Performance comparative study of machine learning algorithms for automobile insurance fraud detection. *Third International Conference on Intelligent Computing in Data Sciences (ICDS)* (pp. 1-4). IEEE.

Lei, J., & Ghorbani, A.A. (2012). Improved competitive learning neural networks for network intrusion and fraud detection. *Neurocomputing, vol. 75, no. 1*, pp. 135-145.

Li Y., Ya C., Liu W, & Li M. (2018). A principal component analysis-based random forest with the potential nearest neighbor method for automobile insurance fraud identification. *Applied Soft Computing, vol. 70*, pp. 1000-1009.

Nembrini, S., König, I.R., & Wright, M.N. (2018). The revival of the Gini importance. *Bioinformatics, vol. 34, no. 21*, pp. 3711-3718.

Ngai, E., Hu, Y., Wong, Y.H., Chen, Y., & Sun, X. (2011). The application of data mining techniques in financial fraud detection: A classification framework and an academic review of the literature. *Decision support systems, vol. 50, no. 3*, pp. 559-569.

Panigrahi, S., & Palkar, B. (2018). Comparative analysis on classification algorithms of auto-insurance fraud detection based on feature selection algorithms. *Int. J. Comput. Sci. Eng., vol. 6, no. 9.*

Šubelj, L., Furlan, S., & Bajec, M. (2011). An expert system for detecting automobile insurance fraud using social network analysis. *Expert Systems with Applications, vol. 38, no. 1*, pp. 1039-1052.

Taha, A., & Malebary, S.J. (2020). An intelligent approach to credit card fraud detection using an optimized light gradient boosting machine. *IEEE Access, vol. 8*, pp. 25579-25587.

Wang, Y., & Xu, W. (2018). Leveraging deep learning with LDA-based text analytics to detect automobile insurance fraud. *Decision Support Systems, vol. 105*, pp. 87-95.

Weisberg, H., & Derrig, R.A. (1991). Fraud and Automobile Insurance: A Report on Bodily Injury Liability Claims in Massachusetts. *Journal of Insurance Regulation, vol. 9, no. 4.*

Yadav, A., & Sora, M. (2021). Fraud detection in financial statements using text mining methods: A review. *In IOP Conference Series: Materials Science and Engineering, vol. 1020, no. 1*, p. 012012. IOP Publishing.

INDUSTRIAL MODELING AND PROGRAMMING LANGUAGE (IMPL) FOR COMPLEX DATA ANALYTICS AND DECISION-MAKING PROBLEMS

Brenno Menezes[1], Jeffrey Kelly[2], Munier Elsherif[3] and Robert Franzoi[1]
[1]*Division of Engineering Management, College of Science and Engineering, Hamad Bin Khalifa University, Qatar Foundation, Doha, Qatar*
Education City, LAS Building
[2]*Industrial Algorithms Limited., Toronto, Canada*
[3]*Department of Chemical Engineering, Faculty of Engineering, University of Tripoli, Tripoli, Libya*

ABSTRACT

The Industrial Modeling and Programming Language (IMPL) is a sophisticated computational system for tackling large-scale and complex-scope data analytics and decision-making problems in the engineering and operations research fields. Although the software provides both scalar-based (e.g., MATLAB) and set-based modeling (GAMS, AIMMS, AMPL, MOSEL, OPL) as found in most of the modeling programming languages (MPL), IMPL is mainly built as ad hoc and specialized proprietary industrial software platform (closed-source). This is made by built-in structured- and semantic-based modeling that rely on the Unit-Operation-Port-State Superstructure (UOPSS) constructs (for the structure) and Quantity-Logic-Quality Phenomena (QLQP) concepts (for the semantics). Besides the data analytics package included in the IMPL-DATA version, this mathematical programming language enables the modeling and solving of industrial-scale discrete, nonlinear, and dynamic optimization, estimation, and simulation problems found in both the batch and continuous process industries. IMPL's data analytics (DA) includes several functions to concatenate, substitute, sort, cluster, regress, etc., datasets in order to categorize, reduce, track, etc., the given data. IMPL's decision-making (DM) is suitable to support the modeling and solving of design, planning, scheduling, coordinating production, process, operations, optimization, and control problems as well as parameter identification, estimation, and data reconciliation problems. IMPL includes links to various community and commercial LP, QP, MILP and NLP solvers. To summarize, IMPL may be considered as a confluence with the scientific disciplines of applied engineering, management, information and computer science, statistical and data science.

KEYWORDS

IMPL, Programming Languages, Data Analytics, Decision-Making, Structured and Semantic Programming.

1. INTRODUCTION

The Industrial Modeling and Programming Language (IMPL) is an enabler of complex modeling in a simpler programming of constructs (for the flowsheet structures) with regards to concepts (of how the structural objects behave in the semantics). It permits to overcome the barrier of implementing advanced data-analytics (DA) and decision-making (DM) applications in industrial on- and off-line environments. By making better decisions in a state-of-the-art formulation for large-scale and complex-scope problems integrated with advanced data analytics. where IMPL can considerably improve a business bottom-line especially inside its production-chain (Kelly, 2003, 2004, 2005). With such an advanced DA-DM combination found in IMPL, complexity issues are most often the least understood, and IMPL's proposed modeling and solving algorithms can be tailored for each scenario and situation. The combination of making good decisions using good data is well-known and is part of the continuous-improvement revolution also known as Kaisen in Lean Manufacturing. When poor data is used to make decisions then larger than expected "plan versus actual" deviations or steady-state offsets result which increases the overall uncertainty of the system and erodes the likelihood of making the best decisions possible (Kelly and Zyngier, 2008).

At the core of IMPL's DM is its ability to maximize profit (hard benefits) and performance (soft benefits) and to minimize penalties (i.e., infeasibilities and inconsistencies if they exist). It is typical to think of planning as optimizing the economics of the plant (revenues minus costs) (Kelly, 2003 and Kelly, 2004) whereby scheduling as optimizing the efficiency and effectiveness of the plant (Zyngier and Kelly, 2009).

2. MATHEMATICAL PROGRAMMING MODELING AND LANGUAGES

Established on how itemized constraints are coded with respect to the sets of the elements of the flowsheet network and semantics of the problems to be reproduced, mathematical programming modeling languages can be classified based on their built-in structural and semantic elements coded using various sets and scalars. The main MPL can be grouped as seen in Figure 1. These mathematical modeling languages allow the configuration or codification of real-world business problems transformed into mathematical formulations to be optimized (maximized or minimized) for an objective function subject to constraints (as in Figure 1) from where theoretical and numerical analysis can provide insight, interpretation, and guidance beneficial for the originating application (Kallrath, 2004).

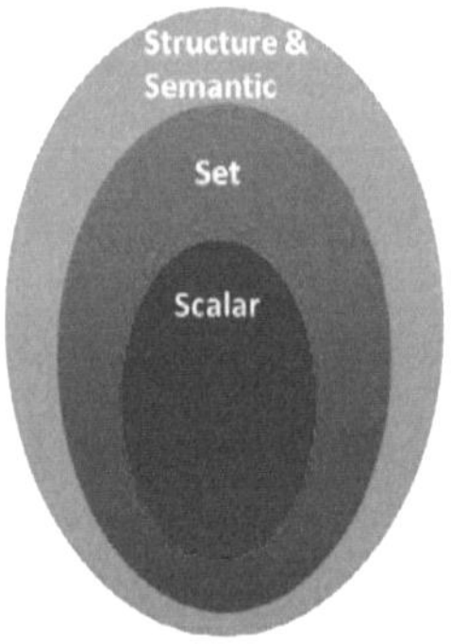

Structure & Semantic: IMPL and anyLogistix

Set: AIMMS, AMPL, GAMS, LINGO, MOSEL, MPL, OPL Pyomo and JuMP (open-source)

Scalar: MATLAB and IMPL-DATA

$$\min z = \sum_t \left(c_t x_t + d_t^T y_t\right)$$

$$\begin{aligned} s.t. \quad & g_t(x_t) + B_t y_t \le b_t \ \ \forall\, t \\ & h_t(x_t) = 0 \ \ \forall\, t \\ & A_t y_t \le a_t \ \ \forall\, t \\ & x_t \in X_t, y_t \in Y_t \end{aligned}$$

Figure 1. Mathematical programming languages

2.1 Scalar-Based Modeling

This represents the system using mathematical scalars, vectors, and matrices of inputs (independent), outputs (dependents) and states (both independent and dependent) where states are by definition unmeasured variables. This is the simplest method to start the modeling process where the state variables provide the transparency to model more complex systems such as graphs, networks, circuits, and flowsheets with transshipment nodes (i.e., both inputs and outputs). Scalar-based modeling can also be considered as *matrix generation* found in for example oil-refinery planning optimization systems. MATLAB and IMPL-DATA (a light version of IMPL) are examples in this group.

2.2 Set-Based Modeling

This can be found in algebraic mathematical modeling languages (AML) where the lists, parameters, variables, constraints, and coefficients/derivatives are indexed, addressed, keyed or pointed to by one or more sets representing its multiple dimensions. This type of modeling can be considered as a more sophisticated scalar-based modeling paradigm. Set-based modeling requires high-skill to code an industrially relevant model especially to manage large networks or superstructures of modeling objects or constructs, referred to as a set-indexing capability of the AML (Fragniere and Gondzio, 2002). The main commercial software in the group is AIMMS, AMPL, GAMS, LINGO, MOSEL, OPL and the open-source Python-Pyomo and Julia-JuMP.

2.3 Structured- and Semantic-Based Modeling

This type of modeling is the evolution or next-step beyond the previous modeling paradigms described but still encompassing all of their intricacies of having sets, lists, parameters, variables, constraints, derivatives, etc. It is similar to a *visual programming language* (VPL) whereby the network, circuit, flowsheet or more appropriately the superstructure is represented pictorially, figuratively or allegorically (Kelly, 2003, Kelly, 2004; Kelly, 2005; Kelly and Menezes, 2019). Structure-based modeling is semantic versus syntactic in the sense that it focuses on how to configure or construct the system as opposed to how to code it. In this sense, structure-based modeling can also be considered as a *domain-specific and declarative language* given that it is focused on a particular class of problems to be modeled and solved of industrial relevance and significance. There are two software with these attributes: anyLogistix and IMPL.

2.3.1 anyLogistix

The software anyLogistix is a supply chain domain MPL for linear and mixed-linear programming (LP and MILP) problems, linked exclusively to CPLEX IBM, that helps the management and organization of supply chain networks in its design, planning, risks analysis, etc. The optimization and simulation capabilities of anyLogistix enable the user, for example, to create plans with network optimization and use simulation modeling to test and develop them. Optimization and simulation combine to extend supply chain analytics. anyLogistix software tool can help transform logistics networks, including supply chain network design, transportation planning, inventory optimization, supply chain risk assessment, inside four walls facility analysis, supply chain master planning, production capacity planning, bullwhip effect quantification, last-mile distribution, etc.

2.3.2 Industrial Modeling and Programming Language (IMPL)

The software IMPL is a full engineering scope and operations research domain MPL for linear, mixed-linear and non-linear programming (LP, QP, MIP and NLP) problems, linked to several solvers such as GUROBI, CPLEX, XPRESS, COIMP for LP and MILP problems as well as IPOPT for NLP problems. IMPL also presents its exclusive SLPQPE (sequential linear programming quadratic programming engine) for NPL solutions. The fundamental philosophy in IMPL is made by the Unit-Operation-Port-State Superstructure (UOPSS) representation of industrial flowsheets to uniquely and unambiguously name all the modeling objects, shapes or structures where these names inherently provide the index-sets from which to assign, associate or attach the semantic-based Quantity-Logic-Quality-Phenomenological (QLQP) attributes over time.

In IMPL, graphically or visually constructing a flowsheet or superstructure using the open-source DIA software as the drawing tool (similar to Microsoft Visio) and the open-source Python as the programming language to write out the construction data (object and connectivity sets) of the flowsheet into a file. The benefit of using a drawing package such as DIA is that it is a graphical or visual representation of the construction and connectivity data of the industrial optimization problem (IOP) with respect to its flow network, graph or diagram i.e., nodes and directed arcs. The alternative is to configure or populate the structures, shapes or objects in a spreadsheet or data file which can be problematic and difficult to interpret i.e., "a picture is worth a thousand words".

A flowsheet is a common term used in chemical engineering and other fields to describe the nodes and directed arcs of a graph, network, or superstructure and is widely used in process design simulators. The IMPL flowsheet is similar but in order to more comprehensively model or construct flowsheets suitable for advanced planning and scheduling (APS), advanced production/process control (APC) and advanced production/process monitoring (APM) applications.

Figure 2 provides a list of the various UOPSS shapes available in DIA and these can be arranged in any arbitrary topological order where the unit-operation shapes can only be connected to in- and out-port-state shapes and out-port-states (upstream) can only be connected to in-port-states (downstream) as further described below.

Figure 2. UOPSS Sheet and Shapes in Dia

Figure 3 shows a simple flowsheet with an inbound "Supply" perimeter and an outbound "Demand" perimeter (unit) for a "Feed" and a "Product" (operation) respectively. There are two internal streams from the unit-operations to/from the port-states and one external stream from the out-port-state "out" to the in-port-state "in". This is a simple supply-demand chain flowsheet given that there is no production or transportation value-add i.e., no pools, processes, pipelines, etc.

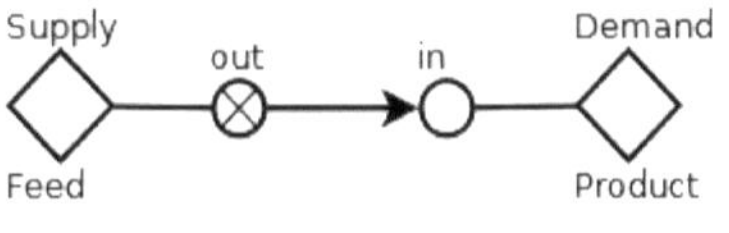

Figure 3. Simple Supply-Demand Chain Flowsheet with no Value-Add

The lines between the UOPSS shapes were drawn using DIA's "Standard - Line" object to construct connections between unit-operations and port-states (internal streams) and upstream unit-operation-port-states to downstream unit-operation-port-states (external streams). Each of these line types will recognized as valid connections when drawn between the appropriate UOPSS shapes and can be used to construct easier to interpret and better-looking flowsheets. However, towards advanced modeling and programming skills in a progressive pace, there is a combination of configurations and codifications with its internal mathematical and integrated computer programming languages in IMPL (Kelly and Menezes, 2020). They are: IML (Industrial Modeling Language), OML (Output Modeling Language), Industrial Linear/Logistics Programming Language (ILP), Industrial Nonlinear Programming Language (INP), IPL (Industrial Programming Language) and IMPC (Industrial Modeling and Programming Code).

To put IMPL into perspective with respect to its built-in, internal, intrinsic or standard modeling capabilities related to its structural and semantic UOPSS-QLQP constructs-concepts and computer programming calls, IMPL has over six hundred (630+) sets, lists and parameters, one hundred and ninety plus (190+) variables and three hundred plus (315+) constraints. There are twenty-seven (27) flags useable by IMPL's console executable, two hundred and fifty-two (253) IML frames, three hundred plus (300+) IPL functions and subroutines, over fifteen (15+) third-party solver interfaces including its own successive or sequential linear programming (SLPQPE), successive equality-constrained quadratic programming (SECQPE) and supplemental observability, redundancy and variance estimator (SORVE) algorithms (optimization and estimation) and finally IMPL is easily callable from eleven (11) computer programming languages.

3. IMPL'S DATA ANALYTICS AND DECISION-MAKING FUNCTIONS

3.1 IMPL's Data Analytics

IMPL-DATA is a small subset of IMPL which does not include the UOPSS-QLQP standard (structure-/flowsheet- and semantic-/formulation-based) modeling and solving capabilities of IMPL although IMPL-DATA does support scalar-based modeling and solving via foreign-files suitable for both optimization and estimation (ILP and INP foreign-files). IMPL-DATA includes the settings, calc, data, text, data-calc, data-data, calc-group/list, data-group/list, text-group/list and include-file frames of the Industrial Modeling Language (IML) only and the Output Modeling Language (OML) and may be considered as an Industrial Scripting Language (ISL). Since IML and OML's output data files are comma-separated-value (CSV) formatted, the integration of IMPL-DATA using CSV readers/writers, ETL, MQTT, IIoT, etc., data transfer technologies found in both Information Technology (IT) and Operational Technology (OT) is very straightforward enabling applications such as industrial/integrated data studio's and viewers (IDS and IDV's) to provide integrated data connectivity with the trend and tabular views, etc. as well as static but graphical drawing capabilities. Direct data source connectors to relational and real-time data sources can also be achieved using ODBC (Open DataBase Connectivity) and OPC (Object linking and embedding (OLE) for Process Control).

The primary purpose of IMPL-DATA is to provide users, modelers, and analysts such as engineers, scientists and technologists the ability to pre-and post-process scalar and vector industrial data quickly, efficiently and transparently in both off-line (near real-time) and on-line (real-time) environments using a straightforward syntax and symbology although absent of IMPL's UOPSS-QLQP structures and semantics as mentioned. Basic use of IMPL-DATA is to implement explicit and usually engineering-based data calculation/computation units or blocks for soft/virtual sensors or inferential measurements in industrial OT and/or IT environments which are simply ad hoc calculation and computation expressions/formulas involving multiple measurements, coefficients/parameters and logical/conditionals also known as industrial data fusion. These types of relatively basic but fundamental data calculations and computations may be considered as Industrial Data Programming/Processing (IDP) in a calculator/computer. More advanced use of IMPL-DATA and IMPL is its on-going application in both Engineering Technology (ET) and Analytics Technology (AT) we collectively call "Data Engalytics" which includes (calculation, computation) simulation, estimation and optimization (cf. the ILP and INP) also known as predictive and prescriptive analytics (estimation and optimization) and makes IMPL-DATA ideal for "fit-for-purpose" or "purpose-driven" applications involving data calculations, computations, simulations, estimations (regressions and reconciliations), optimizations, etc.

Ultimately, IMPL-DATA is intended to be easy to learn, light weight, reliable and low cost for basic data engalytics especially suited for off-line and on-line monitoring but is highly extensible for advanced data engalytics involving complex industrial estimations and optimizations invoking the same solving technologies as IMPL. Presented below are some interesting and useful IMPL-DATA examples that should provide the user, modeler, or analyst with a good and solid understanding of its capabilities and potential applications.

3.1.1 Data Concatenating and Combining (SPLICE)

The IMPL-DATA allows for the capability to concatenate, consolidate or combine multiple data-vectors into a single data-vector similar to the SPLICE() data function where SPLICE() only concatenates together two (2) data-vectors per statement i.e., two (2) at a time. However, the IMPL's data frame allows for any number of data-vectors to be combined where calc-scalar expressions may be injected as required between any of the configured data-vectors. For example, see the X data-vector below with 1000.0, 2000.0 and 3000.0 inserted or injected using the pipe separator before data-vector Y is concatenated. It should be pointed out that this data frame is also useful to convert, combine or cast multiple calc-scalars into a single data-vector especially using the pipe ("|") character as the value separator.

3.1.2 Data Swapping (SWAP)

The capability to swap, switch, substitute, modify, revise, update or replace any single data-vector row, point or element in any data-vector i.e., one (1) element, point or row at a time using the SWAP (value; index) data function. The value and index arguments may also be any valid calc-scalar and data-vector-element expression or formula.

3.1.3 Data Substituting (SUBSTITUTE, SCRAPERANGE, SCATTER)

A simple extension of the SWAP() data function to substitute several or multiple data-elements / -rows / -points of an existing data-vector with a data subset, sublist or subvector of real values with an accompanying data subvector containing the specific index numbers, with arbitrary order, in the existing data-vector using the SUBSTITUTE(values, indexes) data function. For example, if X is the existing data-vector requiring a subset of its data elements to have different replaced, revised, updated or modified values, XV is the data subvector of different data values for substitution and IX is the data subvector of chosen index numbers or indices of X to be substituted, then the SUBSTITUTE() function simply performs the straightforward array indices exchange of X(IX) = XV. As mentioned, the SUBSTITUTE() data function is simply a multi-value version of the mono-value SWAP() data function to provide the capability to swap or substitute many or multiple values at the same time.

3.1.4 Data Sorting and sequencing (SORT, SEQUENCE)

The purpose of the SORT() data operation explicitly returning the sorted permutation set, list or vector of index numbers only is to enable the capability of sorting the rows, points or elements of multiple related data-vectors sometimes referred to as parallel-arrays which is very common when representing sparse matrices as three (3) parallel-arrays for the row indexes, column indexes and its real non-zero sparse values. This is also useful for piecewise continuous model (PCM) estimation or regression with multiple inputs or independent variables where one and only one input is configured for ordering, sequencing, segmenting, partitioning, grouping or piecing the input space or region based on the primary sorted single input's tread profile with the same sorting required for the output trend profile as well as the other secondary inputs. The SORT() data function returns the sorted permutation indexes or indices in the data-vector I for the primary 1D array to be sorted which in this example is X. Then, both X and Y are sorted according to the sorting permutation retained in I where the SEQUENCE() data function returns or retrieves the sorted data in U and V, respectively.

3.1.5 Data Desorting and Desequencing (DESORT)

The reverse, inverse or reciprocal sorting problem also known as unsorting or desorting with a notion that is simple, if we sort a data-vector say X using I, the sorted permutation index-set / -list / -vector returned from SORT(), then permutate the 1 to N rows, points or elements of X according to I, we arrive at the sorted data-vector XS = X(I) using SEQUENCE() where XS(1) = X(I(1)) (smallest) and XS(N) = X(I(N)) (largest). Now, to unsort or desort XS back to X and store into the data-vector XUS, with X and XUS being equal, we require an unsort or desort index-set, -list, -sequence, -series, -1D-array or -vector as shown below in K returned by the DESORT() data function. The DESORT() function simply desorts the sorted permutation index-vector according to the following statement K(I) = J where J = 1..N = 1:N = {1,...,N}.

3.1.6 Data Scraping (SCRAPERANGE, CONUNTRANGE)

This is a straightforward concept of scraping a data-vector over a lower and upper bound range or interval of a data-vector's real values to obtain the arbitrary index numbers or indices of its data-elements, -points or -rows within the configured range. The data function SCRAPERANGE() requires an input data-vector and the lower and upper real bounds of the data to be scraped where the COUNTRANGE() data-calc function simply returns the count or cardinality number of the subvector of indexes.

3.1.7 Data Shifting (SHIFT)

The IMPL-DATA also provides the capability to lag/lead or time- / trial-shift any data-vector using the SHIFT() data function especially relevant when the data-vector is a time-series or trial-sequence. In this function, we simply shift down (lag) and shift up (lead) by one (1) and two (2) time- / trial-index numbers replacing the top and bottom data-vector-elements respectively with the configured impute default value argument which in the case is zero (0.0). The SHIFT() data function is useful to time-shift any time-series, time-signal, time-indexed or time-ordered data-vector when performing dynamic data regression i.e., dynamic models representing dead- / delay-times and the degrees of numerator and denominator rational polynomials found in what is known as deterministic and stochastic transfer functions. The SHIFT() function is also useful to time-shift data-vectors in dynamic principal component analysis and regression (DPCA and DPCR).

3.1.8 Data Scanning (SCANBELOW, SCANABOVE, SCANFREEZE, SCANJUMP)

The capability to scan or survey any data-vector and to check for four (4) simple and rudimentary tests using the data-calc functions SCANBELOW(), SCANABOVE(), SCANFREEZE() and SCANJUMP(). These SCAN functions are useful to verify the validity of the actual, measured or hard- / soft-sensed variable values against rudimentary data validation rules known as the range and rate-of-change checks. The below and above scans check for data-vector values that are less than a lower limit and are greater than an upper limit whilst the freeze and jump scans check for data values that change too little or too much from their previous values indicating that these values are suspect and infer the suspicion that they could be bad, faulty, defective, etc.

3.1.9 Data Stacking and Stretching (STACK, STRETCH)

To both stack and stretch a data-vector in IMPL-DATA using the STACK() and STRETCH() data functions which ultimately expands the data-vector. Data stacking means taking an existing data-vector and simply repeating or replicating its vector of scalars several times in a stacked formation as specified by the length argument. Data stretching means taking an existing data-vector and stretching each of its data elements, -rows or -points by the length argument. Stretching of course is a form of stacking as it stacks one data-vector-element at a time in sequence over the length number set on the right-hand-side (LHS) of the STRETCH() data function or operation.

3.2 IMPL's Decision Making

IMPL Decision-Making or IMPL (not IMPL-DATA) refers to as the Quantity-Logic-Quality Phenomena (QLQP) in the structure and semantic modeling programming language domain. The QLQP provides a suitable phenomenological break-down of the problem semantics and complexity where the quantity dimension details quantities such as flows, rates, holdups, and yields where the quantities can be related to any stock or signal including time. The other two dimensions are logic data with setups, startups, switchovers-to-self, shutdowns and switchover-to-others (sequence-dependent transitions) and quality data with densities, components, properties and conditions. In addition to the QLQP, IMPL also has what it calls the Unit-Operation-Port-State Superstructure (UOPSS) determined by the flowsheet network as in Figure 3 using the shapes, constructs or objectsseen in Figure 2. This provides the arbitrary, ad hoc or anywhere-to-anywhere connectivity generally referred to as a flowsheet, topology, mapping, routings or block flow diagram of the IOP / IEP in terms of the various shapes, objects or structures necessary to construct and configure it. The UOPSS is more than a single network given that it is comprised of two networks we call the physical network and the procedural network. The physical network involves the units and ports (equipment, structural) and the procedural network involves the operations (tasks) and states (activities, functional). The combination or cross-product of the two derives the *projectional* superstructure and it is these superstructure constructs or UOPSS keys that we apply, attach or associate specific QLQP attributes to where our projections are also known as hypothetical, logical or virtual constructs.

Brunaud et al. (2020) show large-scale problems solved within a minute by better modeling and solving algorithms when using the unit-operation-port-state superstructure (UOPSS) from Kelly (2005) and better settings of the solvers to explore solution algorithms, e.g., the use of lazy constraints. The authors compare the UOPSS to the state-task network (STN) (Kondili et al., 1993, Shah et. al., 1993) and resource-task network (RTN) (Pantelides, 1994) formulations, which reduces four-fold the optimization time. Additionally, by varying the settings of commercial solvers, the total CPU reduction is in the order of eight times when comparing the UOPSS to the STN and RTN.

Ultimately, when we augment the superstructure with the time or temporal dimension as well as including multiple scenarios or sites (echelons), i.e., sub-superstructures, we essentially are configuring what is known as a *hyperstructure*. It should be noted that in IMPL, multiple scenarios are modeled and solved simultaneously into one problem where certain variables are commoned, coupled, connected, balanced, linked or tied together to find essentially one solution to multiple sub-problems simultaneously (cf. common data) i.e., one solution to a family, group, or collection of problems.

4. CONCLUSION

We have presented the constructs and concepts of the structured- and semantic-based modeling platform Industrial Modeling and Programming Language (IMPL). This is built-in modeling language that uses the structures of the unit-operation-part-state superstructure (UOPSS) and the semantics of the quantity-logic-quality phenomena (QLQP) for modeling the details of industrially relevant optimization and estimation problems for any type of manufacturing system. The data analytics capabilities of the IMPL-DATA integrated to the decision-making features of the IMPL can be integrated to solve large-scale and complex-scope problems which eliminates the necessity of the underlying model at each decision-making cycle in order to empower automation in both off-line and on-line. IMPL has been applied successfully in practice covering a broad range of industrial sectors, including (but not limited to) oil and gas, chemicals, mining and minerals, pulp and paper, energy, and food and beverage.

REFERENCES

Fragniere, E. and Gondzio, J., (2002), Optimization modeling languages. In: Handbook of Applied Optimization, pp. 993–1007.

Kallrath, J., (2004), Modeling Languages in Mathematical Optimization, Vol. 88. Springer Science & Business Media, US.

Kelly, J. D. and Mann, J. L., (2003), Crude-oil blend scheduling optimization: an application with multi-million dollar benefits – parts I and II, *Hydrocarbon Processing*, June/July.

Kelly, J. D. and Menezes, B. C., (2019), Industrial Modeling and Programming Language (IMPL) for Off- and On-Line Optimization and Estimation Applications. In: Fathi M., Khakifirooz M., Pardalos P. (eds) Optimization in Large Scale Problems. Springer Optimization and Its Applications, 152, 75-96.

Kelly, J. D. and Menezes, B. C., (2020), Industrial Software for Computer Aided Process Engineering (CAPE) Modeling and Programming Skills Development. *Computer Aided Chemical Engineering*, 48, 2035-2040.

Kelly, J. D. and Zyngier, D., (2007), An improved MILP modeling of sequence-dependent switchovers for discrete-time scheduling problems, *Industrial and Engineering Chemistry Research*, Vol. 46, pp. 4964.

Kelly, J. D. and Zyngier, D., (2008), Continuously improve the performance of planning and scheduling models with parameter feedback. In Foundations of Computer Aided Process Operations, FOCAPO, Boston, MA, United States, 29-2 July.

Kelly, J. D., (2004), Production modeling for multimodal operations, *Chemical Engineering Progress*, February.

Kelly, J. D., (2005a) Modeling production-chain information, *Chemical Engineering Progress*, February, 28-31.

Kelly, J. D., (2005b), The unit-operation-stock superstructure (UOSS) and the quantity-logic-quality paradigm (QLQP) for production scheduling in the process industries, In G. Kendall, L. Lei, & M. Pinedo, eds. Proceedings of MISTA2005. NY, USA, p. 327-333.

Menezes, B. C. et al., (2015), Phenomenological decomposition heuristic for process design synthesis of oil-refinery units. *Computer Aided Chemical Engineering*, 37, 1877-1882.

Zyngier, D. and Kelly, J. D., (2009), Multi-product inventory logistics modeling in the process industries. In Optimization and logistics challenges in the enterprise, pp. 61-95. Springer, Boston, MA.

SAFETY-RELATED COMPUTERIZED EMBEDDED SYSTEMS WITH HETEROGENOUS REDUNDANCY

Joseph Khattar, Eike Hahn, Samer Telawi, Michael Schwarz and Josef Boercsoek
ICAS, Institute for Computer Architecture and System Programming, University of Kassel
Kassel, Germany

ABSTRACT

Recent advancements in the embedded systems field have resulted in more complicated systems with application-specific blocks (IP cores), often known as System on Chip (SoC) devices. Several redundancy-based embedded designs provide reliability and safety for SoC in aeronautics, automotive, industrial automation, railway, and space. In this paper, a Safety System-on-Chip heterogenous1oo2 architecture is presented. The design is based on two open-source and proven in-use cores, LEON3 from Cobham Gaisler and RISCV processors SweRV EH1 from Western Digital. The SoC is implemented on a Xilinx FPGA system and supplemented with conventional peripherals from the Xilinx IP library and Cobham Gaisler. A software comparator is included for a diagnostic. Each core has independent IPs, and the software comparator evaluates data from both cores; in case of deviation, the system is rendered to an energized safe state.

KEYWORDS

Safety-Related Computerized Systems, Redundant Computing, Safety System on Chip, Functional Safety.

1. INTRODUCTION

Existing computerized embedded systems include all necessary interfaces on a single chip, known as a system on a chip (SoC), resulting in significant space and cost savings. Furthermore, the high demand for more processing power in real-world systems has led to multiprocessors performing a specific task. In that regard, with a high level of processing capability, the entire system performance is improved.

An SoC can comprise a processor to run the different components combined on the chip, such as software system, on-chip memories, memory controllers to interface external memories, DSP functionality, particular co-processors, communication peripherals like PCI/PCIe, USB, Ethernet, UART, SPI, and I2C, as well as other application-related components. This type of device can be found in various product categories, including cell phones that require low-power programmable processors, telecommunication and networking that demand high-speed and high-complex systems on a single chip, and digital televisions with high-resolution requirements (*MELECON 2014 - 2014 17th IEEE Mediterranean Electrotechnical Conference* 2014 - 2014; Hayek & Borcsok 2014 - 2014).

Moreover, the Multiprocessor System-on-Chip (MSoC) concept emerged in response to the increased speed and processing power demand to achieve the desired performance. The principle is similar to that of an SoC but with more processors to increase and improve the computerized performance. Another crucial consideration for SoC or MSoC is where it should be implemented. Only Integrated Circuits (ICs) manufacturers using Electronic Design Automation (EDA) technologies to produce Application Specific Integrated Circuits may create such systems (ASICs).

Regarding the advancement of new powerful and feature-rich Field Programmable Gate Arrays (FPGAs) and the Complex Programmable Logic Devices (CPLDs), the development of MSoCs can be done more efficiently. The configurable feature of such computerized systems reduces overall system space and weight and provides high performance with the lowest power consumption compared to standard ICs, rendering these devices ideal for high-performance computerized embedded systems.

Nowadays, the dual-core or quad-core multiprocessor systems are utilized in desktops and laptops. However, these devices are not ideal for computerized embedded systems or designs with high customization. Some areas can now benefit from the excellent performance and low power consumption of such system designs. The advantages of such a new approach in designing embedded digital systems make them essential in various industries, including space, aerospace, military, automotive, medical, and autonomous systems, where system reliability is a significant concern. Furthermore, the design tools for developing multiprocessor systems for embedded designs are now available, with support for FPGA devices written in Hardware Description Languages such as VHDL or Verilog (eds Wolf & Jerraya 2005).

Accordingly, utilizing the Safety System-on-Chip (SSoCs) in a safety-critical application where human safety is the biggest concern requires that these systems fulfill specific safety-related requirements following the related standards. IEC61508 is a widely used standard in electrical, electronic, and programmable electronic safety-related systems. Furthermore, the International Electrotechnical Commission has created several adaptations based on this standard to cover a wide range of applications. The IEC61508 standard provides a roadmap for developing computerized systems used in critical environments and defines the management life cycle for developing such systems. According to this standard, a safe state is the state of a system where safety is achieved; a safe state can be either energized or de-energized. The standard defines attributes or system characteristics that manufacturers should follow. One of the main attributes is "dependability," the ability of a computerized system to fulfill the reliability, availability, maintainability, and safety requirements (Börcsök 2007). In that regard, reliability is the probability of a system to perform the intended functionality over a given period of time whereas availability is the probability of a system to execute its intended functionality over a given instance of time. Moreover, redundancy is the means through which one of these parameters can be increased.

Important to mention is that redundancy is an essential means of achieving the reliability of a system. It can be defined as the additional presence of functionally identical or comparable technical resources, not usually required for trouble-free operation. In other words, redundancy means inserting the same equipment but not necessarily entirely identical for performing the same or part of the safety function. As a rule, these additional resources serve to increase operational safety. Having more engines than needed for a flight is an example of system redundancy; if one of the engines fails, the airplane can rely on the remaining engines to execute a safe landing with no casualties. Another example of redundancy in communication is sending information or data from a sensor to a computing unit in two independent ways. In general, there are two main types of redundancy," homogeneous redundancy" utilizing the same hardware or software and "diversity redundancy," where different hardware or software are used (Börcsök 2007).

Furthermore, the IEC61508 defines the concept of Hardware Fault Tolerance (HFT) which is a measure that indicates how many defects in components or a set of components lead to the loss of safety features in a redundant system. Therefore, redundancy helps to increase the system's capacity to prevent single failures from escalating into total system failure. Redundancy helps the system tolerate potential faults. From a theoretical point of view, it depends upon the architecture. The IEC61508 defines multiple architectures that can be adopted to develop safety-related systems. Accordingly, if the architecture is M out of N (MooN), the HFT is calculated as N–M. Suppose the HFT of a system is 1; it implies that even when there is one fault, the system can maintain the safety function intended. However, if there is more than one fault, the component or subsystem may fail to provide safety (Börcsök 2007).

Safety-related systems are commonly developed based on a one out of two (1oo2) system to improve their reliability. The 1oo2 architecture consists of two channels connected in parallel, such that either channel can process the safety function. Thus, both channels would have necessitated a dangerous failure before a safety function failed on-demand (IEC International Electrotechnical Commission 2010b).

In any system, two types of functions exist; safety-related functions (SRF) which are responsible for rendering the system to a safe state in case of a failure, and non-safety-related functions (NSRF) which execute other functionalities. Most systems rely on a de-energized safe state, where on the one hand, reliability is increased, but on the other hand, availability is not affected or even decreased. This is because in the occurrence of a failure in one channel, the system is generally switched off, and no functionality can be resumed. Modern systems require some functionalities to be available regardless of the failure. For example, in autonomous driving, medical equipment, and industrial systems, restricted functionality is usually more beneficial than no functionality. Thus, availability must be respected in developing SSoC.

In addition, most SSoC implements homogeneous redundancy to lower the cost and the overhead of research and development. This is disadvantageous, in the sense that a failure in one channel might be duplicated in the redundant channel since an identical system is utilized (A. Hayek et al. 2014; Texas Instruments, Incorporated [SPRY178 & *] n.d.).

To resolve these problems, this paper introduces a design of 1oo2 heterogenous microprocessors for a safety-related system based on the requirements of the IEC61508 standard. Two different processors, Leon3 and RISCV, are coupled and synthesized on Artix7 FPGA to implement the 1oo2 architecture and achieve an HFT of 1. Both cores possess independent clock inputs and peripherals as well as outputs. Furthermore, the safety-related functions are executed by both processors in parallel to assure failure-free operation. A software comparator accompanies this redundancy to compare and detect deviations between the two processors. In case of divergence, any core can mitigate the system to a safe state. Moreover, this implementation that adopts the hardware redundancy with a software comparator enables this computerized system to perform safety-related functions as well as different non-safety functions that can be executed by each processor independently.

This paper is organized as follows. Firstly, the paper introduces functional safety stating the current design problems and proposes a heterogenous redundant system to counter these problems. Secondly, it describes the architectural design and the software comparator used between the two processors. Thirdly, it describes the implementation of the design. Finally, the paper concludes with recommendations and an outlook for future designs.

2. ARCHITECTURAL MODEL

Safety microcontroller systems are increasingly being constructed as fully integrated systems, referred to as SSoC. Depending on the application, an HFT of at least 1 is mainly targeted for safety-critical architectures. This paper utilizes a 1oo2 heterogeneous architecture, as illustrated in figure 1. When following 1oo2 architecture, a system consists of two independent connected channels, where only one channel is sufficient for a dangerous failure to bring the system to a safe state via the second channel. However, most of today's systems include duplicated processor architectures; nonetheless, the same peripherals are employed, resulting in lower reliability (Hayek & Borcsok 2014 - 2014; Texas Instruments, Incorporated [SPRY178 & *] n.d.).

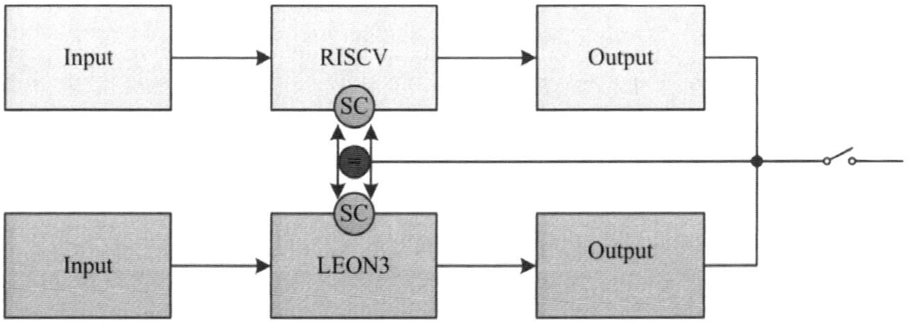

Figure 1. THE proposed 1oo2 architecture

The systems that employ the homogenous hardware redundancy to improve the reliability might be exposed to some errors that can lead these systems to fail to achieve the safety functions; this type of error is the common cause of failure. The redundant systems can keep running even if many hardware or software components fail based on the HFT. However, when the same cause leads individual components to fail on their own, common-mode failures threaten the system. Furthermore, the common-mode failure is the unplanned failure of two or more similar components in separate channels of a redundant system due to a common cause such as power loss or high temperature. For example, in a redundant system where two identical processors are used, a design flaw that exists in one and results in failure of the channel is inevitably duplicated in the second processor thus generating a similar hazardous event.

Therefore, this paper utilizes heterogeneous redundancy with two independent power domains to overcome and reduce the effect of common cause failures on the proposed system and thus improve the system's reliability.

Additionally, the IEC 61508-2 recommends utilizing diverse hardware redundancy to resolve systematic failures that are essential failures in any system (IEC International Electrotechnical Commission 2010a). Accordingly, by utilizing diversity, the impacts of system failures can be better controlled. A systematic failure is deterministically linked to a single cause, and it can only be removed by changing the design or manufacturing process, operational procedures, or documentation. For example, the software may contain errors that manifest when some piece of code is run under some specific conditions. However, considering that many redundant aspects are created and configured utilizing various design processes and components, the various channels have different characteristics, behaviors, and statistics on reliability. In this case, diversity protects the redundant channels in the system from systematic failures.

Furthermore, the redundancy of channels in safety instrumented systems logic solvers as well as field devices has been explored for high availability. Maintaining the mandatory safety integrity while keeping the operational process increases the availability of safety-related systems. The availability is a quality criterion of a system, and it is a system's ability to perform a specified function under a given condition at a given instant of time (Edgar C. Ramirez n.d.).

Hardware redundancy can range from essential duplication to complex architectures that automatically switch in spare units when the active ones fail. Moreover, hardware redundancy in SoCs can take several forms, including lockstep replication of cores doing safety-critical operations, delayed lockstep, one out of one system (1oo1), asymmetrical lockstep, and triple-voting based on two out of three systems (2oo3). These types of hardware redundancy come with much overhead; thus, they are usually only used in essential systems where the cost is warranted. The approaches were generally based on the Electronic Shut Down (ESD) with lockstep principle, which most research institutions and industries also choose. These methods were solely focused on ensuring the redundancy of central processing units (Börcsök 2004). Furthermore, the hardware lockstep is a notion that has been around for a long time, and various manufacturers such as Texas Instruments (Texas Instruments, Incorporated [SPNU511 & D] n.d.), Infineon (*AURIX 32-bit microcontrollers for automotive and industrial applications-Highly integrated and performance optimized* n.d.) and NXP (Semiconductors n.d.) have utilized the hardware lockstep concept to develop safety-related solutions (Borcsok et al. 2021 - 2021).

Accordingly, the cores conducting the safety-critical operations are replicated in high-level safety compliance devices where the applications run both cores in lockstep mode, comparing the results to ensure that the redundant processing produces identical outputs. If the same outcome is not attained, it is assumed that something went wrong. Further, the identical inputs are supplied to both cores simultaneously in lockstep, and they conduct the same calculations in the same clock cycle, and a hardware comparator compares the execution of each command of the redundant subsystems. The results are regularly compared to discover when a failure has occurred, whether momentary, intermittent, or permanent, and the entire system is rendered to a de-energized safe state when any deviations are detected. Also, lockstep mode troubles the system in handling non-safety-related functions because both cores must be synced at all times. Furthermore, the instruction memory should be shared in most cases, making the system susceptible to common cause failure.

The IEC61508 dictates on a 1oo2 system with HFT of 1 that in case of failure, the system must mitigate to a safe state, and most of the time a de-energized state, due to the decrease in safety integrity level (SIL) after a hazard has occurred. The aforementioned unveils that even though the system's reliability is improved dramatically in a 1oo2 system, the additional redundancy of the processing units does not affect availability since the system is shut down and non-safety-related functions are prohibited from executing their intended functionality.

In contrast, utilizing a software comparator for a 1oo2 architecture increases the system availability where the software comparator is responsible for synchronizing both units regularly. The software comparator running on both cores compares the values for the safety instrumented function (SIF); in case a failure occurs, the system mitigates to a safe state. Since both cores utilize independent peripherals, inputs, outputs, and clock, the system is capable of achieving an energized safe state. The SIF is not utilized due to the loss of the required SIL. However, non-safety-related functions could continue to perform, thus increasing the system's availability. For example, consider a compressed air generator system. In case of failure, the system will shut down and open safety valves to reduce pressure in the tank and close the isolation valve to avoid a more significant threat, along with shutting down all-electric functionality. However, measures like pressure, temperature, ambient sensor, communication, and data storing functions could help detect what went wrong and keep monitoring the system even when shut down, therefore increasing the system's availability.

This paper proposes a 1oo2 heterogeneous processor followed by a software comparator to detect errors and mitigate to a safe state while maintaining non-safety-related functions running. The software installed on both cores executes the same functionality. First, the initialization of the peripheral is accomplished. Next, communication is established, followed by the primary function where safety-related and non-safety-related functions are utilized. Each core possesses its independent clock source, architecture, and peripherals. Thus, data handling is different in both cores, and the timings are not synched. In other words, one core might read the data from a sensor twice, with the other still fetching the first value. The processes must be synchronized to compare data between the cores. The software comparator handles this subprocess and notifies the system of the results by a message for verification. The comparison follows a successful sync. The software comparator flow chart is represented in figure 2.

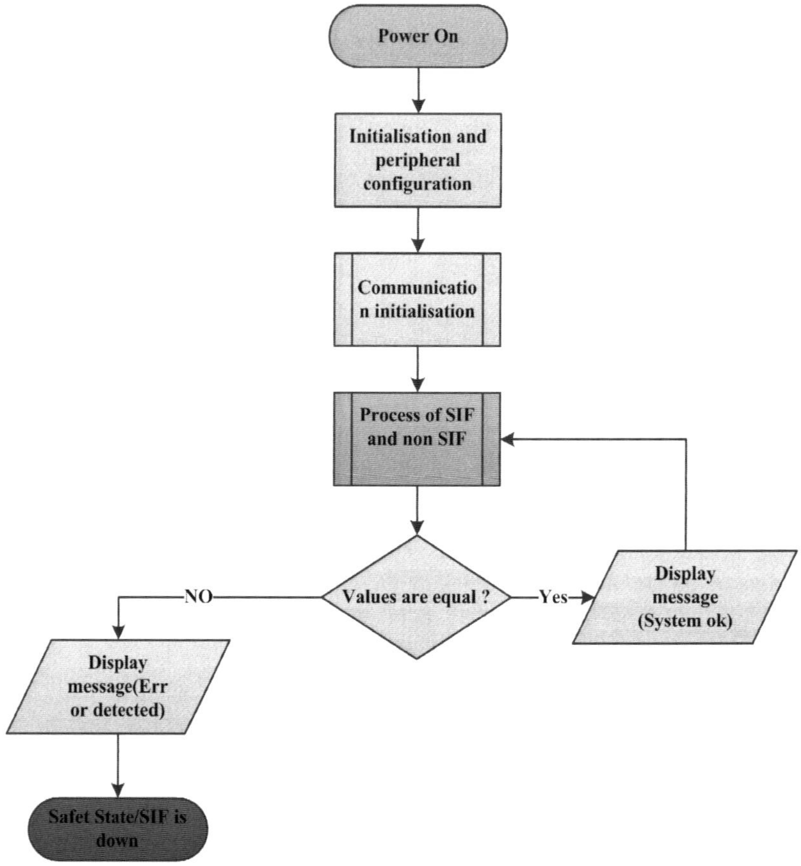

Figure 2. THE software comparator flow chart

Moreover, safety-related systems are commonly built with proven in-use technology. Novel production techniques, such as manufacturing procedures and fault models, induce uncertainty because of the limited amount of experience needed to identify risks. As a result, the application of state-of-the-art processes in the consumer sector would have limited applicability (Hayek & Borcsok 2014 - 2014). IEC61508 approves using proven in-use product software or hardware provided that the requirements are met. Only when an element's functionality is restricted and specified, and there is sufficient documentary evidence to show that the likelihood of any dangerous systematic faults is low enough, is the technology considered proven in use. The evidence must be based on examining operational experience with a specific configuration of the element and suitability analysis and testing (IEC International Electrotechnical Commission 2010a). The use of proven-in-use hardware in functional safety is critical to eliminate structural flaws in hardware components as much as possible. Both RISCV and Leon3 processors meet these standards because different companies already use them (Abdelawwad et al. 2018 - 2018; Habinc 2022).

3. CONCEPT AND IMPLEMENTATION

This paper utilizes the RISCV architecture which is developed based on previous work of The SweRV EH1 from Western Digital. The company has developed four RISCV cores that will be used in a variety of Western Digital products shortly (RISC-V International 2022). Additionally, a modified SweRV EH1 from Hahn et al. in 2022 (Hahn et al. 2022) was selected and altered to meet this design's requirement where the ethernet module is eliminated from the design to be added in the future based on AXI ethernet lite provided by Xilinx Vivado. A secondary AXI (Advanced eXtensible Interface) UART (Universal asynchronous receiver-transmitter) is added for internal communication, and the final RISCV architecture is shown in figure 3.

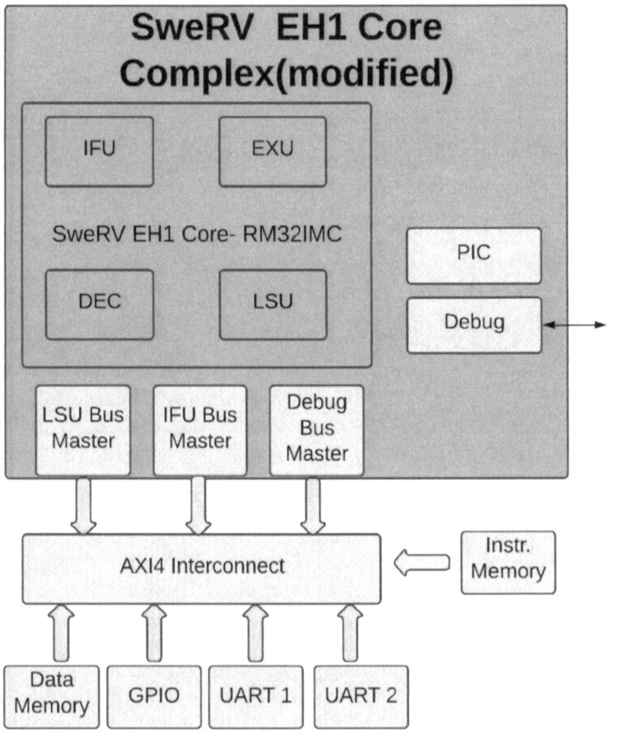

Figure 3. RISCV design

Furthermore, to achieve the heterogeneous redundancy, the Leon3 core is generated from the GRLIB library available on Cobham Gaisler's website. The Leon3 core is established mainly through three files, the Top-file "leon3mp.vhd", which generate all VHDL components (IP cores) and executes the AMBA (APB and AHB) bus system interconnection between IPs. The "Top-file" contains the primary entity representing the external pins of the core. The second file, "config.vhd", is a VHDL package that configures the settings and parameters of the intellectual property of the core. The last file represents the constraint file of the design. In Xilinx Vivado, the constraint file is called the XDC file, which indicates to the program which physical pins on the FPGA are intended to be used or connected to the HDL code to define the designed functionality. Consequently, all of these files were modified to meet the requirements and demands of the project. An alternative "Top-file" was created that incorporates the cores, Leon3 and RISCV, as components. Both cores needed adequate reconfiguration to be included in the "Top-file". Furthermore, the central concept requires full redundancy, so each core has independent peripherals, a GPIO module and I2C, and an SPI. Moreover, a different clock supply for both cores ensures their independence. In the Artix Ac701 FPGA, there exist three clock sources. The AC701 board has a 2.5V LVDS differential 200 MHz oscillator (U51) soldered onto the backside of the board and another differential clock programmable low-jitter 3.3V differential oscillator (U34) with an output frequency of 156.250 MHz.

The GPIO and UART module development is straightforward, following the GRLIB library for the Leon3 and utilizing the Vivado AXI reference guide. Two UART modules were added to the design, enabling internal communication between the two processors (Administrator 2022; Xilinx & Inc. n.d.). Figure 4 represents the architectural concept of the proposed design.

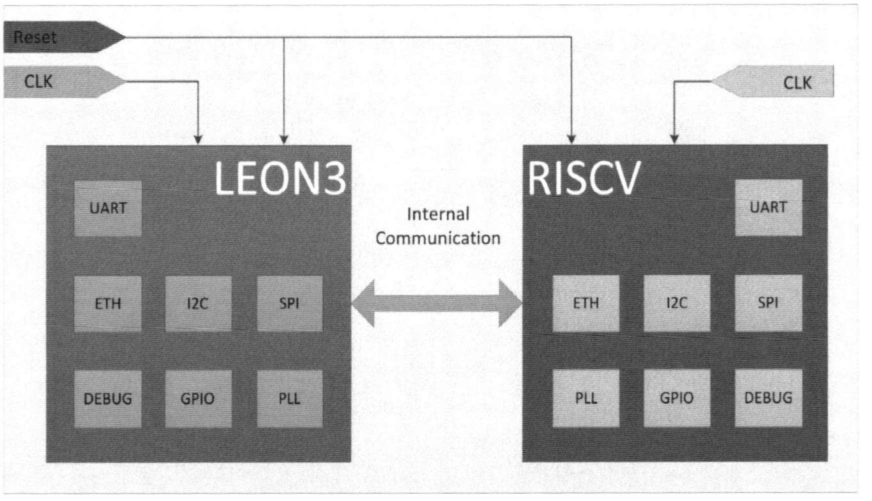

Figure 4. ARCHITECTURE design of the SSoC

In order to test the design, the software comparator is loaded in the RAM of both cores, and a simulation is made. The test consists of general purpose inputs/outputs (GPIOs). Their values are forced using a VHDL testbench and the software comparator loaded in the memory of each core handles the outputs. Different input feeds the processors; each core respectively reads this input and sends it internally to the other to compare it with its own. Three outputs exist, two of which represent the safety function handled by both cores, and the third represents a non-safety function handled by one of the processors – in this simulation, the LEON3 processor.

A testbench is created and simulated using Xilinx simulator, where the value of two switches that represent the inputs to the cores are the same, and the safety function on both cores is working along with the non-safety function. If there is a difference between the two inputs, the safety functions shut down on both cores, whereas the non-safety related function handled by Leon3 processor continues to work normally. The non-safety related function can only be stopped by a global reset. Figure 5 represents the simulation made. After a reset, the signals from RISCV and Leon3 are compared by the software: if they are equal, the SRF and the NSRF is high; if there is a difference, the SRF is low and the NSRF is still high. This simulation shows that availability can be increased in a redundant system. This simulation is then translated to the FPGA. The inputs are replaced by switches, the SRF by leds, and the NSRF by a simple motor for further testing. A discrepancy is noticed during simulation, due to different clock frequencies on each core, thus generating different response times of the processors, and creating a problem which will be handled in future work.

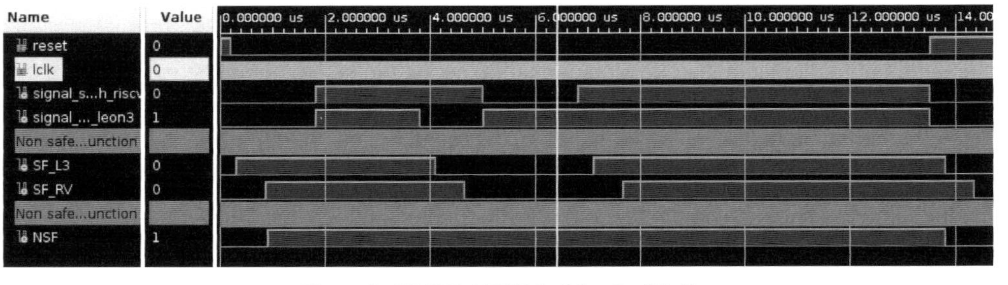

Figure 5. SIMULATION of the the SSoC

4. CONCLUSION AND FUTURE WORK

Because of the rapid advancement of semiconductor technology, the use of chips in various control applications is becoming increasingly appealing. Current research is focused on the use of system-on-chips in safety-related applications. A single on-chip safety system can combine and integrate all components of a safety system. SSoC results in a lower component count, which improves the system's reliability. Additionally, the system's costs are decreased. Besides, the usage of chips in electronic applications is supported by decreased power consumption and a more compact system design.

In this paper, the architecture of a 1oo2 diverse microprocessor is presented. The design consists of two processor cores, two sets of inputs and outputs, and communication through a software comparator mounted on both. The architectural concept is described. The hardware configuration of the proposed method was then presented. An assessment was given, highlighting the benefits of the proposed method. A simulation was made to prove functionality and show the increased availability.

Future research should place a greater emphasis on the mathematical safety evaluation of the introduced system. The safety parameter calculation must be addressed, analyzed, and compared with other systems. The system could be upgraded to a 1oo2D architecture enabling higher reliability against random hardware and systematic failures. A 1oo2D heterogeneous redundancy increases the system's reliability and reduces CCF (common cause failures). Having independent clock input, peripherals, and I/O overseen by a software comparator that detects a difference between the processors, ensure an HFT of 1. In case of hazards, the software comparator triggers an energized safe state where non-safety-related functions maintain their functionality.

REFERENCES

A. Hayek, B. Machmur, M. Schreiber, J. Börcsök, S. Gölz & M. Epp 2014, 'HICore1: "Safety on a chip" turnkey solution for industrial control', *2014 IEEE 25th International Conference on Application-Specific Systems, Architectures and Processors*, 2014 IEEE 25th International Conference on Application-Specific Systems, Architectures and Processors, pp. 74–5.

Abdelawwad, M, Hayek, A, Alsuleiman, A & Borcsok, J 2018 - 2018, 'FPGA Implementation of a Safety System-on-Chip Based on 1oo4 Architecture Using LEON3 Processor', *2018 International Conference on Computer and Applications (ICCA)*, 2018 International Conference on Computer and Applications (ICCA), Beirut, 8/25/2018 - 8/26/2018, IEEE, pp. 231–5.

Administrator 2022, 'GRLIB IP Library', 18 March, https://www.gaisler.com/index.php/downloads/leongrlib.

AURIX 32-bit microcontrollers for automotive and industrial applications-Highly integrated and performance optimized n.d.

Borcsok, J, Muller, W, Hahn, E, Schwarz, M & Abdelawwad, M 2021 - 2021, 'Safe-System-on-Chip for Functional Safety', *2021 18th International Multi-Conference on Systems, Signals & Devices (SSD)*, 2021 18th International Multi-Conference on Systems, Signals & Devices (SSD), Monastir, Tunisia, 3/22/2021 - 3/25/2021, IEEE, pp. 619–24.

Börcsök, J 2004, *Electronic safety systems: Hardware concepts, models, and calculations* (eng), Hüthig, Heidelberg.

——2007, *Functional safety: Basic principles of safety-related systems / Josef Börcsök* (eng ger), Practice, Hüthig, Heidelberg.

Edgar C. Ramirez n.d., 'Diverse Redundancy used in SIS technology to acheive higher safety integrity', viewed 18 March 2022, https://library.e.abb.com/public/c8ebe6fed0204975852575ac0061e959/1462_DiverseRedundancy_Final.pdf.

Grob, T n.d., 'Seminar', https://d-nb.info/1057871729/34.

Habinc, S 2022, 'CAES', 18 March, https://www.gaisler.com/index.php/component/content/article/38-news/events/471-porting-pikeos-to-noel-v-and-leon-sysgo-and-cobham-gaisler-extend-cooperation-around-risc-v.

Hahn, E, Kalinowski, D, Mueller, W, Abdelawwad, M & Boercsoek, J 2022, 'RISC-V Based Safety System-on-Chip with Hardware Comparator', in A Tallón-Ballesteros (ed.), *Proceedings of CECNet 2021*, Frontiers in artificial intelligence and applications / faia, vol. 345, IOS Press, Washington.

Hayek, A & Borcsok, J 2014 - 2014, 'On-chip safety system for embedded control applications', *MELECON 2014 - 2014 17th IEEE Mediterranean Electrotechnical Conference*, MELECON 2014 - 2014 17th IEEE Mediterranean Electrotechnical Conference, Beirut, Lebanon, 4/13/2014 - 4/16/2014, IEEE, pp. 315–9.

IEC International Electrotechnical Commission 2010a, *Functional safety of electrical/electronic/programmable electronic safety-related systems: Part 2: Requirements for electrical/electronic/programmable electronic safety-related systems*, General standard.

——2010b, *Functional safety of electrical/electronic/programmable electronic safety-related systems: Part 6: Guidelines on the application of IEC 61508-2 and IEC 61508-3*, General standard.

MELECON 2014 - 2014 17th IEEE Mediterranean Electrotechnical Conference 2014 - 2014, MELECON 2014 - 2014 17th IEEE Mediterranean Electrotechnical Conference, 4/13/2014 - 4/16/2014, Beirut, Lebanon, IEEE.

Pinkle, C 2016, 'The Why and How of Differential Signaling', *All About Circuits*, 17 November, https://www.allaboutcircuits.com/technical-articles/the-why-and-how-of-differential-signaling/.

RISC-V International 2022, 'RISC-V Exchange - RISC-V International', 8 March, https://riscv.org/exchanges/.

Semiconductors, NX n.d., 'MPC5744P Data Sheet', viewed 18 March 2022, https://www.nxp.com/docs/en/data-sheet/MPC5744P.pdf.

Texas Instruments, Incorporated [SPNU511 & D] n.d., 'Safety Manual for TMS570LS31x/21x Hercules ARM-Based Safety Critical MCUs (Rev. D)', viewed 18 March 2022, https://www.ti.com/lit/fs/spnu511d/spnu511d.pdf?ts=1647613357050&ref_url=https%253A%252F%252Fwww.google.com%252F.

Texas Instruments, Incorporated [SPRY178 & *] n.d., 'Hercules™ Microcontrollers: Real-time MCUs for safety-critical products', viewed 15 May 2022, https://www.ti.com/lit/wp/spry178/spry178.pdf?ts=1652629344679&ref_url=https%253A%252F%252Fwww.google.com%252F.

Wolf, M & Jerraya, AA (eds) 2005, *Multiprocessor systems on chips* (eng), Morgan Kaufmann series in systems on silicon, Morgan Kaufmann; Elsevier Science, Boston, https://learning.oreilly.com/library/view/-/9780123852519/?ar.

Xilinx 2022, 'Xilinx Artix-7 FPGA AC701 Evaluation Kit', 18 March, https://www.xilinx.com/products/boards-and-kits/ek-a7-ac701-g.html#resources.

Xilinx & Inc. n.d., 'Vivado Design Suite: AXI Reference Guide (UG1037)', https://www.xilinx.com/support/documentation/ip_documentation/axi_ref_guide/latest/ug1037-vivado-axi-reference-guide.pdf.

SYMBOLIC MODEL CHECKING FOR MODULAR SYSTEMS

F. Ouazar, M. C. Boukala and M. Ioualalen
MOVEP, Computer Science Department, USTHB
BP, 32 El-Alia, Algiers, Algeria

ABSTRACT

Model checking verification is a formal and fully automatic method widely used for checking critical and complex systems. It is based on reachability analysis, which often encounters the state space explosion problem. In this paper, we present our approach to mitigate this problem; we propose to use a hybrid solution based on symbolic representation of a system in a modular way. We proposed a symbolic method for CTL\X properties check on modular systems.

KEYWORDS

Model-Checking, Modular Systems, CTL\X, Symbolic Representation.

1. INTRODUCTION

One of the most powerful approaches and methods of analysing the behaviour of a critical system is the reachability analysis. By constructing the set of reachable states we can decide about the correctness of important properties such as liveness. Perhaps the most flexible analysing method we can use is the so called model checking (Clarke et al., 1999). The model checking is a powerful and automatic technique used for the verification of system's properties, expressed as logical formulae, by exploring all the possible behaviours and states of the system. However, the main issue and drawback of this approach is the state space explosion problem (Valmari, 1998), as, in general, the size of the state space that the model checker must handle increases exponentially with the number of states that constitute the system. This is the case of reactive systems, since they are composed of many parallel and concurrent processes. Several techniques have been proposed to reduce and cope with state space explosion problem. Among them, we can cite techniques and approaches that use a compact and a reduced representation of the system known as symbolic presentation (Edmund, et al.,1996) distribution methods (Boukala et al.,2007), aiming to use a cluster of machines for the representation of system states, the modularity technique on which the system is represented as a set of modules and components (Petrucci, Lakos, 2005) to which we are interested, Although one of the chief motivations for using modular specifications is to ease the design of complex systems, another reason is facilitating compositional reasoning. Compositional analysis aims to cope the problem of the explosion states by considering each module in isolation and then reason about the whole system.

In this paper, we present an hybrid framework for checking properties expressed by CTL\X logic (minus next operator) using symbolic representation of the system in a modular way. We present a solution which builds, in a modular way, an observation graph represented in a non-symbolic manner but where the nodes are composed from symbolic sets of states and the edges are labelled by the synchronization actions (observed actions) between the system components. Due to the small number of events to be observed (observed actions), the observation graph has a very moderate size and thus the time complexity for the verification is negligible w.r.t. the time to build the observation graph. To summarize:

- We have used the (SOG) symbolic observation graph (Klai, Petrucci 2008) for system modelisation, on which the nodes are symbolic sets of states and the edges labelled by the observed actions (the synchronized actions) between the system's components.
- We proposed an alternative CTL\X semantics, which is given in terms of actions of the SOG.
- We proposed model checking algorithms for CTL\X operators verification.

The rest of the paper is structured as follows. In Section 2, we recall the modular construction of the symbolic
observation graph approach. We recall CTL definition and present our alternative semantic in Section 3. We present our technique of symbolic verification and algorithms proposed for CTL operators in Section 4, we present some experimentation results in section 5, discussion and related works outlined in section 6, then we conclude the paper and give some perspectives in the last section.

2. SYMBOLIC OBSERVATION GRAPH

We recall the definition of the symbolic observation graph (SOG) defined in (Haddad et al., 2004) as an abstraction of the reachability state graph of concurrent systems. The construction of the SOG is based on the set of synchronized actions. Such actions are said to be observed while the other actions of the system are unobserved. Then the SOG is a graph, where each node is a set of states linked by unobserved actions (internal actions) and each arc is labelled by an observed action (synchronized action), the nodes of the SOG are called meta states and may be represented and managed efficiently using decision diagram techniques (BDDs for instance). Even though the number of meta-states of a SOG is exponential w.r.t. the number of states of the original system, the SOG has a very moderate size that allows the verification of large and complex systems.

The technique presented in this paper can be applied to different models, that can be mapped to (LTS) labelled transition systems, e.g. Modular Petri nets (Christensen, Petrucci, 2000) (Lakos, Petrucci, 2004). Since the formalism is simple, we chose to present it for labelled transition systems, and for the sake of generality.

2.1 Definition 1

A labelled transition graph (LTG) is a 4-tuple (Γ, Act, $\rightarrow$, I) where (Haddad et al., 2004):

- Γ is a finite set of states.
- Act is a finite set of actions.
- $\rightarrow \subseteq \Gamma\times(Act \cup\{\varepsilon\})\times\Gamma$ is a transition relation
- $I\subseteq \Gamma$ is a set of initial states.

We use s, s' to denote states in Γ, S, S' subsets of Γ and a an action in Act.

Intuitively, a node represents the state of the LTG, the labeled transition $s \xrightarrow{a} s'$ means that (s, a, s') $\in\rightarrow$, when the LTG is in state s, its state can change to s' while the action a is performed. A state s is called terminal if there is no transition from s to any other state in Γ ($s\not\rightarrow$). $S\xrightarrow{a}S'$ denotes that ($\forall s\in S$, $\exists s'\in S'$ s.t $s \xrightarrow{a} s'$ $\wedge$ $\forall s'\in S'$, $\exists s\in S$ s.t $s\xrightarrow{a}s'$). Enable(s) denotes the set of actions a such that $s \xrightarrow{a}$.

For the meta states definition we used the one defined in (Klai, Petrucci 2008).

2.2 Definition 2 (Meta State)

Let (Γ, Act, $\rightarrow$, I) be a labeled transition graph. Let Act = Obs $\cup$ UnObs be partitioned into observed and unobserved actions. Then, a meta-state is a M=< S, l, d> where:

1. S is a non empty subset of Γ where:
   - $\forall s\in S$, $\exists i\in I$ and $\exists \delta\in Act^*$ s.t $i \xrightarrow{\delta} s$; that means, a meta state contains only reachable states.
   - $\forall s\in S$, $\exists s'\in\Gamma$, $\forall \delta \in UnObs^*$: $s \xrightarrow{\delta} s' \Rightarrow s' \in S$; which means, for each state $s\in M.S$, all states s' reachable from s by a sequence of unobserved actions are also in M.S.
2. l = true iff the subgraph induced by S contains a cycle.
3. d= true iff the subgraph S contains a dead state.

Notation: M.S, M.l, M.d denotes the attributes of a meta state M.

2.3 Definition 3

A symbolic observation graph is a LTG Υ=(Γ', Act', →', I') associated with a LTG (Γ, Obs∪UnObs, →, I) such that:

1. Γ' is a finite set of meta states, (which means that the nodes of the SOG are meta states)
2. Act' =Obs; (that means that each arc of the SOG is labeled by an observed action)
3. $\rightarrow' \subseteq \Gamma' \times (Act') \times \Gamma'$ is a transition relation such that :
   - $\forall M, M' \in \Gamma'$ s.t $M \xrightarrow{a}' M'$ for some $a \in Act'$ if one of the following conditions holds:
   - i) $M \neq M' \Rightarrow \forall s \in M.S, \forall s' \in \Gamma, s \xrightarrow{a} s' \Rightarrow s' \in M'.S$; (that means M and M' are different, then each state of M enabling a has its successor in M')
   - ii) $M = M' \Rightarrow$ let $Pred = \{S \subseteq M.S \mid S = I \vee \exists M' \in \Gamma', \exists S' \in M'.S$ and $\exists a' \in Act'$ s.t $M' \xrightarrow{a'} M \wedge S' \xrightarrow{a'} S\}$, then $\forall S \in Pred, \exists s \in S, \exists s_1 \in M.S$ s.t $s \xrightarrow{\delta 1} s_1 \xrightarrow{\delta 2} s_1$ with $\delta_1 \in UnObs^*$, $\delta_2 \in (UnObs \cup \{a\})^+$. (that means the presence of a loop).
   - $\forall s, s' \in \Gamma, \forall a \in Obs$ $s \xrightarrow{a} s' \Rightarrow \exists M, M' \in \Gamma'$ s.t $s \in M.S$, $s' \in M'.S$ and $M \xrightarrow{a} M'$. (This means that all the observed arcs in the original LTS are preserved in the SOG).
4. $I' = \{M_0\}$, where M_0 satisfies $I \subseteq M_0.S$ and $\neg \exists M \in \Gamma' \setminus M_0$ s.t $M_0.S \subseteq M.S$. (that means that all the initial states of the original labeled transition system are in the initial meta-state of the symbolic observation graph).

For the modular system, each module is represented as a SOG and for modular construction of the SOG, the approach consists in synchronizing symbolic observation graphs of all modules, therefore a product of two meta states is defined $M = \langle S, l, d \rangle = M_1 \times M_2$ with respect to $Obs_1 \cap Obs_2$ and $S = S_1 \times S_2$, $l = l_1 \vee l_2$, and d=true iff $\exists (s_1, s_2) \in S$ s.t (s_1, s_2) is a dead state of the 2 LTSs. A detailed algorithm with more explanation is given in (Klai, Petrucci 2008).

2.4 Example

Figure 1 illustrates an example of LTS (Figure 1(a)) and the corresponding SOG (Figure 1(b)) for Obs = {Sync, obs}. The obtained SOG consists of 3 meta-states M1 with state A1B1, M2 with states A4B3, A5B3 and M3 with state A4B3, an arc from M1 to M2 labeled by Sync and one from M2 to M3 labeled by obs. Meta-state M1 contains loops but no dead state, whereas M2 and M3 have both a loop and a dead state. Note that state A4B3 is stored in both M2 and M3.

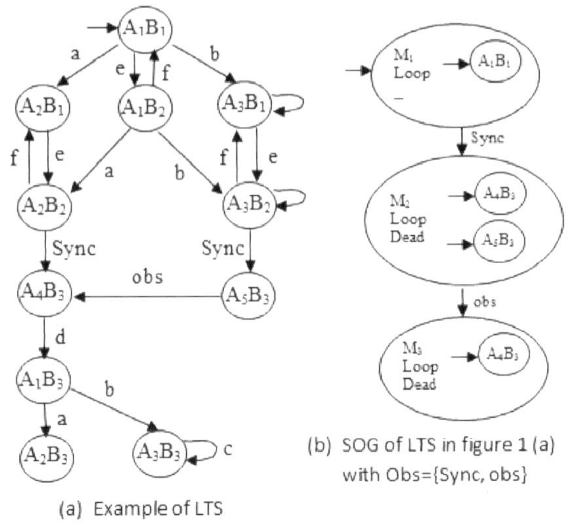

Figure 1. a LTS and its SOG

3. CTL LOGIC

Temporal logic is a language used to describe and specify qualitative and quantitative properties of systems using axiomatic expressions, and express specific properties of systems, such as mutual exclusion property. The syntax of this language is built from atomic propositions, propositional logic and temporal operators.

3.1 Definition

CTL logic is a branching-time temporal logic, introduced by Clarke and Emerson (Clarke et al.,1986). It is used to specify the usual properties of systems such as safety and vivacity.

The CTL formulas are defined as follows:

- Each atomic proposition is a CTL formula.
- If f and g are CTL formulas, so $\neg f$, $f \wedge g$, AXf, EXf, E(fUg), A(fUg) are CTL formulas

3.2 CTL Semantic

The interpretation of CTL formulas is defined over Kripke structures (Park 1994).

Definition: a Kripke structure is quadruple M = (S, T, λ, s_0) with:

- S a finite set of states
- $T \subseteq S \times S$ associates each state $s \in S$ with its successors.
- $\lambda : S \Rightarrow 2^{AP}$, associates to each state $s \in S$ a set of valid atomic propositions in s.
- $s_0 \in S$ the initial state.

Let $p \in AP$ be an atomic proposition, M = (S, T, λ, s_0) a Kripke structure, $\delta=(s_0, s_1, s_2,\ldots)$ a sequence of execution of M, $s_0 \in S$, φ and ψ CTL formulas. The satisfaction relation $|=$ is defined as follows:

$s \models p$ iff $p \in \lambda(s)$

$s \models \neg\varphi$ iff $\neg(s \models \varphi)$

$s \models \varphi \vee \psi$ iff $(s \models \varphi) \vee (s \models \psi)$

$s \models EX\varphi$ iff $\exists\delta$ such that $\delta(0)=s$, $\delta(1) \models \varphi$

$s \models AX\varphi$ iff $\forall\delta$ such that $\delta(0)=s$, $\delta(1) \models \varphi$

$s \models E[\varphi\ U\ \psi]$ iff $\exists\delta$ such that $\delta(0) = s$ and $\exists\ j \geq 0$, $\delta(j) \models \psi \wedge (\forall\ 0 \leq k < j, \delta(j) \models \varphi)$

$s \models A[\varphi\ U\ \psi]$ iff $\forall\delta$ such that $\delta(0) = s$ and $\forall\ j \geq 0$, $\delta(j) \models \psi \wedge (\forall\ 0 \leq k < j, \delta(j) \models \varphi)$

3.3 CTL\X Semantic Over a SOG

In this part, we give our interpretation of CTL semantic on the SOG. CTL semantic over Kripke structure is defined in term of states. For the SOG we define it in terms of actions. So we will consider the set of atomic propositions to be the set of actions of the SOG.

Let $\Upsilon=(\Gamma', Act', \rightarrow', I')$ be a SOG of all modules, φ and ψ CTL formulas, M a meta state of Υ, $a \in Act'$, $\delta=(M_0 \xrightarrow{a1} M_1 \xrightarrow{a2} \ldots \xrightarrow{an} M_n \xrightarrow{an+1} \ldots)$ a sequence of meta states of Υ.

So the $|=$ is defined as below for CTL\X operators (CTL minus next operator as the meta states are symbolic)

- $M \models a$ iff $\exists s, s', \in M.S$ st $s \xrightarrow{a} s'$ and M.d=false.
- $M \models \neg\varphi$ iff $\neg(M \models \varphi)$
- $M \models \varphi \vee \psi$ iff $M \models \varphi \vee M \models \psi$

- M |= E(φ U ψ) iff ∃ δ ∈ϒ, such that δ(0) ∈M.S and ∃j≥0, st δ(j) |=ψ ∧ ∀ 0 ≤ k <j, δ(j) |= φ and δ(k).d=false.
- M |= A(φ U ψ) iff ∀ δ ∈ϒ, such that δ(0) ∈M.S and ∀j≥0, st δ(j) |=ψ ∧ ∀ 0 ≤ k <j, δ(j) |= φ and δ(k).d=false ∧ δ(k).l=false.

3.4 Explanation

For the first case, the action a is correct if there exists a meta state M that executes it with the condition that no dead state exists in M (M.d=false). For the last case, we should ensure that there is no cycle in all the paths leading to the meta state on which ψ is true.

4. SYMBOLIC MODEL CHECKING

In this section, we present our algorithms of CTL\X operators defined over a SOG.

The state space is composed of all meta states of the synchronized SOGs of all the modules. The complexity of the algorithms is linear with the size of the SOG and the formula.

Let ϒ=(Γ', Act', →', I') be a SOG, the main objective of each algorithm is to compute the set of states sat(φ) that satisfy φ.

4.1 Model-Checking of CTL Propositional Formula

The purpose of this algorithm is to calculate all meta states satisfying φ.

Algorithm 1 sat(φ)

```
Begin
sat(φ)=ϕ
switch(φ) do
case φ = a
    For all M ∈ Γ' do
        If M executes a and M.d = false then
            sat(φ) ← sat(φ) ∪ M
        Endif.
    Endfor
case φ = ¬ψ
    For all M ∈ Γ' do
        If M ∉sat(ψ ) then
            sat(φ) ← sat(φ) ∪ M
        Endif.
    Endfor
case φ = φ1∨ φ2
    For all M ∈ Γ' do
        If( M ∈ sat(φ1 ∨ φ2))
          then sat(φ) ← sat(φ) ∪ M
        Endif.
    Endfor
Endcase
End
```

4.2 Model-Checking of φ=Eφ1 U φ2

The goal of this algorithm is to check on the SOG's meta states, if there is a path in which φ1 is true until φ2 becomes true, then label these states by φ.

Algorithm 2 sat(φ=Eφ1 U φ2)

```
Begin
sat(φ)=sat(φ2), Snew = sat(φ2)
while Snew ≠ ϕ do
M' ← oneelentof Snew
Snew ← Snew \ {M'}
  Foreach M predecessor of M' do
      If( M ∈ sat(φ1) \ sat(φ)
          Then sat(φ) ← sat(φ) ∪ M, Snew = Snew ∪ M
      Endif
   Endfor
Endwhile
End
```

4.3 Model-Checking of φ=Aφ1 U φ2

The goal of this algorithm is to check on the SOG's meta states, if in all paths φ1 is true until φ2 becomes true, then label these states by φ

Algorithm 3 sat(φ=Aφ1 U φ2)

```
Begin
sat(φ)=sat(φ2), Snew = sat(φ2)
Foreach M' ∈ Snew
Snew ← Snew \ {M'}
  Foreach M predecessor of M' do
      If( M ∈ sat(φ1) \ sat(φ))
          Then sat(φ) ← sat(φ) ∪ M, Snew = Snew ∪ M
      Endif
   Endfor
Endfor
End
```

4.4 Model-Checking of φ=EFψ

The principle of this algorithm is to find all meta states labelled by ψ and mark by φ all the predecessors of all these meta states.

Algorithm 4 sat(φ=EFψ)

```
Begin
sat(φ) = ϕ
  For all M, M' ∈ Γ' do
   If ( M' ∈ sat(ψ)) and M ∈ { the ancestors of M'} ∧ M.d= false // all the predecessors of M'
          then sat(φ) ← sat(φ) ∪{M}
   Endif
  Endfor
End
```

To decide whether the property is correct on the system or no, we check if the initial meta state is included in sat(φ). For the other operators as AG, we can use the equivalence of CTL operators.

Example

We will check the formula φ = ***AGAFobs*** on the system represented in figure 1, which expresses that always the action obs is eventually executed in the future.

$\varphi \equiv \neg EF \neg A(true\ U\ obs)$

By applying the above algorithms we find:

- Sat(obs)=ϕ
- Sat(A(trueU obs))=ϕ
- Sat($\neg$A(trueU obs))= {M_1, M_2, M_3}
- Sat(EF$\neg$A(trueU obs))={M_1}, (M_2.d=true, M_3.d=true).
- Sat(φ)=Sat($\neg$EF$\neg$A(trueU obs))={M_2, M_3}.
- The initial meta state M_1 can't be labeled by φ, ($M_1 \notin$Sat(φ)) so the formula can't be hold on the system above.

5. EXPERIMENTATIONS

As first experimentations, the above algorithms were implemented within a prototype tool. Given a SOG, and then a CTL property is verified.

In this part, we provide the first results obtained for the example cited above with comparison with the results obtained for a LTS in term of the time execution and a waiting the generalisation of the implementation for known and complex problems such as dining philosophers, data base managers...

Table 1. Some formulas checked

The formula	result	Time execution on the SOG (ms)	Time execution on the LTS (ms)
AGAFobs	false	0.01	0.32
AGAFsync	false	0.01	0.40
EFsync	true	<0.01	0.25

6. DISCUSSION AND RELATED WORKS

During the last 20 years, many researchers have worked on the use of abstraction and techniques to tackle the explosion problem of model-checking on concurrent systems, the modularity is one of these techniques allowing verifying large systems, Modular state spaces were studied in (Petrucci, 2005) (Ouazar et al.,2014), the idea there was to start from a system designed in a modular way and construct the state space of the complete system in a similar fashion: one local state space per module and a synchronization graph showing their interactions, the technique was applied to several problems and proved the interest of the modularity approach in representing systems weakly coupled and proved the good results obtained comparing with the ordinary method, in term of memory and time used to generate the state spaces. In (Klai, Petrucci 2008) and (Latvala, Makela, 2004), the authors interested to the verification of properties expressed with LTL logic and proposed the construction of the symbolic observation graph in a modular way, interested results obtained also. In (Lakos, Petrucci, 2008) the authors interested only to the general properties such as reachability, deadlock, etc...

7. CONCLUSION

In this paper, we presented our idea which is the symbolic verification of CTL formulas of modular systems, so the system is divided on components or modules and each module is represented by a Petri net or an LTS, each LTS is transformed to a SOG, then the verification will be ensured on the synchronized SOG of all modules with observed actions. So, we proposed a new semantic of CTL\X properties and operators within symbolic representation of the system, we proposed also model checking algorithms for CTL operators, then we implemented the algorithms on a prototype tool for simple examples. In the next step, we will apply the algorithms for large and complex systems and integrated theme to an existing model-checking tool to prove that this approach avoids the state space explosion problem.

REFERENCES

Boukala M.C, L. Petrucci, 2007, Towards distributed verification of Petri nets properties. *In Proc. 1st International Workshop on Verification and Evaluation of Computer and Communication Systems (VECOS'07)*, Algiers, Algeria, eWiC, pages 15-26. British Computer Society.

Christensen S and L. Petrucci, 2000. Modular analysis of Petri nets. *The Computer Journal*, 43(3) :224242.

Clarke M.E, E. A. Emerson, and A. P. Sistla, 1986. Automatic verification of finite state concurrent systems using temporal logic specifications. *ACM Transactions on Programming Languages and Systems*, pages p. 244_263.

Clarke, E., Grumberg, O., Peled, D, 1999, MODEL Checking. *MIT Press*, Cambridge, Massachusetts.

Edmund M. Clarke, Kenneth L. McMillan, Sérgio Vale Aguiar Campos, and Vassili Hartonas-Garmhausen, 1996, Symbolic model checking. *In Int. Conf. on Computer Aided Verification (CAV)* 1996, volume 1102 of Lecture Notes in Computer Science, pages 419_427. Springer.

Haddad S, Jean-Michel Ilié, and Kais Klai, 2004, Design and evaluation of a symbolic and abstraction-based model checker. *In Int. Conf. on Automated Technology for Verification and Analysis (ATVA)*, volume 3299 of Lecture Notes in Computer Science. Springer.

Klai K and Laure Petrucci, 2008, Modular construction of the symbolic observation graph. *In ACSD, IEEE*, China pp. 88-97.

Lakos C, L.Petrucci, 2004, Modular Analysis of Systems Composed of Semiautonomous Subsystems. *ACSD2004*, Ontario, Canada pages 185-196.

Latvala T, M. Makela, 2004, LTL Model Checking for Modular Petri Nets. *In ICATPN*, pages 298-311.

Ouazar F, M.Ioualalen, M.C.Boukala, 2014: vérification des systèmes modulaires, *Conférence sur les Architectures Logicielles CAL*, paris, France.

Ouazar F, M.Ioualalen, M.C.Boukala, 2014: verification of modular systems, *conference on Information Technology for Organizational Development*, Tebessa, Algeria, pages 246-251.

Park D, 1994. Concurrency and automata on infinite sequences. *In Springer, editor, In Deussen, P. (ed.). Theoretical Computer Science, Proceedings of the 5th GIConference Karlsruhe*, volume 104 of *Lecture Notes in Computer Science*, pages 167_ 183.

Petrucci L, 2005, EXPERIMENTS with Modular State Spaces. *Petri Net Newsletter* 68.

Petrucci L, C.Lakos, 2005, Distributed and modular state space exploration for timed Petri nets, *LIPN, CNRS UMR 7030*, Université Paris VIII.

Valmari, A.1998: The state explosion problem. *In: Lectures on Petri Nets I: Basic Models*. Volume 1491 of LNCS. Springer 429_528.

DESIGN OF PRODUCTS AND SERVICES FOR THE AUTOMATION OF CELL CULTURE IN THE PRODUCTION OF ADVANCED THERAPY MEDICINE

Dalia Gallico and Pietro Fissore
Università San Raffaele Roma, Italy

ABSTRACT

A cure for what until now was incurable. Tumors, arthrosis, regeneration of diseased tissues or those that have suffered a trauma. It sounds like science fiction but medicine is advancing and, thanks to the intertwining with biotechnologies, it is starting to propose innovative therapies that are proving to be effective. But. Half a million people are queuing (unfortunately constantly expanding) and even less than 1% are able to access these therapies every year. Production capacity is in fact held back by exorbitant costs, complex processes and organizational difficulties. This analysis aims to investigate the different and intertwined causes of the problem and is followed by the presentation of a project and development of a possible solution. The project involved an entire company and a Balanced Scorecard system made it possible to set up and maintain a balance in the internal dynamics between the many and various departments involved. For constant and clear internal communication, graphic and summary artifacts of Service Design such as Customer Journey Maps and Service Blueprints were used. The skills involved ranged from Business Development to regulatory different areas, from biotechnology to mechatronics and software, from communication to sales and post-market. The "Genesis" model was therefore chosen to structure and manage an Innovation Team in order to collect and filter an exhaustive map of ideas and to translate it into a Minimum Viable Product over a short period of time. The use of Design Thinking proved to be crucial and made it possible to immediately involve potential customers (consum-actors) and to empathize with their problems, deepening the search for hidden needs and allowing the formulation of solutions focused on creating real value and real benefit. The attention paid to correctly targeting business objectives has accompanied - and in some way even helped to amplify - the attention to satisfy not only the "company" customer but also the "person" customer. In fact, throughout the management of the User Experience we have tried to pay extreme attention to and leverage on "Design for All" to ensure both physical and cognitive ergonomics. The Nielsen-Norman Group's usability heuristics were used but also the stringent regulations for the usability of medical devices (despite the fact that the product is not configured as such) in order to increase the general comprehensibility of the instrument and reduce the error. human thanks to the cycle of "perception / cognition / action".

KEYWORDS

Quality-of-Service, Scientific Computing, Advanced Therapy Medicinal Products, Biotechnologies.

1. INTRODUCTION

Advanced Therapy Medicinal Products (abbreviated to ATMP) are biotech drugs based on cells, tissues or genes. They are part of the "medicine of the future" and o ff er very interesting opportunities for the treatment of both trauma from accidents or sports injuries and serious diseases such as leukemia, prostate cancer, cartilage defects and osteoarthritis. Every year, research brings out new therapeutic applications and thus the context is ever-expanding.

Compared to traditional drugs, ATMPs are mostly personalized drugs. By removing a small amount of adipose tissue or bone marrow from the patient, a small number of his adult stem cells can be obtained. These, cultivated according to precise procedures to make them grow in number, can be re-grafted locally in the patient himself, starting a natural process of regeneration of the diseased tissues and therefore of healing.

The global market stood at 11 billion dollars in 2021 with a projection of 21 billion in 2026. The diffusion is widespread all over the world with three main nuclei: Europe, USA and China.

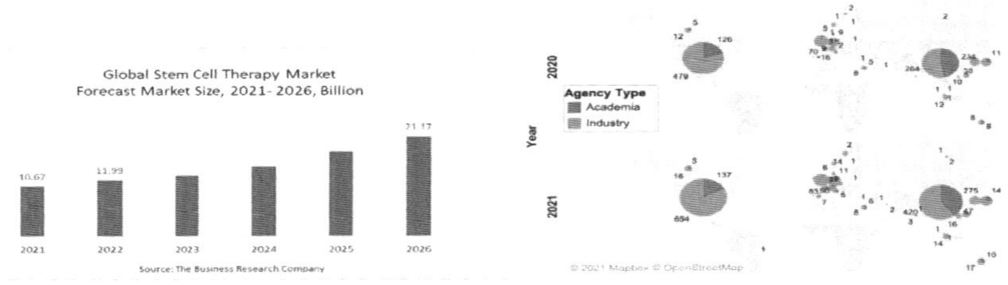

Figure 1. Global Stem Cell Therapy Market. The diffusion all over the world with three main nuclei: Europe, USA China

The production of ATMP is regulated by local agencies such as the Food and Drug Administration (FDA), the European Medicines Agency (EMA) and the National Health Commission of the PRC (NHC), which are responsible for ensuring the strict regulatory constraints. and control.

Within the 2030 Agenda, this international context has both a "healthcare" and a "productive" nature and therefore falls into two points: 3 - Health and Wellness; 9 - Businesses, Innovation and Infrastructures.

2. THE PROBLEM

The manufacturers of these therapies are called Cell Factory and are laboratories with highly specialized personnel equipped with sterile environments ("Cleanroom") and with a high technological content. Unlike traditional drugs, which are produced in large batches, advanced therapies are personalized drugs and therefore require many minute and separate small-scale productions. Although the potential of these therapies is enormous, the resulting problem is that very few people can still access them every year due to the prohibitive costs and organizational difficulties to produce them. Referring to 2021, less than 1% of patients waiting for a dose were able to receive it. The market trend is therefore that of optimizing production processes. The main strand is that of migration from manual to automated processes. In recent years, the main trade fairs and congresses of the sector such as ASCO (Chicago), Advanced Therapies (London), EORS (Rome) and EBHT (Trieste) have in fact more and more automated devices - called "Bioreactors" - whose purpose is precisely that of increasing standardization and at the same time optimizing resources, all in the direction of being able to produce more therapeutic doses every year at a lower cost. Being a relatively new and constantly evolving context, still no one seems to have found the winning formula in terms of features, performance and flexibility, so the race is still widely open.

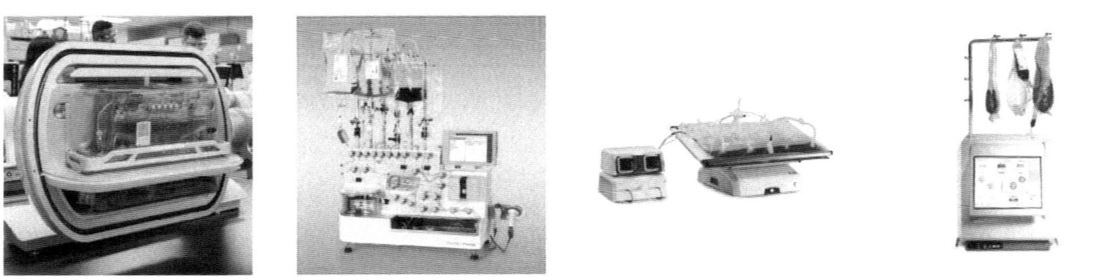

Lonza **Cocoon** | Miltenyi **CliniMACS** | GE **Wave** | Terumo **Quantum**

Figure 2. Automated devices - called "Bioreactors

Above all in terms of flexibility, the market continues to show needs that are not yet sufficiently satisfied. First of all, the possibility on the part of therapy manufacturers to be able to make changes on the fly during the development of production processes in order to find the optimal and most sustainable formula both for patients and for the laboratories themselves.

3. OBJECTIVES AND CONSTRAINTS

Compared to the automated devices currently on the market, it is therefore intended to study an alternative solution that is able to at least equal (and hopefully overcome) the reduction in production costs of the single therapeutic dose as well as increase the flexibility and customization of processes by users.

It is decided to create a network of Consumers-Actors involving various potential customers in order to collect concrete requirements first and to have the results evaluated at the end of the design.

From the analysis of the requirements it was concluded that the production costs of ATMP are excessive for the following reasons.

1. The production spaces ("Cleanroom") are structures that must ensure air sterility, where access to the areas is highly regulated given the critical risk of contamination and the equipment is numerous, heterogeneous and expensive.

2. Due to the risk of contamination, it is not possible to prepare more than one dose per patient at a time, a complication that affects production scalability.

3. The staff must be highly specialized and, due to tiring schedules and work rhythms, it is difficult to keep them for a long time, a complication that extends the training periods and efforts for new recruits.

4. Production takes place by means of still mostly manual processes where the numerous operations to be performed are prone to errors and numerous iterative checks are required to ensure repeatable and standard quality within the strict regulatory constraints.

The main operational constraints within which Cell Factories are obliged to operate are contained in guidelines called Good Manufacturing Practices (abbreviated GMP). At a high level, the following are the main principles.

1. Manufacturing facilities must maintain a clean and hygienic manufacturing area.

2. Manufacturing facilities must maintain controlled environmental conditions in order to prevent cross-contamination from adulterants and allergens that may render the product unsafe for human consumption or use.

3. Manufacturing processes must be clearly defined and controlled. All critical processes are validated to ensure consistency and compliance with specifications.

4. Manufacturing processes must be controlled, and any changes to the process must be evaluated. Changes that a ff ect the quality of the drug are validated as necessary.

5. Instructions and procedures must be written in clear and unambiguous language using good documentation practices.

6. Operators must be trained to carry out and document procedures.

7. Records must be made, manually or electronically, during manufacture that demonstrate that all the steps required by the defined procedures and instructions were in fact taken and that the quantity and quality of the food or drug was as expected. Deviations must be investigated and documented.

8. Records of manufacture (including distribution) that enable the complete history of a batch to be traced must be retained in a comprehensible and accessible form.

9. Any distribution of products must minimize any risk to their quality.

10. A system must be in place for recalling any batch from sale or supply.

11. Complaints about marketed products must be examined, the causes of quality defects must be investigated, and appropriate measures must be taken with respect to the defective products and to prevent recurrence.

This list therefore represents the scenario in which it is necessary to move during the study of a series of solutions and serves as a guide in the final phase of product validation.

4. PLANNING AND DEVELOPMENT

A design approach of Service Design is chosen (rather than just "Product Design") as the relationships with the consumer-actors have shown that the operational context of the product is actually a complex ecosystem.

The main high-level characteristics that must be respected to ensure a result capable of bringing real benefit to the customer are defined below.

1. The device must automate the greatest number of currently manual steps, incorporating various existing instruments and thus combining and simplifying the technology involved.

2. The device must allow to prepare several doses in parallel without risk of contamination in order to decrease the production capacity.

3. The device must make it possible to reduce the continuous intervention of staff to reduce access to the Cleanroom and thus limit the risk of contamination, constantly monitoring the processes and automatically providing all the detailed data acquired during crops.

4. The device must allow personnel to design robust automated processes that can be used in a standard manner throughout the production line to increase the quality of the final result and to reduce the manual workload, while allowing an easy and rapid iteration in the modification and in the optimization of processes.

Development goes through four main innovation sectors which we explore below.

5. AUTOMATION OF MANUAL STEPS

A cell culture lasts approximately two weeks. During this period, the main manual steps to perform include:

1. create and maintain a controlled temperature and CO2 environment where cells can grow;
2. manage the transfer of liquids, ie nutrients for growth and waste produced during the same;
3. photograph the cells under a microscope to determine their real state of growth, a parameter that determines the repetition of specific steps up to a precise value or, upon reaching the same, the actual continuation of the process;
4. carry out sampling of liquids to carry out detailed quality controls in itinere;
5. collect the cells at the end of the culture to prepare them for the subsequent stages of drug preparation.

The first component of the solution is an automated tool, called a Bioreactor, capable of responding to these needs. It is a benchtop instrument that encompasses a series of technologies capable of satisfying the listed requirements.

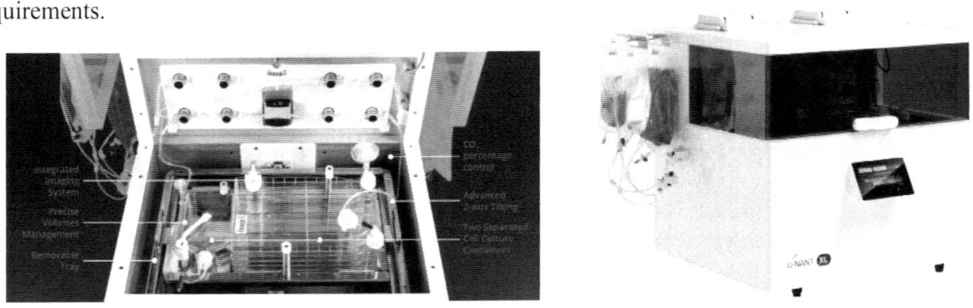

Figure 3. Automated tool, called a Bioreactor

The main compartment, called the culture compartment, contains: heaters to generate the necessary temperature; a pump to insure CO2 at the necessary percentages; a pump and valves to manage the flow of liquids; a microscope capable of acquiring images of the cells and autonomously determining, thanks to an intelligent algorithm, the state of growth; a series of sensors to acquire on-going process control parameters. The functionality of the microscope is perhaps the most innovative of all as it allows real automation since the cells are alive and always behave differently from one culture to another. Determining the progress of the process is therefore more complex than, for example, managing the production of a graph where the steps are always identical and easily predetermined. The intelligent algorithm is able to analyze the photo and numerically determine the growth parameter thus allowing the Bioreactor to decide independently how to proceed with the crop.

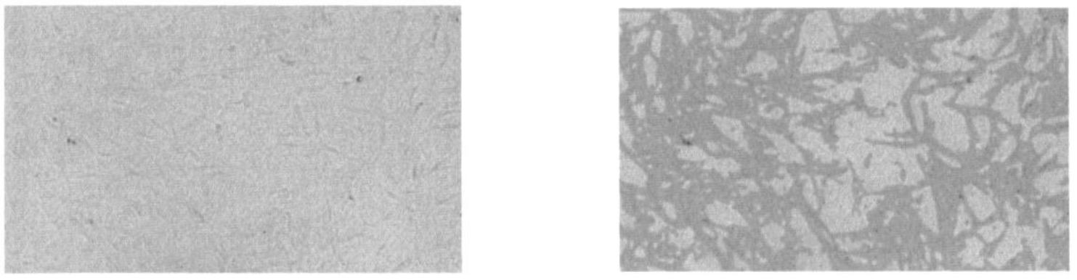

Figure 4. Functionality of the microscope allows real automation since the cells are alive and always behave differently from one culture to another

The Bioreactor embodies the functionalities of different instruments (incubators, laminar flow hoods, benchtop microscopes ...) and integrates and optimizes their use in a single environment that the cells never leave from the beginning to the end of the culture (in manual processes, to carry out these operations in sequence, the cells must be transported to different places in the Cleanroom with the risk of disturbing their correct growth).

Like any tool that automates processes up to now carried out manually by highly specialized skilled hands, the staff could certainly have problems to trust. The physical design of the object must therefore also take into account this possible "wall" of mistrust. For this reason the instrument has a large transparent glass, a sort of "o ff er of peace" towards the operators, a real declaration of transparency to all effects, as if to say: "I do everything automatically but look, you can check everything whenever you want ".

The general aesthetics of the Bioreactor stems from a design and construction approach "from the inside out", so the final shape was obtained by following exactly the geometries and spaces rationally necessary for the functioning of the various internal mechanisms. The absence of frills and the rigorous reduction of surfaces up to almost a primitive, as well as being a necessity to facilitate cleanability - a fundamental characteristic for this area - aims to simplify the advanced complexity of internal technologies to o ff er its user in the lightest and friendliest way possible.

The conception of the device, which started from a white board, was followed, over the course of a few months, by the CAD design and the construction of the very first prototypes with the aid of construction materials that are easy to find and work at home (such as wooden profiles for the structures and flat panels in wood and aluminum for the paneling), as well as the use of 3D printing for the more complex functional components. Actuators such as motors and levers were controlled by a series of Arduino boards on which the first basic software was also installed to arrive at a first series of experiments for proof of concept. Functional tests with typical users have made it possible to study the user interfaces on the integrated front display, in the continuous search to give the right shape to the potential mental schemes typical of end users. In the following months, we moved to a more specific design with the creation of a network of suppliers for key processes, the optimization of software and electronics as well as the necessary safety certification for market introduction.

Multiple Doses in Parallel Without Risk of Contamination

The second component of the solution is a closed and sterile circuit, called Disposable Cartridge, made up of tubing, bags and components specific to the conduct of a cell culture.

The Cartridge is mounted inside the Bioreactor and allows the cells of a specific patient to be safely stored - for the entire two weeks of culture - without the risk of contamination with those of another patient.

Its disposable nature allows you to quickly switch from one patient to the next without having to spend excessive time on cleaning and sterilization. For the most part it is composed of components on the market (to give a sense of familiarity to the operators), joined with specific tubing and completed by small customized elements and produced in injection molds.

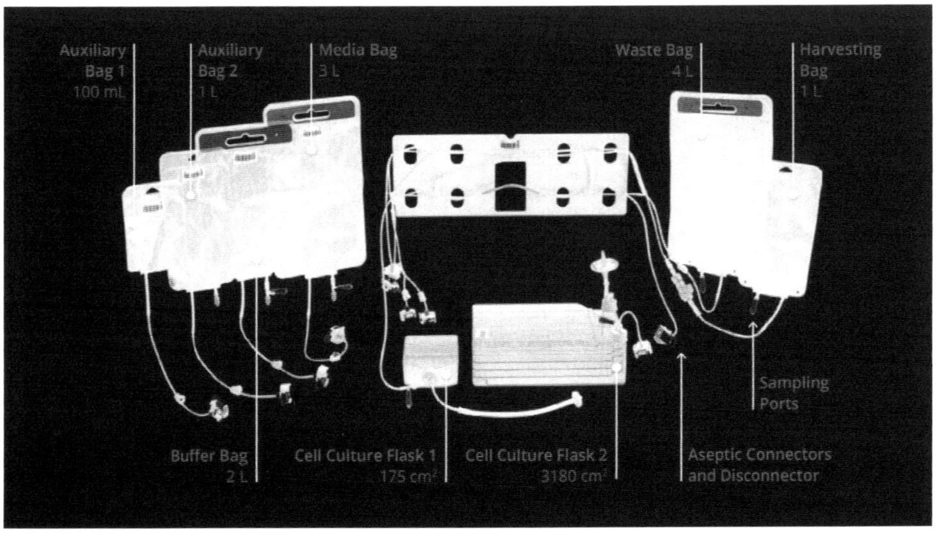

Figure 5. Disposable Cartridge, consisting of tubing, bags and components specific to the conduct of a cell culture

The most interesting optimization is that the Cartridge project has made it possible to reduce the use of components compared to the processes performed manually, thus also resulting in a lower final impact of consumption and disposal of plastic material which is not yet recyclable as biological waste.

6. CUSTOMIZATION OR OPTIMIZATION OF PROCESSES

The entry into the Cleanroom to check the progress of the processes, in addition to amplifying the risk of environmental contamination, involves lengthy preparations and dressing (gloves, coats, gowns ...) which result in significant costs.

To overcome this problem, the solution provides for remote monitoring of processes via desktop, phone or tablet. A web-based application allows staff to check all the process parameters in progress at will and even visually check the cells thanks to the images acquired by the microscope.

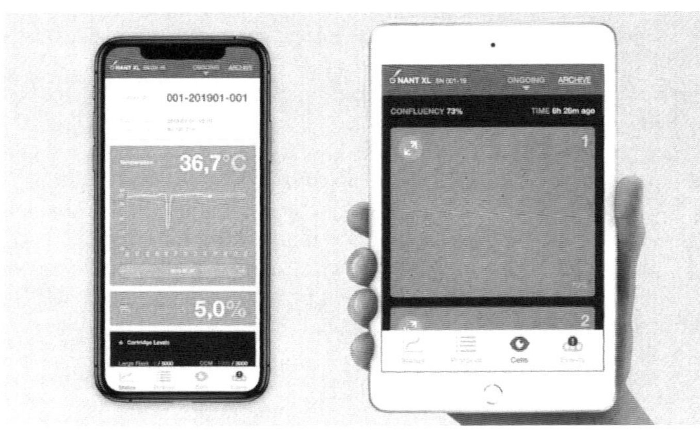

Figure 6. Remote monitoring of processes via desktop, phone or tablet to check all the process parameters in progress and even the cells thanks to the images acquired by the microscope

Each drug requires various research and optimization cycles and, in any case, is always different from Cell Factory to Cell Factory.

One of the services offered is a web-based cloud software that allows operators to build from scratch, with very simple clicks, the sequence of operations of their specific cell culture, upload it to the Bioreactor and quickly optimize it between one development test and another.

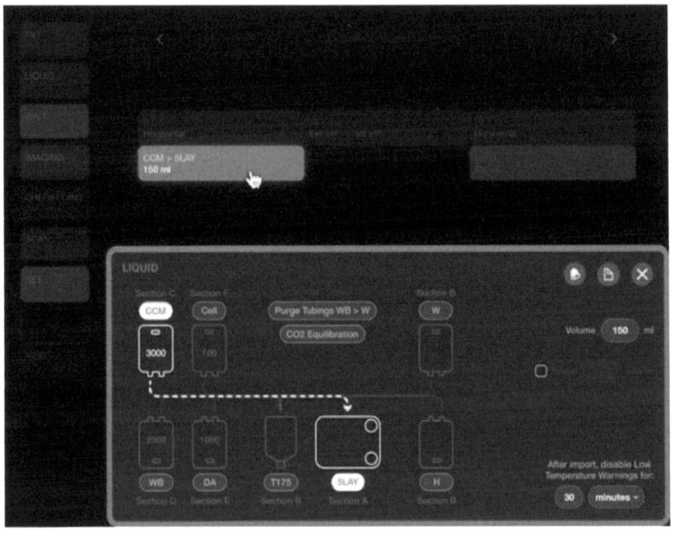

Figure 7. Web-based cloud software that allows to build from scratch, with very simple clicks, the sequence of operations of their specific cell culture

To summarize, we remind that the essential metrics for design and development evaluation are the following.

1. The device must produce every single dose at least equalizing the cost reduction offered by the competition.

2. The customer must be able to customize processes with extreme simplicity and speed in order to ensure the best optimization for both patients and the laboratory itself.

To evaluate the first point, a cost model was developed, in collaboration with a partner of the network, which shows how, by using two Bioreactors to replace the manual process, it is possible to reduce costs by 24%. Using four Bioreactors it is even possible to triple the production without having to increase the production facilities and staff, reducing costs by half.

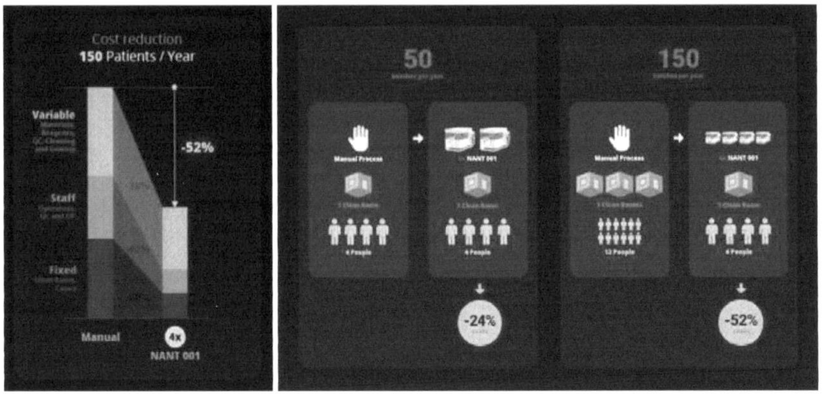

Figure 8. The satisfaction questionnaire about customer to be able to customize processes with extreme simplicity and speed

For the evaluation of the second point, a satisfaction questionnaire was submitted to all members of the network. The results highlighted a satisfactory ease of use and a great versatility of the design and process optimization software, also and above all in relation to the alternatives offered by the competition.

7. CONCLUSION

The project involved an entire company and a Balanced Scorecard system made it possible to set up and maintain a balance in the internal dynamics between the many and various departments involved. For constant and clear internal communication, graphic and summary artifacts of Service Design such as Customer Journey Maps and Service Blueprints were used.

The skills involved ranged from Business Development to regulatory different areas, from biotechnology to mechatronics and software, from communication to sales and post-market. The "Genesis" model was therefore chosen to structure and manage an Innovation Team in order to collect and filter an exhaustive map of ideas and to translate it into a Minimum Viable Product over a short period of time.

The use of Design Thinking proved to be crucial and made it possible to immediately involve potential customers (consum-actors) and to empathize with their problems, deepening the search for hidden needs and allowing the formulation of solutions focused on creating real value and real benefit. Indeed, it is only thanks to Design Thinking that the numerous multi-disciplinary efforts, repeated for different construction / feedback / redesign iterations, have managed to converge in a balanced and sustainable product.

The attention paid to correctly targeting business objectives has accompanied - and in some way even helped to amplify - the attention to satisfy not only the "company" customer but also the "person" customer. In fact, throughout the management of the User Experience we have tried to pay extreme attention to and leverage on Design for All to ensure both physical and cognitive ergonomics. The Nielsen-Norman Group's usability heuristics were used but also the stringent regulations for the usability of medical devices (despite the fact that the product is not configured as such) in order to increase the general comprehensibility of the instrument and reduce the error. human thanks to the cycle of "perception / cognition / action".

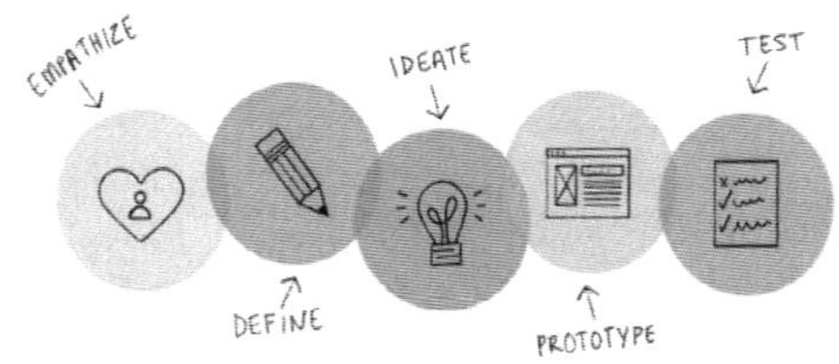

Figure 9

REFERENCES

England, J.L. (2013). Statistical physics of self-replication. The Journal of Chemical Physics, 139(12), 09B623_1. http://www.englandlab.com/uploads/7/8/0/3/7803054/2013jcpsrep.pdf

Mayumi, K. (2009) Nicholas Georgescu-Roegen: His Bioeconomics Approach to Development and Change. Development and Change, 40(6), 1235-1254.

Mayumi, K. (2009). Nicholas Georgescu-Roegen: His Bioeconomics Approach to Development and Change. Development and Change, 40(6), 1235-1254. https://onlinelibrary.wiley.com/doi/full/10.1111/j.1467-7660.2009.01603.x

Morris, J. et al. (2019). Biology: How Life Works, 3rd edition, p. 3098.

Schrodinger, E. (1944). What is life? The Physical Aspect of the Living Cell. http://www.whatislife.ie/downloads/What-is-Life.pdf

See http://statisticstimes.com/economy/gross-world-product.php

See https://earthlogic.info/wp-content/uploads/2019/12/Earth-Logic-eversion.pdf

See https://www.nationalgeographic.com/magazine/2020/03/how-a-circular-economy-could-save-the-world-feature/Goerner S, Fiscus D, & Fath, B.D. (2015). Using energy network science (ENS) to connect resilience with the larger story of systemic health and development. Emergence: Complexity and Organization, 17 (3), 1-21.See https://www.chemforward.org/stacy-bio

See https://www.quantamagazine.org/a-new-thermodynamics-theory-of-the-origin-of-life-20140122/

Van Der Heijden, M., Martin, F., Selosse, M., and Sanders, I. (2015). Mycorrhizal ecology and evolution: the past, the present, and the future. New Phytologist, 205(4), 1406-1423.

SHORT PAPERS

TRANSDISCIPLINARY EDUCATIONAL CASE: DEVELOPING A MESH (MUNICIPAL-ENVIRONMENTAL-SOCIAL-HEALTH) PLATFORM

Meira Levy[1], Sivan Spitzer[2] and Michal Pauzner[3]
[1]*School of Industrial Engineering and Management, Shenkar, College of Engineering Design, Art, 12 Ana Frank St., Ramat-Gan, Israel*
[2]*Azrieli Faculty of Medicine, Bar Ilan University – BIU, 8 Henrietta Szold St., Safed, Israel*
[3]*Visual Communication Department, Shenkar, College of Engineering Design, Art, 12 Ana Frank St., Ramat-Gan, Israel*

ABSTRACT

The paper presents an on-going research program that aims to develop a MESH (Municipal-Environmental-Social-Health) platform that will facilitate the prevention of type 2 diabetes and promote healthy life and people well-being. The MESH platform exhibits the realization that the ecological aspects that are caused by humans influence our health. The ecological determinants are coupled with the social determinants of health which are the non-medical health factors that influence health outcomes and reflect the conditions in which people are born, grow, live, work and age. The MESH comprehensive framework includes methods and tools for MESH platform development. The first phase of the on-going research is a collaborative transdisciplinary course of the design, engineering, and medicine faculties. Students from the different domains collaborate and practice the design thinking methodology to come up with innovative solutions for the MESH platform. In this short paper we present the research and the challenge the students face as well as the course pedagogical vision and structure.

KEYWORDS

Health, Environmental Determinants, Social Determinants, Requirements Engineering, Design Thinking, Diabetes.

1. INTRODUCTION

"It is becoming increasingly clear that the Earth's natural systems are under threat from human activity, and this threatens the health of the human population of the Earth [...] Responding to this situation has to be a priority for those working in health promotion." (Hancock, 2019).

The World Health Organization (WHO) points to the linkage between Environmental determinants (Pritchard, 2019) and Social Determinants of Health (Friedman and Banegas,2018). The environmental aspects that are caused by humans influence our health, are entitled the Ecological Determinants of Health, call not only to reduce the human footprint (e.g. replacing meat consumption with fruits, vegetables, nuts, and legumes), but also to improve the quality of our water and decrease air pollution. Social Determinants of Health are the non-medical health factors that influence health outcomes and reflect the conditions in which people are born, grow, live, work and age. The linkage between environmental sustainability and health challenges can be demonstrated by the need to decrease private transportation and increase public ones (for improving air quality), which resembles the need to increase physical activity (for reducing stress and improving community, family connections, and general well-being).

The WHO[1] calls for pursuing initiatives in the urban domain. Despite variations in what they are and how they operate, municipalities possess features that position them (to varying degrees) to address population health inequities as their responsibilities include culture & leisure, education, environment, health & social

[1]https://www.who.int/teams/social-determinants-of-health/urban-health

services, housing, planning, public safety, transportation, water, and/or waste (Mapar et al., 2017). However, the performance of public sector organizations including municipalities, and the degree to which they focus on the integration of health, safety, and environmental (HSE) determinants to improve the lives of their residents has remained underexplored (Collins and Hayes, 2010; Meroni et al., 2021).

2. RESEARCH STATEMENT

Personal and environmental responsibilities have been found to lead to both healthier life and well-being. This hypothesis underlies our main research objective that aims to build awareness to both sustainable and health concerns, that will eventually lead to behavioral change and responsibility. To achieve this objective, we will recruit municipalities as pivots of change and will examine diverse perspectives of different stakeholders for creating a circle of change in the community. The study is unique as it addresses requirements beyond the technological ones in order to foster behavioral change and create healthier and sustained communities. It follows the concept of the "City as-a-Platform" (Repette et al., 2021) and the Knowledge-based Urban Development (KBUD) conceptual framework (Chang .2018). The study uses the case study of diabetes, as urban environments not only impact people's risk of developing type 2 diabetes but can also influence people's ability to manage it effectively. With rising obesity and sedentary lifestyle, access to green spaces, walkability, and a lifestyle promoting platform is critical. With an estimated 640 million people by 2040, type 2 diabetes poses a global challenge in the HSE interface and the role of municipalities. Existing data shows us that the lack of health promoting infrastructure is grossly exacerbated in municipalities at the social-geographic peripheries.

The research aims to develop innovative methodologies and tools for a trans disciplinary requirements engineering (RE) process for developing such platforms thereby addressing RE-related challenges in the social context with a large group of heterogeneous stakeholders (Doerr et al., 2018; Villela et al., 2018). Former studies have addressed the need to educate requirements engineers for sustainability awareness (Duboc et al., 2020), but we did not find studies suggesting methods and tools for developing platforms that promote health and sustainability.

The study will apply the Service Design (SD) approach that brings together a human centered, holistic perspective and methods with service systems thinking to design complex service Systems (Eun, 2020). It greatly increases the ways in which people can explore, express, and evaluate their current experiences and future lifestyles (Sanders and Stappers, 2014). Borrowing Design Thinking (DT) and Service Design (SD) methodologies and tools to facilitate transdisciplinary co-creation, allows for participation at different levels and ranges to effectively achieve value co-creation in dealing with social issues (Yang and Sung, 2016; Brenner et al., 2016).

In our research we apply the DT methodology which includes: (1) mindset, (2) process, and (3) toolbox (Brenner et al., 2016). As a mindset, it exhibits three key principles: (1) a combination of divergent and convergent thinking, (2) a strong orientation towards both explicit and implicit needs of users, and (3) prototyping. As a process it combines a micro- and a macro-process. The micro-process—as an innovation process per se—consists of five steps: (1) define the problem; (2) find needs and synthesize; (3) ideate; (4) create a prototype; and (5) test. The macro-process consists of managing milestones while developing prototypes that must fulfill defined requirements. As a toolbox, DT refers to the application of numerous methods and techniques taken from various disciplines: design, engineering, informatics, and psychology (Brenner et al., 2016). Moreover, we aim to develop new DT methods and techniques that are inspired by best practices of disciplines such as sociology, film studies, and journalism (Hess et al., 2021).

Following the design study and conceptual MESH (Municipal-Environmental-Social-Health) prototype validation, the study will focus on service design research (Eun, 2020;), hence, defining the solution requirements and building a working prototype of the MESH platform, and studying its usefulness and acceptance. The prototype will be tested on its effectiveness for addressing the health challenge of diabetes. The data obtained will help realize the impact of the solution in building communities that promote sustainable personal and community health.

The research workplan will be comprised of four phases:

1. Study municipalities in social-geographic peripheries in Israel for developing the framework and defining the requirements for the MESH platform that promotes healthier and sustainable life.

2. Design and develop the platform according to the defined requirements.
3. Validate the developed platform by piloting it in communities facing the challenge of preventing diabetes as well as improving management and reducing complications for those already sick.
4. Analyze the implementation process and outcomes and enhance the platform accordingly.

We will conduct our case study mainly in Israel in The Russell Berrie Galilee Diabetes SPHERE (Social Precision-medicine Health Equity Research Endeavour) which aims to promote health in Israel's northern social-geographic periphery, reducing the gap of diabetes morbidity and mortality, by focusing on urban infrastructure. In its first phase the project will implement a complex intervention to prevent the onset of disease and improve management in 5 cities. The cities chosen include diverse ethnic populations including Arab Muslim and Christians, Druze, and Ultra-orthodox Jews.

3. EDUCATIONAL SETTING

Beyond developing the MESH platform, our research targets to educate the next generation of engineering, design, and medical students about the importance of transdisciplinary effort in solving complex social, health and sustainable challenges. In this regard, the first phase of our on-going research is divided to three stages:

1. A transdisciplinary course where engineering, design and medical students study the research agenda and create conceptual prototypes that advances the theoretical approach of the MESH platform in the context of diabetes in Israel's northern social-geographic periphery.
2. Build a working prototype in a summer lab.
3. Validate the working prototype in a real setting.

The course includes 14 sessions in which 4 groups of students from the different domains will work according to the Double Diamond framework (Design Council, 2007). The Double Diamond is a clear, comprehensive, and visual description of the design process. Launched in 2004, it has become world-renowned with millions of references to it on the web. As well as highlighting the design process, Design Council's framework also includes the key principles and design methods that designers and non-designers need to take, and the ideal working culture needed, to achieve significant and long-lasting positive change. The Double Diamond framework (Figure 1) is formed from four distinct phases, which are: Discover, Define, Develop and Deliver. The framework places emphasis on the Discover phase as one of the most critical, and the one which makes best use of the designer's knowledge and skills. The figure represents the divergent and convergent stages of the design process, showing the different modes of thinking that designers use.

The course will work closely with relevant stakeholders from the medical and municipal institutes as well in collaboration with the relevant communities in order to develop solutions for Diabetes preventive challenges and address cultural as well as social barriers.

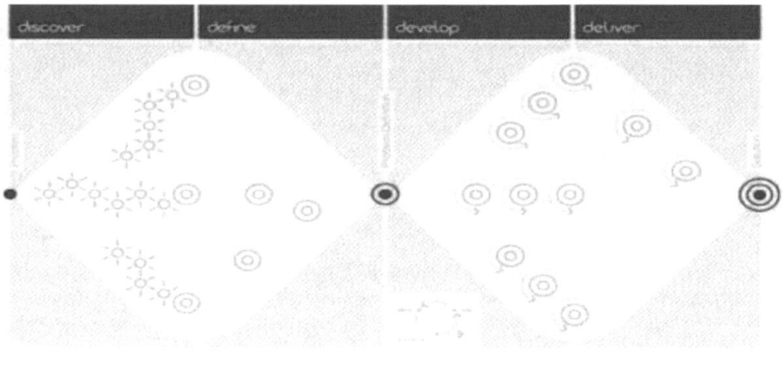

Figure 1. The Double Diamond Framework (Design Council, 2007)

4. PRELIMINARY RESULTS

The course we developed is currently being implemented. Over the past weeks, students have been working to address four major challenges of The Russell Berrie Galilee Diabetes SPHERE working with the relevant stakeholders presented in Section 3:

1. The Municipality
2. High-School students
3. Pregnant women with risk to develop gestational diabetes
4. Physicians who treat and manage patients with type 2 diabetes

We used the Miro[2] digital whiteboard platform as a place for collecting both the course materials as well as students' work. Medical students participated in the course via Zoom[3] video meetings, given the geographical distance between Shenkar located in the center of country and the Azrieli Faculty of Medicine located in Israel's northern periphery. The concepts developed by student teams addressed diverse aspects and needs, ranging from clinical measurement and reporting of tests; physical aspects, such as infrastructure to encourage physical activities, environmental concerns, such as promoting the use of solar energy in sports' fields; emotional support for pregnant women, for example, by creating virtual support of clinicians and mentors as well as improving the well-being of children and empowering for health lifestyle choices through gamification and cooking contests.

5. CONCLUSION

Our short paper describes an on-going research agenda and the first step of a transdisciplinary educational setting where design, engineering and medical students collaborate to develop the first MESH platform. Our pedagogical vision promotes transdisciplinary approach, involving students from various domains to tackle a "wicked" problem that can't be addressed solely from one perspective and requires human-centered and systemic design in order to facilitate behavioral change that last in the long-run.

Our experience to date shows that addressing the The Russell Berrie Galilee Diabetes SPHERE challenges through multidisciplinary student teams, actually manifested the MESH (Municipal-Environmental-Social-Health) PLATFORM. The conceptual solutions developed by the students tackle SPHERE's complex challenges through clinical, municipal, environmental, and social perspectives. A follow-up study will develop MVPs of the best solutions, assessing the feasibility and effectiveness of the proposed conceptual solutions.

REFERENCES

Brenner, W. et al., 2016. Design Thinking as Mindset, Process, and Toolbox, in Brenner, W. and Uebernickel, F. Eds., 2016. *Design thinking for innovation research and practice*, ch 1, Springer, NY.

Chang, D.L. 2018. Knowledge-based, smart and sustainable cities: A provocation for a conceptual framework. *J. Open Innov. Technol. Mark. Complex*, 4.

Collins, P.A. and Hayes, M.V., 2010. The role of urban municipal governments in reducing health inequities: A metanarrative mapping analysis. *Int J Equity Health* 9, 13.

Council, Design, 2007. Eleven lessons: Managing design in eleven global companies-desk research report.

Doerr, J. et al., 2018. RE and Society - A perspective on RE in times of smart cities and smart rural areas. *Proceedings of IEEE 26th International Requirements Engineering Conference (RE),* pp. 100-111.

Duboc, L. et al., 2020. Requirements engineering for sustainability: an awareness framework for designing software systems for a better tomorrow. *Requirements Eng* 25, 469–492.

Eun Y., 2020. Toward an Integrative Service Design Framework and Future Agendas. *Design Issues*, 36, 2, 41–57.

Friedman, N. L. and Banegas, M. P., 2018. Toward Addressing Social Determinants of Health: A Health Care System Strategy. *The Permanente Journal*, 22, 18-095.

[2]https://miro.com/
[3]https://zoom.us/

Hancock, T., 2019. Webinar 8: Health in the anthropocene: health promotion 2.0 and healthy cities 2.0. *World Health Organization*.

Hess, A. et al., 2021. From screenplays to podcasts - new perspectives on improving requirements communication in interdisciplinary teams. *Proceedings of IEEE 29th International Requirements Engineering Conference (RE)*, 162-172.

Mapar, M. et al., 2017. Sustainability indicators for municipalities of megacities: Integrating health, safety and environmental performance. *Ecological Indicators*, 83, 271–291.

Meroni, G. et al., 2021. The relationship between air pollution and diabetes: A study on the municipalities of the Metropolitan City of Milan. *Diabetes Research and Clinical Practice*, 174, 108748.

Pritchard, S., 2019. The Eat-Lancet Commission report: my favourite eight take-aways

Repette, P. et al., 2021. The Evolution of City-as-a-Platform: Smart Urban Development Governance with Collective Knowledge-Based Platform Urbanism. *Land*, 10, 33.

Sanders, E., Stappers, P. J. (2014). Probes, toolkits and prototypes: Three approaches to making in codesigning. *CoDesign*. 10.

Villela, K., et al., 2018. Towards ubiquitous RE: A perspective on requirements engineering in the era of digital transformation, *Proceedings of IEEE 26th International Requirements Engineering Conference (RE),* 205-216.

Yang, C.F. and Sung, T.J. 2016. Service design for social innovation through participatory action research. *International Journal of Design*, 10. 21-36.

DEVELOPING USER- AND TECHNOLOGY-DRIVEN USE CASES FOR SMART CITY APPLICATIONS

Robert Otto, Myriam Guedey and Dieter Uckelmann
University of Applied Sciences Stuttgart
Schellingstraße 24, 70174 Stuttgart, Germany

ABSTRACT

Within the transformation and digitalization in the area of smart public buildings and infrastructures, finding, selecting and implementing the "right" use cases is an actual challenge for cities, public utilities, and other stakeholders. The question is where to start, what knowledge and capacities are available and what should be prioritized. This paper introduces a first concept for a methodology that supports the co-development of use cases with respect to current activities, existing infrastructures, and know-how on behalf of the public partners. As a preliminary result, three use cases were identified that represent the current priorities of the involved partner smart cities.

KEYWORDS

Smart City, Smart Public Buildings, Internet of Things, Use Case Development, Semiotic Ladder.

1. INTRODUCTION

The term "smart city" describes a wide field of intelligent solutions for actual and future problems of urban areas. Digitalization and especially the availability of a wide range of Internet of Things (IoT) technologies generate a huge potential for data-based improvements for cities and public institutions. From the multitude of possible innovations, the task is to find those that offer the greatest economic, ecological and social advantages. To this end, the first step is to consider new technologies and possible use cases, align them with one another and prioritize them on the basis of criteria. In addition, an iterative process model must be selected to enable the sequential implementation of the prioritized use cases. This paper introduces a methodological concept for developing IoT-based use cases in close collaboration with partners from the city government and other public facilities. The use cases should be of high relevance for the public partners but also fit into their current activities (know-how, infrastructures, technologies) and take into account technological dependencies as well as possible synergies. The latter improves the chances of reusability and collaboration between different cities to minimize development costs and increase experience in the same areas and technologies. The proposed concept is carried out along current research activities on smart public buildings and infrastructures. Public buildings offer a great potential for IoT-based applications, e.g. in terms of energy efficiency and the use of other limited resources (Guedey & Uckelmann, 2020).

In research, several approaches for the development and selection of technology-based use cases have been introduced. Hofmann et al. (2020) propose an iterative process of six activities (Narrow, Prepare, Explore, Understand, Design, Introduce) to identify valuable AI use cases for companies. According to the authors, the first two steps (Narrow, Prepare) are crucial to limit the outcome of possible use cases and to focus only on those that generate added value for the company. Hofmann et al. also underline the importance of rating the generated use cases, because an implemented use case is likely to become the baseline for future projects and processes. This approach has been further developed towards an AI Toolbox for utility companies by the Fraunhofer IAO (2020). Kohl et al. (2019) present a multi-staged model to identify and select Industry 4.0 use cases in logistics. The model is based on cataloged searches, clustering, profiling and an evaluation scheme to identify the most suitable use cases for the respective company-specific context. Gianni und Divitini (2017) developed a practical toolkit related to the Design Thinking approach to generate new ideas for IoT applications addressing societal challenges in the smart city. They focus on a workshop-based collaboration with the public (non-experts). As in Design Thinking they aim for human-centered solutions, not technology-driven ones. In a smart city, stakeholders such as planners, citizens, and municipals are truly important when it comes to organizational as well as social impacts of technological innovations. From a methodological point of view, there is still a lack in the systematical development of use cases that detects synergies as well as technological dependencies and at the same time considers them in a social and organizational context. An established approach for the integrated description of information technology systems is offered with the "Semiotic Ladder" by Stamper (1973). This concept has been transferred to the Internet of Things and its specific applications by Herion et al. (2020).

Increasing energy efficiency and user comfort as well as reducing financial investments and safety risks are the goals of many IoT use cases in the field of smart (public) buildings and thus have been subject of research. Mylonas et al. (2019) show an IoT-based energy monitoring for public schools that visualizes potential energy savings in a graphical dashboard; the system reduces the energy demand up to 20 percent. With the consequences of climate change, smart cities and their buildings need to take measures to predict extraordinary events to avoid damage. Projects in this discipline gather and analyze sensor-based data such as temperature, rainfall, water level and other environmental measurements (Ivanov et al., 2020; Loftis et al., 2018; Soest Digital [Stadt Soest], 2021). During the COVID19 pandemic, safety precautions such as wearing masks and a regular ventilation of stale air in closed spaces have proven to be essential to keep infections to a minimum. For this purpose, researchers at HFT Stuttgart (2021) have developed an open-source CO_2 measurement box, that displays the actual CO_2 load and thus indicates the right time to ventilate. There have been many more researches on IoT-based applications for smart buildings. Nevertheless, the scope of this paper is not to find novel use cases for smart buildings but rather to co-develop use cases with municipal partners to identify those that promise the most benefit for the partners and thus are very likely to be more sustainable.

In the following section 2 (methodology) of this paper, the methodological concept as well as the process gone through, which is not yet complete, will be described. Section 3 (conclusions) finally reflects on the proposed use case development process and its preliminary outcomes.

2. METHODOLOGY

For the ongoing use case development in the research on Smart Public Buildings and Infrastructures at the University of Applied Sciences Stuttgart (HFT Stuttgart), the technology-driven approach of Fraunhofer IAO has been adopted and modified towards an iterative process. It furthermore has been extended by tools for each of the four stages (*Figure 1*), such as Design Thinking workshops (user- and problem-oriented view) and the use of a Semiotic Ladder based on Stamper and Herion et al. to describe the IoT systems in a holistic way. The four stages of the process, their related activities and tools are presented in the following.

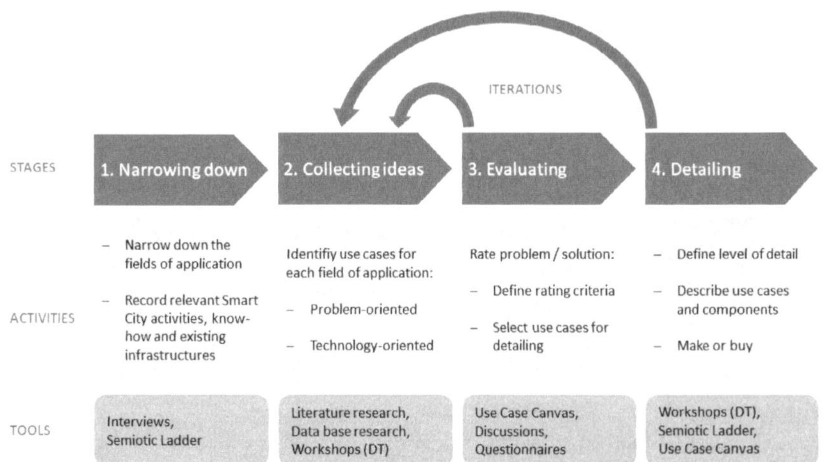

Figure 1. Iterative process of the use case development based on Fraunhofer IAO (2020)

2.1 Narrowing Down (Stage 1)

To reduce the search space for the possible use cases, specific fields of application are determined during this phase. In the ongoing research project on Smart Public Buildings and Infrastructures, the municipal partners from the cities of Ludwigsburg and Solingen (Germany) were interviewed regarding their current and planned smart city activities, digital strategies and already implemented technologies and services. Derived from these interviews, several fields of application with common interest could be identified: 1) increasing public buildings' energy efficiency, 2) strengthen resilience to climate and storm events, and 3) optimizing public infrastructures. In addition, the already implemented IoT systems in both partner cities have been mapped to an adapted Semiotic Ladder (Figure 2) to obtain a unified and structured description of the status quo in Ludwigsburg and Solingen. Therefore, the Semiotic Ladder was used as a table where the existing IoT systems each are entered in columns. This way, commonalities regarding know-how and system components (infrastructures, data formats, applications…) become apparent and can be used to refine the use cases accordingly (stage 4).

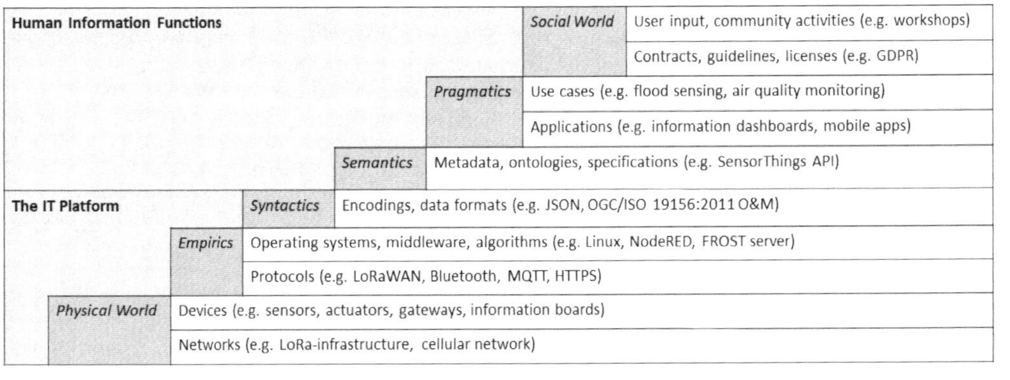

Figure 2. Semiotic Ladder for the description of IoT systems based on Stamper (1973) and Herion et al. (2020)

2.2 Collecting Ideas (Stage 2)

In this stage, ideas for possible use cases in each field of application are collected. Fraunhofer IAO suggest an either problem- or technology-oriented search. To find use cases, literature and relevant data bases can be queried. Additionally, for a problem-oriented co-development, Design Thinking workshops are a feasible tool to generate ideas together with stakeholders from different backgrounds. In the present case, the first collection of ideas was built on literature and data base research, taking into account projects from academia as well as from practice. Here, typical problems of the defined fields of application were used to think of potential solutions within the given framework (interviews from stage 1). The collected ideas were then adapted to the respective situation in the partner cities and processed by a procedure based on Kohl et al., including clustering and listing the ideas as use cases in canvases (cf. Table 1). The application of canvases is also suggested by Fraunhofer IAO, as they enable a uniform presentation of the use cases for the following stage 3 (evaluation). In this research, a total of about ten different use cases could be identified, among them an energy monitoring for public buildings, an early weather warning system for public buildings, a monitoring application for smart parks, an indoor air quality monitoring, the utilization of public infrastructures, and an intelligent sensor management system.

Table 1. Template of a use case canvas based on Fraunhofer IAO (2020)

Use case	Name of the use case
Fields of action	e.g., from the DIN SPEC 91387:2020-08 (2020)
Problem	Description of the problem that needs to be solved
Idea/Solution	Brief description of the idea/solution
Objectives/Benefits	What should be achieved with the implementation?

Target group	Who benefits from this use case?
Usage scenario	Short description of a typical scenario from a user's view
Requirements	What resources are needed?
Status quo	What can be built on?
State of the art	Technical state of the art (academia, technology providers, other smart city projects)
Solution approach	A more detailed description of the proposed solution (methods)
Possible technologies	Technologies that may be used to solve the problem
Risks	Risks that may hinder a successful implementation (e.g., financial risks, missing knowledge)
Extensibility	After implementation, can this use case be an enabler for other use cases?

2.3 Evaluating (Stage 3)

The goal of stage 3 is the selection and prioritization of the most promising use cases for implementation. Therefore, evaluation criteria have to be defined and weighs added if necessary. Based on the canvases (stage 2), the use cases can then be discussed and prioritized according to the criteria. Kohl et al. suggest a quite elaborated evaluation process that may be adopted, if the number of collected use cases is high. Furthermore, if the group of relevant stakeholders for the co-development is large, the discussion may be replaced by an online questionnaire. The ladder was performed in another research group at HFT Stuttgart, where the use cases should be evaluated by several departments in a large company. In case that the group cannot agree upon a small number of use cases, an iteration to stage 2 is recommended to collect more ideas that may fit the criteria. In the present research, the use cases were evaluated together with the municipal partners during a workshop-like discussion. Again, common interests and activities of the partner cities were a major criterion for the selection, but other parameters have also been reflected, such as economics, social compatibility, ecological impact, technological usability, and feasibility. Finally, three use cases were selected and prioritized: 1) energy monitoring of public buildings, 2) utilization of public infrastructures, and 3) intelligent sensor management for a public smart home lab.

2.4 Detailing (Stage 4)

In this stage, the selected and prioritized use cases will be further elaborated. According to Fraunhofer IAO, objectives, resources and relevant stakeholders for the implementation should be defined at this point. Again, iterations back to stage 2 (collecting ideas) can be made, if obstacles to implementation (e.g., lack of resources) arise during the detailing process. Design Thinking workshops that refine the initial use case ideas from the user's perspective can be also a valuable tool in this stage. Furthermore, the use case can be described in more detail in the canvases and transferred to the Semiotic Ladder, each use case in a separate column. This way, the Semiotic Ladder depicts the status quo (stage 1) as well the use cases side by side. Synergies (e.g., existing infrastructures, data and protocol standards, applications…) then become obvious and can be utilized to make the system design more sustainable. Aspects that have not yet been considered appear as "gaps" in the Semiotic Ladder and can be cleared at this point. In the ongoing research, the joint definition and delineation of the system boundaries for the use cases were developed in a collaborative Design Thinking workshop. Relevant stakeholders could be identified, the users' perspective could be integrated, and the respective problem definition as well as first prototypical designs could be outlined. In a next step, these concepts will be mapped to the canvases and the Semiotic Ladder to make use of these tools as described. After the detailing phase, they will serve as basis for the planning of the implementation.

3. CONCLUSION

The development of IoT use cases for smart cities requires different tools that can be planned and implemented depending on the participation of third parties and decision-makers. In this project, thanks to a small team and direct coordination with the responsible public partners, three use cases that reflect the common interests of the involved smart cities were co-developed relatively quickly. The identified use cases are 1) energy monitoring and saving in public buildings (schools and swimming baths) through observation and actuation, 2) analysis of the utilization of infrastructures in those public buildings (e.g., classrooms, shared spaces, water slide tower) to make the buildings more efficient, and 3) sensor management for a public smart home lab that supports an intelligent maintenance and servicing.

Stage 4 and the planning of the use case implementation are going to be completed in a next step, followed by a first evaluation of the proposed methodology. In a follow-up project, the use cases will then be implemented, evaluated and assessed, and the methodology further elaborated. Though the proposed process turned out to be effective and efficient so far, different conditions (group size, backgrounds, starting points, number of ideas…) should be considered and the overall process systematized in form of a step-by-step guideline. The Semiotic Ladder has proven to be a very helpful tool as the IoT systems are analyzed and mapped in a holistic way. On the other hand, it had to be supplemented by non-expert tools, as the municipal project partners found it challenging to apply the Semiotic Ladder without instructions (guided interviews, workshops). Its further potential when modified towards a Semiotic Circle (iterative application) and designed more accessible will also be part of the future research.

ACKNOWLEDGEMENT

The authors thank the Federal Ministry of Education and Research of Germany (BMBF) for supporting the research on Information and Communication Technologies for the Intelligent City - ICT4iCity (13FH9I02IA).

REFERENCES

DIN SPEC 91387:2020-08 (2020). Kommunen und digitale Transformation: Übersicht der Handlungsfelder. Berlin. Beuth Verlag GmbH.

Fraunhofer IAO. (2020). KI-Toolbox für Versorgungsunternehmen: Modul Use Cases. https://www.kodis.iao.fraunhofer.de/de/ki-toolbox-fuer-versorgungsunternehmen/use-cases.html

Gianni, F. & Divitini, M. (2017). Designing IoT Applications for Smart Cities: extending the Tiles Ideation Toolkit. undefined. https://www.semanticscholar.org/paper/Designing-IoT-Applications-for-Smart-Cities%3A-the-Gianni-Divitini/0d0791bdc42667e701b0a82e8531b7f0b6a65f41

Guedey, M. & Uckelmann, D. (2020). Exploring smart home and internet of things technologies for smart public buildings. In P. Davidsson & M. Langheinrich (Hrsg.), Proceedings of the 10th International Conference on the Internet of Things (S. 1–8). ACM. https://doi.org/10.1145/3410992.3411009

Herion, L., Hunecke, C. & Uckelmann, D. (2020). LoRa-Technologie in der Logistik (Bd. 2020). https://www.researchgate.net/publication/344029964_LoRa-Technologie_in_der_Logistik https://doi.org/10.30844/FS20-3_41-44

HFT Stuttgart. (2021). co2ampel [Computer software]. HFT Stuttgart (Eric Duminil et al.). https://transfer.hft-stuttgart.de/gitlab/co2ampel

Hofmann, P., Jöhnk, J., Protschky, D., Stähle, P., Urbach, N. & Buck, C. (2020). KI-Anwendungsfälle zielgerichtet identifizieren. Wirtschaftsinformatik & Management, 12(3), 184–193. https://doi.org/10.1365/s35764-020-00257-z

Ivanov, V., Ivanov, R. & Bande, C. M. (2020). Real time alert system in Smart Home. International Journal of Scientific and Research Publications (IJSRP), 10(9), 676–682. https://doi.org/10.29322/IJSRP.10.09.2020.p10580

Kohl, M., Malik, B., Lopitzsch, J. & Fottner, J. (2019). Auswahl- und Priorisierungsmodell für Industrie 4.0-Use Cases in der Logistik. Logistics Journal: Proceedings. Vorab-Onlinepublikation. https://doi.org/10.2195/lj_Proc_kohl_de_201912_01

Loftis, D., Forrest, D., Katragadda, S., Spencer, K., Organski, T., Nguyen, C. & Rhee, S. (2018). StormSense: A New Integrated Network of IoT Water Level Sensors in the Smart Cities of Hampton Roads, VA. Marine Technology Society journal, 52. https://doi.org/10.4031/MTSJ.52.2.7

Mylonas, G., Amaxilatis, D., Tsampas, S., Pocero, L. & Gunneriusson, J. (2019). A Methodology for Saving Energy in Educational Buildings Using an IoT Infrastructure: 15-17 July 2019, Patras, Greece. IEEE. https://ieeexplore.ieee.org/servlet/opac?punumber=8893976 https://doi.org/10.1109/IISA47616.2019

Soest Digital. (2021). BürgerWOLKE: Klimasensoren in der Stadt Soest. https://digital-soest.de/projekte/13-infrastruktur/57-buergerwolke

Stamper, R. (1973). Information in Business and Administrative Systems. Wiley & Sons, Inc.

MOBILITY DATA PRODUCTS FOR SMART CITY ECOSYSTEMS – A GREENHOUSE GAS BALANCING CASE STUDY

Johannes Sautter[1], Dominik Lis[2], Jan Kräck[3], Andreas Helsper[4], Kai Erlenhardt[5], Fabienne Schnieders[2] and Udo Lambrecht[3]

[1]*Fraunhofer Institute for Industrial Engineering IAO, Nobelstr. 12, 70569 Stuttgart, Germany*
[2]*Fraunhofer Institute for Software and Systems Engineering ISST, Emil-Figge-Str. 91, 44227 Dortmund, Germany*
[3]*Institute for Energy and Environmental Research (IFEU), Wilckensstr. 3, 69120 Heidelberg, Germany*
[4]*Municipality of Wuppertal, Johannes-Rau-Platz 1, 42275 Wuppertal, Germany*
[5]*Municipality of Solingen, Walter-Scheel-Platz 1, 42651 Solingen, Germany*

ABSTRACT

Smart cities need high-quality data products in order to shape societal challenges such as the transformation of transportation and mobility. Trusted Data intermediary concepts are an important tool for enabling the sharing of data via standardized interfaces and ensuring trust and data quality. The ecosystem of a smart city comprises numerous organizations and extends far beyond the city's own boundaries, especially with regard to data products. Based on related work, this paper elaborates key terms of a data intermediary ecosystem concept that is planned to be applied at the interface between smart city and mobility on the one hand, and between municipalities and their municipal companies, science and industry on the other. The nucleus for this eco-system is the Klingenstadt Solingen in Germany that serves as a case study to explore ecosystem data governance concepts.

KEYWORDS

Data Product, Ecosystem, Data Governance, Mobility Data, Data Quality, Trusted Data Intermediary.

1. INTRODUCTION

Data are the key to sustainable urban mobility. Intelligently used and linked, they offer a huge opportunity: in the future, we can travel much more efficiently, in a more climate-friendly way, and at the same time more comfortably – while measuring impacts on the environment even more directly. The "Urban Data Space" contains a large amount of data, the combination of which is still difficult from a technical, organizational, or legal point of view, which so far has had to be processed, quality-assured and brought together separately for each specific application.

Numerous initiatives are currently dealing with mobility data – either politically driven or with a focus on data platforms (Pretzsch, Drees and Rittershaus 2020, VDA 2022). Both technological (e.g., sensor technology, autonomous driving, 5G) and social developments (e.g., urban mobility revolution, climate protection, new mobility offerings) highlight the need to share data and use it in a value-creating way to develop intelligent data products. Data products are the result of a value-added approach to data. Various data users don't have to repeat the underlying processing of data.

Currently, smart cities projects often suffer from a patchwork of incompatible products and components that are difficult to integrate into a holistic urban ecosystem (Tcholtchev et al., 2021). Therefore, smart cities need high-quality data products. For future sustainable data excellent smart cities, trusted data intermediary concepts may play an important role to enable data sharing via standardized interfaces and to ensure trust and data quality.

This paper aims to serve as a starting point for the determination whether in alliances, a trusted data intermediary concept can take over tasks for data management and provision. Possible archetypes are, for example, data centers in research data management (e.g., in the digital humanities) or transport associations that already collect public transport data from their member companies and make it openly available (e.g., OpenVRR). Therefore, the following chapters first describes related work on data excellence, its relevance for smart cities as well as on ecosystem data governance. Second, methodical aspects are described, followed by a first draft of a data intermediary concept by means of key terms. Finally, the greenhouse gas balancing data product case study is described as a scenario evaluation, followed by a conclusion and an outlook.

2. RELATED WORK

Data excellence, unlike data quality, refers not to an individual data object, but to the capability how data is managed within an organization (Sautter et al. 2018). Challenges to data consumers and users include process quality, compliance, data quality as well as operational excellence (ibid.). Thereby, especially behind the process quality aspect is the concept of treating data like products (Wang and Strong 1996). Data products eliminate the need to perform labor-intensive operations (e.g., preparing data) on a per-use-case basis.

Vienna already has a data excellence strategy (Lutz, 2020). German smart cities also face data challenges and currently discuss how to address them (BBSR 2020). Within the smart city community, data governance is increasingly gaining importance as means of establishing a managed and controlled data flow (Cuno et al. 2019). As multiple participants in the smart city context are involved in utilizing data or delivering novel value propositions that are driven by data, there is an increasing need to enable coordination while ensuring that the interests of data providers are protected (Grafenstein et al. 2019).

When a data governance instance is centrally located, it can decentralize aspects of data management to achieve more flexibility in the conduct of data-related tasks and the realization of a smart city ecosystem. Key elements of data governance in the context of the smart city are the definition of data ownership, decision-making rights, responsibilities, and the establishment of guidelines for the management of data (Cuno et al. 2019). The goals are to promote and ensure desirable behavior in the use of data and maximize value by improving data quality (Weber et al. 2020).

James Moore initially applied the ecosystem concept in the business context to explain new forms of economic activity between companies in terms of a "business ecosystem" (Moore, 1993). Due to the increasing penetration of digital technologies and the strategic relevance of data, this analogy is today increasingly reflected in so-called data ecosystem (Oliveira et al. 2019).

However, the consideration of data governance in the sense of sharing data products among multiple actors in ecosystems is still immature (Lis and Otto 2020). Existing concepts do not provide satisfactory detail when clarifying evolving systems with complex interactions where the balance of control and authority in terms of data is uncertain (Lis and Otto 2021). A data ecosystem is characterized by the interaction of several actors who directly or indirectly use, generate or provide data and other related resources (Otto and Jarke 2019). Interaction creates new forms of organization that are not only beneficial to the individual member, but to the system as a whole, value propositions can be realized through innovative data products (Lis and Otto 2021).

A universally accepted definition of data ecosystems has not yet emerged. Nor has the role of data governance been adequately considered in this context. The trusted data intermediary is described as a role that acts as a trustworthy and neutral authority in the interaction to foster collaborative value creation-based data. His or her task is to avoid conflicts of interest and to identify a balance between control and willingness to share data assets (Kühling, 2021). The Trusted data intermediary concept is an essential pillar of the European Data Strategy and is strengthened at the political level by the development of the recently published draft legislation of the "Data Governance Act " of the EU Commission (European Commission 2020).

3. METHOD AND RESEARCH QUESTIONS

The smart city provides fertile grounds to enable innovative data products because the collaboration between providers of data and services can fosters access, provision and the utilization of distributed data sources. Based on related work in the field of data governance, ecosystems and data in smart cities this paper proposes key terms as an initial step towards a data intermediary ecosystem concept. In the research field of organization, ecosystem, architecture and data trust the following guiding questions will be examined: (i) How can existent operative services at research institutes and municipal administrations as well as apps and website benefit of high-quality data products hosted by a trusted intermediary ecosystem? (ii) What are key terms of such a cross-organization concept?

Based on these small first steps, a Greenhouse gas balancing case study is discussed. The smart city of Solingen, linked with two research institutes, serves as both testbed and benefitting early-adopter. Following the "Design Science" methodology framework by Hevner et al. (2004), the key terms of a data intermediary ecosystem can be understood as a basic artefact (cf. chapter 4). Further, the described use case study serves as early scenario evaluation (chapter 5).

4. KEY TERMS OF A DATA INTERMEDIARY ECOSYSTEM

Data intermediary ecosystems for data topics, such as mobility and environmental issues, could provide easy-processable data products for data users in various organizations. The following key terms serve as a basis for a data intermediary ecosystem model dedicated to fulfilling trusted data intermediary tasks:

Trusted data intermediary concept: Based on the EU definition (EC 2020), we distinguish Data intermediary concepts in such that propose an individual organization that serves as intermediary for others (bundesdruckerei, 2022) and in concepts that propose a federation of multiple organizations. We aim for establishing a concept for the latter. Its major objective is to permanently moderate the maintenance of purpose-oriented “least common denominator” data products able to be applied for multiple use-cases. Independence and neutrality following strategic guidelines along both, public welfare standards and business goals of the multiple organizations, as well as compliance with legal requirements are crucial to be considered.

Data users: Users of data that elaborate solutions, reports, apps etc. for data consumers such as citizens, executives etc. Examples for data users are municipal servants working on municipal services and reports, data scientists in research organizations as well as programmers and data scientist in startups and enterprises.

Data product: Data products denote a processed intermediate result, which in turn can be used by further users without having to repeat the process underlying the data product. They can be distinguished in dynamic and static data products. Dynamic data products may for instance base on smart city sensors that measure e.g., humidity with a clock of one minute. Examples for static data are geographic data e.g., on parking spaces.

Data Ecosystem: The ecosystem of a smart city comprises numerous organizations and extends far beyond the city's own boundaries, especially regarding data products. We understand an ecosystem to be a network of several organizations. Data ecosystems focus on data and systems. On the one hand, a data architecture including identity and access management must ensure data protection and data security, but on the other hand, it must also fulfil easy-to-use requirements and align with the processes of data governance.

Use Case: A use case from a practitioner’s view is understood as a particular report, app, interactive map etc. or a particular aspect of an information system operated by citizens, municipality servants, faculty clerks in enterprises.

5. THE GREENHOUSE GAS BALANCING CASE STUDY

Current assessments of the environmental impact of urban or municipal traffic are often based on simplified assumptions due to the quality of public available traffic or transport statistics data, such as the number of registered passenger cars with their corresponding national average mileage or are derived of traffic simulations that rely on a few local and irregular traffic counts. These approaches often lead to a rather rough or outdated estimation of the traffic volume and sources on site, which also affects the estimation of traffic-induced emissions. Causes of traffic and thus starting points for targeted measures can often not be evaluated with the available traffic data. Sensor data (e.g., vehicle detectors or occupancy level detection systems) and differentiated motor vehicle movement data provide an excellent basis for carrying out more precise analyses. For example, greenhouse gas accounting, deriving measures and monitoring could be carried out for different relation types like source-destination, domestic or commuter traffic more accurately and specific. The further development of a basic high-quality database, that provides all the available data of the and regarding the local transport system could be used by many actors involved in environmental monitoring and transport planning.

To tackle the greenhouse gas use case, based on existing internal and external data, one or several valuable data products shall be identified. These could on the one hand serve as a basis for both existing analysis systems and reports created by and for municipalities as use cases. On the other hand, it could be accessed by a smart city app that citizens use to find their multi-modal path to their destination that is both, most emission-avoiding and short as another use case. A particular role (e.g., a data steward), based in one of the closely cooperating trusted data intermediary ecosystem organizations, ensures the maintenance and permanent data quality for the data product. It can serve with dynamic minute-accurate value-series for dynamic use cases as e.g., the mentioned app, as well as with one-request data for data reports.

6. CONCLUSION AND OUTLOOK

Smart city projects often suffer from a patchwork of incompatible data and systems. Ecosystem data governance could address this issue, however there is a lack of concepts from a research perspective. This paper proposed basic terms of a data intermediary ecosystem concept and proofed its relevance by a case study.

Based on these preliminary results, the aim of the project MobiDataSol is to develop and test such a trusted data intermediary ecosystem by establishing a pilot at the interface between smart cities and mobility on the one hand, and between municipalities and their municipal companies, science and industry on the other.

ACKNOWLEDGEMENT

We kindly thank Michael Kubach (Fraunhofer IAO) for his expert review as well as Aleyna Kilicaslan (Fraunhofer IAO) for her valuable formatting work. The MobiDataSol project, funded by the German Federal Ministry of Education and Research (funding code 16DTM103B) and supervised by VDI/VDE, aims at elaborating a concept for ecosystem data governance for mobility data products in the context of smart cities.

REFERENCES

Bundesdruckerei (2022): Datentreuhänder. Datentreuhänder-Plattform mit Vertrauensstellendienst on demand. Der neutrale Vermittler zwischen Datengebern und Datennutzern. Available online at https://www.bundesdruckerei-gmbh.de/de/loesungen/datentreuhaender.

Bundesinstitut für Bau-, Stadt- und Raumforschung (BBSR) (2020): Themenpapier Datenkompetenzen. Ergebnisse aus dem Fachworkshop „Datenkompetenzen" der Nationalen Dialogplattform Smart Cities am 22.10.2020. Ed. v. Bundesinnenministerium. Available online at https://www.smart-city-dialog.de/wp-content/uploads/2021/03/Datenkompetenzen_Fachworkshop_bf_n.pdf, last checked 14.05.2021.

Cuno S, Bruns L, Tcholtchev N, Lämmel P, Schieferdecker I. (2019): Data Governance and Sovereignty in Urban Data Spaces Based on Standardized ICT Reference Architectures. Data, 4(1):16.

European Comission (2020): Regulation of the european parliament and of the council on European data governance (Data Governance Act). Ed. v. European Comission. Available online at https://ec.europa.eu/digital-single-market/en/news/proposal-regulation-european-data-governance-data-governance-act, last updated 25.11.2020.

Grafenstein, Max; Wernick, Alina; Olk, Christopher (2019) : Data Governance: Enhancing Innovation and Protecting Against Its Risks, Intereconomics, ISSN 1613-964X, Springer, Heidelberg, Vol. 54, Iss. 4, pp. 228–232, http://dx.doi.org/10.1007/s10272-019-0829-9

Hevner; March; Park; Ram (2004): Design Science in Information Systems Research. In: MIS Quarterly 28 (1), p. 75. DOI: http://doi.org/10.2307/25148625.

Kühling, Jürgen (2021): Der datenschutzrechtliche Rahmen für Datentreuhänder. Zeitschrift für Digitalisierung und Recht. In: Zeitschrift für Digitalisierung und Recht, S. 1–26.

Lis, Dominik and Otto, Boris (2020): Data Governance in Data Ecosystems – Insights from Organizations. AMCIS 2020 Proceedings.

Lis, Dominik and Otto, Boris (2021): Towards a Taxonomy of Ecosystem Data Governance, HICSS 2021 Proceedings.

Lutz, Brigitte (2020): Warum Städte und Kommunen "Data Excellent" werden sollten. Stadt Wien. Available online at https://www.slideshare.net/DigitalesWien/warum-stdte-und-kommunen-data-excellent-werden-sollten.

Moore, James F. (1993): Predators and prey: a new ecology of competition. In: Harvard Business Review (May-June Issue). Available online at http://blogs.harvard.edu/jim/files/2010/04/predators-and-prey.pdf.

Oliveira, M.I.S.; Barros Lima, G.d.F.; Farias Lóscio, B (2019): Investigations into Data Ecosystems: a systematic mapping study, Knowledge and Information Systems 61, pp. 589–630.

Otto, Boris and Jarke, Matthias (2019): Designing a multi-sided data platform: findings from the International Data Spaces case, Electronic Markets 29, pp. 561–580.

Pretzsch, Sebastian; Drees, Holger; Rittershaus, Lutz (2020): Mobility Data Space. Eine sicherer Datenraum für die souveräne und plattformübergreifende Bewirtschaftung von Mobilitätsdaten. Ed. v. Fraunhofer-Institut für Verkehrs- und Infrastruktursysteme IVI. Available online at https://www.ivi.fraunhofer.de/content/dam/ivi/de/dokumente/broschuere/Whitepaper_Mobility_Data_Space_Web.pdf, zuletzt aktualisiert am 2020, last checked 04.07.2021.

Sautter, Johannes; Litauer, Rebecca; Fischer, Rudolf; Klages, Tina; Wuchner, Andrea; Müller, Elena et al. (2018): Beyond Data Quality: Data Excellence Challenges from an Enterprise, Research and City Perspective. In: Proceedings of the 7th International Conference on Data Science, Technology and Applications. 7th International Conference on Data Science, Technology and Applications. Porto, Portugal, 7/26/2018 - 7/28/2018: SCITEPRESS – Science and Technology Publications, pp. 245–252, DOI: 10.5220/0006912902450252, http://publica.fraunhofer.de/documents/N-506685.html.

Tcholtchev, Nikolay; Lämmel, Philipp; Raabe, Jacob (2021): Ein Überblick urbaner Datenplattformen: Eine Evaluierung nach Designprinzipien der DIN SPEC 91357. Stuttgart. Available online at http://publica.fraunhofer.de/documents/N-635039.html.

VDA (2022): Plattform Urbane Mobilität. Ed. v. Verband der Automobilindustrie e.V. (VDA). Available online at https://www.plattform-urbane-mobilitaet.de/de/, zuletzt aktualisiert am 22.04.2022, last checked 22.04.2022.

Wang, Richard Y.; Strong, Diane M. (1996): Beyond accuracy. What data quality means to data consumers. In: Journal of management information systems 12 (4), pp. 5–33.

Weber, Kristin; Otto, Boris; Lis, Dominik (2021): Data Governance. In: Daten- und Informationsqualität: Springer Vieweg, Wiesbaden, pp. 271–291. Available online at https://link.springer.com/chapter/10.1007/978-3-658-30991-6_16.

HARNESSING WEAK SUPERVISION TECHNIQUES IN WEB MINING TO IMPROVE OVERALL DATA QUALITY

Allen O'Neill
Web DataWorks Ltd, Carlow, Ireland

ABSTRACT

Good data quality is imperative to support robust information analysis and decision making. Predictions based on low quality training data can have a serious impact on outcomes for both data consumers and organizations. It has been established that determining if data is of sufficient high-quality and therefore 'fit for use' depends on the context and use-case of the target data. The research presented in this paper outlines a 'work in progress' novel method to use weak supervision techniques to improve data quality. This is achieved by identifying patterns in existing datasets and mapping these to input data, thereby performing a low-cost bootstrapping technique to help overcome the problem of expensive data annotation for machine learning training datasets. The research described is a work in progress primarily focusing on the web-based eCommerce data area but has implications and relevance for other non-related domains. The contribution of this work, when completed, is expected to be an improved approach to evaluating and building models for monitoring data quality.

KEYWORDS

Data Quality, Web Mining, Schema Mapping

1. INTRODUCTION

Big data as a term is used to describe extremely large amounts of both structured and unstructured data, both at rest (historical) and in motion (real-time). Big Data is heavily used in modern analytics and many critical decisions are made based on the output (Dilsizian & Siegel, 2014; Yin & Kaynak, 2015; Kwon, et al., 2014). With any form of decision making, the quality of the decision is only as good as the data analyzed, and so there is a need to ensure that the highest quality data is available for analysis. The term Data Quality is often described as "fitness for use" (Wang & Strong, 1996), but can mean different things in different domains. Research in specific areas has been carried out in numerous domains (Gudivada, et al., 2017), and a range of domain specific techniques have been developed to evaluate and improve Data Quality (Batini, et al., 2009; Ganti & Sarma, 2013; Loshin, 2010).

Apart from general analysis using Big Data, other factors have focused a new lens on Data Quality, including the reliance of AI and Machine Learning on high quality input (Sessions & Valtorta, 2006) and legislation (Hoeren, 2018). Research relating to Data Quality in the field of Machine Learning normally focuses on aspects of missing data (Sessions & Valtorta, 2006), but this is only one of the dimensions of Data Quality that have been identified by many (Batini & Scannapieco, 2016) including the Data Management Association (DAMA, 2008). Data quality is a multi-dimensional concept, and organizations must deal with the objective measurements based on the data set in question (Pipino, et al., 2002).

Recent work carried out in the area includes (Juddoo, 2015) who examines challenges and future research areas for data quality management relating to Big Data, (Taleb, et al., 2016) who propose a Big Data evaluation scheme for Data Quality using sampling, and (Li, et al., 2018) who define a rule-based taxonomy of dirty data. Woodall et al (2014) have examined the on-going trend of Big Data analytics and find that 'new Big Data paradigm opens new questions about the role of data quality management that need to be addressed'. Other researchers suggesting the need for further research in the area include (Cai & Zhu, 2015; Hashem, et al., 2015; Liu, et al., 2016; Batini, et al., 2016).

It is clear from the review of literature that data quality cannot be measured in isolation (apart from certain specific cases) and must be evaluated in the context of how the data is being used. From this perspective, there is a potential benefit from examining data already available in the organisation that may first demonstrate how data under investigation exists in the organizations data catalog and second, determine what rules may be inferred from existing data that may inform the quality of new data being ingested for analysis.

In this regard, the research examines two interconnected areas:

(a) schema analysis of existing data to extract observations of interest that may be used to inform weak supervision annotation and

(b) automatic extraction of relevant data in a structured manner to map back to the weak supervised annotation

While this work is ongoing, the research contribution describes a framework for analysis of both existing data, and new target data, and the generation of training rules that can be used to create a mapping between the two. In particular, the hypothesis of this part of research is that data in an existing dataset can be leveraged to assist with a text based weak supervision approach to annotating data by labelling for machine learning training purposes. The benefit of this approach is that it can dramatically reduce the amount of time required in human dataset annotation and improve overall data quality by ensuring alignment of new unseen data with existing validated data.

2. RELATED WORK

Strategies for schema analysis have been proposed by numerous researchers. One of the earliest relevant works to this investigation (Wang & Liu, 1997) proposes using an object exchange model to describe data in a labelled graph. Other work of note considers using Ontology based information extraction, structuring and learning (Maedche & Staab, 2001) and (Embley, et al., 1998). On a more fundamental level, other research uses techniques such as discovering conditional functional dependencies (Fan, et al., 2008) and the application of conditional functional dependencies for data cleaning (Bohannon, et al., 2007) to help surface underlying rules in a dataset to which incoming new data should adhere to maintain data consistency and quality. More recently, a considerable amount of work has been carried out at large eCommerce organizations such as Amazon (Lockard, et al., 2018; Dong, et al., 2020), Walmart (More, 2016), Rakuten (Kikuta, et al., 2022) and Google (Zhou, et al., 2022) in relation to attribute extraction and the automatic creation of knowledge graphs. The general goals of this recent research have been to improve data quality for better precision in the areas of knowledge discovery, eCommerce search, product recommendations and review insight analysis.

3. METHODS

3.1 General Approach

Given a dataset or table of structured data 'A' that is the target of incoming data 'B,' carry out a basic analysis of the data contained in 'A' to discover general patterns of acceptable data to which 'B' can be mapped into. Specifically, use the patterns discovered in 'A' to generate weak supervision data labelling rules that can be applied to an incoming data corpus 'B' to indicate a match and thus enable quality data mapping from a previously unseen data source 'B' to the target data destination 'A.' In the experiments the open-source NLP library 'spaCy' (Explosion.AI, 2022) has been used for rule-based annotation and model generation.

3.2 Schema Discovery

Given a dataset A, for each field B carry out an analysis to discover distinct groups of data and generate rules to be used to annotate data. Figure 1 illustrates the process for field analysis, where for each field a set of functions is executed to derive a pattern of knowledge about the data the field contains.

```
Algorithm 1: Field type analysis
procedure ANALYZEFIELD(FieldName)
    select distinct values
    select distinct value data-types
    select percent distribution of value sets
    select value set clusters
    select min/max values
end procedure
```

Figure 1. Algorithm to analyze sample dataset

Figure 2 illustrates the step of taking the pattern of knowledge discovered from Algorithm 1 and using distinct options to generalize and extract alternatives to the exact values discovered. This process not only takes observed values from the sample dataset, but also enriches it by proposing lemmatized word values, and other similar words, phrases, and synonyms among other techniques.

```
Algorithm 2: Create wide word-net
procedure GENERATEWIDENET(FieldMetaData)
    Set TokenNet = array
    if Option contains value then
    |  TokenNet ← Process(Option.Lemma)
    |  TokenNet ← Process(Option.Antonym)
    |  TokenNet ← Process(Option.Synonym)
    |  TokenNet ← Process(Option.Similar)
    end

end procedure
```

Figure 2. Algorithm to create wide word-net to generate rulesets

The output from Algorithm 1 and Algorithm 2 result in a set of rules that can be transformed into the spaCy ruler-pipeline format (Explosion.AI, 2022).

Rules in spaCy are expressed in JSON notation as per the example in figure 3.

```
{"LOWER": "i"}, {"LEMMA": {"IN": ["like", "love"]}}
```

Figure 3. Example of spaCy rule notation in JSON format.

3.3 Information Extraction and Preparation

The next step in the process is to extract information from data sources and prepare for data mapping, the last step in the process. The current research focuses on eCommerce data and builds on work carried out by a team active at Amazon (Dong, et al., 2020) who use the "Autoknow" system to dynamically analyze web data sources and extract information in rich key/value pairs. The insight realized from this research groups work is that such rich information extraction can be valuable for building contextually relevant data, especially when used in conjunction with techniques that use this context to generate proximity-based vector embeddings.

Figure 4 illustrates the embedding generation process. Given a series of webpages WP, for each page P, execute an information extraction process that generates output target document(s) of in key/value/list format, that can be used to generate proximity-based vector embeddings.

Figure 4. Embedding generation process

3.4 Data Mapping

The last step in the process is to take the output from step 3.2 and use the output step 3.4 to generate an annotated set of training data that is subsequently used as the training data from which the spaCy framework uses to build a model. Figure 5 offers a summary of the overall workflow. The key to achieving the successful mapping of entity objects observed and collected from the sample dataset to the enriched data collected from the collection of webpages is harnessing the observed word relationship between the information 'in context' from the web-data with the entity stored in the sample dataset that has been made richer by expanding its context using the automatically generated 'wide net' of entity tokens.

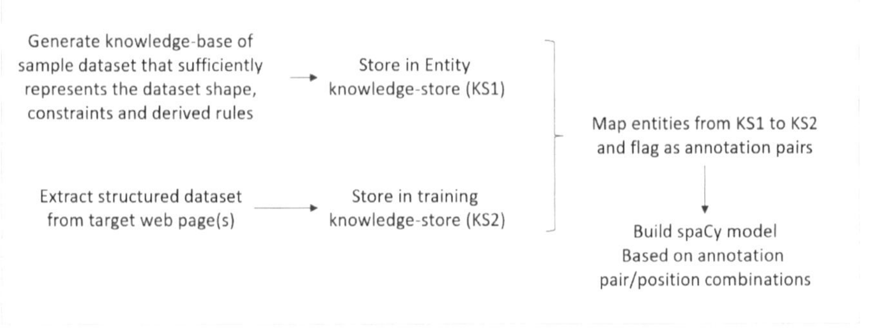

Figure 5. Overall workflow summary

4. CONCLUSION

The research discussed in this paper is a work in progress, however, has already produced very encouraging early results. Compared to manual methods of annotation and information enrichment observed in industry, the methods under investigation have clear advantages in both terms of speed of execution and accuracy of data delivered to the end user. The main application of this work is in the field of data quality, harnessing automated weak supervision to improve the outcomes of data ingestion to large datasets.

Further work that needs to be carried out includes investigating the application of the solution in non-eCommerce domains to determine its wider suitability and moving beyond the area of linguistic analysis to evaluate if similar techniques could be applied to multi-modal datasets. The next stage of this research will be to carry out extensive experimentation to measure the performance of the described solution against current state of the art.

REFERENCES

Batini, C., Cappiello, C., Francalanci, C. & Maurino, A., 2009. Methodologies for data quality assessment and improvement. *ACM Comput. Surv.*, 41(3), p. 16:1–16:52.

Batini, C., Rula, A., Scannapieco, M. & Viscusi, G., 2016. From data quality to big data quality. *Big Data: Concepts, Methodologies, Tools, and Applications,* pp. 1934-1956.

Batini, C. & Scannapieco, M., 2016. Data and Information Quality: Concepts, Methodologies and Techniques. *Springer International Publishing.*

Bohannon, P. et al., 2007. Conditional functional dependencies for data cleaning. *IEEE 23rd international conference on data engineering,* pp. 746-755.

Cai, L. & Zhu, Y., 2015. The Challenges of Data Quality and Data Quality Assessment in the Big Data Era. *Data Science Journal,* Volume 14, p. 2.

DAMA, I., 2008. DAMA-DMBOK Functional Framework. *DAMA International. Technics Publications.*

Dilsizian, S. & Siegel, E., 2014. Artificial intelligence in medicine and cardiac imaging: harnessing big data and advanced computing to provide personalized medical diagnosis and treatment. *Current cardiology reports,* 16(1), p. 441.

Dong, X. et al., 2020. *AutoKnow: Self-driving knowledge collection for products of thousands of types.* s.l., ACM SIGKDD, pp. 2724-2734.

Embley, D., Campbell, D., Smith, R. & Liddle, S., 1998. Ontology-based extraction and structuring of information from data-rich unstructured documents. *Proceedings of the seventh international conference on Information and knowledge management,* pp. 52-59.

Explosion.AI, 2022. *spaCy - Entity Rular PIpeline documentation.* [Online] Available at: https://spacy.io/api/entityruler[Accessed 10 6 2022].

Explosion.AI, 2022. *Spacy - Industrial-strength Natural Language Processing (NLP) in Python.* [Online] Available at: https://github.com/explosion/spaCy [Accessed 10 6 2022].

Fan, W., Geerts, F., Jia, X. & Kementsietsidis, A., 2008. Conditional functional dependencies for capturing data inconsistencies. *ACM Transactions on Database Systems,* 33(2), pp. 1-48.

Ganti, V. & Sarma, A. D., 2013. Data Cleaning: A Practical Perspective. *Synthesis Lectures on Data Management. Morgan & Claypool Publishers.*

Gudivada, V., Apon, A. & Ding, J., 2017. Data Quality Considerations for Big Data and Machine Learning: Going Beyond Data Cleaning and Transformations.. *International Journal on Advances in Software,* Volume 10, pp. 1-20.

Hashem, I. et al., 2015. The rise of "big data" on cloud computing: Review and open research issues. *Information systems,* Volume 47, pp. 98-115.

Hoeren, T., 2018. Big data and Data quality. *Big Data in Context. Springer, Cham,* pp. 1-12.

Juddoo, S., 2015. Overview of data quality challenges in the context of Big Data. *International Conference on Computing, Communication and Security (ICCCS). IEEE,* pp. 1-9.

Kikuta, D. et al., 2022. *Knowledge Graph Embedding with Smoothing Effects of Graph Convolutions for Recommendation.* s.l., arXiv preprint arXiv:2205.12102..

Kwon, O., Lee, N. & Shin, B., 2014. Data quality management, data usage experience and acquisition intention of big data analytics. *International journal of information management,* 34(3), pp. 387-394.

Li, L., Peng, T. & Kennedy, J., 2018. A rule based taxonomy of dirty data. *GSTF Journal on Computing (JoC),* 1(2).

Liu, J., Li, J., Li, W. & Wu, J., 2016. Rethinking big data: A review on the data quality and usage issues. *ISPRS Journal of Photogrammetry and Remote Sensing,* Volume 115, pp. 134-142.

Lockard, C., Dong, X., Einolghozati, A. & Shiralkar, P., 2018. Ceres: Distantly supervised relation extraction from the semi-structured web. *arXiv preprint,* Volume arXiv:1804.04635.

Loshin, D., 2010. The Practitioner's Guide to Data Quality Improvement. *Burlington, Massachusetts: Morgan Kaufmann.*

Maedche, A. & Staab, S., 2001. Ontology learning for the semantic web. *IEEE Intelligent systems,* 16(2), pp. 72-79.

More, A., 2016. Attribute Extraction from Product Titles in eCommerce. *arXiv preprint arXiv:1608.04670..*

Pipino, L., Lee, Y. & Wang, R., 2002. Data quality assessment. *Communications of the ACM,* 45(4), pp. 211-218.

Sessions, V. & Valtorta, M., 2006. The Effects of Data Quality on Machine Learning Algorithms. *Conference: Proceedings of the 11th International Conference on Information Quality, MIT, Cambridge, MA, USA,* pp. 485-498.

Taleb, I. et al., 2016. Big data quality: a quality dimensions evaluation. *Intl IEEE Conferences on Ubiquitous Intelligence & Computing, Advanced and Trusted Computing, Scalable Computing and Communications, Cloud and Big Data Computing, Internet of People, and Smart World Congress.*

Wang, K. & Liu, H., 1997. Schema Discovery for Semistructured Data. *KDD,* Volume 97, pp. 271-274.

Wang, R. & Strong, D., 1996. Beyond accuracy: What data quality means to data consumers. *Journal of management information systems,* 12(4), pp. 5-33.

Yin, S. & Kaynak, O., 2015. Big data for modern industry: challenges and trends. *Proceedings of the IEEE,* 103(2), pp. 143-146.

Zhou, Y. et al., 2022. *Learning Transferable Node Representations for Attribute Extraction from Web Documents.* s.l., Proceedings of the Fifteenth ACM International Conference on Web Search and Data Mining, pp: 479-1487.

AN EFFECTIVE HYBRID DATA ANALYTICS TECHNIQUE FOR A 360-DEGREE VIEW OF CUSTOMER DATA

Majdah Al Nefaie[1,3], Siva Muthaly[2,4] and Siva Muthaly[1,5]

[1]*Dr.*
[2]*Professor*
[3]*Executive Manager, Riyadh, Saudi Arabia*
[4]*Head School of Business, Melbourne Institute of Technology, Australia*
[5]*College of Business and Law, RMIT, Australia*

ABSTRACT

Digital transformation has increased the importance of big data analytics. The growth of customer data generated through multiple sources, such as physical stores, online stores and services, social media platforms and multimedia applications, has created complexity in understanding customer behaviours and other related business patterns, such as sales and revenue growth. This means that organisations need a 360-degree view of their customer data from multiple sources to create customer journey recommendation systems and gain business, sales and revenue insights. Big and quantitative data, such as data collected from face-to-face surveys from customers in physical stores, have played a critical role in organisational decision making. However, big data requires precise analytical methods and techniques to ensure its credibility and the efficiency of its outputs to the related business. This research paper presents a hybrid big data analytics technique that uses multiple sources of big data from online services and quantitative data collected from face-to-face physical semi-government customer service centres. The study model has been implemented in mega projects such as COVID vaccine centres for semi-government organisations in Saudi Arabian. The output of the study is presented a 360-degree customer view for top management and business developers that helps provide a reliable view of and access to the customer information that businesses and organisations need, such as information on the customer journey combined with sales and revenue forecasts.

KEYWORDS

Big Data, Online Services, 360-Degree Customer View, Data Analytics, Digital Transformation

1. INTRODUCTION

This research paper presents hybrid big data analytics techniques that have been implemented in mega projects such as COVID vaccine centres in semi-government organisations in Saudi Arabia. In this research paper, big hybrid data is identified as a large data gathered using quantitative surveys and user data imported from online services. The number of digital services has greatly expanded, leading to increased customer usage in the digital domain. Customer use of digital services creates a pool of valuable data about their customer journey, from data on recent purchases to day-to-day interactions with companies (Mohamed et al. 2020). Today, companies offer customers multiple online services along with physical stores or service centres to fit with the digital transformation. Again, this leads to multiple sources from which data can be generated.

To make better sense of the complex customer journey, which now occurs online and in person, companies are building 360-degree views of their customer data from multiple data sources. This 360-degree view helps companies increase the efficiency of big data once companies have aggregated customer information, behaviour and data in one place. This has assisted organisations in driving marketing and sales growth, better understanding customer behaviour and, most importantly, delivering a more personalised customer experience.

The complexity of big hybrid data increases daily in alignment with the growth of customer usage in the market. Therefore, hybrid data requires precise analysis methods and techniques to increase its credibility and efficiency for the related business (Mohamed et al., 2020). This study presents analytics methods and techniques that have been implemented using structural equation modelling for quantitative analysis of face-to-face surveys and Python to analyse the big data collected from semi-government online services.

The analytics methods and techniques presented in this paper were utilised from 2021 to 2022 in mega projects in different sectors of the Saudi Arabian mark, for example, logistics, information technology and health. The use of the study's analytics model assisted in generating a 360-degree customer view in semi-government organisations in Saudi Arabia. It provides a reliable view of their customers and relevant attributes so that any employee or system would have access to the customer information they need to move the customer along the customer journey and enable accurate sales and revenue forecasts.

The remainder of this paper has been organised in the following ways. First, the discussion has been presented on Hybrid dada analytics methods and techniques. The analytical methods of the study are defining the business needs for the data, as well as data selection, data quality analysis, data collection, data cleaning (removing duplication and irrelevant data), data analysis, and data interpretation and reporting. Lastly, the paper presents a conclusion and future implications.

2.1 Defining the Business Needs for the Data

Identifying business needs is an essential phase of big data analytics (Pappas et al., 2018). This will assist the organisation in gaining deeper insight to develop a clear conceptual framework to harness the prospective of big data analytics. In this study, business needs were defined by applying the following elements: identifying strategic objectives, identifying factors that influence business performance and growth, prototyping the expected business insights, segmenting the market and clients into individuals (B2C); businesses and enterprises (B2B); and government (B2G). These elements were utilised in different government and private organisations in Saudi Arabia to assess the current situation of the organisations and its future direction. This also helped to increase the efficiency of the business insights of the big data to enable organisations to understand different aspects of factors such as their target clients, revenue and growth. In this phase of the analysis, the business needs must be classified based on different hierarchical levels in the organisation, including those of top leaders at the management level, middle-management level, and the development and operational levels (Carlsson 2017). This must be achieved because every employee in an organisation's hierarchy has their mission and authority concerning data use; for example, top leaders have access to the company's financial data, whereas middle management does not have access to this data because of the sensitivity of the information.

2.2 Data Selection

To achieve the aims of the analytics techniques, the company needs to identify the type of data needed; that is, it must state what types of data are required. The data types needed can be defined from the business objectives (Pappas et al. 2018). This study provides the data selection of semi-government organisations in Saudi Arabia that aimed to gain a 360-degree view of customer data, including customer behaviours and needs and data on sales and revenue growth. Therefore, the face-to-face quantitative questionnaire method is utilised to obtain data on large-scale populations more quickly and can provide a clear understanding of targeted clients' behaviours in physical service centres (Zhao and Tang, 2021). On the other hand, big data readily available within the organisation, such as sales data and customer demographics from registration details, assist in providing insights on sales and revenue growth.

2.3 Data Quality Check

The effectiveness of prediction models and insights depends on the quality of the data used in building the models that analyse the data (Gudivada et al., 2017). The researcher in this study used the big data quality check techniques developed by Zhao and Tang (2021) to overcome big data's information threshold and discover big data's information value. These covered the data platform, analysis platform and display platform. The data platform is responsible for the collection and classification storage management of big data. The data gathered has to be filtered and re-marked. Marked data should be cleaned up and updated, and it shows most of the research value of massive data. The analysis platform is responsible for big data analysis and is an important way to value the visualisation. To ensure the data quality in this study, the researcher analysed 5% of the data to confirm that the potential insights were relevant to the business objectives (Zhao and Tang 2021). After data quality analysis, the initial outputs were checked though the strategic data team, whose mission was to ensure that the outputs answered the business objectives questions. In addition, the strategic team checked whether the hybrid data offered a clear view of the business needs and had the potential to offer new insights.

2.4 Data Collection

This study collected data from the government system and face-to-face questionnaire interviews. The target samples were Saudi nationals and residents who use government services. Males and females were surveyed, with a sample size of more than 1,000,000. The data were collected in 2021 and 2022.

This study developed the hybrid data collection techniques listed below to ensure the validity and relevancy of the data to the business objectives:

1. Time: The quantitative research data was collected during the same period that the big data was collected from the organisation's system.
2. Factors and keywords: The data collected using the survey was based on factors that were relevant to the organisation's needs and on using keywords associated with these factors while importing the big data from the organisation's system.
3. Data collection tools and storage: It is important to ensure that the tools used to collect traditional marketing research data and big digital data can be stored in files that can be easily integrated for final analysis and visualisation.

2.5 Data Cleaning

Every data set required cleaning because uncleaned data usually result from human error, scraping data or combining data from multiple sources (Gudivada et al. 2017). The researcher's clear understanding of the business objectives and what insights were planned to be gained from cleaning and analysing the data helped in deploying appropriate data cleaning methods. This assisted in establishing a guide to identify the relevant data within the data and prevented the need to clean up a lot of inconsistencies. The study used two steps to clean the data. First, duplicates were removed. When big data is collected from multiple sources, the data will likely have duplicate entries (Gudivada et al. 2017). These duplicates might generate from human error, such as when the individual filling out a form caused a mistake. Second, irrelevant data was removed to avoid confusion during the data analysis process. Therefore, identifying relevant and non-relevant data is important before data cleaning begins (Gudivada et al., 2017).

2.6 Data Analysis

The main goal of analysing hybrid data is to segment that data into unified themes and factors that will be used to create a model that can help answer business questions and achieve the proposed business objectives. Therefore, structural equation modelling (Mueller and Hancock 2018) was used to analyse the quantitative data to identify, examine and understand the relationships among the latent attributes (Zhao and Tang 2021). The digital data was analysed using Python to identify patterns and relationships and find insights and predictions. The study developed guidelines for data analysis that include the following classifications: segmentation: this reflects the sectors of the organisation's services, such as health and finance; category: this reflects the different services under the organisation's sectors; the central theme: this indicates the main factors that impact customer usage as analysed from the data; subtheme: this indicates the elements describing the central theme's influence on the business. An example of applying these classifications is segmenting (health); category (health certification service); central theme (certification issues); and subtheme (technical issues).

2.7 Data Interpretation and Reporting

The hybrid data presents an integrated scenario revealing different factors that influence the business and its customers' demands. The hybrid data report should be designed by selecting the appropriate charts and graphs to present to decision-makers and stakeholders in a compelling and easy-to-understand way (Tsujimoto et al. 2017). This is created by applying data storytelling by converting the data into a compelling narrative relevant to the business objectives. To achieve this, this study utilised data interpretation team with different skills, including business strategy, marketing research, data analysis and business intelligence analytics. The strategy team created the model design for the dashboard where it shows. The marketing researcher ensured the data's quality by assessing the statistical results' validity. The advanced analysis and data science team were responsible for analysing the data to align it with storytelling. The technical consultant worked on data integration in power business intelligence (BI), adding interactive dashboard tools such as filtrations. The quality assurance team tested the added features in the dashboard and ensured that all the figures in the data showed correct and valid results. In addition, this team assessed the ease of using the dashboard for decision-makers and stakeholders.

3. CONCLUSION

This study presented a continuing development of hybrid data analytics techniques to enable a 360-degree view of customer data insights utilised in Saudi Arabia's semi-government organisations. The study techniques assisted these organisations in effectively utilising data gathered from multiple sources (i.e. big data from online services and quantitative data from a face-to-face customer survey). The analytics techniques applied in the study included data collection, data analysis, and interpreting the data into themes that reflect patterns influencing the organisations and their market growth. These techniques assisted the organisations in overcoming the complexities inherent in analysing big hybrid data by effectively collecting data on customer usage of the services offered. The output of the study is the provision of a 360-degree customer view reflected in a dashboard for semi-government organisations in Saudi Arabia. This allowed top management and business developers a reliable view of their customers' behaviours, needs and desires and of important business attributes, including sales and revenue growth. This 360-degree view allowed the organisations to monitor their current performance, set strategies to maintain their business strength and set strategies for future growth and direction.

This study has demonstrated that effective data analytics techniques are vital for organisational development in today's digital transformation. Organisations must invest in different resources, such as human capital and technology, to compete in the digital economy for data collection and analytics (Carlsson 2017). Researchers such as Gupta and George (2016), Loebbecke and Picot (2015) and Mikalef et al. (2017) consistently demonstrate that big data has become a necessary resource in creating value. Big data analytics capability is defined as the ability of a data actor to effectively deploy technology and talent to capture, store and analyse data, towards value creation, business change, and societal change'. The impact of hybrid big data analytics in developing organisations in today's digital transformations will increasingly attract research and business attention in the coming years. Therefore, to enhance the potential of data, it is important to increase understanding of the different sources that generate customer data, and how these sources interact to improve organisational capabilities, including human skills and business growth.

REFERENCES

Deng, L., 2018. Structural Equation Modeling with Many Variables: A Systematic Review of Issues and Developments. *Frontiers in Psychology*. Vol. 9.

Gudivada, V. et al, 2017. Data Quality Considerations for Big Data and Machine Learning: Going Beyond Data Cleaning and Transformations. *International Journal on Advances in Software*. Vol. 10. No. 1, pp. 1-20.

Mohamed, A. et al, 2020. The State of the Art and Taxonomy of Big Data Analytics: View from New Big Data Framework. *Artificial Intelligence Review*. Vol. 53, pp. 989-1037.

Mueller, R.O. and Hancock, G.R., 2018. Structural Equation Modeling. *The Reviewer's Guide to Quantitative Methods in the Social Sciences*. Routledge, pp. 445-456.

Pappas, I.O. et al, 2018. Big Data and Business Analytics Ecosystems: Paving the Way towards Digital Transformation and Sustainable Societies. *Information Systems and e-Business Management*. Vol. 16, No. 3, pp. 479-491.

Tsujimoto, M. et al, 2017, A Review of the Ecosystem Concept—Towards Coherent Ecosystem Design. *Technological Forecasting and Social Change*. Vol. 136, pp. 49-58.

Zhao, Y. and Tang, Q., 2021. Analysis of Influencing Factors of Social Mental Health Based on Big Data. *Mobile Information Systems*. Vol. 2021.

SOCIAL MEDIA DATA VISUALIZATION: A REVIEW

Hanan Asiri and Mehmet Sabih Aksoy
Department of Information systems
King Saud University, Riyadh, Saudi Arabia

ABSTRACT

With the huge amount of data available on social media, it will be challenging to analyze, summarize, and present useful information extracted from social media in an understood, effective, and communicable form, which facilitates the decision-making process. In this paper, the visual analytics of social media is discussed. Started with a brief description of the social media concept. Then, a review of a piece of works in social media data analysis is shown. Finally, we summarize state-of-the-art visual analytics of social media data since 2015 categorized based on their applications into four categories: geographical information visualization, text visualization, disasters management, general-purpose visualization tools of social media data.

KEYWORDS

Social Media Data Visualization, Data Analytics.

1. INTRODUCTION

Social media generate a large amount of data characterized by its volume, velocity, and variety. It has been observed that the monthly amount of data produced is equivalent to approximately thirty billion pieces of content (Chen et al., 2017). These data available on social media can provide great insights that can be helpful in different fields using proper techniques and methods for data analysis. Therefore, using techniques such as data visualization enable users to not only interpret vast quantities of these data effectively but also to gain insight, identify trends and spot flaws within the data. One perfect way for human to grasp the knowledge faster is visualization. Data visualization offers much more than graphics. It converts complex data into is a powerful way for exploring data and communicating information in an easy-to-understand way specifically for a massive amount of data such as data generated by social media. In This paper, a brief description of social media is presented in section (I). In section (II), the previous literature reviews of social media data analysis are presented as a guideline of the recent works in social media analysis. In the last section (III), we summarize recent state-of-the-art social media data visualization tools, frameworks, and approaches since 2015 categorized based on their applications into four categories: geographical information visualization tools, text visualization tools, disasters management visualization tools, and general-purpose visualization tools.

2. SOCIAL MEDIA

In this part of this section, the definition of social media and its classification are shown.

2.1 Social Media Definition

Social media is defined as a collection of internet-based applications build based on the concept of web 2.0 that allows the creation and the exchanging of user-generated content (Kaplan & Haenlein, 2012). The term social media relates two terminologies: Web 2.0 and User Generated Content (Kaplan & Haenlein, 2010). Web 2.0 can be described easily as the "network as a platform". Where the applications and content are not just created and published, but the software is published as a service that is updated and modified by users continuously in a collaborative way. And these content and applications become better when they are used by more people (Kaplan & Haenlein, 2010) (O'reilly, 2005). User-generated content described as the content that comes from regular people who contribute information, data, or media voluntarily that appears to others in an entertaining and useful form (Krumm et al., 2008). Social media has seven functional building blocks that defines the functionality of the social media. And they are: presence, identity, sharing, relationships, reputation, conversation, groups (Kietzmann et al., 2011). Social media has three components according to (Howard & Parks, 2012):

- The tools and infrastructure for producing and distributing content.
- The digital content in form of news, ideas, messages, and cultural products.
- People, industries, and organizations who produce and consume the content and the tools.

2.2 Social Media Classification

Social media can be categorized based on its content into six categories: wiki, blogging, micro-blogging, question answering, opinion review, and social networking (Hou et al., 2020). The description and the example of each category are provided in Table 1.

3. SOCIAL MEDIA DATA ANALYSIS

The ninth edition of the Data Never Sleeps report that was published in 2020 shows the enormous growth of data despite the spread of the COVID-19 pandemic worldwide. The report shows that there is no sign of data growth slowdown in fact the opposite is quite true. For instance, there are about approximately 157 million users watch clips on TikTok, 575 thousand tweets on Twitter, 65 thousand tweets on Twitter, 65 thousand photos shared on Instagram, and about 2 million snaps on Snapchat, and all that in one minute.

Table 1. Social Media Classification

Category	Description	Example
Wiki	Allows collaborative editing	Wikipedia
Blogging	Allows regularly posting articles about events and topics	WordPress
Micro-blogging	Is a shorter version of blogging	Twitter
Question answering	Serves as platforms for users to exchange questions and answers	Stack Overflow
Opinion review	Allows sharing reviews of services	Yelp
Social networking	Connects users	Facebook

The creation and the exchanging of the content generated by the users produce an enormous volume of data, which known as big data that provide valuable insights and values for different fields when they analyzed. The analysis of the big data is a challenging task due to its following characteristics: volume, velocity, variety, veracity, value. Authors (Gole, & Tidke, 2015) summarize each characteristic of big data, the challenges that face each characteristic and the techniques and the tools that used to overcome the big data characteristics' challenges.

An extensive number of studies and research were conducted on social media such as studying users' behavior, analyzing the relationship, etc. A comprehensive survey presents the previous literature and the current applications from a practical view and outline the pipeline used commonly in building social media-based applications (Howard & Parks, 2012). There are -several artificial intelligence and machine learning algorithms that have been developed to provide an effective analysis of big data in social media. A summarization is provided by Ghania et al. which shows recently used machine learning algorithms in social media big data analytics especially the applications of artificial neural networks, deep learning, swarm intelligence, fuzzy systems, and evolutionary computation (Ghani et al., 2019).

4. VISUAL ANALYTICS OF SOCIAL MEDIA DATA

Data visualization is an effective way for data exploration and information communication in a graphical way that is easy to understand (Chen et al., 2007). The visualization of social media data is one of the trends of data visualization (Aparicio & Costa, 2015). Here we summarize state-of-the-art social media data visualization tools, frameworks, and approaches since 2015 based on their applications into four categories: geographical information visualization, text visualization, disasters management, and general-purpose visualization tools. Table-2 provides a summarization of the presented works in this paper.

Table 2. Summary of Social Media Visual Analytics

Reference	Year	Application	Category
[10]	2015	Geolocated audial visualization	Geographical information visualization tools
[4]	2015	Real-time interactive exploration system of movement dynamics of location-based data	Geographical information visualization tools
[8]	2015	Interactive analyzing sparsely sampled trajectory data	Geographical information visualization tools
[29]	2019	Reducing the clutter of overlapped elements in the geographical representation	Geographical information visualization tools
[25]	2017	Discovering trends	Text visualization
[27]	2016	Predicting and visualizing the orientation of customers' opinions.	Text visualization
[9]	2017	Analyzing and visualizing trends	Text visualization
[24]	2019	Detecting and predicting fake news with visualization techniques	Text visualization
[19]	2019	Exploring of both the data of social media and the categorical output from the natural language processing and machine learning systems.	Disaster Management Visualization Tools
[28]	2016	Real-time processing and visualizing system of social media data for emergency management purposes, considering the ethical and privacy issues of the collected data.	Disaster Management Visualization Tools
[26]	2018	Analyzing disaster information with a geo-visualization.	Disaster Management Visualization Tools
[3]	2017	Content analyzing of geotagged text data on social media and visual it	Disaster Management Visualization Tools
[1]	2018	Analyze and visualize social media data for both expert and non-expert users	General Purpose Visualization Tools
[6]	2021	Detect and editing flaws in already-built visualizations	General Purpose Visualization Tools
[12]	2019	Visual analysis of massive heterogeneous data.	General Purpose Visualization Tools

4.1 Geographical Information Visualization Tools

Geospatial information visualization depicts the complicated spatial and attributes data into images, charts, maps, and three-dimensional dynamic roaming allowing the user to get a clear perception of the data (Qi et al., 2015). Many works were developed to provide effective visual analytics of social media data, the most recent works are shown in this section. One of these works is a web-based geolocated audial visualization tool. The tool provides a summary of the data collected from the web animatedly and interactively. The tool provides an interactive map of the sentiment of the tweets on the Twitter platform (Dahyot et al., 2015). Another computational framework was developed by (Cao et al., 2015) to provide spatiotemporal analysis of location-based data available on social media by applying space-time trajectories. The framework allows for real-time interactive exploration of movement dynamics of location-based data in social media. To reduce the uncertainty time traveling extracted from the social media, (Chen et al., 2015) propose an interactive analytics visual system that helps in analyzing sparsely sampled trajectory data from social media. In addition, they developed an uncertainty model to reduce the uncertainty of time traveling extracted from social media by helping the analysis to understand the distribution of the temporal data. In other words, the visual analytics system enables the analyst to analyze the microblogs' content, location, and the posting time to analyze the movements of social media users. In some cases, when the social media data is visualized in a map, the visual elements overlap with each other creating visual disturbing of the semantic features and their distribution geographically. A doc2vec model developed by (Zhou et al., 2019) can be used to transform geographical data of social media into high dimensional vectors, and hence the semantic correlation can be recognized easily in the dimensionality reduction space.

4.2 Text Visualization Tools

Text visualization basically consist of text analysis, data mining, data visualization, human-computer interaction, computer graphics, cognitive science theory and methods, and other discipline data (Qi et al., 2015). Here the recent works in text visualization of social media are presented. RIVA is a real-time information analysis and visualization platform. It collects data from the social network using Spark computing platform to discover trend topics around the world with a visualization interface using a web browser. RIVA can discover people's sentiments via sentiment analysis (Wu et al.,2017). To predict the orientation of the customers' opinion, a framework developed by (Zhang et al., 2016) to predicts and visualizes the orientation of customers' opinions based on their relationship with the other customers whose opinion are known for using collective classification algorithm that can predict customers' opinion orientation. Some computational social science requires real-time analysis and visualization of the trends in social media such as political elections. For this purpose, a GPU accelerated project was developed by (Ch'ng et al.,2017). Among the huge number of opinions available on social media, there is disinformation such as fake news that spread for financial or political purposes. FakeNewsTracker is a system that can understand and predict fake news with effective visualization techniques (Shu et al., 2019).

4.3 Disaster Management Visualization Tools

Social media contain useful information in disaster management embedded in the users' text messages, pictures, videos, or news. Due to that many disasters management systems developed. SAVIS is an interactive visualization platform that can accommodate the social media data and the categorical output from the natural language processing and machine learning systems such as sentiment analysis and situation labeling. It is compatible with many existing crisis intelligence platforms, which can render easily using a web browser (Kejriwal & Zhou,2019). Another web-based disaster information system can collect, extract, recognize, classify disaster information, and provide a geo-visualization of the analyzed information developed by (Xie & Yang, 2018). The collection of data from social media for analysis purposes and emergency management may arise many ethical and privacy issues due to that The Slandail Monitor ware developed by (Zhang et al., 2016). It is a real-time processing and visualizing system of social media data for emergency management purposes. The system analyses the message content using the spatial and temporal data included in it for summarizing the emergency events reported in social media. The analyzed result then visualized for quickly accessing the events by topic, time, and location. The system addresses the ethical and privacy issues of the collected data computationally. In the crisis management field, the analysis of time and location of social media data may not provide enough information about the situation. For a comprehensive analysis of disasters data, a tool can cluster the content of geotagged text data on social media and visualize the clusters on the map, rather than analyzing the location and the time data only, it was improved by 0et al., 2017).

4.4 General Purpose Visualization Tools

In this section, the recent visual analytics social media tools are presented which then can be used for different visualization purposes. Novice people may want to analyze and visualize the social media data and may they will face difficulty in doing that. FireAnt is an example of the software that ware developed by (Anthony, 2018) to overcome this problem, which is a freeware, multi-platform, stand-alone tool to analyze and visualize social media data as time series plots, geo maps, and network graphs. It can be used by expert and novice computer users. The automated visualization tool may provide a result that does not meet the required specifications and hence the there is a need for manual adjustment, and it is difficult especially when the users do not have sufficient skills. To solve this problem, VizLinter developed by (Chen et al., 2021) can assist users in detecting the flaws and editing flaws in already-built visualizations. Produced data from social media are heterogeneous and massive, and it is necessary to have an environment capable of analyzing heterogeneous data in a combined view. VAMD is a visual analysis system supports analyzing massive heterogeneous data, it was improved by (Fallon & Crouse, 2019).

5. CONCLUSION

It is not easy to interpret massive amount of information in an easy-to-understand way. Data visualization works as a powerful solution for this problem, and one of the current data visualization trends is the visualization of social media data. In this paper, we presented the latest visual analytics of social media data, and we classified them based on their applications into four categories: geographical information visualization, text visualization, disasters management, and general-purpose visualization tools, which provided a guideline to recent visual analytics of social media.

REFERENCES

Anthony, L. (2018). Introducing Fireant: A Freeware, Multiplatform Social Media Data-Analysis Tool. IEEE Transactions on Professional Communication, 61(4), 428-442.

Aparicio, M., & Costa, C. J. (2015). Data visualization. Communication design quarterly review, 3(1), 7-11.

Barnard, S. A., Chung, S. M., & Schmidt, V. A. (2017, November). Content-based clustering and visualization of social media text messages. In 2017 International Conference on Data and Software Engineering (ICoDSE) (pp. 1-6). IEEE.

Cao, G., Wang, S., Hwang, M., Padmanabhan, A., Zhang, Z., & Soltani, K. (2015). A scalable framework for spatiotemporal analysis of location-based social media data. Computers, Environment and Urban Systems, 51, 70-82.

Chen, C. H., Härdle, W. K., & Unwin, A. (Eds.). (2007). Handbook of data visualization. Springer Science & Business Media.

Chen, Q., Sun, F., Xu, X., Chen, Z., Wang, J., & Cao, N. (2021). VizLinter: A Linter and Fixer Framework for Data Visualization. IEEE transactions on visualization and computer graphics.

Chen, S., Lin, L., & Yuan, X. (2017, June). Social media visual analytics. In Computer Graphics Forum (Vol. 36, No. 3, pp. 563-587).

Chen, S., Yuan, X., Wang, Z., Guo, C., Liang, J., Wang, Z., ... & Zhang, J. (2015). Interactive visual discovering of movement patterns from sparsely sampled geo-tagged social media data. IEEE transactions on visualization and computer graphics, 22(1), 270-279.

Ch'ng, E., Chen, Z., & See, S. (2017, October). Real-time GPU-accelerated social media sentiment processing and visualization. In 2017 IEEE/ACM 21st International Symposium on Distributed Simulation and Real Time Applications (DS-RT) (pp. 1-4). IEEE.

Dahyot, R., Brady, C., Bourges, C., & Bulbul, A. (2015, October). Information visualisation for social media analytics. In 2015 International Workshop on Computational Intelligence for Multimedia Understanding (IWCIM) (pp. 1-5). IEEE.

Domo Resource - Data Never Sleeps 9.0. (2020). https://www.domo.com/learn/infographic/data-never-sleeps-9

Fallon, J., & Crouse, R. J. (2019, October). VAMD: Visual Analytics for Multimodal Data. In 2019 IEEE 9th Symposium on Large Data Analysis and Visualization (LDAV) (pp. 93-94). IEEE.

Ghani, N. A., Hamid, S., Hashem, I. A. T., & Ahmed, E. (2019). Social media big data analytics: A survey. Computers in Human Behavior, 101, 417-428.

Gole, S., & Tidke, B. (2015, January). A survey of Big Data in social media using data mining techniques. In 2015 International Conference on Advanced Computing and Communication Systems (pp. 1-6). IEEE.

Hou, Q., Han, M., & Cai, Z. (2020). Survey on data analysis in social media: A practical application aspect. Big Data Mining and Analytics, 3(4), 259-279.

Howard, P. N., & Parks, M. R. (2012). Social media and political change: Capacity, constraint, and consequence.

Kaplan, A. M., & Haenlein, M. (2010). Users of the world, unite! The challenges and opportunities of Social Media. Business horizons, 53(1), 59-68.

Kaplan, A. M., & Haenlein, M. (2012). Social media: back to the roots and back to the future. Journal of Systems and Information Technology.

Kejriwal, M., & Zhou, P. (2019, August). SAVIZ: Interactive exploration and visualization of situation labeling classifiers over crisis social media data. In Proceedings of the 2019 IEEE/ACM International Conference on Advances in Social Networks Analysis and Mining (pp. 705-708).

Kietzmann, J. H., Hermkens, K., McCarthy, I. P., & Silvestre, B. S. (2011). Social media? Get serious! Understanding the functional building blocks of social media. Business horizons, 54(3), 241-251.

Krumm, J., Davies, N., & Narayanaswami, C. (2008). User-generated content. IEEE Pervasive Computing, 7(4), 10-11.

O'reilly, T. (2005). Web 2.0: compact definition.

Qi, Y., Shi, G., Yu, X., & Li, Y. (2015, June). Visualization in media big data analysis. In 2015 IEEE/ACIS 14th International Conference on Computer and Information Science (ICIS) (pp. 571-574). IEEE.

Shu, K., Mahudeswaran, D., & Liu, H. (2019). FakeNewsTracker: a tool for fake news collection, detection, and visualization. Computational and Mathematical Organization Theory, 25(1), 60-71.

Wu, Y. T., Hsieh, H. Y., Sigalingging, X. K., Su, K. W., & Leu, J. S. (2017, November). RIVA: A Real-Time Information Visualization and analysis platform for social media sentiment trend. In 2017 9th International Congress on Ultra Modern Telecommunications and Control Systems and Workshops (ICUMT) (pp. 256-260). IEEE.

Xie, J., & Yang, T. (2018, September). Using social media data to enhance disaster response and community service. In 2018 International Workshop on Big Geospatial Data and Data Science (BGDDS) (pp. 1-4). IEEE.

Zhang, L., Yuan, H., & Lau, R. Y. (2016, November). Predicting and visualizing consumer sentiments in online social media. In 2016 IEEE 13th International Conference on e-Business Engineering (ICEBE) (pp. 92-99). IEEE.

Zhang, X., Kelly, S., & Ahmad, K. (2016, August). The slandail monitor: Real-time processing and visualisation of social media data for emergency management. In 2016 11th International Conference on Availability, Reliability and Security (ARES) (pp. 786-791). IEEE.

Zhou, Z., Zhang, X., Zhou, X., & Liu, Y. (2019). Semantic-Aware Visual Abstraction of Large-Scale Social Media Data with Geo-Tags. IEEE Access, 7, 114851-114861.

CLASSIFIER RANK - A NEW CLASSIFICATION ASSESSMENT METHOD

Ningsheng Zhao[1], Jia Yuan Yu[1] and Krzysztof Dzieciolowski[1,2]
[1]*Concordia University, Montreal, Quebec, Canada*
[2]*DAESYS, Canada*

ABSTRACT

Most of the commonly used confusion matrix-based classification performance metrics, such as f1_score, MCC, and PRC, are sensitive to the class imbalance. To address this problem, we propose a novel classifier evaluation method, called classifier rank which provides the rank of the classifier in the space of all possible classifiers. To rank a classifier, we find the distribution of performance metrics conditional on arbitrary class ratio. However, some metrics like PRC are functions of a large sequence of confusion matrices whose joint distribution is difficult to estimate. Hence, we propose a directed binary tree model to effectively represent this large-scale joint distribution. As a result, we can estimate the classifier rank using graphical inference algorithms, such as Monte-Carlo algorithm.

KEYWORDS

Confusion Matrix, Class Imbalance, Performance Metrics, Graphical Inference, Classifier Rank.

1. INTRODUCTION

There are two kinds of confusion matrix-based classification performance metrics: *deterministic metrics* and *scoring metrics*. The deterministic metrics, such as recall, precision, f1_score, and MCC, are computed from a single confusion matrix related to the predicted labels. On the other hand, the scoring metrics are computed from a sequence of confusion matrices obtained by varying the thresholds applied to the predicted classification scores. The scoring metrics can be visualized by curves such as *Receiver Operating Characteristics (ROC)* and *Precision-Recall curves (PRC)* which are often quantified by the *area under the curves (AUC)*.

In binary classification, where the two classes are labeled *positive* and *negative*, we can construct a binary confusion matrix with four elements $\{TP, FN, FP, TN\}$, counting the true positive, false negative, false positive and true negative, respectively. Furthermore, let $m = m_p + m_n$ denote the data size, where $m_p = TP + FN$ is the positive class size, and $m_n = TN + FP$ is the negative class size. Let $\lambda_p = TP/m_p$ be the true positive rate, $\lambda_n = TN/m_n$ be the true negative rate, and $\pi = m_p/m$ be the positive class ratio measuring the imbalance rate. The confusion matrix can be normalized by dividing all its elements with the data size m as follows

$$\frac{1}{m} \times \begin{bmatrix} TP & FN \\ FN & TN \end{bmatrix} = \begin{bmatrix} \pi\lambda_P & \pi(1-\lambda_P) \\ (1-\pi)(1-\lambda_n) & (1-\pi)\lambda_n \end{bmatrix} \tag{1}$$

The normalized confusion matrix can thus be represented by a 3-dimension random variable $C = (\lambda_p, \lambda_n, \pi)$. Due to the dependence on the positive class ratio π, the corresponding performance metrics, such as f1_score, MCC and PRC, are sensitive to class imbalance. Often, a lower value of π may cause a relatively low value of these metrics, thus invalidating their effectiveness as universal criteria of model evaluation and selection. For example, the value of $f1 = 0.6$ represents a poor classifier performance when data is balanced, i.e., $\pi = 0.5$, but a good classifier performance when $\pi = 0.1$.

Study of Amalia L. et al, 2019 attempts to find the impact of class imbalance on performance metrics by analysing the distribution of the confusion matrix and the bias resulting from the class imbalance. However, it does not suggest a method to address the problems caused by class imbalance. In addition, this study focuses only on the deterministic metrics. To address these issues, in our research, we propose a novel classifier evaluation method, called *Classifier Rank (CR)*, based on graphical inference of the distribution of confusion matrix-based performance metrics. The suggested Classifier Rank method is robust to class imbalance, so it can be used as a universal criterion for classifier evaluation and selection. A concept of the space of all possible models and ranking of the classifier was brought up by Mazzanti (2020) but no general solution for estimating the model space was proposed.

2. RANKING A CLASSIFIER

According to "No-Free-Lunch Theorem" (Shai S. and Shai B., 2014), no classifier can perform well on all datasets. Hence, we can only assess a classifier's performance on a given data. To address this data-dependency, we adopt the following definition of Classifier Rank.

Definition 1 (Classifier Rank) *In a binary classification task, given data D, if a performance metric X returns a value of x for a selected classifier, then the corresponding classifier rank (CR) with respect to X on data D can be defined as:*

$$CR_X(x|D) \doteq P(X < x|D).$$

The definition describes that, given metric X and data D, CR is the probability that the selected classifier outperforms a randomly selected classifier. We can interpret it as the rank of the selected classifier in the classifier space which contains all possible candidates for the classification task. To compute CR, we first need to find the classifier space. We can then infer the distribution of performance metric $X \in \mathcal{X}$, where $\mathcal{X}$ is the domain of X. We know that X is a function of a confusion matrix C for deterministic metrics, or a sequence of confusion matrices $(C_1, ..., C_J)$ for scoring metrics. Given data D, both C and $(C_1, ..., C_J)$ are determined by the selected classifier. Therefore, the classifier space can be projected onto the domain of C, denoted by $\mathcal{C}$ including all possible confusion matrices, or the domain of $(C_1, ..., C_J)$, denoted by $\mathcal{C}_1 \times ... \times \mathcal{C}_J$ including all possible sequences of confusion matrices, respectively. Now, what we must solve is to find the joint distribution over $\mathcal{C} \times \mathcal{X}$, or $\mathcal{C}_1 \times ... \times \mathcal{C}_J \times \mathcal{X}$, then infer the marginal distribution over $\mathcal{X}$.

3. CLASSIFIER RANK FOR DETERMINISTIC METRICS

The deterministic metrics can be expressed as a function of a single confusion matrix, formulated as $X = X(\lambda_p, \lambda_n, \pi)$, and the joint distribution over $\mathcal{C} \times \mathcal{X}$ can be represented by a simple directed acyclic graph (DAG) in Figure 1. Given data $D = d$, the positive class ratio $\pi = \pi^d$ is a constant, and we assume that λ_p, λ_p are uniformly distributed on [0,1] (Amalia L. et al, 2019) with CDF denoted by $F(\cdot)$. Then, the CR_X can be directly computed by variable elimination as:

$$CR_X(x|D = d) \doteq P(X < x|D = d) = \int_{X(\lambda_p, \lambda_n, \pi^d) < x} dF(\lambda_p)\, dF(\lambda_n). \quad (2)$$

For example, the formula of f1_score can be written as

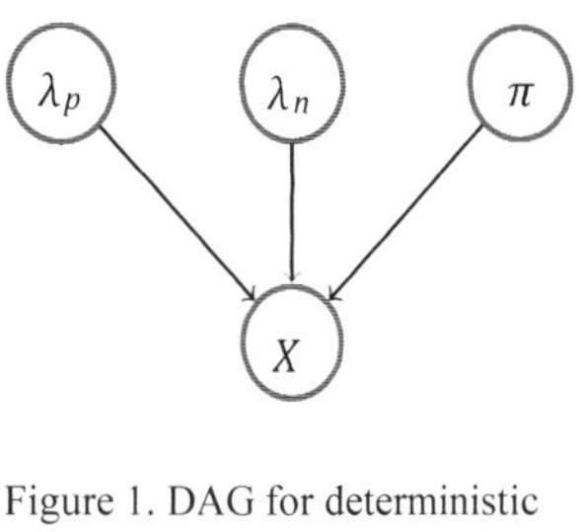

Figure 1. DAG for deterministic Metrics

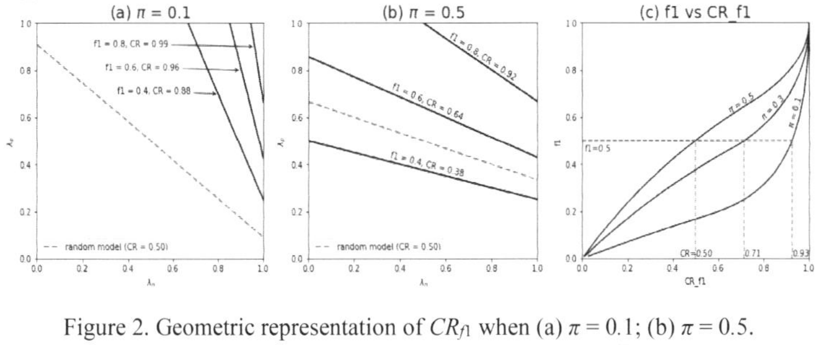

Figure 2. Geometric representation of CR_{f1} when (a) $\pi = 0.1$; (b) $\pi = 0.5$. (c) The relation between *f1_score* and CR_{f1} for different π

$$f1(\lambda_p, \lambda_n, \pi) = \frac{2\pi\lambda_p}{\pi(1+\lambda_p) + (1-\pi)(1-\lambda_n)}. \quad (3)$$

Then, given data $D = d$, the function of classifier rank with respect to f1_score can be computed as:

$$CR_{f1}(x|D=d) = \begin{cases} \frac{(1+\pi^d)x}{2\pi^d(2-x)}, & if \quad 0 \le x \le \frac{2\pi^d}{1+\pi^d} \\ \frac{(1+\pi^d)x}{2\pi^d(2-x)} - \frac{\left[(1+\pi^d)x - 2\pi^d\right]^2}{2\pi^d(1-\pi^d)x(2-x)}, & if \quad \frac{2\pi^d}{1+\pi^d} < x < 1. \end{cases} \quad (4)$$

The geometric representation of f1_score can be found in Figure 2 (a) and (b). Given π, the domain $\mathcal{X}$ can be represented as a unit square including all possible pairs of (λ_p, λ_n). For a given $x \in [0,1]$, the straight line $f1(\lambda_p, \lambda_n, \pi) = x$ divides the unit square into two parts, where the right part indicates better performance ($f1 > x$), and the left part indicates worse performance ($f1 < x$). It is trivial to find that CR_{f1} is the area of the left part. Moreover, as shown in Figure 2 (c), for the same value $f1 = 0.5$, the value of CR_{f1} increases, hence the quality of the classifier improves, as π decreases. Hence, lower values of the f1_score could be satisfactory for highly imbalanced data while inadequate for balanced data.

4. CLASSIFIER RANK FOR SCORING METRICS

4.1 Graphical Representation

Instead of a deterministic label, most popular classifiers return a numeric score, such as a predicted probability, for each item in the data. A sequence of dependent confusion matrices $(C_1, \ldots, C_J)$, with each $C_j = (\lambda_{pj}, \lambda_{nj}, \pi)$, can be obtained from a sequence of J thresholds. A scoring metric is defined as a mapping $L: C_1 \times \ldots \times C_J \rightarrow \mathrm{R}^{2\times J}$. Specifically, let $\phi_L = \{\phi_1, \phi_2 : C \rightarrow \mathrm{R}\}$ contain two specific functions mapping from a confusion matrix into a real number, for example, for the Precision-Recall Curve (PRC), we have

$$\phi_1(\lambda_p, \lambda_n, \pi) = \lambda_p,$$

$$\phi_2(\lambda_p, \lambda_n, \pi) = \frac{\pi\lambda_p}{\pi\lambda_p + (1-\pi)(1-\lambda_n)}.$$

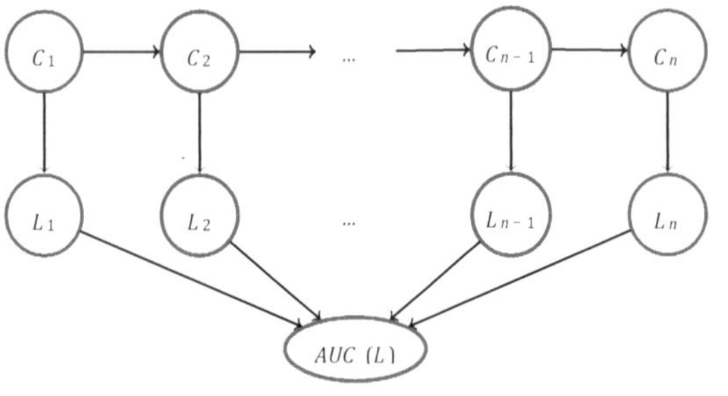

Figure 3. DAG for scoring metrics

Hence, we can define $L(C_1, \ldots, C_J) = \phi_L \otimes (C_1, \ldots, C_J)$, which can be visualized by a curve, drawn from points $L_j = \left(\phi_1(C_j), \phi_2(C_j)\right)$. L can be quantified by the area under it, i.e., $AUC(L)$. Now, given data D, the corresponding classifier rank with respect to scoring metrics L can be written as:

$$CR_L(x|D) = P\{AUC(L) < x|D\}.$$

Intuitively, the large-scale joint distribution of L and $(C_1, \ldots, C_J)$ can be represented by the DAG in Figure 3. However, this graph cannot be used for inference since we do not know the local distribution $P(C_1)$ and $P(C_j|C_{j-1})$ for $j \ge 2$. Instead, we propose a more appropriate and inferable graphical model: *Directed Binary Tree (DBT)*. In DBT, we let $\theta = (a_p, b_p, a_n, b_n) \in [0,1]^4$ denote a parameter set, representing the range of (λ_p, λ_n). For each confusion matrix C_j, we assume that $\lambda_{pj} \in \text{uniform}[a_{pj}, b_{pj}]$, and $\lambda_{nj} \in \text{uniform}[a_{nj}, b_{nj}]$.

We set each (C_j,θ_j) as a node of DBT. Figure 4 shows a simple example of DBT with depth=4. In practice, we usually choose depth ≥ 7 so that we have more points to draw the curve more precisely.

When data D is given, π is a constant, then to build a DBT, we need to specify three local distributions: (1) $P_{\theta_1}(C_1)$for the root, (2) $P_{\theta^l|C',\theta''}(C^l|C',\theta')$for the left child, and (3) $P_{\theta^r|C',\theta''}(C^r|C',\theta')$ for the right child of any node (C',θ'). At the root, let C_1 be obtained by selecting the optimal threshold on the global data D, so it follows the same distribution as in the deterministic case. After choosing a threshold, D is split into two parts, predicted positive and negative respectively, which are called *local data* for the children. Then for each child node, its range parameter set Θ is determined by its local data, and the local data is determined by the value of its parent as shown in Figure 4.

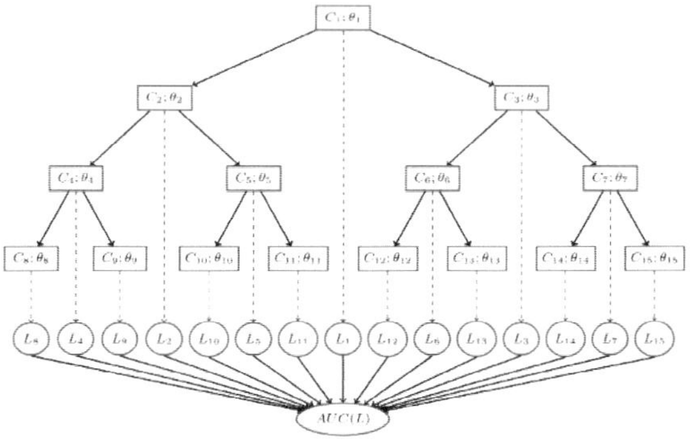

Figure 4. Directed Binary Tree model with depth=4

4.2 Graphical Inference

The CR_L can be approximated by the Monte-Carlo inference algorithm. The algorithm first samples K curves from the DBT based on the given π and ϕ_L, and calculate the AUC for each curve, then the corresponding classifier rank can be approximated as

$$CR_L(x|D) \approx \frac{1}{K}\sum_k I(AUC_k < x). \tag{5}$$

The implementation is very simple. However, due to the large number of random variables, a huge sample set is needed to reduce the variance of the approximation for different data or tasks, so it is a loss of time and samples. To reuse the samples for future different classifier evaluation tasks, we can view CR_L as a value function of x and π, i.e., $v(x,\pi)$, then train a model, like a neural network, to fit it. In this way, we only spend time and use the samples to learn this model once, then it can be reused to estimate the CR_L for all tasks.

5. EXPERIMENTS

The effectiveness of the proposed CR method can be verified by an experiment on the Bank Marketing data set from the UCI Machine Learning Repository (https://archive.ics.uci.edu/ml/datasets/Bank+Marketing). Two testing datasets were generated from the original data, with $\pi_1 = 0.1$(imbalanced data) and $\pi_2 = 0.5$ (balanced data) respectively. Then, the rest of the data was used to train an Xgboost classifier, where its performance with f1_score and PRC can be seen in Figure 5 (a). It exhibits that the classifier performs much better on the balanced data than the imbalanced one, with maximal $f1$: 0.89 > 0.61, and AUC(PRC): 0.915 > 0.606. However, is that the true story? And what do these values tell us about how good the classifier here is? To answer these questions, we apply the proposed Classifier Rank method to evaluate this Xgboost classifier. The results in Figure 5 (b) and (c) shows that both CR_{f1} and CR_{PRC} keep almost unchanged with the similar differences of about 1.4% on the two testing data sets, even though both f1_score and PRC show large differences. Therefore, these large differences can be explained by the data imbalance. Furthermore, the values of CR_{f1} and CR_{PRC} demonstrate that the selected Xgboost classifier outperforms at least 96% of all possible candidates, indicating an excellent performance.

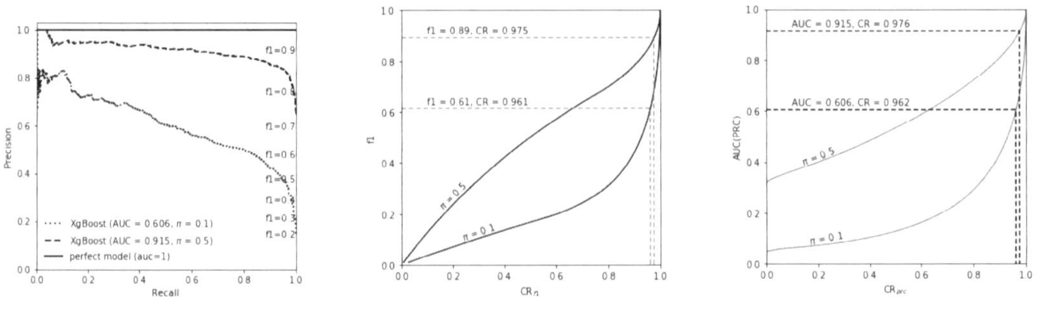

(a) PRC and f1 curves (b) CR_{f1} (c) CR_{PRC}

Figure 5. Experiments' results

6. CONCLUSIONS

The proposed novel classifier rank method addresses a common problem of class imbalance in measuring the performance of binary classifiers. It allows for a robust assessment of classifiers in presence of imbalanced data. The classifier rank estimation is based on the graphical representation of the joint distribution of confusion matrices and related performance metrics. In applications, the classifier rank can be used as a universal criterion for classifier evaluation and selection. In the included experiment, we demonstrated that the classifier's performance on balanced and imbalanced data are similarly good when assessed by a classifier rank despite large differences in their performances when assessed by the traditional metrics such as PRC and f1_score. The proposed classifier rank approach can be extended to a multi-class evaluation problem by averaging classifier ranks for all classes, weighted by their class ratios.

ACKNOWLEDGEMENT

The first two authors gratefully acknowledge the financial support from Mitacs and Daesys Inc.

The third author gratefully acknowledge the financial support from Concordia University Part-time Faculty Professional Development of CUPFA.

REFERENCES

Alaa T., 2021. Classification assessment methods. *Applied Computing and Informatics*, Vol. 17 No. 1, pp. 168-192.

Amalia L. et al, 2019. The impact of class imbalance in classification performance metrics based on the binary confusion matrix. *Pattern Recognition*, Vol. 9 No. 1, pp. 216-231.

Daphne Koller and Nir Friedman, 2009. *Probabilistic graphical models: principles and techniques.* MIT press.

Jorge M. et al, 2008. Auc: a misleading measure of the performance of predictive distribution models. *Global ecology and Biogeography*, Vol. 17 No. 2, pp. 145-151.

Mazzanti, S., 2020. *Why you should stop using the ROC curve.* Towards Data Science.

Mohamed B. et al, 2013. Evaluation measures for models assessment over imbalanced data sets. *J Inf Eng Appl*, Vol. 3 No. 10, pp. 27-38.

Nathalie J. and Mohak S., 2011. *Evaluating learning algorithms: a classification perspective*. Cambridge University Press.

Shai S. and Shai B., 2014. *Understanding Machine Learning - From Theory to Algorithms.* Cambridge University Press.

Takaya S. and Marc R., 2015. The precision-recall plot is more informative than the roc plot when evaluating binary classifiers on imbalanced datasets. *PloS one*, Vol. 10 No. 3, e0118432.

POSTER

ODIN: A FRAMEWORK FOR ERROR DIAGNOSIS OF DNNS

Rocio Nahime Torres, Federico Milani, Niccolò Zangrando and Piero Fraternali
Politecnico di Milano
Piazza Leonardo da Vinci, 32, 20133 Milan, Italy

ABSTRACT

Methods for the analysis of Deep Neural Networks (DNNs) use two approaches: open- and black-box. The formers apply explainability techniques to assess the relationship between the input, the inner layers, and the output. Black-box approaches exploit semantic properties of the input additional w.r.t. those used for training. They enable the characterization of performance metrics and errors and help scientists identify the input features responsible for prediction failures and focus their model improvement efforts. In this demo we provide a guided tour of the functionalities of ODIN, an open-source framework for black-box DNN model diagnosis. We show how to investigate the behavior of classification and object detection models using a broad range of metrics and performance reports, easily extensible by the model developer.

KEYWORDS

Error Diagnosis, Computer Vision, Model Evaluation, Black-Box, Error Categorization.

1. ODIN DEMO

Deep Neural Networks (DNNs) are evaluated in a black-box manner by means of standard metrics such as Accuracy, Precision, Recall, Average Precision, or F1-score. While such metrics played a key role in the progress of Deep Learning, they do not provide insights on the potential flaws or strengths of the models. Deeper analysis of model behavior can be pursued in different ways. One line aims at improving model explainability, by characterizing the relation of the internal representations of deep models to the input and output (Tjoa and Guan, 2020, pp. 4793-4813). An alternative option is to consider the model as a black-box and analyze the impact that the properties of the input have on performances and on the errors. In this demo we provide a guided tour of ODIN, an open-source error-diagnosis framework that integrates into a unique solution the previous approaches to DNN black-box diagnosis for classification and computer vision tasks. ODIN allows the addition of custom properties to the input, supports the plug-in of user-defined performance indicators, and implements many metrics and analysis reports off-the-shelf. It also enables the error categorization with a fine granularity and the comparative study of multiple models. It can be used to investigate both model performance and data set bias and combines error impact sensitivity and confidence calibration. ODIN is developed in Python and offers a Jupyter Notebook interface for visualizing the data set and the analysis reports and annotating the data (e.g., to add classes, bounding boxes, instance segmentation masks, or semantic properties). ODIN is publicly available on GitHub: *https://github.com/rnt-pmi/odin.*

2. FUNCTIONALITIES

2.1 Annotator and Visualizer

ODIN supports class annotation and bounding box and instance segmentation masks creation and allows associating *properties* to the input samples, i.e., annotations that do not contribute to model training but can be exploited for error diagnosis. Examples include object viewpoint, occlusion, or domain-specific properties.

A visualization interface enables the inspection of the data set and of the diagnosis. The GUI supports the browsing of the GT, by displaying all the observations or a subset filtered by a class and/or a property value. If the predictions of the model are available, it visualizes them filtered by user-defined criteria (e.g., by error type). These functionalities allow the assessment of the quality of the data set annotations and bias presence.

2.2 Analyzer

The analyzer implements 15 types of analysis (per-property, per-class, reliability, false positive error categorization, sensitivity and impact of properties etc.) and supports 9 standards metrics (accuracy, precision, recall, average precision etc.). Figure 2 shows three plots from the tutorial[1]. The one at the left (figure 2. (a)) displays the sensitivity and impact analysis. It shows that the area size property is the one with the highest impact on the AP metrics and that by addressing the sensibility of the model to this property the AP could have an increment of +0.2 (0.890 - 0.678). The Figure 2 (b) shows the analysis of the aspect ratio property for a subset of the classes: train, dog and person. In this case, the train class exhibits the worst performances when the bounding boxes are taller (XT, T) than wider (W, XW). This depends on the shape of a train because a train bounding box can be taller only when the object is truncated or seen from the front. The opposite happens with the class person because a wider bounding box can happen only when the object is occluded, or the person is lying down. The dog class instead does not present much variation. The figure 2 (c) presents a similar analysis considering the area size instead. In this case, for the three classes a higher performance is achieved when the bounding boxes are bigger. Here the designer might consider to improve the model by adding multi-scale (e.g., RetinaNet (Lin et al, 2017, pp. 2980-2988) or attention (Guo et al, 2022, pp. 1-38) components.

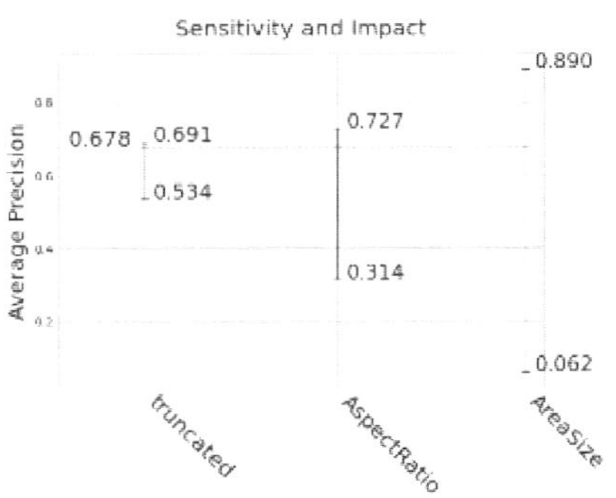

(a)

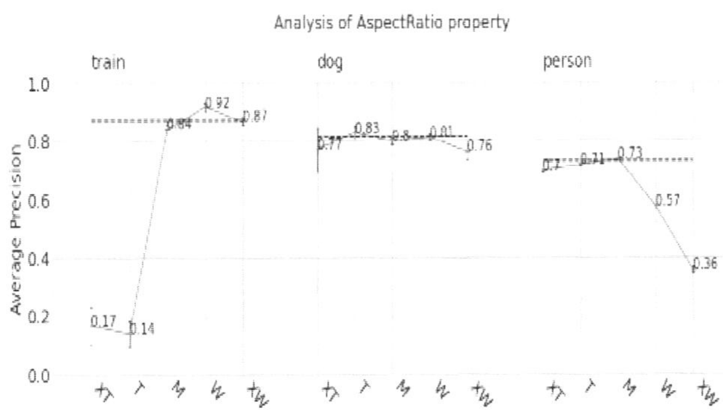

(b)

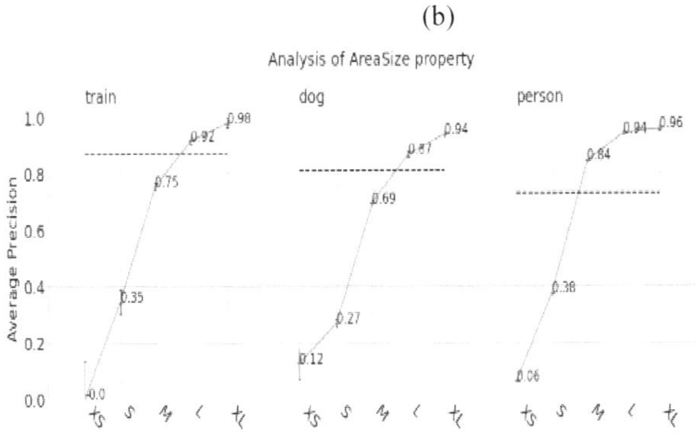

(c)

Figure 2. (a): Sensitivity and impact analysis. (b): aspect ratio analysis. (c): area size property analysis

[1]Pascal VOC analysis using FasterRCNN-Mobile Net model with the weights provided by PyTorch

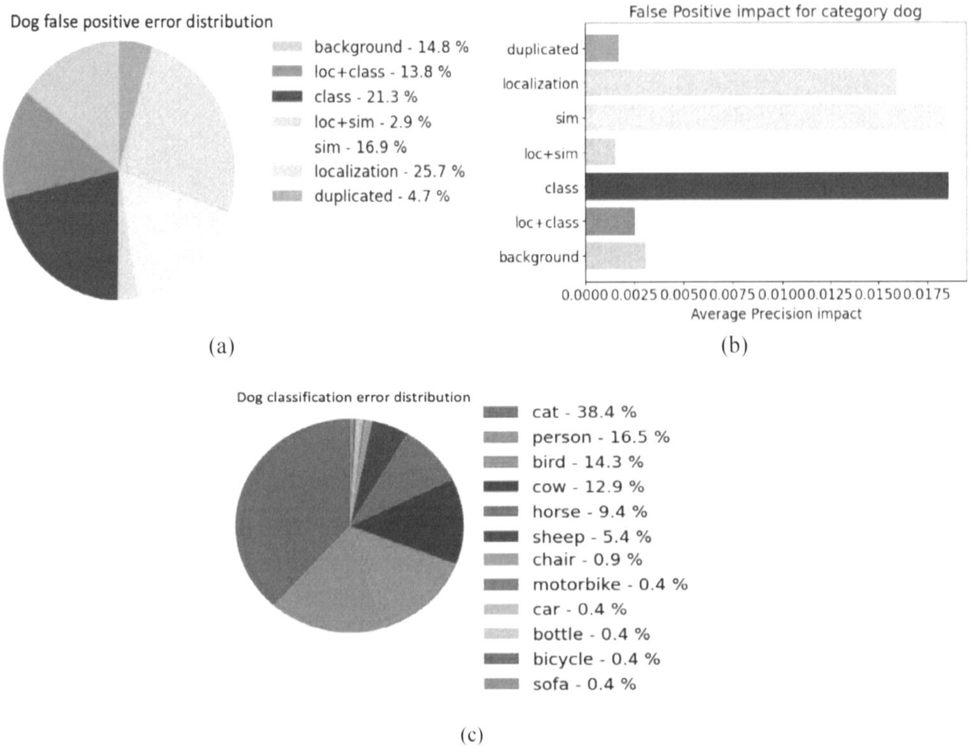

Figure 3. (a): Distribution of FP errors. (b): impact of FP errors. (c): Distribution of classification errors

Another analysis showcased in the demo is error categorization. Figure 3 shows three plots that visualize FP error analysis. The demo will also showcase models comparison to verify if two models are equally sensitive to the same properties of the input or exhibit similar distribution and impact of the error types.

ACKNOWLEDGMENT

This work is partially supported by the project "PRECEPT - A novel decentralized edge-enabled PREsCriptivE and ProacTive framework for increased energy efficiency and well-being in residential buildings" funded by the EU H2020 Programme, grant agreement no. 958284.

REFERENCES

Guo, MH. et al, 2022. Attention mechanisms in computer vision: A survey. *Computational Visual Media*, Vol. 8, pp. 1-38.

Lin, T. Y. et al, 2017. Focal loss for dense object detection. *In Proceedings of ICCV*. Venice, Italy, pp. 2980-2988.

Tjoa, E. and Guan, C., 2020. A survey on explainable artificial intelligence (xai): Toward medical XAI. *IEEE TNNLS*. Vol. 32, No. 11, pp. 4793-4813.

International Association for Development of the Information Society (IADIS)
Rua Sao Sebastiao Da Pedreira
No. 100, 30, 1050-209
Lisbon, Portugal

ISBN 978-1-7138-6091-4

CURRAN ASSOCIATES INC.
proceedings.com

Animal Nutrition Conference of Canada (ANCC 2022)

Feed Production and Formulation Technologies: Considerations for a Sustainable Industry

Saskatchewan, Canada
10 – 12 May 2022

Animal Nutrition Association of Canada
ANAC
Association de nutrition animale du Canada